Cyberspace Security and Defense:
Research Issues

NATO Science Series

A Series presenting the results of scientific meetings supported under the NATO Science Programme.

The Series is published by IOS Press, Amsterdam, and Springer (formerly Kluwer Academic Publishers) in conjunction with the NATO Public Diplomacy Division.

Sub-Series

I. **Life and Behavioural Sciences**	IOS Press
II. **Mathematics, Physics and Chemistry**	Springer (formerly Kluwer Academic Publishers)
III. **Computer and Systems Science**	IOS Press
IV. **Earth and Environmental Sciences**	Springer (formerly Kluwer Academic Publishers)

The NATO Science Series continues the series of books published formerly as the NATO ASI Series.

The NATO Science Programme offers support for collaboration in civil science between scientists of countries of the Euro-Atlantic Partnership Council. The types of scientific meeting generally supported are "Advanced Study Institutes" and "Advanced Research Workshops", and the NATO Science Series collects together the results of these meetings. The meetings are co-organized by scientists from NATO countries and scientists from NATO's Partner countries — countries of the CIS and Central and Eastern Europe.

Advanced Study Institutes are high-level tutorial courses offering in-depth study of latest advances in a field.
Advanced Research Workshops are expert meetings aimed at critical assessment of a field, and identification of directions for future action.

As a consequence of the restructuring of the NATO Science Programme in 1999, the NATO Science Series was re-organized to the four sub-series noted above. Please consult the following web sites for information on previous volumes published in the Series.

http://www.nato.int/science
http://www.springeronline.com
http://www.iospress.nl

Series II: Mathematics, Physics and Chemistry – Vol. 196

Cyberspace Security and Defense: Research Issues

edited by

Janusz S. Kowalik
University of Washington,
Seattle, WA, U.S.A.

Janusz Gorski
Gdansk University of Technologies,
Gdansk, Poland

and

Anatoly Sachenko
Institute of Computer Information Technologies,
Ternopil Academy of Economy, Ternopil, Ukraine

 Springer

Published in cooperation with NATO Public Diplomacy Division

Proceedings of the NATO Advanced Research Workshop on
Cyberspace Security and Defense: Research Issues
Gdansk, Poland
6—9 September 2004

A C.I.P. Catalogue record for this book is available from the Library of Congress.

ISBN-10 1-4020-3380-X (PB) Springer Dordrecht, Berlin, Heidelberg, New York
ISBN-13 978-1-4020-3380-3 (PB) Springer Dordrecht, Berlin, Heidelberg, New York
ISBN-10 1-4020-3379-6 (HB) Springer Dordrecht, Berlin, Heidelberg, New York
ISBN-10 1-4020-3381-8 (e-book) Springer Dordrecht, Berlin, Heidelberg, New York
ISBN-13 978-1-4020-3379-7 (HB) Springer Dordrecht, Berlin, Heidelberg, New York
ISBN-13 978-1-4020-3381-0 (e-book) Springer Dordrecht, Berlin, Heidelberg, New York

---

Published by Springer,
P.O. Box 17, 3300 AA Dordrecht, The Netherlands.

Printed on acid-free paper

Printed in the Netherlands.

Table of Contents

Part 1   General Security Issues

Part 2   Dependability

Part 3   Networks

Part 4   Early Warning Information Systems and Secure Access Control

Part 5   Cryptography

Part 6   Intrusion Detection

Preface

This volume contains a selection of papers presented at the NATO sponsored Advanced Research Workshop on "Cyberspace Security and Defense" held at the Politechnika Gdanska in Gdansk, Poland, from September 6th to 9th, 2004.

The purpose of the workshop was to assess the state of the art in this area of information technology and identify key research issues. The papers collected in this volume represent a wide spectrum of topics with the main focus being practicality and real life experiences.

The workshop was an opportunity for many top experts from the North America, the Western and Eastern Europe for discussing their technical approaches to securing and defending cyberspace against many potential threats.

We wish to thank the NATO Scientific Affairs Division in Brussels for their generous financial support and sponsorship of the workshop, and to the Administration of the Politechnika Gdanska for being an excellent host.

Many individuals helped to organize the workshop. Among them are Mr. Huang Ming-Yuh from The Boeing Company in Seattle and Mr.Philip Attfield from The Seattle University who were responsible for the technical program.

Several persons provided an excellent office and technical support for the workshop. We thank Mrs. Alfreda Kortas and Mr. Marcin Olszewski for this invaluable help.

In the final assembly of the manuscript we were helped by Mr. Ray Benson from The Boeing Company. We thank him for his time, effort and his great attention to details.

But above all we are deeply grateful to the participants of the workshop, especially those who have contributed their papers to this volume.

December 2004.

Janusz S. Kowalik

Janusz Gorski

Anatoly Sachenko

PART 1

GENERAL SECURITY ISSUES

IT SECURITY DEVELOPMENT
Computer-Aided Tool Supporting Design and Evaluation

Andrzej Białas
Institute of Control Systems, 41-506 Chorzów, Długa 1-3, Poland
abialas@iss.pl

Abstract: The paper presents a prototype of the software tool for IT (Information Technology) security development and evaluation according to Common Criteria (ISO/IEC 15408) family of standards. The main goal of developing the tool is to make these activities easier. The tool is based on the enhanced concept of generics, advanced functionality, compliant to ISO/IEC DTR 15446 and the recent information security management standards, and on the risk analysis as well.

Key words: Common Criteria; IT security; design; evaluation; development; computer-aiding; security engineering

1. INTRODUCTION

The paper deals with a prototype of the software tool aiding IT (Information Technology) security design and evaluation according to Common Criteria (ISO/IEC 15408) [1–3] and related standards [4–6], although it is focused on functionality offered to developers. Common Criteria (CC) impose a rigorous development and evaluation methodology on any security-related product, depending mostly on the declared Evaluation Assurance Level (in range: EAL1–EAL7). Basically, more strict discipline in development and evaluation means better assurance. Thus the development and evaluation processes are very complicated due to many details, dependencies and feedbacks, which should be taken into consideration, and rather difficult rationales. That is why the need of computer-aided tools is important and growing. There are three main groups of the tools designed for the IT security developers and evaluators.

The first one supports Common Criteria IT security development process in a less or more detailed way [7–9]. These applications help to manage design stages and related documentation. All of them have CC functional and assurance components implemented and allow to define mnemonic

---

J. S. Kowalik et al. (eds.), Cyberspace Security and Defense: Research Issues, 3–23.
© 2005 *Springer. Printed in the Netherlands.*

descriptors expressing IT security features, called "generics." Some of them [7–8] have predefined only a basic set of generics with relations between them, some offer the possibility of defining them by the user [9] only. These tools need also to improve their basic functionality offered to developers, allowing them:

- not only to manage the development process but also to better support the design trade-offs dealing with developed security-related product,
- to better focus on the problems solving (better design decision support),
- to issue designs that are more precise and compliant to the created IT security standards and also development and evaluation to be more cost effective.

These tools are designed rather for lower EALs and can be useful for commonly used products, like COTS (commercial off-the-shelf).

The second group of tools, designed for higher EALs, is enhanced but also application specific (usually for Java smartcards). The tools focus mainly on proper implementation of ADV class [3] (Development assurance), based on semiformal or formal approach, like UML, OCL, B-method and tools [10], Autofocus [11], Spark [12], Eden [13]. As a good example one can [14] consider an extended version of [9]. The works dealing with UML extension, called UMLsec [15], are very promising, providing unified approach to security features description.

The third group, designed for the evaluators, supporting implemented evaluation scheme, like [16], will be not considered there.

Some of the tools are developed as a part of know-how of the IT development or evaluations laboratories, and for this reason, their description as well as the tools, are not often publicly available.

The software presented below belongs to the first group of the tools. Compared to the previously mentioned, the tool has three general features, ensuring not only effective management, but also providing improved assistance of the IT security development process, especially for COTS and low assurance protection profiles:

- enhanced commonly used generics library, horizontally and vertically ordered, allowing better aiding of design decisions by the tool, operations on generics, parameterization and its reusability,
- advanced assistance of the development process, and also compliant to the created ISO/IEC 15446 standard, including extra features, like a risk analyzer, project data relationships visualization, reporting and evaluation modules,
- improved compliance with information security managements systems—always creating the working environment for security-related products.

The tool features are consistent with the recent researches and trends focusing on: creating unified assurance frameworks mostly for COTS, implementing risk management features and evaluating non-IT components [17–18], issuing products of low cost of evaluation [19], being more compliant to security management standards [20–22] and basing on XML.

The development of the presented software has also a common meaning: promoting CC and secure COTS, providing contribution to the CCRA (CC Recognition Arrangement) deployment (the experience of the other countries [23], shows it is not easy), as well as it can be used for training purposes.

The SecCert [24] presented there was significantly improved, basing mostly on the following experiences:

1. Validation on the COTS-type PKI application for digital signature and encryption, based on Microsoft CryptoAPI® (SecOffice [24]); The result was generally positive, but needs and discovered gaps have enforced new options, like: risk analyzer, XML generator improving (designers drawings attachment), extension of the generic libraries and its better management, supporting trade-off between security objectives declared for the security related product, for its environment or for both.

2. Case study based on early certified products of Philips® smart card; In conclusion, the visualization of the generics/components and their relationships (beside the existing correspondence matrices), and improved evidence material management were implemented.

3. Compatibility checking with ISO/IEC DTR 15446 discovers not properly implemented the so called "SOF—Strength of Functions claims" and operations on components, and also numerous, but rather small, discrepancies dealing with development process implementation.

4. The features improving compatibility with information security management standards were implied basing on experiences in software development compliant to BS-7799-2 standard (SecFrame [24]).

2. AN INTRODUCTION TO IT SECURITY DEVELOPMENT PROCESS

To better understand the tool features and functionality, a concise introduction to IT security development process is needed. All secured IT hardware or software products and systems are called Target of Evaluation (TOE) which are created on the basis of the security requirements specifications: Security Target (ST)—an implementation-dependent and Protection Profile (PP)—an implementation-independent. Development process (Figure 1) consists of 4 (3 for PP) phases and transitions rationales:

- establishing security environment, defined by sets of assumptions, threats and organizational security policies (OSP), worked out during an analysis: TOE assets, purpose and physical environment;

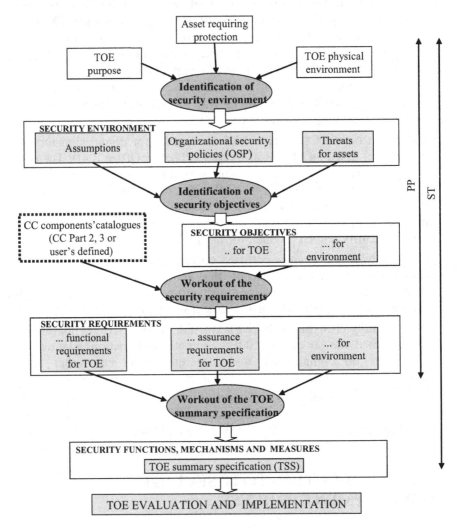

Figure 1. General Scheme of IT Security Development Process.

- setting security objectives—for the TOE and its environment;
- using CC components catalogues and analyzing the above objectives, working out the sets of functional and assurance requirements for the TOE and for the environment;
- using functional and assurance requirements, preparing the TOE summary specification (TSS)—deals with ST specification only.

3. IT SECURITY DEVELOPMENT TOOL FEATURES

On the basis of a general TOE development process (Figure 1), a more detailed scheme of elaborating Protection Profiles and Security Targets was worked out and implemented, presented in the Figure 2 [8], [25–26].

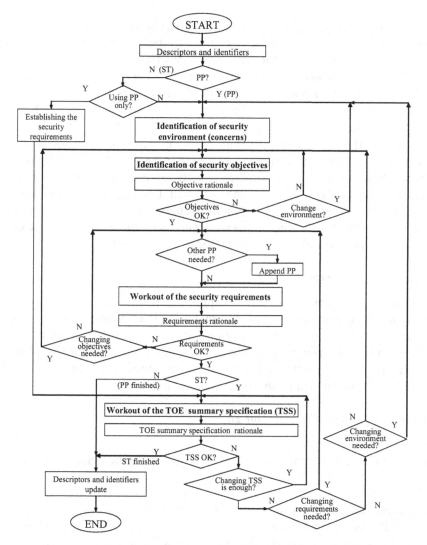

Figure 2. Security Target (ST) and Protection Profile (PP) Development Process.

These different ways of creating ST or PP specifications according to [1] were encompassed by the presented tool. The TOE can be designed:

- straight on the basis of consumer needs,

- using consumer needs, and additionally in compliance with given PPs,

- based only on the requirements defined within the earlier evaluated PPs.

3.1. Enhanced Data Model and Data Libraries

A more enhanced design library means more effective support for developers. For this reason it encompasses not only functional [2] and assurance [3] components, but also a set of generics [27]. It should be noticed that the paper presents an extended concept of a generic. The numerous and ordered set of generics allows to specify different aspects of IT security for the large group of the security-related products (assuming COTS). The set is compliant, albeit considerably larger than those included in informative annexes in [6]. It is ordered horizontally—by domains of the application, and vertically—by security design aspects, corresponding to the development phases, like: security environment, objectives, requirements or functions. Additionally, generics representing different types of assets and subjects were introduced, together with generics representing such security aspects, like risk, vulnerability and impact—never met before. They can express security features, mostly threats and policies, more precisely.

Definition 1 (General, Descriptive):

Generic is a mnemonic name, expressing the set of common features, behaviors or actions, relating to different aspects or elements of IT security system, like subjects, objects, assumptions for the security environment, organizational security policies, threats, security objectives for the TOE and its environment, security requirements for the environment, security functions, as well as vulnerabilities, risks and impacts.

Definition 2 (More Formal, Open):

Generic =
[Domain.]Type.Mnemonic[.Derived].Description.Refinement[.Attributes],

where:

„**Domain**" deals with the area of applications, like:
    GNR – common aspects,
    CRP – specific cryptographic applications,
    COM – communication, networks aspects, firewall/IDS/IDP specifics,
    DAB – Database Management Systems (DBMS),
    TTP – specific applications for Trusted Third Party (TTP),
    SCR – smart cards,

„**Type**" deals with the group of IT security aspects (concerns), like:
— different form of assets:
    DAD – data objects and other assets,
    DAS – asset as service,
    DAE – asset as TOE IT environment,
    DAP – asset as TOE including IT physical environment of the system,
— different form of subjects:
    SNA – represents an unauthorized subject (individual, user, process); may be internal or external to the TOE; usually expresses threat agents;
    SAU – represents an authorized subject; may be internal or external to the TOE; usually expresses legal users or administrators;
    SAH – deals with the source of an undesirable event caused by accidental human actions or errors;
    SNH – deals with an undesirable event caused by non-human actions, deals with physical environment, like fire, flood, earthquake, different disturbances or technical failures;
— threats to asset protected by the TOE, or placed within the TOE or its environment, assumed as a set:
<asset, threat agent, attack method or event, exploited vulnerability>:
    TDA – concerns direct attacks made by hackers and other intruders,
    TUA – deals with users' activities,
    TAA – concerns administrators' activities,
    TIT – deals with software (flaws, malicious codes, etc.) and hardware (failures, power disruption, tampering, line tapping, electromagnetic emanation, etc.) aspects,
    TPH – deals with technical infrastructure and physical security of the TOE environment,
    TFM – concerns force majeures, accidents, catastrophes, terrorism acts, other undesired events, and failures possible within the TOE environment,
— OSP (Organizational Security Policies):
    PIDA – deals with identification and authentication,
    PACC – specifies access control and information flow control rules,
    PADT – concerns accountability and security audit,
    PINT – concerns integrity,
    PAVB – concerns availability,
    PPRV – deals with privacy,
    PDEX – specifies general secure data exchange rules,
    PCON – deals with confidentiality,
    PEIT – deals with the right use of software and hardware within the TOE environment,

PEPH – deals with technical infrastructure (media) and physical security of the TOE environment,

PSMN – encompasses security maintenance (management) aspects,

POTL – concerns technical solutions and legislation, obligatorily used within the organization,

— different form of assumptions for the environment:

AX – deals with the relevance of the considered threat,

AU – deals with the intended usage of the TOE,

AE – must be satisfied by the TOE environment (i.e., in a physical way),

AC – deals with the connectivity aspects of the TOE,

AP – deals with the personnel,

AA – leads to a choice-given assurance requirement,

— IT security objectives for the TOE or its IT environment:

OIDA – deals with identification or authentication,

OACC – deals with access control,

OADT – concerns audit and accountability,

OINT – concerns integrity,

OAVB – concerns availability,

OPRV – deals with privacy,

ODEX – concerns data exchange,

OCON – concerns confidentiality,

OEIT – deals with software or hardware aspects of the TOE environment,

OEPH – concerns technical infrastructure, physical security of environment,

OESM – deals with security management—all non-IT aspects,

— security requirements for the environment, impossible or difficult to express by functional or assurance components:

REIT – security requirements for the environment— general IT aspects, difficult to express with the use of functional components,

REPH – security requirements for the environment dealing with technical infrastructure and physical security,

RENIT – non-IT security requirements for the environment— difficult to express with the use of assurance components,

— other elements:

F – security functions, expressed on general level of abstraction,

V – vulnerabilities,

RI – risk scenarios;

„**Mnemonic**"— a concise expression of a feature, behavior or action; may include parameters to be a generic too, usually of DA-type or Sx-type;

„**Derived**" is ""(empty) for the basic version, and "Dn" for the version derived from the basic one, according to developers' needs, where n means a successive derived version number;

„**Description**"— a full description, expressing mnemonic meaning, displayed separately when needed;

"**Refinement**"— details and interpretations dealing with the "description," a field attached by the developer, matching the meaning of a generic to the TOE reality; not included in the library but added to the project;

„**Attributes**"— a list of attributes, expressing auxiliary aspects.

NOTES:

1. Name within [], like [*element*] means an optionally presented *element*.
2. Examples of attributes for:
   - assets: *AssetValue*;
   - threat: *ExploitedVulnerability, AttackMethodOrEvent*;
   - risk: *EventLikelihood, AssetValueLoss, RiskValue*;
   - security objectives: *Influence* (preventive, corrective or detective).

The enhanced data model is based mainly on:
   - extended concept of a generic, expressed by the above definition,
   - parameterization of generics and allowing operations on them,
   - generics refinement and derivation, adding new ones and their relations,
   - creating a common set of generics containing default relations, allows to support the development process, especially COTS and low assurance PP.

Example 1: Generics

GNR.OCON.DataEncrypt	*Use data encryption*
CRP.F.DataIntegrityCtrl	*Data integrity control function (module).*
DAD.StoredData	*Data stored on media*
DAD.StoredData.D1	*Data stored on flash memory*

-- derived (more compliant with the designer's needs) version of the above;

SNA.CleaningPers	*Internal personnel, not authorized*

-- refinement: " to access the server room"

Generics can be parameterized, i.e.,they can include other generics. Parameter can be left uncompleted, meaning "any of," or completed, using other generic as assignment, similarly to the operations on the CC components.

Example 2: Parameterized Generics, Iteration

TPH.MediaDisposal(1) Data [DAD-parameter] is disclosed or inferred from the disposal medium by [SNA-parameter <= SNA.CleaningPers]

-- the SNA-parameter represents one of the threat agents, for example SNA.CleaningPers could be assigned in the same way as it was assumed for the component, but for the DAD-parameter, there was no assignment – it means "any of data assets";

TPH.MediaDisposal(2) Data [DAD-parameter] is disclosed or inferred from the disposal medium by [SNA-parameter <= SNA.ExternalIndruder]

-- iteration (numbered): this generic is used with different SNA-parameter.

Default and user defined relationships between generics, belonging to a given design phase from the generics belonging to the previous one, are allowed to support designers' decisions dealing with the covering of one security aspect by other, i.e., to facilitate decisions, like: "What security objectives should be set to counter a given threat or to be suitable for a given policy?," "What security requirement meets a given security objective?," "What threats are countered by a given security function?," "What threats can compromise a given asset?"

The tool is able to visualize all these relationships, so that the designer should know what depends on a given generic or component, and what other generics or components depend on the pointed one. All relationships built-in the tool are rather complex so the presentation of this idea will be restricted to a simplified example (Figure 3).

The developer pointing to given OIDA-type generic can see all existing dependencies influenced or implied by it. Basing on this concept, the entire design can be visualized, starting from assets and subjects and ending on security functions, helping also a coverage analysis during the rationale.

Example 3: Dependencies and Their Visualization in PP (UML notation)

To counter the direct attack (TDA) to the system services (DAS) provided by the external intruder (SNA), OIDA-type security objective satisfying also PIDA-type policy rules was set. It is satisfied by the subset of functional[2] and assurance components [3]. Pointing at OIDA-type generic the developer can analyze all these dependencies.

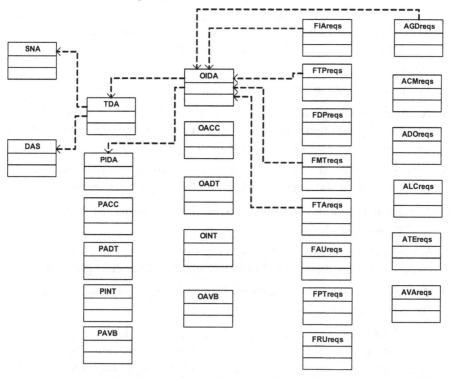

Figure 3. Relationships Between Design Elements (OIDA-type generic is pointed).

3.2. Advanced Assistance of the Development Process

The improving support of IT security development process implies more precise designs, easier rationale and documenting, lower development and evaluation costs. To achieve these, the following features were implemented:

1. The structures, content and presentation of security specifications are enforced by the tool on a detailed level, helping to avoid most of the common CC developers' problems [28].

2. The design stages are wizard driven, ensuring flexibility mostly for:

   - the security environment specification—the tool supports trade-off between its elements, especially between threats and policies.

   - the security objectives specification—the tool supports trade-off between objectives set for the TOE, for its environment or for both,

- the security requirements for the environment specification—the tool allows to express them by CC components as well as by generics representation.

3. The built-in simple risk analyzer, supporting developers in countermeasures, and its assurance requirements selection (see 3.3 below).

4. Enhanced two phase rationale (item justification, CC rationale).

5. A simple coverage status control (a given threat by the objective, an objective by the requirement, etc.) was implemented, helping to resolve if any item is necessary and sufficient during rationale.

6. Visualization of the relationships, starting from security environment generics to security functions, can be useful for problem tracing.

7. Management options allowing traceability of assurance measures and applied security mechanisms and techniques.

8. Evaluation module with status and progress statistics, allowing developers to be aware how their work will be evaluated and to detect gaps early.

9. All possible ways of elaboration of security specifications, supported by the design tree and XML documents generator.

The IT security development process, compliant to [6], corresponds to the step by step creation of ST or PP specifications. It encompasses 6 stages, presented below, each having wizard driven steps. Wizard functionalities represent the essence of IT security development methodology. For each step, the developer, aided by the tool and provided with necessary input data to analyze it, specifies output data. For attaching items to the specification, a short justification and coverage status can be added. The wizards, itemizing the actions, suggest sequential nature of the development process. It is not true – it is complex, rather recursive and incremental.

3.2.1. Introductory Part

The developer prepares the TOE description, including its concise presentation for consumers. It contains the following kinds of data: identifiers, product type and functionality, logical and physical boundaries and the TOE operational environment.

3.2.2. Establishing the Security Environment

The first main development stage is establishing the TOE security environment. Its purpose is to define the nature and scope of the security needs, to be addressed by the TOE [1]. For this stage it is very important to provide the trade-off between its elements, especially between threats and policies, albeit generally the threat specification has higher priority.

The security environment wizard enforces the following steps:

1. *Using TOE description, identify TOE assets and assets protected by the TOE, and specify them by DA-type generic; try to assess its value.*

2. *Using the TOE description, specify AX-type generics, excluding some threats within the TOE boundary and its environment.*

3. *Using the TOE description, specify AU-type generics dealing with the TOE intentional usage.*

4. *Assign an AP-type to define appropriate personnel behavior during the use of the TOE within its environment.*

5. *Assign an AE-type to the environment responsibility in the TOE protection.*

6. *Assign AC-type generics (if needed) reflecting connectivity aspects.*

7. *Analyze special needs, like considerable protected assets value, assign AA-type generics if needed.*

8. *Define a basic set of subjects of SAU-, SNA-, SAH-, SNH-types.*

9. *Analyze assets requiring protection (DA-type), their value and vulnerabilities, potential threats agents, sources of undesirable events, define a list of possible threats dealing with the TOE and/or its environment, try to assess their likelihood and impact (percentage of the asset value loss).*

10. *Review specified threats against the security concerns, revealing topics not covered, not fully covered, or difficult to cover by threats, and cover them by defining OSPs, usually together with AU- or AP-type generics.*

3.2.3. Security Objectives Elaboration

The security objectives elaboration is also aided by the implemented generics library. The objectives provide a concise statement of the intended response to the security problem [1], indicating the extent to which the security needs, defined by the security environment, are addressed by the

TOE and its environment. This is the central point of the whole ST or PP, a kind of bridge between security concerns and precise security specification based on components. The trade-off concerning responsibility for security between TOE and its environment is very important there, because it implies the nature and cost of the developed product.

The security objectives wizard enforces the following steps:

1. *Using the TOE threats specification, accepting proposed objectives or adding new ones, assign them to the right group, trying to cover any item.*

2. *Review the TOE OSPs and assign other suitable Ox-type objectives (choose new ones or assign to the previously specified).*

3. *Using the TOE environment threats specification select suitable OEIT, OEPH and OESM to cover any security concern.*

4. *Review the TOE OSPs, find the concerns not fully covered by the TOE and assign other adequate Ox-type objectives, OEIT, OEPH and OESM (choose new ones or assign to the previously specified).*

5. *Assign (if needed) supportive security objectives for the TOE (Ox-type) or its environment, countering some threats or satisfying some OSPs (usually OEIT, OEPH, OESM).*

6. *Assign (if needed) supportive security objectives for the TOE environment satisfying AE, AC, AX, AU, AP, AA (usually OEIT, OEPH, OESM).*

3.2.4. Preparing the Security Requirements

Three main types of IT security requirements should be specified:

- Security Functional Requirements (SFRs) for the TOE—expressed by functional components [2],
- Security Assurance Requirements (SARs) for the TOE—expressed by assurance components [3];
- Security Requirements for the IT environment—expressed by components (for a well defined TOE IT environment) or by REIT- or REPH-type (when more general statements are enough).

Supportive to the above mentioned, and generally optional, are Security Requirements for non-IT environment, expressed by RENIT-type generics.

Besides, there are two main types of SFR:

- principal SFRs, which directly satisfy given TOE security objectives;
- supporting SFRs, which provide support to the principal SFRs, and hence indirectly help satisfy the relevant security objectives for the TOE.

The selected SARs depend on the declared EAL level, respecting the asset and risk value, and on specific needs implied by security objectives. Operations on SFRs, (e.g., iteration, assignment, refinement, selection), and user defined SFRs are allowed too. At this stage SOF (Strength of Function) claims should be attached when permutation or probabilistic mechanisms are presumed. SOF may be: basic, medium or high.

To elaborate the TOE security requirements specification, the wizard offers the following functionality:

1. *Assign (tool proposed on the basis of Ox-type or chosen by the designer) principal security requirements for the TOE.*

2. *Review automatically assigned dependencies and select, as the first group of supporting requirements, these which allow to achieve given security objectives—prepare justification why some of the dependencies can be left unsatisfied.*

3. *Analyze any principal SFR and attach the second group of supporting requirements, regarding the avoidance of bypassing/tampering attacks, audit support, protection of the TOE security functions, supporting security management—unless they were not assigned.*

4. *Review automatically assigned dependencies to these supportive SFRs, and select these really needed—prepare justification why some of them can be left unsatisfied.*

5. *Considering the value of assets, risk factors, feasibility, time and financial constraints, select SARs—usually it is the EAL package with added or replaced assurance components to meet the specific needs.*

6. *Consider SARs implied directly by security objectives and merge them with the above.*

7. *When EAL>1 and probabilistic or permutation mechanisms are implied by SFRs, prepare adjacent SOF claim for each of them, basing on the threat agent capability (knowledge, expertise, time and position to perform the attack successfully, possessing equipment, possibility to gain the TOE access, etc), asset value and adjacent risk value (Figure 4—see below).*

To elaborate security requirements specification for the IT environment (not evaluated during the TOE evaluation) the following steps are proposed:

1. *For a well defined IT environment use functional and assurance components transforming Ox-type objectives to components, like it was presented for the TOE.*

2. For other, more general IT or technical aspects, when it is not suitable to use such components, apply OEIT or OEPH generics.

3. Assign RENIT to OESM (optional).

3.2.5. Workout of the TOE Summary Specification for the ST

The aim of the development of the TOE Sumary Specification (TSS) is to specify the TOE solution and demonstrate how the TOE provides security functions and assurance measures to satisfy the defined TOE security requirements [1]. The TSS specification should include:

- a definition of the IT security functions, expressed by F-type generics, satisfying SFRs and SARs;
- a definition of assurance measures which satisfy the identified SARs.

To elaborate the TOE Summary Specification (TSS) the tool recommends to follow these steps:

1. Analyze principal SFRs, group them according to security concerns and assign a security function to each group or, if it is impossible, assign a single function to a given requirement.

2. Prepare a high level description for this function to meet principal SFRs and update (optionally) the reference list of related mechanisms and techniques to implement it, like cryptographic algorithms, claims of conformance to standards.

3. Analyze supporting SFRs, related to a given function, and refine security function specification.

4. Consider whether security functions will satisfy SOF claims.

5. For every SAR assign applied assurance measures as a reference list.

3.2.6. Rationale Process

At the end of the development process it should be demonstrated that the conformant TOE provided by its countermeasures will be secure in its environment [1]. For these reasons, for IT security development stages rationales must be performed, showing that:

- all aspects of the identified security needs expressed by the TOE security environment are suitably addressed by the security objectives and the assumptions are upheld by them;

- the security objectives for the TOE are suitably met by the identified IT security requirements (SFR, SAR), the requirements are mutually supportive, and SOF claims are consistent with the TOE objectives;
- security requirements (SFR, SAR) are suitably met by the IT security functions and assurance measures (a list prepared by the developer); this rationale step deals with ST only.

Common Criteria assume to perform and document the rationale at the end of the development process, and this may be difficult to carry out. The presented tool offers some flexibility, allowing to reveal any gaps in the design earlier, after each design stage, and distinguishing two phases in each rationale stage:

- current justification of any element when selected, putting "why it is needed to cover a given security aspect" into words,
- rationale, summarizing partial justifications, may be considered as "Common Criteria rationale."

The added current justification phase ensures more consistency, due to the obligatory designer's declaration, but coverage status helps control, if any specification item is necessary and sufficient.

The following steps are enforced during the security objectives rationale:

1. *Check if each security objective covers at least one threat, OSP or assumption (redundancy checking—all of them must be necessary).*

2. *Check if each threat, OSP or assumption is covered by at least one security objective (specification completeness checking—if security objectives are sufficient).*

3. *Check if any security objective addressed to the threat will provide efficient countermeasures (detective, preventing, corrective) to it—a simple built-in risk analyzer may be useful (Figure 4—see below).*

4. *Consider if security objectives dealing with OSPs will provide complete coverage of them.*

5. *Consider if security objectives will provide the upholding of the assumptions related to them.*

6. *Consider the role of those objectives which address both threat and OSP.*

7. *Consider the supportive role of any environmental objectives for the TOE objectives.*

The following steps are forced by the tool for the security requirements rationale:

1. *Check if SFRs are suitable (should be necessary and sufficient, each of the identified SFRs is sufficient to satisfy a given security objective, how environmental objectives support the TOE objectives).*

2. *Check if SARs are appropriate for the TOE (sufficient, not excessive to address security objectives and technically feasible to the TOE).*

3. *Check if SOF claims are appropriate (consistency with security objectives, based on the analysis of attacker's capability).*

4. *Check if security requirements are mutually supportive (SFRs and SAR dependencies satisfaction, internal consistency, avoidance of bypassing or tampering attacks).*

For ST wizard three other rationale activities are necessary:

1. *Demonstration: how IT security functions satisfy the SFRs (should be necessary and sufficient, explanation how particular SFRs are satisfied, considering SOF claims meeting, security mechanisms and techniques).*

2. *Consideration: how assurance measures satisfy SARs (table of reference and justification).*

3. *For ST based on PP, compliance checking with the referred PP.*

3.3. Improved Compliance with Information Security Management Systems and Other Useful Features

The following tool features can be useful to deploy more easily the certified against CC security-related products, by the organization compliant to information security management standards, like ISO/IEC 17799, BS-7799-2, ISO/IEC 13335:

- some of introduced policy objective types are adopted from these standards to improve the above mentioned compatibility,
- compared to the CC, a more comprehensive, based on the security management standards, concept of subjects and assets, assets management, risk analysis, security policy defining, was assumed,
- analogy between "justification" and "SoA—Statement of Applicability" adopted from BS-7799-2,
- built-in simple risk analyzer (Figure 4).

This figure presents basic OSP and threat dependencies and simple risk analyzer elements. It was assumed that all risk scenarios are adjacent to threats and express how the subject, exploiting the vulnerability and using a specific attack method, can compromise the asset, having its value. A simple risk formula was applied: risk value depends on the asset value, percentage of the asset value loss due to incident and its likelihood. The value of the assessed risk can be helpful during security requirements identification. It should be mentioned that the concept of risk scenarios using generics has a broader meaning and can be applied not only for this CC based tool.

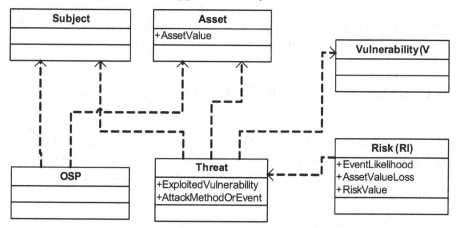

Figure 4. The Security Environment—Risk Analyzer Elements (UML Notation).

The tool has two additional features—a full evaluation module and an XML reports generator—not discussed there.

4. CONCLUSIONS

The paper presents the concept of the computer-aided tool for the IT security products development and evaluation, according to Common Criteria and related standards. The prototype of the tool meets basic IT security developer's needs:

- expresses security design needs, as the input to the TOE security model,
- supports the model refinement process—starting from ideas and needs, through risk assessment to security functions specification, and delivering and managing assurance measures,
- supports rationale processes between each of the design stages,
- makes documentation creating and management easy,
- supports reusability of elaborated security models,
- evaluation module compliant to [4–5] was built in the tool too.

The results achieved up until now indicate that design and evaluation processes seem to be considerably facilitated, but the tool SecCert [24] needs more verification in real operation and more user feedbacks. Some useful features, like: packages management, composite and complex TOE features are under development. Library improvement is very important and should be considered as permanent process. The tool seems to be not enough for higher EALs designs due to the absence of a semiformal or formal method built-in or associated with it, but it can be considered as a basis for the development of such a tool in the future.

PERMISSION AND ACKNOWLEDGEMENT

The author wishes to thank for the support from Ms Irena Styczeń, Mr Oleksandr Pidlisny, Mr Dariusz Rogowski, Mr Krzysztof Fałek, Mr Jacek Bagiński—key members of the SecCert development team. The preliminary version of this software [8] was supported in part by a grant from the State Committee for Scientific Research.

REFERENCES

1. ISO/IEC 15408-1, Information Technology—Security techniques—Introduction and general model (*Common Criteria Part 1*).

2. ISO/IEC 15408-2, Information Technology—Security techniques—Security functional requirements (*Common Criteria Part 2*).

3. ISO/IEC 15408-3, Information Technology—Security techniques—Security assurance requirements (*Common Criteria Part 3*).

4. Common Evaluation Methodology for Information Technology Security, Part 1: Introduction and General Model, CEM-97/017, v.0.6, 1997.

5. Common Evaluation Methodology for Information Technology Security, Part 2: Evaluation Methodology, CEM-99/045, v.1.0, August 1999.

6. ISO/IEC DTR 15446, Information Technology—Security Techniques—*Guide for the Production of Protection Profiles and Security Targets*.

7. CCToolbox: **http://cc-control.sparta.com/**

8. POZIT: Białas A. Praca zbiorowa pod red.: Metodyka prowadzenia bada i oceny rodków teleinformatycznych, Projekt celowy KBN pt. System wspomagania projektowania i oceny zabezpiecze teleinformatycznych, Instytut Systemów Sterowania, Chorzów, 2002–2004 (target project reports: „*IT Security Development and Evaluation,*" in Polish).

9. TL SET: **http://trusted-logic.fr**

10. B-METHOD/TOOLS: **http://www.b-core.com**

11. AUTOFOCUS: **http://autofocus.informatik.tu-muenchen.de**

12. Chapman R.: SPARK—a state-of-the-practice approach to the common criteria implementation requirements, 2nd International CC Conference, Brighton, July 2001.

13. Lavatelli C.: EDEN: A formal framework for high level security CC evaluations, e-Smart' 2004, Sophia Antipolis 2004.

14. TL FIT: **http://trusted-logic.fr**

15. Jürjens J.: UMLsec: Extending UML for Secure Systems Development, UML 2002, Dresden, LNCS, Springer-Verlag, 2002.

16. AGTER: Hwa-Jong S.: Development and utilization of automatic generation tool for evaluation report, 5th International CC Conference, Berlin, September 2004.

17. Naaman N.: A unified framework for information assurance, 5th International CC Conference, Berlin, September 2004.

18. Melton R.: Integration of risk management with the Common Criteria (ISO/IEC 15408:1999), 5th International CC Conference, Berlin, September 2004.

19. Nash M.: Simpler security targets, 5th International CC Conference, Berlin, September 2004.

20. Pattinson F.: BS 7799-2 and Common Criteria—Supporting the business of software development, 5th International CC Conference, Berlin, September 2004.

21. Krueger B.: Application of the Common Criteria to Information Security Management Systems—A study, 5th International CC Conference, Berlin, September 2004.

22. ARENA: Cakir M.: Evaluation of organizational information systems according to CC and ISO 17799, 5th International CC Conference, Berlin, September 2004.

23. Jung-Shian Li: Development of CC in Taiwan, 5th International CC Conference, Berlin, September 2004.

24. SecCert, SecOffice, SecFrame: **http://www.iss.pl**

25. Białas A.: Wprowadzenie do problematyki projektowania i oceny zabezpiecze teleinformatycznych, Studia Informatica vol. 22, Number 1(43), Silesian University of Technology Press, Gliwice 2001, pp. 263–287 (*„Introduction to IT Security Development and Evaluation,*" in Polish).

26. Białas A.: Modelowanie i ocena zabezpiecze teleinformatycznych, Studia Informatica vol. 23, Number 2B(49), Silesian University of Technology Press, Gliwice 2002, pp. 219–232 (*„Security Modeling and Evaluation,*" in Polish).

27. Białas A.: Sposób formalnego wyra ania własno ci bezpiecze stwa teleinformatycznego, Studia Informatica vol. 24, Number 2B(54), Silesian University of Technology Press, Gliwice 2003, pp. 265–278 (*„Formal Description of the Security Features,*" in Polish).

28. Apted A.J., Carthigaser M., Lowe Ch.: Common Problems with the Common Criteria, *Proceedings of the 3rd International Common Criteria Conference*, May 2002. **http://www.expotrack.com/iccc/english/proceedings.asp**

A CASE FOR PUBLIC AND PRIVATE REVIEW OF DEVELOPING IT SECURITY STANDARDS

Roger Allan French,
ASE

Timothy Grance
National Institute of Technology and Science
U.S. Department of Commerce

Abstract: Standards are important. International IT Security Standards are critical. This paper presents the benefits of getting involved in the development of some standards, the risks of leaving such development to others, and the process of deciding which development efforts an organization should focus on .It spells out the types of involvement available to organizations, paying detailed attention to public and private reviews as the most beneficial and least expensive alternative for many standards. It suggests methods for becoming a reviewer and provides pointers to several important Standards Development Organizations (SDOs).

Keywords: IT security; Information Technology; International Standards; Standards Development; SDO; Public Review; Private Review; NIST; FIPS

1. INTRODUCTION

"Standards are not just for other people and other companies. Some, but not all, are or should be important enough to you for you to track them, track their development, and, in some cases, influence their development and the final standards."

— Roger Allan French, Guest Lecturer,
Technical University of Szczecin, May 2002.

Every individual, every company, every government agency/ministry, every non-profit, in fact every organization that uses networked computers,

J. S. Kowalik et al. (eds.), Cyberspace Security and Defense: Research Issues, 25–42.
© 2005 *Springer. Printed in the Netherlands.*

especially Internet connected computers, should care about international IT Security standards. In fact, every individual or organization that uses the data of such systems should care about international IT Security standards, just to know how much faith, how much assurance can be placed in that data.

The above paragraph seems to include a large number of organization and individuals. And in fact, it does. It includes every government in the world. It includes almost every government agency/ministry. It includes almost every company. It includes most of the non-profits. It includes most of the higher level educational facilities around the world. It may even include or soon include, most, meaning more than half, of the people in the world.

Standards are important; in fact, they have become necessary in our time. This paper briefly addresses that importance, that need. Then it addresses a small subset of all standards, ones that apply to IT, ones that apply to the security aspects of IT, ones that are or are intended to be internationally accepted. The focus is on international IT Security standards.

This paper makes two cases. First, it makes a case that those who should care about international IT Security standards should care enough to get involved in the process of developing those standards. To that end, it presents both the benefits of involvement and the risks of leaving such development to others. It briefly presents the range of involvement options with a short rationale for picking the appropriate one. And it focuses on the two that provide the most benefit to the most participants for the least cost and effort; public and private review.

Because the purpose of this paper is to be both informative and persuasive, it presents methods of initiating contact with Standards Development Organizations (SDOs) and an appendix with some web site addresses.

2. THE NEED FOR STANDARDS

To understand the need for standards, the easiest method is to envision a world without them. In that world, riders change trains at every national border or even city border because different railroad track widths require different railroad cars and engines. Crossing the border is difficult if you are not from one of the two countries because there is not standard format for identification. Manufacturers make dozens or hundreds of versions of each product because of different electrical or mechanical requirements and must charge for the differences and for huge inventories. Credit cards can only be used for a single chain of stores and banks charge a lot of money to process them. And there is no telephone service across borders. The Internet is both an interesting academic idea and an impractical science fiction. Fortunately, the world without standards is the fiction.

Organizations from government agencies/ministries to companies to institutions of higher education seek to minimize their costs in terms of money, time, effort, and talent. They also seek insight and assurance of possible futures that are relevant to their areas of interest (i.e., markets, manufacturing, distribution, IT, regulation, finance, health, environment, etc.). Many of these areas have their own standards.

Standards seem to have been in use for centuries. In fact, they have been in use for millennia. The cubit, a stone and wood cutting measure from the elbow to the tip of the middle finger, was used for nearly 4,400 years, from approximately 2400 BCE until the 1960's AD. The Lydo-Milesian Weight Standard (Lydia and Miletus were cities in ancient Asia Minor) for electrum, an alloy of gold and silver, was used for different sizes of coinage in 546 BCE, more than 2,500 years ago. Most standards go unnoticed, like the distance between railroad tracks, like electrical outlets for many large regions or groups of countries, and like CD and DVD formats. Certainly these standards benefit consumers who can buy CDs or DVDs without regard to which manufacturer produced them or produced their individual players. Standards also benefit manufacturers who make products to a single national, industry, or international standard with the knowledge that everyone in their market is a potential customer. They need not constantly survey their markets where there are accepted standards to determine the dominant players and then develop, distribute, and store multiple versions of their products.

3. THE NEED FOR INTERNATIONAL IT SECURITY

The need for international IT Security standards is, or should be, obvious. While the case for standards in general demonstrates the values of having them and using them, IT security has its own added requirements and benefits.

IT security must be pervasive. Some technologies are point products or highly bounded services. But IT security, like most security, requires pervasive protection. The analogy of a fence that covers less than all of a perimeter or a castle with walls on only three sides illustrates the need for pervasiveness in security. The same is true of IT security. Protecting some but not all of the entry points to a network is not enough. While protecting against every threat is usually cost and performance prohibitive, what protection is provided must take into account the pervasive nature of IT security.

IT security must be far sighted. The nature of computer networking makes threats at a distance into potential threats near by. Some threats propagate exponentially, a virus for example. Others are broadcast, software product and patch errors for example. And others travel at a more sporadic unpredictable pace, Trojan horses and worms for example. For networked systems, IT security must address threats from every system connected to or ever connected to the system by any means.

IT security must be standardized. Some standardization involves nothing more than the use of common terms and common definitions. It is dangerous to have different names for the same component, the same service, the same threat, etc. It is more dangerous to have different definitions for the same term. Such differences contribute to misunderstandings of what is needed and what is provided. And those misunderstandings can lead to mismatches of protection measures, gaps in security, and a false sense of security from the individual and company level to the national and international level. Some comprehensive standardization involves the specifics and extent of security requirements and capabilities. The Common Criteria is an example of a standard that covers IT security terms and definitions and provides a uniform method of evaluation of IT security functions. It also provides a standardized way of describing IT security needs (called Protection Profiles). Other examples are specific standards like IPV6 and FIPS 185 (NIST Digital Signature Standard), which are technical standards. These allow communication between systems with a clear understanding of the requirements of specific formats and of the security provided.

4. WHY GET INVOLVED IN SDO PROCESSES?

There are two major reasons why an organization should be involved in standards, including the international IT Security standards that are important to it. The first concerns the advantages such participation provides and the other concerns the risks that failure to participate allows. For international IT security standards, the results may have minor or major effects on different types of organizations. It must be obvious that IT vendors and particularly IT security vendors have a major stake in these standards. They effect their markets, business, profits and survival. For users, from countries to companies to individuals, the stakes are often less important but not in all cases. Countries are interested in their own protection, in the protection of their own investments, in the protection of their own industries and commerce, and in the protection of their own cultures. Companies have their own markets to protect, their own investments to leverage, and relationships with partners, customers, their countries, and their industries to consider.

Individuals need to protect their freedoms and rights and their economic futures and to minimize their own costs.

If these interested parties get involved in the development processes, they will as a minimum know what is possible and maybe what is probable that the developing standard will require. At higher levels of involvement, they can provide their own alternatives, their own reasons for change, their own compromises. Sometimes a standard can be a benefit or a liability based on a single word or phrase. That change or lack of change can be either intentional or unintentional. Unintentional errors can come when some aspect of the standard is unimportant to the experts developing the standard. For example, the TCPA (Trusted Computing Platform Alliance) standard (and Protection Profile) would have defined 'binding' of the trust module only in terms of drops of epoxy had the phrase not been noticed by a reviewer whose company used cryptographic binding.

The risks of not being involved in a standard that is or will be important to an organization or to a government, is the opposite of the benefits. "If you are willing to live by the standards developed by others, then there is no need to be involved on its development." The operative term here is "developed by others." There are two categories of others to consider. One set of "others" is a group of people who are unconcerned about the benefits or damage the standard will cause to your organization. The second set of "others" is a group who is concerned that the standard not benefit your organization. The decision not to be involved in the process for a specific standard is to accept those groups and their resultant standard in advance. That decision, even by default, means accepting the risks.

One added risk is that there may be gaps in current and future standards and those gaps will cause uncertainty, increase costs, limited markets, lost opportunities, and could cause a later need for quick, poorly researched standards.

5. WHICH STANDARDS TO FOCUS ON?

There are good reasons for getting involved in the development of standards that affect a company or organization. The reasons and the benefits of involvement or the risks of not getting involved vary not just from company to company or organization to organization, but within each of them. For an organization, some standards will not influence how they do business or how their markets react. Other standards will have more importance while still others may be critical to the short term or long term health of the company, or on the national level, to an economy. It is important to note that the set of important standards may change over time, as may the importance of any one of them. For these reasons, organizations need to decide on the level of their involvement in the development processes of new IT Security standards and of new versions of existing ones.

The need to decide requires many decisions, not just one. For each standard in development or soon to be in development, a decision is needed. An organization need not and in fact should not decide on a single uniform level of involvement for each and every standard that has or will have an effect on it. There are a large number of standards and a wide spectrum of possible levels of involvement and their respective amounts of effort. This document makes no recommendation of whether such involvement and the decisions that support those levels are centralized in an organization or those decisions are made individually by the members and managers most effected by the benefits and risk of such involvement. Each decision ought to be the result of careful consideration of each development effort, the importance of the possible result, the risks involve, and the cost of involvement versus the less easily determined cost of not being involved.

6. WHAT DOES INVOLVEMENT MEAN?

There is a wide range of types of involvement in the development processes of international IT Security standards, both new ones and revisions. To provide focus, six levels are highlighted. Since involvement is a spectrum, there is a range of options within each level and the borders of each level are not well defined.

6.1. Level 0: No Interest/No Involvement

At one end of the spectrum of involvement is no involvement, caused by the perception that the standard is not and will not be important. As long as the perception and the reality are the same, then no action is the correct action. Also in this category are standards that are not expected to change. There is, therefore, no development to track or influence. Unfortunately, the most common reason for an organization to have no interest or no involvement in some or even all IT Security standards is that new standards are not considered. That situation may change when the standards appear fully developed or when interested parties including customers, partners, suppliers, and regulators inquire of the organization's compliance with them. In the former case, it is too late to anticipate them and far too late to influence them. "Not deciding is a decision." For many organizations, ignoring them by default is not an appropriate level selection criterion.

6.2. Level 1: Tracker

Some standards are more important, but their particulars are not important to a specific organization. An organization may want to know the details of an upcoming standard or may want to know what possible options are being considered for the standard in order to be prepared for whichever option is selected. For example, if a major customer group, an industry consortium, or a government regulatory agency is going to select a specific instance of a technology (a new encryption algorithm or a set of security management standards) many organizations have no need to influence the selection criteria or the final selection, but do need to know what possible options exist (which finalists remain) or even less specific information like when the new technology or the new management techniques or new certification will be required. These are sufficient reasons to track the development of such standards and tracking that development may be sufficient. That should provide an expected implementation date as well as an understanding of what the standard will require. The risk of not tracking them is that the organization will not be prepared to use or comply with a new standard. Sometimes it is a matter of needing enough notice, enough lead-time, to make a few changes. At other times, it is a matter of making certain that the partnerships, licensing, training, purchasing, set up, and certification is done in time to meet a specific market, to retain a technology leadership position, or comply with a regulation.

6.3. Level 2: Public Reviewer

For something more important, the organization might want to be a reviewer, simply to be more assured of the details and the dates. Instead of simply tracking the major actions of the SDO, like setting new dates, releasing drafts, etc., an organization could be interested in the details within the developing standard. In these cases, the reviewer is interested in the details which could effect how and when his organization responds, but not interested in altering or influencing the standard. One reason for this need to review without a need to influence is that the net outcome will not be significant to the organization as long as it is knowledgeable about the details and has sufficient time to prepare, to convert, and/or to market/promote it. In many instances, there is an advantage to compliance, to be evaluated against a new standard, to be seen as 'open', 'interoperable', and/or 'current.' The risk of not reviewing the developing details of standards during the development is twofold. First, its market may have to wait, if it will, while the company gears up, tests, evaluated, and distributes. Second, the market will not have to wait if the organization's competitors were reviewing the development documents and are ready. Not all risks are sales and marketing risks. There are risks that an organization will not be able to use the benefits of the new standard when its partners and its own personnel want it. There is the risk that a new standard signals a security exposure simply because it 'fixes' something and that exposure remains until the organization complies. There are reasons why a reviewer may not influence a standards development. One reason might be that some decisions are made by governments or by large organizations with substantial influence. Another reason is that the decision will be made by consortia or user groups which the organization wants to encourage. A third reason is that all the proposed alternatives in the standard are acceptable to the organization. Even without the desire or ability to influence changes, it is important that organizations get and stay informed on all the details that may affect them.

6.4. Level 3: Private Reviewer

As the benefits and risks increase, an organization may want to influence the final document using a range of possible input methods. It may join or already belong to an alliance or consortia that provides input, requested or at will, to the developers. It may belong to a standards organization that has a formal liaison status with the SDO. It may become a formal reviewer that provides its own inputs by notifying the SDO of its interests. A private reviewer returns comments and suggestions to the development body. It may be more important to an organization that the resulting standard takes into account its needs and the needs of its customers, partners, supplies, etc. In some cases, it will be most important that they protect an organizations technology, its markets and future markets, its investments, and its own plans for its future. That importance becomes more obvious when an organization considers the possible risks of not influencing a new or updated standard that is critical to its performance. One risk is that competitors will protect their interests at a cost to others not represented. Another risk is that the results will be developed by experts who are not experts in all aspects covered by the standard or who simply do not consider certain aspects as important. If an organization has reasons to care about the output of an SDO, it has reason to input into that SDO, and that means investing in at least the review and comment process.

6.5. Level 4: Member

For the standards that are or may be critical to an organization, that organization may become a member of the SDO. "Standards are developed by those with a stake in the outcome." This means more than influencing the developing standards or even influencing the developers. It means being one of the developers. SDOs have members because there is a need for new standards or revisions of existing ones and member companies have a stake in what is standardized, on how it is standardized, and on how a standard is specifically worded. For critical ones, it is not enough to review and forward comments. There is no magic formula or secret process for developing standards. People, who range from interested parties to experts, sit around a table or collaborate by phone and email, and write a new standard or modify an existing one. Each SDO has its own processes and rules and its own review policies and balloting requirements. But the bottom line is the people at the table make the standards and if an organization has a major stake in the outcome, it should have someone at the table. The costs are the price of membership, the time and pay of an expert or experts, travel costs, the cost of hosting some meetings, the availability of other personnel to consult with the company experts, etc. It is not unusual to see, at a development or ballot meeting where companies or countries often send one or two members, for a single company or country to send a half dozen representatives ten thousand miles to make its point. The risk of not being a developer or of not investing in the development process commensurate with the organizations stake in the new standard, can be increased time-to-market, loss of existing or future markets, increased development and/or manufacturing costs, added marketing expenses, higher distribution costs, dissatisfied customers and partners, non compliance with regulations, and more.

6.6. Level 5: Driver

For the most important standards in development or for new versions or even completely new or competing standards, an organization may choose to be its driver. Such an effort may entail proposing the initial work, negotiating the approval of the SDO (or finding another SDO or even starting a new SDO) for the work, managing and often editing the effort, and publishing the final document. One reason for an organization to become the driver is that its stake in the results is extremely high. Another reason is that driving such development efforts is a part of its charter, its mission. That would apply to users groups and industry consortia that are chartered to protect and promote a certain technology or an application or a cross technology interest like privacy or the environment protection. The same holds true for many of the efforts by governments around the world that understand that standards can help or hinder, depending on how they are written and implemented, their major goals or the specific goals of individual agencies and ministries. While driving the development of a specific standard or update is not a guarantee that the results will be perfectly satisfactory to the driver's sponsor, it increases the chances that it will, and if not, it ensures that a more favorable outcome will occur. This is an effective demonstration of receiving value for investment, as the major stakeholder in the results should invest more in its development. The risk of not driving a new standard or update is that there will not be one when it is needed or when it would be most beneficial. Another risk is that there will be one, but it will not be beneficial to some major stakeholders or it will not be widely accepted.

7. TWO LEVELS, THE BENEFITS AND COSTS OF REVIEW

Each organization and each individual must make its or his/her own decisions on each standard in development regarding how much involvement in the process is beneficial and possible. For many, the most attractive in terms of costs versus benefit is that of a reviewer, either as a public reviewer or a private reviewer. As a public reviewer, providing comments is optional. As a private reviewer, providing comments is mandatory and often includes providing corrections and/or alternatives.

7.1. Public Review

While different levels of involvement are appropriate for an organization based on the importance of the standards to it, the minimum reasonable involvement in any standard with the potential to effect an organization in more than a superficial way is to take advantage of the standard's public review. Standards in development and revisions in development are often published for public review, to the limited benefit of both the developers and the reviewers.

7.1.1. Public Review is Important for the Developers

Developers have clear goals for the final standard that they develop. One goal is that it be widely accepted by a full range of stakeholders. Another goal is that the final standard provides the originally intended results. For those reasons, the final drafts of standards near completion are often published for public review. Some government-generated standards are published for public review by law. But even without that requirement, many SDO's publish their final drafts for review, to get the opinions of the stakeholders.

Wide acceptance is important to all stakeholders. At the high end of the range of stakeholders are the vendors that develop, manufacture, and sell products based on the standard. Also on the high end are nations whose interests range from the utility and fit of the standard in current and future plans and objectives to the protection of national industries and the protection of processes and advantages. An example is the protection of the countries' or its agencies'/ministries' investment in existing technologies and its plans for the future based on those technologies.

At another level of stakeholders are the companies that use the technologies that are affected by the standard. For example, vendors that make peripheral products or provide services related to the technologies covered by the standard. Certain changes in such standards can cause increased business. Other changes can cause increased investment in reengineering products and additional training for technical support and for offered services. And certain changes can obsolete existing inventories and even restrict or remove an entire market segment.

Even at the individual level, there are stakeholders. For some, it is as a customer for whom the standard may represent an unnecessary expense. For others, it may represent a peripheral or related change, such as environmental or privacy issues.

The goal of wide acceptance by the standard's developers in easily understood. A standard that is not widely accepted is not much of a standard by definition. The more widely it is accepted, the more value it has in defining markets, predicting future usage, and leveraging even wider sales. In many languages other than English, the word for standards is a local derivation of the word "normal." And there is nothing normal about something not widely used. Another reason developers want their standard widely accepted is that they don't want to have to develop another one. Most important is that few or none of the benefits expected to accrue from a standard, often accruing to their company or their government, will materialize.

Developers often have a wide range and varied set of reasons for developing a new standard or for revising an existing one. There are too many to address all those reasons here. What should be clear, and may seem redundant to state, is that they have a goal for the standard to satisfy their original intentions. It is also clear to those involved in the development processes and especially by those who must conform to the standards, is that there is no guarantee that original intentions are the correct balance of possibilities or that the resultant standard meets the intention. Part of the reason for such discrepancies is that the developers may be too close to the problem or may have too narrow a view of its requirements or its effects. That problem is easily countered by independent reviews. And public review offers the widest reviews at the least cost to the developers.

7.1.2. Public Review is Important for the Reviewers.

As stated, standards and revisions in development are often published for public review, to the limited benefit of both the developers and the reviewers. The benefits are limited most often by the failure of most potential reviewers to actually review the drafts. And yet the benefits are more for them than for the developers.

The rationale for reviewers is easily understood, making the absence of more reviewers difficult to understand. Reviewers get the information they need to know what is coming and usually when. They get to comment of the draft, a draft that is likely to remain unchanged if they don't comment. And they get to build a critical mass of resistance to the draft if they see the need. The absence of those reviewers absents those benefits from the development process.

Reviewing a draft standard is more than just reading it. Public reviews usually provide status information about the standard and the process that answer important questions like:

- What standard(s) will it or is it expected to replace?

- Are/were the replaced standards mandatory or critical to the organization?

- When is the new standard expected to be published? Will it go into immediate effect, either as a mandatory requirement or a customer demand?

- How can comments be submitted and by what date?

- Who is being asked to review the draft?

These and similar draft status questions should generate answers that help an organization decide if a draft standard gets reviewed, and if so, by whom, by what date, with what results and actions. Without those answers, without review, the standard will get designed, developed, and implemented by others.

In addition, reviewers get to study the draft, noting not only the general purposes of the standard, but the details including how the standard goals are to be implemented and the wording used. This is the time, before the standard is finalized, to question everything from the general goals to the methods to the wording to the gaps to the ambiguities.

A sample of the questions to consider is:

- Are the intentions of the standard obvious? Are they the right intentions for your organization? Are they a balance with other business, technological, political, and organizational needs? Are they fulfilled by the draft?

- Are the methods or restrictions appropriate and necessary? Are they unfair to some segments covered by the standards? Are they unnecessarily restrictive?

- Is the wording correct? Is it clear and concise? Does it support the goals clearly? Will it be understood by all the parties, industries, nations that it will affect?

- Does the standard have gaps in it? Are parts of the intended goals not covered?

- Is the draft comprehensive and consistent? Or it is vague and unenforceable?

- What unintended consequences have not been addressed by the draft?

Beyond the information provided to the reviewing organization, the review allows a further benefit, the opportunity to change the standard before it becomes a standard. This is the opportunity to have an organizations concerns and preferences heard by the developers.

And beyond being heard, beyond expressing concerns and possible alternatives, reviewers get a chance to consider the effects of the draft on others and to get them involved in the review or to point out the concerns and provide a broader and stronger response.

7.1.3. Reviewers Responsibilities

Reviewers have several responsibilities and a few options. They should approach a standards draft review with a review plan. They need to pass on to the appropriate people in their organization what they learn from the draft status data and from the draft itself. They may have the requirement or desire to provide feedback to the developers. And they may choose to pass on their review result to others that will be affected, perhaps negatively, if the unchanged draft becomes a standard.

7.2. Private Review

Not all draft standards are published for public review. And even those that are published are usually close to the end of the development process with considerable investment in the draft. That creates a bias toward little change between the final draft and the actual standard.

For each potential standard that is or could be relevant to an organization, that organization should decide what are possible consequences and then decide on appropriate action. The range of consequences covers a good standard, with 'good' defined by their needs, and a bad standard, with 'bad' defined as anything from a damaging or ambiguous or non-existent standard. If a standard is important and if either a public review is not expected or would be too late for significant changes, the organization needs to get involved in the review formally. It may need to establish an external review process.

There are many types of development organizations and within them there are different types of review process. Most but not all, encourage external reviews. Some of the others tolerate them. Regardless of the preference, external review is usually beneficial to all interested parties.

The major differences between public and private reviews involve the selectivity of reviewers, the number of reviews, and the requirement for comments, and commitment.

7.2.1. Selectivity of Reviewers

SDO's understand the range of parties that will be effected by a new standard or revision and often reach out to a sampling of those parties for input and comment. In those cases, this is formally done from the beginning of the process. Unlike public reviews which are almost exclusively for final drafts, private reviews involve work-in-process drafts during the entire development process.

The set of reviewers comes from three sources. All organizations and individuals holding a liaison relationship with the SDO are expected to review and comment of each review draft from their own perspective. This is the salient reason for establishing liaison relationships. To fill in any gaps in perspective, specific organizations are signed up as reviewers based on the concern with the upcoming standard. These may include some organizations that are opposed to the standard, for example privacy or other rights groups in some cases. It can be useful to work with such groups to lessen the opposition or at least to understand it. And finally there are the volunteers, the organizations that have their own concerns and want to be heard before it's too late.

7.2.2. Number of Reviews

Unlike public review, which are almost exclusively for final drafts, private reviews cover several drafts of a single standard, drawing inputs to help its refinement through most of the process. There is a reluctance in everyone, not just developers, to hold up their early attempts, their unfinished work, to public scrutiny. That makes private reviews of early draft more valuable than public reviews. At each major revision of the standard, in many SDO's, the draft is distribution to the members for review and comment. For example, within ISO, each Committee Draft, CD, is sent to each national body for review, for comment, and for ballot. Liaisons and other interested reviewers, experts in some aspect of the standard, are also asked to participate in the review. The end result is that more aspects of the standard are considered throughout the development process. In addition, those external reviewers have a say and therefore a stake in the resultant standard.

For the developers, the total effort is reduced as problems are identified earlier in the process, allowing for earlier resolutions. This reduces or eliminates the need to backtrack, to rewrite other parts of the standards affected by the change in or withdrawal of some parts, some sentences, and some language. While it sometimes means more work, more comments to check, it often does not significantly increase the total work. And it may spread out the need for changes over several drafts.

For the reviewers, it means more work, but that often improves the likelihood that the reviewers comment will affect the standard. It gives the reviewer more time to research the possible ramifications of the standard part by part and in total as well as those of its alternatives. And it allows for a process that refines in steps the standard from major points down to the actually wording.

7.2.3. Requirement to Comment and Commitment

As important as a comprehensive set of reviewers is to the development process, the requirement to comment adds the most value to the private reviewer process. Public review allows everyone and anyone to review the final draft, but requires no one to comment. Public review can be the most comprehensive output method and the least comprehensive input method. Private review reverses those parameters.

The purpose of private reviews is to produce a better, more widely accepted, more useful standard. The reviewers are selected for a reason beyond providing them with a warning of what to expect. They are selected for a reason beyond allowing them to read the details. They are selected for a reason beyond reviewing the draft and forming opinions and alternatives. They are selected to provide their feedback directly to the developers. It is a requirement of those that are allowed to review the early drafts, are allowed to follow the logic that is producing the drafts and the standard, allowed to ensure that they are heard. Since reviewers are selected for their sometimes unique perspectives on the standard and its effects, the likelihood that their comments will affect the developer's decisions is very high.

Private review is an agreement between the developers and the reviewers. It is a commitment, usually for the entire development process. That is another significant difference between public and private reviews.

8. HOW TO BECOME A REVIEWER

Some of the information in this paper was prepared for and taken from a US NIST project in process, an IT Security Standards and Guidelines Roadmap. For more details on becoming a standards draft reviewer and in fact on all levels of involvement in the development processes, please refer to the NIST document once it becomes available. It is also recommended that the NIST document be referenced for descriptions of types of SDO's, for SDO methods and processes, for SDO membership requirements, and for an overview of salient standards and guidelines important to IT Security.

There are many ways to become a reviewer including, but not limited to:

- Check public review announcements;
- Check the web sites of the SDO, determine if they have a review policy, determine which organizations have liaison status with them, and find out who to contact;
- Check with internal organization people and groups to determine if the organization is already a member of the SDO or is considering becoming a member;
- Contact the SDO directly;
- Contact a liaison organization that may be reviewing drafts as part of their liaison activities;
- Look for user's groups or other interest parties that have commented on the output of the SDO in the past;
- Use the Internet search engines to find such connections and such organizations;
- Contact other organizations with similar interests in the drafts and determine what they have done to become reviewers or if they want to become reviewers.

The benefits of standards draft reviews are high. The costs of such reviews are low. More organizations should become reviewers to their own benefit.

APPENDIX

ISO/IEC JTC 1 (SC 6, SC 17, SC 27, SC 37)
  http://www.jtc1.org/

ISO TC 68
  http://www.tc68.org/

IETF
  http://www.ietf.org

INCITS (TC, B10, M1, T3, T4)
  http://www.incits.org/

X9
  http://www.x9.org

IEEE
  http://standards.ieee.org/

Center for Internet Security (CIS)
  http://www.cisecurity.org

Internet Security Alliance
  http://isalliance.org

Network Reliability and Interoperability Council VI (NRIC VI)
  http://www.nric.org/

Partnership for Critical Infrastructure Security (PCIS)
  http://www.pcis.org

NIST ITL
  http://www.itl.nist.gov/

NIST ITL Computer Security Resource Center
  http://csrc.nist.gov/

NIST ITL Biometrics Resource Center
  http://www.nist.gov/biometrics

NIST ITL Smart Card
  http://smartcard.nist.gov

NIST Special Publication 800 Series
  http://csrc.nist.gov/publications/nistpubs/index/html

NIST ITL Computer Security Bulletins
  http://csrc.nist.gov/publications/nistpub/index.html

Federal Information Processing Standards
  http://www.itl.nist.goc/fipspubs/

NIST Critical Information Infrastructure Brochure
   http://www.itl.nist.gov/itlcipbrochure.pdf

ASSURING CRITICAL INFORMATION INFRASTRUCTURE

Sokratis K. Katsikas
Information & Communication Systems Security Laboratory
Department of Information & Communication Systems Engineering
University of the Aegean
Karlovassi GR-83200
ska@aegean.gr

Abstract: Critical Information Infrastructure constitutes a subset of public and private information systems whose continuing operation is of grave importance to the well being of the society. In view of their importance, the security risks that these information systems face are deemed to be very high; therefore, these systems need to be protected against cyber threats. Governments must undertake action to this end, focusing in five operational areas.

Keywords: Critical Information Infrastructure; Information Society; Information Systems; Risk Management; Protection Strategies; Government Actions

1. INTRODUCTION

The Information Society permeates the whole of our lives, not only affecting, but also giving shape to our ways of working, living, entertaining, doing business, socializing, looking after our health etc. In this setting, information systems have proliferated within almost every aspect of human life, changing it (hopefully to the better) and facilitating it, but also, at the same time, making it more dependent upon the underlying Information and Communication Technologies. According to the OECD, the development of web-enabled services is expected to affect the productivity increase rate in the European Union by as much as 30%, as shown in Figure 1. Indeed, as indicated in the figure, the expected productivity growth rate, based on data of the last decade, without web-enabled services is 1.3%, whereas the respective rate with web-enabled services is 1.7%. On the other hand, the number of incidents reported to the US CERT, shown in Figure 2, has

43

J. S. Kowalik et al. (eds.), Cyberspace Security and Defense: Research Issues, 43–55.
© 2005 *Springer. Printed in the Netherlands.*

increased from 6 in 1998, to 137.529 in 2003, as shown in Fig. 2 (CERT2004).

The more our society depends upon ICT, the more significance it is likely to assign to securing these technologies. However, securing information systems is not cost-free; indeed, the cost of securing an information system can be, in particular circumstances, very high. As no society can afford to assign unlimited budget to any activity, no matter how significant this may be, some prioritization needs to be made with regards to which information systems should be more carefully protected. Clearly, one of the factors – perhaps the most crucial- to be considered in determining such priorities is the importance of the information system to the society at large. Not all information systems are of equal importance; those that are recognized as being more important are referred to collectively with the term Critical Information Infrastructure. According to the US Dept. of Homeland Security, Critical Infrastructure Assurance Office, "Critical Information Infrastructure pertains to and encompasses the organizations, the networks and the distribution systems that provide for the continuous provision of goods and services that are necessary for the defense of the state, for its economic security, as well as for the health, well-being and security of its citizens" (US Government2003).

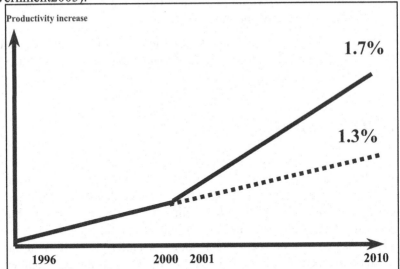

Figure 1. Increase in EU Productivity

By definition, Critical Information Infrastructure (CII) encompasses both the public and the private sector and also encompasses systems in agriculture, food, water, public health, emergency services, government, defense industry, information and telecommunications, energy, transportation, banking and finance, chemicals and hazardous materials, postal and shipping. The common ground and nervous system of all these dissimilar and diverge systems is the Cyberspace; this, then, is what we need to protect.

In this paper we argue, in Section 2, that CII needs to be protected, using a qualitative argumentation inspired from principles of risk analysis and management. Subsequently, in Section 3, we propose a set of actions that governments need to undertake in order to protect CII and we comment briefly on the state of these actions in the particular case of Greece. Finally, Section 4 summarizes our conclusions.

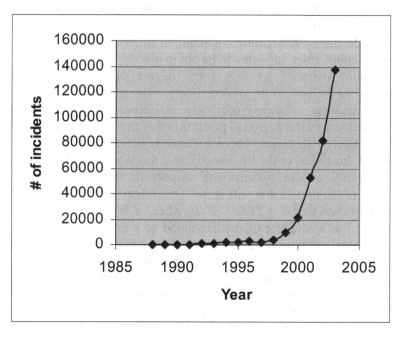

Figure 2. Number of Incidents Reported to the U.S. CERT

2. RISK ASSESSMENT

Any information system consists of hardware, software, communications equipment, environmental control equipment, documentation and staff. It manages, i.e., processes, transmits and stores information. All of the above are called the "system assets", and must be protected.

Any information system, no matter how well designed, has vulnerabilities. Besides, the system is exposed to a number of different threats, which are defined as acts or events that can harm an asset. Vulnerabilities are defined as weak points in the system that can be exploited by threats to cause a security breach. When a threat successfully exploits one or more vulnerabilities of the system, it leads to one or more impacts, which in turn result in consequences to the system and, consequently, to the organization that uses the system. These consequences are clearly a function of the value (not only in the narrow monetary sense) of the system assets that have been affected. Figure 3 depicts graphically the concept of risk and related concepts.

The objective of the security policy is to either minimize the likelihood of impact occurrence or to at least minimize the consequences that an undesirable event may have. The former can be done either by reducing the system vulnerabilities or by decreasing the likelihood that a threat will successfully exploit some vulnerability. Clearly threats cannot be controlled, being outside the system control domain. In order to achieve these goals, appropriate countermeasures should be put in place.

Any countermeasure provides some degree of protection, which is proportional to the cost of its implementation. Because of this, the selection of countermeasures is always (not only in information systems security) made on the basis of the degree of protection that they offer, in relation to the reasonably likely risk factor. The risk factor is determined as a function of the value of the assets, of the likelihood that a threat will occur, of the degree of vulnerability of the system with respect to this threat, and of the seriousness of the impact that will occur if the threat succeeds. Therefore, we can formally state that $R = f(A, T, V, I)$, where R is the risk factor, A is the asset value, T is a measure of the likelihood of a threat occurring, V is the degree of vulnerability of the system with respect to the particular threat, and I is some measure of the likely impact that the threat will bear upon the system if it succeeds. R is an increasing function in all its parameters.

Even though the exact risk that an Information System is exposed to should be determined through the application of a rigorous risk analysis and management exercise that will, inter alia, allow for the subsequent compilation of the security policy, the design of the appropriate countermeasures and a proposal for mitigating the remaining risk, it is not difficult to qualitatively assess the risk associated with critical information infrastructures as very high. Indeed, by looking at the elements of risk, as previously defined, the following considerations apply:

- The wide proliferation of ICT that we witness today leads to increased dependence upon the very same technology, which in turn leads to increased dependence upon the Internet. The largest portion of the added value of today's information systems, in particular those serving e-government, lies in their connectivity. Therefore, there would be little sense or usefulness in building stand-alone information systems. Likewise, an information system that has been designed for use in the networked world would lose most of its functionality if forced to operate on its own. This loss of functionality of elements of the critical information infrastructure would certainly result in disruption of critical operations, causing severe loss of revenue, intellectual property, government malfunction, or even loss of human life. Therefore, the anticipated impact of a security breach of elements of the critical information infrastructure is very high.

- The Internet, as good a communication medium as it may be, it is also notorious for its inherent vulnerabilities. The Internet was not designed originally for the purpose it has come to exclusively serve today; this is the main reason for it being vulnerable 'by design'. Consequently, there is at least one element of the critical information infrastructure whose vulnerability rating is "very high."

- The Internet, the very same element that has made the Information Society a reality has also allowed all kinds of hacker communities to flourish, by providing them with increased and inexpensive communication means. This not only has resulted in vast increase in the numbers of potential attackers, but has also led to a wide proliferation of malicious tools and techniques that are now available to any interested party, literally one click away. Thus, the threats against the critical information infrastructure are many and the likelihood of their appearance is very high. Similarly, considering that attacks are becoming all the more sophisticated, one concludes that the likelihood of a serious attack to succeed is also very high.

- Finally, the definition of the critical information infrastructure itself easily leads to the conclusion that the assets involved are extremely precious.

The concept of risk

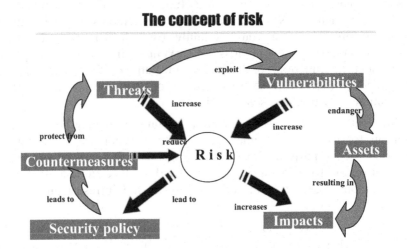

Figure 3. The Concept of Risk

The above discussion reveals that all elements of risk associated with critical information infrastructure are rated as "very high". Consequently, we can safely qualitatively assert that the risk itself is "very high". This recognition leads inevitably to the conclusion that critical information infrastructure must be protected. Moreover, its protection is critical. The question then is "how do we go about protecting critical information infrastructure?" Clearly, the answer to this question is multidimensional, ranging from policies to strategies to measures. In the next section we will attempt to answer the question at the policy and strategy levels.

3. PROTECTION STRATEGIES

Complete and absolute security is a theoretical construction; no information system can be made totally secure, unless it is locked in a room with no access at all and nobody is allowed to use it. On the other hand, security measures carry a cost, which is usually proportional to their effectiveness. Therefore, the best we can do is to secure information systems as best as possible within a given, finite, monetary budget. The purpose of all protection strategies is to reduce the risk that the information infrastructure is exposed to and, as some risk will always remain, to mitigate or accept this remaining risk. To do this, because the risk function is increasing in all its elements, one must reduce one, more, or all the elements of risk. As it is meaningless to reduce the value of assets, one must attempt to reduce the threat, vulnerability and impact levels.

In the particular case of critical information infrastructure, reducing the threat level implies effectively countering cyber attacks; reducing the vulnerability level implies making systems more secure; and reducing the impact level implies minimizing damage and recovery time in the event of a security breach. There are several levels of action that should be undertaken in order to achieve the above; these comprise action at the legal, technical, physical, procedural and organizational levels. In the sequel, we will outline key action lines that should be undertaken with increased priority. These have been synthesized out of guidelines, recommendations and resolutions on the subject made by national governments, international administration and international bodies (U.S. Government 2003, Commission of the EC 2001, OECD2003). As to who should provide leadership in this effort, one realizes that government is a key stakeholder and, hence, should be a key player in the process of securing CII. Indeed, government functions in a multiplicity of roles with regards to CII: first, it is the prime responsible for the development of public policy, second, it is, itself, a large-scale owner and operator of systems and networks, and third, it is, itself, a large-scale user of such systems and networks. Providing leadership does not, naturally, mean exclusive responsibility. In fact, public policy development is a unique role of government but one that should be carried out in a transparent fashion and in consultation with other participants and concerned parties; on the other hand, as owner, operator and user of information systems and networks, most of which are now privately owned and/or managed, government shares a role with businesses and other organizations.

Key action line 1:   National policy on information security and cross-border co-operation

Government should recognize the increasing need for a comprehensive policy and institutional infrastructure to ensure public safety, security and economic well-being in response to the threats and vulnerabilities associated with CII. Such policies include those aiming at combating cyber crimes, such as enhancing law enforcement capabilities against cyber crime by enacting a comprehensive set of substantive criminal, procedural and mutual assistance legal measures to combat cyber crime and to ensure cross-border co-operation, as networks today are international. These legal measures should be at least as comprehensive as, and consistent with, the Council of Europe Convention on Cybercrime (2001). The identification of national cyber crime units and of national and international high-technology assistance points of contact, that would be able to provide expert assistance on assessing and securing emerging systems and on secure Internet mechanisms, and the creation of such capabilities—to the extent they do not already exist—also fall within the range of these policies. The establishment of a national coordination center to which the responsibility for co-ordinating all relevant policies and actions as well as the responsibility for international coordination and co-operation should be assigned is also a condition sine qua non. Such a national coordination center in the setting of the U.S. Government is shown in Figure 4, wherein FBI stands for Federal Bureau of Investigation, NIPC stands for National Infrastructure Protection Center, PCIS stands for Partnership for Critical Infrastructure Security and CIAO stands for Critical Information Assurance Office.

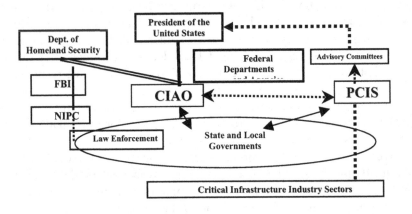

Figure 4. The U.S. Government CII Protection Structure

Key action line 2: Training and awareness

Awareness raise can be achieved through consistently emphasizing the necessity of security at every opportunity. Education, training, press releases, Web sites, public announcements, offering tools and kits are among the currently identified means to raise awareness. Government should emphasize the importance of awareness of the risks and available safeguards. A public information and education campaign should be launched, following the development of an appropriate comprehensive awareness program. Moreover, government should foster security education programs at all education levels. In designing such programs, not only tips to ensure the security of the systems and networks are necessary, but also emphasis on the ethics to promote conduct that recognizes security needs and respects the legitimate interests of others. Government initiated education and outreach programs should also promote conduct that aims at ensuring security in a manner consistent with the values recognized by democratic societies including the freedom to exchange thoughts and ideas, the free flow of information, the confidentiality of information and communication, the appropriate protection of personal information, openness and transparency. Assessing the impact of planned security measures on these values should also be encouraged. Further, government, in close co-operation with businesses should foster training programs in both the public and the private sector. In doing this, care must be taken to ensure that all this effort is undertaken by competent personnel, therefore skills certification procedures must be promoted.

Key action line 3: Security response system

This should aim at providing in-depth attack analysis and threat and vulnerability assessments, at assisting with individual incident management and at facilitating the development of public-private continuity and contingency plans. It should have capability for attack attribution and response; hence a public-private architecture is appropriate, so as to enable public-private security information sharing. It should also stimulate the exchange of best practice among interested organizations and businesses. Government should strengthen their Computer Emergency Response Teams (CERTs) and, in the case of the European Union, improve the co-ordination among them. It goes without saying that the establishment of a national CERT where such does not exist is of paramount priority. At the EU level, optimal organization of the data collection and analysis and of the planning of forward-looking responses to existing and emerging security threats must be examined.

Key action line 4: Technology support

Support for research and development in security, aiming at threat and vulnerability reduction, should be a key element in the national R&D support program and should be linked to the broader strategy for improved network and information security. Likewise, the national standardization organizations should accelerate their work on interoperability, certification, electronic signatures, further development and deployment of IPv6 and IPSec, and should also review and promote the use of all relevant security standards, including but not limited to the Common Criteria for Information Systems Assurance.

Key action line 5:   Security of public information infrastructure

Government must address the principles of risk assessment, security design and implementation, security management, and reassessment, just as any other owner and operator of information systems and networks must. Government should develop policies that reflect best practices in security management and risk assessment. Security management should be based on a risk assessment that identifies threats and vulnerabilities and is sufficiently broad-based to encompass key internal and external factors, such as technology, physical and human factors, policies and third-party services with security implications. Security management within government should also be dynamic, encompassing all levels of governmental activities and all aspects of their operations. It should include forward-looking responses to emerging threats and it should address prevention, detection and response to incidents, systems recovery, ongoing maintenance, review and audit. And, these information system and network security policies, practices, measures and procedures should be coordinated and integrated to create a coherent system of security. Internationally recognized information security management standards, such as ISO, ITU, CEN and ETSI standards and industry-specific standards, may be used to establish an effective system of security management. Because of the size of its operations, government has a special responsibility to become a model owner/operator and to lead by example. Government can thus use its operational expertise to facilitate the development of best practices and other operational improvements for the benefit of all participants. Government can also use its significant purchasing power in information systems and networks to encourage the development and expanded availability of more secure products and services. As a user of information systems and networks, government has a responsibility to ensure that its use is consistent with ethics and democracy principles, and thus contributes to a secure global system. Because individual government employees constitute government use, government must ensure its employees are aware of security concerns, their individual responsibilities and have the capability to respond in an appropriate way to security incidents. Development by government of an appropriate security environment, training, and tools will not only facilitate security in government systems and networks, but can also serve as foundation elements for government's outreach as a public policy matter. In particular, government should incorporate effective and interoperable security solutions in their e-government and e-procurement activities and should introduce electronic signatures when offering public services.

The Council of the European Union, in its Resolution of 6 December 2001 (CoEU2001) "asks the Member States

1. by the end of 2002 to launch or strengthen information and education campaigns to increase awareness of network and information security; to specifically target such actions at business, private users and public administrations; to elaborate such awareness raising actions closely with the private sector, including inter alia Internet Service Providers, and to encourage private sector-led initiatives;

2. to promote best practices in information security management notably in small and medium sized companies based, where appropriate, on internationally recognised standards;

3. by the end of 2002 to strengthen or promote the importance of security concepts as part of computer education and training;

4. by mid 2002 to review the effectiveness of national arrangements regarding computer emergency response, which could include virus alert systems, with a view to strengthening, where necessary, their ability to prevent, detect, and react efficiently at national and international level against network and information systems disruption and attack;

5. to promote the use of the Common Criteria standard (ISO-15408) and to facilitate mutual recognition of related certificates;

6. by the end of 2002 to take significant steps towards effective and interoperable security solutions based on recognised standards where possible—which could include open source software—in their e-government and e-procurement activities, and towards the introduction of electronic signatures to allow those public services that require strong authentication also to be offered on-line;

7. where they choose to introduce electronic and biometrics identification systems for public or official use, to co-operate where appropriate on technological developments and to examine any possible interoperability requirements;

8. with a view to facilitating Community and international co-operation, to exchange information with each other and with the Commission on the bodies primarily responsible within their territory for network and information security matters."

Against this request for action, Greece, regrettably, lags behind: With respect to points 1 and 3 above, there has been no awareness campaign and no specific action targeting the strengthening of education in ICT security. The only exception is the establishment of a MSc Program on Information and Communication Systems Security Engineering at the University of the Aegean (University of the Aegean2004) that followed a successful ERASMUS/SOCRATES Curriculum Development project (Katsikas2000). There are, of course, individual security courses embedded in Informatics and Computer Science curricula of Greek Universities; these, however have not been the result of an "organized campaign" or of targeted "promotion of the importance of security concepts as part of computer education and training". With respect to point 2 above, there has been no promotion of best practices to small and medium enterprises, with the exception of the work performed within the e-Business forum (e-Business forum2004). With respect to point 4 above, there is still no national CERT in Greece; the only CERT in Greece is the one operated by the University of the Aegean on behalf of EDET, the body responsible for the operation of the Greek academic and research network (Greek Research Network2004). With respect to point 5 above, there has been no promotion of the use of the Common Criteria. With regards to point 6 above, satisfactory progress has been made through the active and significant support of the Information Society Programme and the Information Society S. A.. Point 7 above is, for the time being at least, not applicable to Greece. Finally, with regards to the last point above, one must note the absence of a national centre of reference that would, inter alia, facilitate Community and international cooperation.

CONCLUSIONS

Critical Information Infrastructure comprises the subset of information and communication systems whose continuous operation is of paramount significance to the well-being of society. In today's cyber environment, CII faces increased threats, which, combined with its inherent vulnerabilities lead to unbearable impact if successful. Therefore, the risk that CII faces is very high, a fact that makes the protection of CII imperative. National governments and international bodies and administrations have issued recommendations, guidelines and resolutions to this effect. Based on these, a set of 5 priority action lines have been produced and proposed herein. Compared to the mandate of the Council of the EU, progress in Greece has been found to lag behind, despite the fact that security research and education in Greek Universities are rated among the very top worldwide in the field of security. The main reason for this is the reduced awareness and interest of government—which has resulted in complete lack of national coordinated action—as well as the lack of cooperation with the private sector. In addition to these, despite the remarkable performance of Greek Universities and industry in attracting competitive EU R&D funds in the area of security, national R&D funding of research in the field is negligible. Addressing the issue of CII protection is now critical.

REFERENCES

1. CERT, 2004, **http://www.cert.org/stats/cert_stats.html**

2. Commission of the European Communities, 2001, Communication from the Commission to the Council, the European Parliament, the European Economic and Social Committee and the Committee of the Regions, Network and information security: Proposal for a European policy approach, COM(2001) 298 final. **http://www.europa.int/ information_society/eeurope/news_library/pdf_files/netsec_en.pdf**

3. Council of the European Union, 2001, Resolution of 6 December 2001 on a common approach and specific actions in the area of network and information security, **http://www.europa.int/information_society/eeurope/news_library/ pdf_files/netsecres_en.pdf**

4. Council of the European Union, 2001.

5. **http://conventions.coe.int/treaty/EN/ WhatYouWant.asp?NT=185&CM=8&DF=23/04/02**

6. E-business forum, 2004, **http://www.ebusinessforum.gr/english/content/workinggroups**

7. Greek Research Network, 2004, **http://cert.grnet.gr/grnetcertenglish.php**

8. Katsikas, S.K., A Postgraduate Programme on Information and Communication Systems Security, *Proceedings, IFIP SEC 2000*, Beijing, China, pp. 49-59, 2000.

9. Organisation for Economic Co-operation and Development, 2004, Implementation plan for the OECD guidelines for the security of information systems and networks: towards a culture of security, **http://www.olis.oecd.org/olis/2002doc.nsf/ 43bb6130e5e86e5fc12569fa005d004c/ 36896c8a5cb63c7ec1256ca6005cf815/ $FILE/JT00137968.PDF**

10. University of the Aegean, 2004, **http://www.icsd.aegean.gr/index_en.htm**

11. U.S. Government, Department of Homeland Security, 2003, The National Strategy to Secure Cyberspace, **http://www.dhs.gov/interweb/assetlibrary/ National_Cyberspace_Strategy.pdf**

SYSTEMIC CHALLENGES FOR CRITICAL INFORMATION INFRASTRUCTURE PROTECTION

Marcelo Masera
Institute for the Protection and Security of the Citizen
Joint Research Centre, European Commission

Abstract: This paper examines the challenges presented by the need to assure the information infrastructure. First, the concept of critical infrastructures is discussed, along with their features from the security viewpoint. Then, the critical information infrastructure is analyzed, reflecting on the requirements and constraints for its protection, and the different perspectives that can be given to the problem. In particular there is an account of the main questions that have to be answered when determining which type of protection could be appropriate. Finally, the main systemic challenges found in the discussion are summarized with reference to both the information infrastructure internal organization, and the risk-related decision making processes concerned with its protection.

Keywords: Critical information infrastructure; Critical Infrastructure Protection; Security

INTRODUCTION

The assurance of the information infrastructure upon which modern societies rely is recognized as being of growing importance for citizens, businesses and governments. The social and economic fabric of these societies vitally depends upon the secure and reliable flow, storage and access to information managed through electronic means. A key question that has to be solved is about the challenges that may hinder that assurance.

This paper first discusses critical infrastructures, its relation with security concepts, and the features that are relevant for understanding the challenges they pose to society. Then, the critical information infrastructure is analyzed, with reflections on the requirements and constraint for its protection, and the

J. S. Kowalik et al. (eds.), Cyberspace Security and Defense: Research Issues, 57–73.
© 2005 *Springer. Printed in the Netherlands.*

different perspectives that can be given to the problem. Finally, the main systemic challenges found in the discussion are summarized with reference to both the information infrastructure internal organization, and the risk-related decision making processes concerned with its protection

CRITICAL INFRASTRUCTURES

Our society is characterized by the deployment of large, complex infrastructures which are interconnected among them in intricate ways. These infrastructures are composite socio-technical systems-of-systems, whose functioning comes out from the interaction of multiple components and organizations, mostly loosely coupled and weakly coordinated [15].

The web of links that connect the infrastructures expands at different levels: technological as well as organizational—and most of the crucial connections are enabled by information and communication technologies (ICT). This set of underlying ICT systems is normally referred as the *information infrastructure*—which presents critical aspects in its own right, as well as being an essential service provider for the other infrastructures.

What is a Critical Infrastructure (CI)? There is no single, universal definition, but a common understanding is that with this term it is meant a *"complex set of interconnected, interdependent systems on which nations, business and individuals depend for goods and services"* [13].

Therefore CI refers to a specific subset of infrastructures (transport, energy, health, telecommunications) dangerously vulnerable to accidental and malicious events, where the criticality is defined by two factors, namely: a.) products and services that are essential for society; and b.) whose disruption may have adverse societal effects in the short-term (e.g., black out, virus) or in the long-term (e.g., harbour blockade).

As a consequence of the acknowledged criticality of some infrastructures, it has been identified the need for a organized and coordinated approach to their protection, that should encompass all measures (technical, social, economic, etc.) needed for ensuring the dependable functioning of the CIs—the topic now usually known as Critical Infrastructure Protection (CIP).

In the context of CIP, the information infrastructure plays a double role: as the main interconnecting network, it initiates and propagates malfunctions and disturbances; on the other hand, it is an essential tool for managing emergencies. Hence, it is at the same time a key cause of the brittleness of our technological society, and an indispensable means for assuring its resilience to risks—for instance it is now indispensable for deploying incident control and crisis management instruments.

Since the inception of the concept of CIP [4] it has been recognized that it might present many denotations according to the context of reference. This fact has obstructed the ready preparation of relevant policies and the quick development and application of solutions. Many elements have contributed to the difficulties in assembling an effective CIP response:

- A first important element is that the majority of the infrastructures are in private hands, and so governments cannot immediately act or regulate their operation without well founded reasons. There is no single owner, and most often no single regulator—and consequently new governance approaches are required.

- A second is that there is no common body of knowledge and practice on CIP. Many disciplines are relevant for CIP, ranging from social and political, to economics, to technical.

- A third is that most of the infrastructures to be protected—and perhaps the most critical ones—are transnational by nature: they cross borders and are regulated and operated on an international basis.

The same understanding of what is critical, of what is an infrastructure and of what is entailed by the protection measures, have been a matter of discussion within countries and at the international level. These definitions, which are political in nature, more than technological, are influenced by the different perspectives taken by the problem stakeholders: for instance, national defense, law enforcement, business continuity, and information assurance are four different domains that have their say on CIP. Moreover, even within governments there have been disagreements among the various policy standpoints—mainly originating from the requisite to link CIP initiatives with other on-going policies: e.g., anti-terrorism, civil protection, security of supply, etc.

What is universally accepted is that to understand, analyze and manage the risks derived from our reliance upon large-scale, complex and interdependent information-based infrastructures, we need to make use of appropriate policy and technological answers, and that this challenge can only be resolved with the application of trans-disciplinary approaches.

CIP and Security

Broadly speaking, security is the quality or state of a system that keeps anyone (person or technical component) from carrying out unauthorized actions that might cause unwanted incidents with potential risky consequences. The unauthorized actions can occur within, with or from the system, and the consequences can be related to assets internal or external to the system. The damage caused by a security breach can derive from unsafe conditions, from the unavailability of services, or from the violation of the confidentiality or the integrity of the data managed by the system.

The failure of an infrastructural systems can affect a single user (person or organization), or accumulate its negative effects up to the societal level. In this case and when the system that fails to deliver its intended output is providing a critical infrastructural service, it is possible to establish a direct link between CIP and security 0.

CI systems can be the target of malicious attacks or fail due to accidental faults, generating effects that can cause unacceptable losses. That loss can be a catastrophic consequence (physical harm, property damage, etc.—i.e., safety concerns), an impairment of civil/personal rights (e.g., privacy infringement), an economic detriment, or the triggering of social and political unrest. This broad set of cases shows how problematical it can be to assess CIs and to define effective protection instruments.

In addition, it should be considered that the picture is further complicated by the fact that security solutions require the application of additional socio-technical systems, vulnerable themselves, and which can be used themselves as attack means (cf. attack to the Twin Towers on September 11th, 2001).

Methodologies and strategies applied for assessing and managing the security of single, local systems do not scale up for analyzing broadly distributed, massively interconnected ones. For instance, perimeter security solutions are ineffectual for highly interlinked systems, and more in-depth approaches are needed. At the same time, fixed security architectures are not adequate for counteracting dynamic hazards and threats that continuously modify their modus operandi. In conclusion, the protection of infrastructures might benefit from the security practices applied for well-engineered systems, with predictable behavior and whose evolution in time is under control—but that is not sufficient. More is needed, from both the theoretical and practical viewpoints.

A key point is to recognize that it is impossible to thoroughly guarantee the security of complex systems such as an infrastructure: these systems do not have a definite topology or architecture, they might change without notice, their components have varying characteristics (as for instance when new vulnerabilities are discovered), the global consequences of some functions might be unforeseeable, and unexpected events and operating conditions might occur beyond the ones established when engineering decisions were made. Therefore solutions have to be developed with the recognition that security lapses will take place. The question is not to develop solutions that will protect the system once and forever, but to put in place a strategy for adapting to unexpected situations.

CIP Features

Before proposing solutions for CIP, it is essential to understand the problem. The rising risks don't leave space for improvised actions. So much is at stake that a rational, rigorous approach is mandatory.

First of all, it is necessary to recognize that this new scenario of interconnected and broadly distributed infrastructures is characterized by the entanglement of policy, socio-economic, and technical factors. As an example we can refer to the measures taken in many countries for the liberalization of energy markets, which have significantly contributed to the fragility of the electric power provision as generation and distribution companies are forced to operate closer to their technical limits for the sake of securing the short-term profitability.

A further twist of the problem is given by the fact that as important as the protection of CIs, is the reassurance of society: citizens and organizations need to develop and maintain confidence on the security of CIs, because they fundamentally rely on the CI's correct functioning for their everyday living and wellbeing. The perception that a system is too frail might undermine the trust of citizens on a government, and perhaps on the same solidity of their society.

This complexity of the CIP problem and its multiple facets require a firm set of concepts and reference to all the scientific fields concerned. Some of the features that characterize critical infrastructures are:

- Cumulative design and development: infrastructures are systems-of-systems that nobody designs as a whole, either from the very beginning or in a definitive way. The basic, original mechanisms originate from simpler systems, and the infrastructure generally transmutes them, by and large expanding their functionality beyond the initial intentions (e.g., the Internet protocols TCP/IP). New components are added, but rarely making reference to a global project—the only constraint being their interface with other components. For this same reason it becomes difficult to introduce major modification to a given infrastructure configuration that has evolved and firmly structured itself in time. The integration of a new standard (perhaps justified for security motives) might proved unworkable since it might require a coordinated action by many actors (e.g., the adoption of IP v6)

- Multi-ownership: infrastructures do not have a single owner. The many operators of the distinct systems that compose the infrastructure can be public or private (mainly the latter), and the only coordination is given by the regulations that normalize a certain sector. This fact, accentuated by the liberalization of many markets, raises questions about the final responsibility of some functional and meta-functional issues, such as the overall performance and the security of an infrastructure. Private companies will invest in the protection of their systems, so long as this is compatible with their business objectives. But the addition of all the business-induced security measures by all the operators of a given infrastructure would hardly ever match the overall security objectives of society. There will be a surplus of security requirements that have to be satisfied.

- <u>International and cross-jurisdiction</u>: infrastructures run through national and jurisdictional borders—and this is connatural to their value in a globalized economy. But the consequence could be that different regulations can apply to the same object. The real implications emerge when a CIP incident occurs, which might degenerate provoking an emergency or crisis, involving several countries. The nature of the information infrastructure that enables world-wide reachability and the free flow of data further complicate this issue. A great challenge is to reconcile the focus on national approaches, with the recognition of the international facets of the problem.

These features present a testing case without an easy solution. The subject needs the joint consideration of several socio-technical disciplines, which have rarely worked together in the past. In addition, these fields share some risk and security-related concepts; but the semantics of these notions do not always overlap, causing misunderstandings and arguments on the appropriateness of the various theories. For instance, there are discrepancies around the concept of threat, according to the various background and viewpoints on the issue: threats are considered as actors (e.g., terrorists, hackers), as events (e.g., an intrusion in a database), as conditions (e.g., the lack of defense against a particular attack), or as mechanisms (e.g., software means that can penetrate and damage information systems). It is easy to understand that the dialogue that has to be established among the different actors is being mined by this multiplicity of meanings.

As information security is concerned, there is a need to concurrently bear in mind information assurance, technical ICT security (systems and components), cybercrime, infowar, but also aspects of privacy, trust and confidence, and information assurance. This variety of definitions further jeopardizes the communication among analysts and both policy and business decision makers. In any case, multi-disciplinary approaches, although recognized as urgently needed, still remain a remote aspiration.

A central question involves who is responsible and should take decisions about the security and risk management of infrastructures. As said before, infrastructures are mostly property of private companies, but the policy initiatives are obviously in the hands of governments. This can lead to contradictory situations. In many countries this problem has been dealt with the so-called "private-public partnerships" (PPP) [3][7]—but implementing them in a way that yields effective results has proven difficult. The poor state-of-the-art in the security field (that shows a certain inability to keep the pace of the discovery of vulnerabilities and the materialization of new threat agents and means), and the lack of appropriate standards, don't facilitate to agree on which countermeasures should be put in place. As a matter of fact the running PPPs have as main purpose that of gathering and distributing information. This is justified by the fact that any action (either organizational or technical, policy of R&D) needs to be based on confirmable evidence on risks, and on objective proof of what can be gained from the implementation of such actions. But data is scarce, for the same novelty and dynamic nature of many systems. For this reason, two main questions stand:

1. without further measures, individual actors see poor advantages and many dangers from disclosing information (e.g., admitting attacks and poor protections, publicizing business strategies); and

2. the main actors are international companies, with global interests that surmount national borders.

Two extreme situations can be foreseen as government intervention is concerned:

- one in which authorities will force infrastructure operators to implement the security surplus mentioned before;

- a second where objectives are set by governments, leaving the implementation to the private stakeholders. This is for instance the road taken in the USA with the National Strategy for Cybersecurity [2], and the National Strategy for the Physical Protection of Critical Infrastructures and Key Assets [1]

However, it should be considered that security (for its inherent character: if it is successful nothing occurs) is difficult to incorporate into business equations and ROI calculations; and less so when the benefits from any investments will be gathered, not by the implementer alone, but by society as a whole (including the competitors).

At the same time, no single government is able to secure cross-border systems. This has been recognized by, for instance, the eleven guiding principles adopted by the G8 [9]—focused on information infrastructures. The principles are based on the notion that "effective protection... requires communication coordination and cooperation among all stakeholders". This is instantiated in the recommendation 10 which states that "Countries should engage in international cooperation... including by developing and coordinating emergency warning systems, sharing and analyzing information regarding vulnerabilities, threats and incidents, and coordinating investigations of attacks on such infrastructures in accordance with domestic laws."

CRITICAL INFORMATION INFRASTRUCTURES

The critical information infrastructure (CII) is a subset of the critical infrastructure, composed of "the totality of interconnected computers and networks and their critical information flows" [8]0, comprising therefore a vast range of components and systems, extending from hardware (satellites, routers), to software (operating systems, Internet protocols, databases), to data (DNS tables), to the processes and operations applied for running them [16]0. The CII includes typical information systems and telecommunications services, but increasingly now industrial systems (as for instance, the remote control of installations).

A common understanding now is that protecting the CII is not about sheltering cables and wires, but concerns the qualities of some basic services related to the processing and transmission of data. So, although the underlying systems are those supporting fixed and mobile communications, positioning signals and Internet access, what is critical for society, government and industry is the set of CII services. These services have to be as trustworthy as needed for the functions that rely upon the CII: national defense, emergency management, on-line markets, health services, etc. Evidently, as for all infrastructures, the determination of what is "critical" can be very controversial, and should be the object of dedicated and shared risk assessments [14].

The escalating use of networking services, such as the Internet, is continuously changing the scenario of CII. The utilization of information and communication technologies in central functions and procedures by all social and economic elements evolves with the development of technologies, and in different ways—and this is particularly true for the other critical infrastructures. The same policy and technical options for the protection of CII, and as a consequence CIP, are affected: what can be today a sound protection option, might introduce vulnerabilities to be discovered much later.

This is apparent in the case of industrial systems [6]0, which are making increasing use of the capabilities offered by open networks for remotely accessing sensors and actuators for their operation and maintenance. Control and supervision systems are typically embedded in other critical infrastructures: electric power, potable water, oil and gas, railways, etc. The potential advantages from the economic and functional viewpoints are unquestionable; less often studied are the risks that these connections might cause. The application of CII in industrial settings marks a substantial transformation, but systems up to now haven't been design and operated with information and network security in mind. Its assurance from the technical and organizational standpoints is much less evolved than for information other more traditional systems—and therefore of much concern.

CII Features and Requirements

The CII is characterized by some very specific traits, which has to be appraised in order to plan adequate solutions to the critical security issues. Some of these traits result from the CII implementation; others are requirements put forward by the CII users, which shape its development by explicitly demanding (e.g., quality of service contracts) or implicitly expecting some qualities.

The main features of the CII that are relevant for its security implications are: its global scale, the variety of connection means, the emergent dependencies among its components, and its unpredictable evolution [12].

As its scale is concerned, the information infrastructure is global: every point in the world connected to the public infrastructure is reachable from everywhere else. This has clear advantages for business and citizens – but the same capabilities are offered to malicious actors. Networking is about transmitting data between information systems that have independent administrative structures and along loosely coupled network tracts. Global reachability depends upon agreements among network operators who have to share information on the traffic and its routing. This is conditional on the policies of the telecommunications service providers, and on their correct functioning. There is no way to enforce policies, and a successful network is also effective in the propagation of malware (e.g., virus and worms). The resulting structure is also rather vulnerable to attacks such as denial of service and theft of service.

The access points to the CII are increasing with the number of technologies. For instance, there are now numerous means for establishing a wireless connection to the Internet—and some of them are related to geographically wide mobility, such as the use of cellular and satellite phone links. The access to the CII is then immediate and opportunistic: the user might not realize which channels are being activated for directing the communication. The positive side is the possibility to instantaneously be on-line, in whichever place, even while being on the run. The downside is the need to trust many actors.

The CII systems and operators critically depend on each other. From routing to performance, the CII services result from the collaboration among different actors. The network structure is inherently resilient to single failures. For instance, alternative paths can be determined, although not optimal. But there is certain level of homogeneity that makes the system vulnerable to some potential common mode failures; and there exist a limited number of privileged nodes whose failure might cause in especial circumstances the collapse of great parts of the CII (e.g., Internet DNS root services).

Another point is that the CII continuous evolution might complicate the management of the resulting networks and the scaling up of current solutions. The changes accumulate at all levels: routing protocols, algorithms, architectures, applications. The result is a CII that gets more complex and less determined. An important consequence is the difficulty in predicting key security-related characteristics: e.g., the discovery rate of vulnerabilities in the components; the increase of throughput, capabilities gained by threat agents.

From the requirements point of view, users of the CII demand four main characteristics. These, that present positive and negative sides, are:

- Always available and ubiquitous: users would like to access and make use of the CII anytime, anywhere. This might be necessary for enabling some security functions, as for instance the reaction to emergencies. But it is in these crisis situations when the competition for scarce resources might prove challenging. Not just lay people trying to send messages to relatives, but all kinds of business operations flocking over the network for solving urgent needs.

- Compatibility: users would like to just connect and directly draw on all services irrespective of the type of access device. They would also pretend to take advantage of the evolution of terminals, protocols and other technologies, without having to massively reconfigure their systems. The drawbacks come from the uniformity of interfaces, which do not offer alternatives in case of known vulnerabilities, and from the openness of channels to the propagation of malware. More homogeneous the solutions, more susceptible the CII will be to common failures.

- Automation: users would like to apply the CII for automating functions that are crucial for them and for society (this is intrinsic to the definition of "critical infrastructure"). The functions can be related for example to supply chains, production or financial operations. The positive side is given by the possibility to conduct fast and efficient reactions to unwanted conditions (e.g., unsafe states, security breaches). However this exposes those critical functions to the vulnerabilities and uncertainties of the CII – which can neither ensure the availability of the connection, nor the secure treatment of the data.

- Underlined: <u>Intelligence</u>: users would like the CII to be smart enough as to adapt itself to their needs in each situation. In this scenario, the CII will have to be aware of its own status (topology, capacity), and of what the user is pretending to do, for then adjusting itself in order to provide the more satisfactory response. The problem with this will be the false sense of assurance that can derive.

The conclusion is that the more the CII would be tailored to match critical functions, the more it will show its limitations, and the more their users will be exposed to service failures. Security is not an unattainable goal, but it is evident that CII and its applications will require a rigorous approach to their protection based on risk assessments.

CII Protection

The protection of the CII, even taking into consideration all the caveats about the connotations of the term "protection" in this context, is dependent on the assessment of the risks incurred. The problem of determining these risks is rather complex because for the unavoidable lack of proper knowledge on the CII:

- The system is not completely known: the topology and components employed for the delivery of a critical service will always have a certain degree of indetermination until the service is completed—CII is not an engineered system, but a system-of-systems.

- The flaws and frailties of the system and the capabilities and motivations of the possible malicious attackers are only partially known: statistical data and evidence will be sparse—this is not a typical reliability case where probabilities can be computed and applied, or a standard risk management case where hazard sources and their potential are well determined.

- The perception of the risks will be biased by the scarcity of events, and by the level of potential damage to the end users: perception that might greatly vary among the stakeholders.

Consequently the protection of the CII should be based on best available analytical powers, but remain aware of its limitations. It should be founded on:

1. the understanding of the CII service failures that are not acceptable to the CII stakeholders, and that should therefore be considered the critical states that should be avoided;

2. the analysis of the factors (i.e., cyber and physical vulnerabilities, accidental and malicious threats, interdependencies) that might cause those failures;

3. the assessment of the administrative and technical measures that could be taken for countering those harmful factors and therefore assuring the quality of the required services; of the costs incurred in implementing them, and of their limitations.

These can be considered as the standard actions that the responsible of risky systems will undertake. But here, when dealing with an infrastructure, some questions should be answered:

- Who should carry out these tasks?

National governments are the first candidates because they are responsible for public security. But, do they have all the information for determining the risks and the quality of service required? This is not part of the role of governments, who can only define the top level national security goals. Furthermore governments don't have a detailed knowledge of the technical implementation of the CII, and of their utilization. Hence they will have to enquire the private stakeholders: operators and users of the CII. A great level of coordination and trust among the actors would be necessary—without yet considering the cross-border nature of the infrastructure.

- Who will set the criteria for determining what is at risk and the metrics for the criticality evaluation?

Here again the public actor has a central responsibility, but dialogue and collaboration with the private stakeholders is necessary. Conflicts in the appreciation of risks will be unavoidable. The assessments will describe prospective problems, for which few antecedents exist, and therefore with scarce statistical data for supporting the estimation of the probabilities and potential effects of the risk events.

- Who will determine how the security strategy will be implemented? Who should implement the security countermeasures?

We already mentioned the surplus of security that will happen between the business needs of an operator, and the societal needs as defined by public authorities. We can expect that governments will set goals, and the deployment of solutions will be the responsibility of the CII operators. But, in absence of standards and compliance verification, any implementation (or lack of) will be difficult to ascertain. And when a failure will happen, any elucidation will arrive too late.

- Who will pay for the security countermeasures?

For any security means that will exceed their business rationale, private companies will reasonably ask for public funding. However, infrastructures are extended systems-of-systems comprising many actors. How will the funds be distributed among them?

- Who will be responsible for updating the security strategy when new information on vulnerabilities and threats will be available?

The CII and its context are dynamic. Being robust and reliable today doesn't preclude that new conditions tomorrow will not prove that the same architecture and policy are susceptible to critical failures.

Summarizing, we can say that CIIP will prove an arduous task, stressing the links between public and private actors, and demanding innovative governance approaches. How infrastructures will be governed, will determine the level of innovation and investment by the stakeholders [11]0. The three governance courses that can be foreseen are:

1. The public authorities stipulate national regulations setting protection objectives and means, and controlling their implementation by the private sector. Governments decide on the criteria to apply for risk assessment and determine which are the expected benefits and drawbacks of the protection measures. The operators of the CII are responsible and accountable by the government for the implementation of the protection measures.

2. All national CII stakeholders deliberate and reach a collective deal agreeing on obligations and rights of each actor. The resolution can have a mandatory character, and verification mechanisms are established. The operators of the CII are responsible and accountable by the community of stakeholders for the implementation of the protection measures.

3. The national decisions on CII protection are put in the context of international arrangements—which might take precedence in some cases. The trans-national agreements set common criteria and objectives, and mutual verification mechanisms [18]0. The operators of the CII are responsible and accountable by the different countries and actors signing the agreement for the implementation of the protection measures.

CIIP Perspectives

Any solution to the CIIP challenge will have to reconcile the different perspectives on the problem. The perception of vulnerabilities, threats and criticalities might significantly vary among analysts with a different background and conceptual framework of reference.

There is a deficiency in standard terminology, and no recognized reference body of knowledge [14]0. This hinders the possibility to conduct assessments that can reflect all the legitimate viewpoints on the problem. This is not just a theoretical issue: the very capabilities of a country to identify and qualify critical assets, and to develop coherent risk management and CII assurance policies depend on the clarification of these questions.

Which are the perspectives to be considered? At least it is possible to identify four: national security, law enforcement, business assurance and continuity, and technical information and network security [8]0.

The national security is primarily related to the defense objectives of a country. The malicious threats considered are other nation states and other agents that can jeopardize a state (e.g., terrorism). Physical threats are not generally considered. Vulnerabilities are examined at a very high level, with predominance of socio-political factors with respect to technical ones. The targets to be protected are those that could cause extensive catastrophes or have a high symbolic meaning (e.g., government services). The protection measures will include threat intelligence in an international level, and military and civil defense actions.

The law enforcement perspective encompasses all activities related to cyber-crime—in this case, those illegal activities that might impede the CII to deliver their services. Therefore, the threats considered are those malicious agents that violate the quality attributes required for the CII (e.g., availability of connectivity, integrity of data, and confidentiality of communications). Accidental threats originating from the same CII are not considered; threats deriving from natural phenomena are generally responsibility of civil protection departments, and rarely considered in the same framework. The targets are those defined as critical by national authorities but also by private companies (as they would require the protection of their major assets). Law enforcement would only define some external protection measures, relying on the private actors for the security measures, including electronic evidence preparedness.

At the business level, private companies will define their security policies, including the actions to perform in case of a failure of the CII. This will typically be organized in a corporate security policy that will include information assurance and business continuity measures. This document should consider all kinds of relevant treated threats, although for the profiling of malicious agents will have to count on external sources of information (mainly law enforcement and national intelligence). The targets will be those company assets deemed essential for the company operations or of significant economic value. The protection measures implemented will be those judged worthwhile according to apposite risk assessments, including insurance policies.

The technical level will look at the systems from an engineering viewpoint: system will be composed of hardware and software, information and communication technologies, a life cycle spanning from design to operations and maintenance. Threats will be described in technological and procedural terms: attack processes, system failures, human errors, component faults. Vulnerabilities will be identified as weaknesses in the systems structure or functions that can open the way to external breaches or internal pathological behaviors. The security countermeasures will comprise functions and technical assurance means (e.g., configuration management, enforcement and auditing), with reference to technical standards (e.g., ISO 17799 [10], Common Criteria [5]).

CONCLUSIONS: SYSTEMIC CHALLENGES

Can we consider that CII is systemic by nature? Based on the previous discussions, we can conclude that most CII attributes depend on the correlation of multiple components. And this affects both its internal structure, and the risk-related decision making processes concerned with its protection. In the following we will consider both types of systemic challenges and summarize the discussion developed so far on these issues.

CII Intrinsic Systemic Challenges

- Functional and—what is more important here—meta-functional attributes, such as security, are emergent properties.

This means that non-linear phenomena will happen in CII due to the coupling and complex interactions among its components. Not all outcomes to perturbations, even minor, can be predicted. Some of them will prove unmanageable, conducting the system to unwanted states and potential service failures.

- System level vulnerabilities cannot be derived from the lower-level component vulnerabilities.

The interdependencies are related to pathological behaviours where the malfunction of one component is affected by the functioning of another. As the systems are designed and operated independently among them, the collective behaviour is not always predictable—and more so in the presence of local abnormal actions.

- System level failures need to be assessed at the system level, and cannot only be derived from faults and errors at the lower levels.

System failures might originate from the regular functioning of one component in an unanticipated scenario, or the utilization of some capabilities in a context not foreseen by its developers.

The integration, reuse, modification and reconfiguration of basic systems are done with a minor consideration of higher level effects.

CII Protection Systemic Challenges

- There is no global security policy, and therefore no unique definition of threats, protection criteria and risk assessment approaches.

What is unsafe for one CII operator could be considered acceptable by another. This results in the lack of a common definition of illicit uses of the CII. This is further complicated by the potential interactions among accidental and malicious threats, the combination of social and technical aspects in threats, and the interactions among different systems.

At the country level there are potential conflicts between national security objectives and private companies' information and network security objectives. At the international level this problem might acquire important proportions.

- Information on vulnerabilities and threats has to be shared among the major possible number of actors and countries, but taking care of confidentiality and other security criteria.

Three factors affect this: data are scarce and change rapidly; the reaction to risky situations has to be prompt; the security of the CII as a whole will depend on the coordinated action of many operators.

- Standards are falling short of needs and expectations. This hinders the implementation of security solutions, and the compatibility between different solutions.

Standards are deemed fundamental for the development of markets for security devices, methodologies and solutions. Some fields (in particular industrial systems, early warning and cyber-forensics) find themselves in very inadequate situations.

REFERENCES

[1]   Bush, George W., The National Strategy for the Physical Protection of Critical Infrastructures and Key Assets, February 2003

[2]   Bush, George W., The National Strategy to Secure Cyberspace, February 2003

[3]   Clinton, William J., Defending America's Cyberspace: National Plan for Information Systems Protection. An Invitation to a Dialogue, 2000

[4]   Clinton, William J., Protecting America's Critical Infrastructures: Presidential Decision Directive 63, May 22, 1998

[5]   Common Criteria for Information Security Evaluation, Part 1: Introduction and General Model, Part 2: Functional Security Requirements, Part 3: Security Assurance Requirements, version 2.2, January 2004

[6]   Dacey R.F., Critical Infrastructure Protection—Challenges and Efforts to Secure Control Systems, General Accounting Office, March 2004

[7]   Dacey R.F., Critical Infrastructure Protection—Establishing Effective Information Sharing with Infrastructure Sectors, General Accounting Office, April 2004

[8]   Dunn, M. and I. Wigert, International CIIP Handbook 2004, Center for Security Studies, ETH Zurich, 2004

[9]   G8 Principles for Protecting Critical Information Infrastructures, G8 Ministers of Justice and Home Affairs, May 2003

[10] ISO/IEC, International Standard ISO/IEC 17799:2000 Code of Practice for Information Security Management, 2000

[11] Kahin B. and J. H. Keller, Coordinating the Internet, The MIT Press, 1997

[12] Luiijf E., M. Klaver, and J. Huizenga, The Vulnerable Internet: A Study of the Critical Infrastructure of (the Netherlands Section of) the Internet, TNO, The Hague, 2001

[13] Ministry of the Interior and Kingdom Relations, Critical Infrastructure Protection in The Netherlands, 2003

[14] Moteff J., C. Copeland, and J. Fischer, Critical Infrastructures: What Makes and Infrastructure Critical?, Report for Congress RL315556, version January 2003

[15] OECD, Emerging Risks in the 21st Century: An Agenda for Action, May 2003

[16] Personick S. D. and C. A. Patterson (eds.) Critical Information Infrastructure Protection and the Law: An Overview of Key Issues, Committee on Critical Information Infrastructure Protection and the Law, National Research Council, USA, 2003

[17] The Swedish Commission on Vulnerability and Security, Vulnerability and Security in a New Era, A Summary, SOU 2001:41, Stockholm, 2001

[18] Wenger A (ed.), The Internet and the Changing Face of International Relations and Security, Information and Security: An International Journal, Volume 7, 2001

DECENTRALIZED ENERGY SUPPLY TO SECURE COMPUTER SYSTEMS

Igor Tyukhov,
VIESH, Russia, Moscow

Abstract: This paper is devoted to energy security of computer systems and in more general terms security energy supply as important infrastructure component. History of the Internet appearing and developing is similar to the modern tendency in transformation of energy sector. Some of the new tendencies in changing energy sector reflect the exhaustible nature of fossil fuels—the main source of modern power engineering. Other growing demand for changing present power engineering is ecological pressure. Renewable energy sources are practically ecologically clean and by their nature are distributed what can be considered as important factor for supporting distributed computer systems. Appearing problems of high centralized energy systems are connected with terror attacks, man-caused and natural catastrophes. It forces society to pay serious attention to distributed supply energy systems and particularly to renewable energy. Some new developments of photovoltaic systems are discussed.

Keywords: Energy; decentralized energy; renewable energy; Internet; fossil fuels; photovoltaic system; power flow; PV concentrator system; atomic energy

1. GENERAL APPROACH

Energy is the key issue for human beings. It is impossible to imagine a modern civilized man not consuming energy. Energy is the universal

---

75

J. S. Kowalik et al. (eds.), Cyberspace Security and Defense: Research Issues, 75–97.

currency of science, industry, life and also one of the main factors for computer users.

Human civilization deals with power fluxes in a wide range of magnitudes from global to local. At personal level, the flows for computer users would seem small but they cannot be ignored (Table 1).

Mankind was so lucky to discover the great gift from nature—fossil fuels. This generous present gives us to achieve enormous scientific and industrial progress and moves civilization to information society. Energy problems in information society are a new reality. Blackouts in California, for example, stimulated discussion on energy consuming by computers and the infrastructure of the Internet [1]. The appeared relative new word "netizen" reflect a new non-geographically based community of people who are active as members of the network. Distributed computer net is quite a big consumer of electrical energy.

Distributed computer net cannot rely on only high centralized energy system.

Table 1. Power Flow (from global to small level: estimations)

Power Flux	Watts	Fraction to absorbed solar radiation
Global intercept of solar radiation	$1.7 \cdot 10^{17}$	
Solar power absorbed by the earth's surface	$0.8 \cdot 10^{17}$	1
Wind-generated waves on the ocean	$9 \cdot 10^{16}$	0.9
Global Earth heat flow	$4.2 \cdot 10^{13}$	$5.2 \cdot 10^{-4}$
Maximum permissible threshold of disturbance biosphere	???	???
Worldwide fossil fuel combustion	10^{13}	$1.2 \cdot 10^{-4}$
Worldwide installed capacity of earth thermal energy systems	$1.2 \cdot 10^{10}$	$1.5 \cdot 10^{-7}$
Sayano-Shushenskay Hydro Power plant (Russia)	$8.5 \cdot 10^{9}$	$1.1 \cdot 10^{-7}$
Internet electric energy consumption (USA)	$6.7 \cdot 10^{9}$	$8.4 \cdot 10^{-8}$
Big thermal power plant	$5 \cdot 10^{9}$	$6.2 \cdot 10^{-8}$
Four engines of Boeing 747	$6 \cdot 10^{7}$	$7.5 \cdot 10^{-10}$
World largest PV facility (Leipzig, Germany)	$5 \cdot 10^{6}$	$6.2 \cdot 10^{-11}$
ENIAC (1940s ,USA)	$1.7 \cdot 10^{5}$	$2.1 \cdot 10^{-12}$
Power of sprinter	$10 \cdot 10^{3}$	$1.2 \cdot 10^{-13}$
Power for service and technology realization per capita in the USA	$10 \cdot 10^{3}$	$1.2 \cdot 10^{-13}$
Power for service and technology realization per capita in the world	$3 \cdot 10^{3}$	$3.7 \cdot 10^{-14}$
Photocopier	400	$5 \cdot 10^{-15}$
Desktop computers	120	$1.5 \cdot 10^{-15}$

Power Flux	Watts	Fraction to absorbed solar radiation
Basal metabolism of a man	100	$1.2 \cdot 10^{-15}$
Laptop computer	15	$1.9 \cdot 10^{-16}$
Hummingbird flight	0.7	$8.8 \cdot 10^{-18}$

Renewable energy flows are very large in comparison with commercial energy demand. For maximum permissible threshold of disturbance biosphere estimations are very controversial.

Energy efficiency is also an essential element of energy security. The important question is how energy efficiency helps energy security? Energy efficiency reduces pressure on our energy security in many ways. This topic will not be discussed here. Let us only to mention one example [2]. In the 1940s, the ENIAC had 18,000 vacuum tubes and consumed 174 kilowatts—roughly 10 watts per tube. If modern silicon chips required 10 watts per transistor, a Pentium would suck 100 megawatts out of the power grid, and the computer on your desk would easily swallow the entire output of a nuclear plant. Instead, a few tens of watts are enough to power a chip with transistors numbering in the tens of millions.

2. CRITICS OF MODERN POWER ENGINEERING SYSTEMS

The principles of the modern power engineering were created in the last century. Growing of the world population, energy crisis (1973–1974 and 1979), ecological problems, big man-caused catastrophes, terrorists attacks stimulate developing of new energy sources and new principals of power engineering. The question is arising: how to manage the transition to a decentralized power system, which can sufficiently decrease risks. All previous history of mankind was devoted to developing of the energy-intensive technology, industry.

New technologies now are appearing to avoid problems with traditional energy approach which was created in developed countries. These new technology are very suitable from the point of view defense from terrorist attacks, because by their nature it mach with distributed character of computer networks.

2.1. Traditional Energy Supply Disadvantages

2.1.1. Disadvantages of Fossil Fuel Energy

There is a whole list of disadvantages of traditional fossil fuel energy supply. They are listed below.

- High centralization and high concentration of energy and energy flows leads to multiple losses in case of man-caused and natural catastrophes, terror attacks;
- Not only power plants but also oil, gas pipelines and other quite distributed equipment are good targets for terrorists;
- Ecological problems (greenhouses gases, hazardous and dangerous wastes, acid rains);
- Disturbing of natural thermal balance of planet Earth because of internal energy is released;
- Global dimming*;
- High external cost of fossil fuel energy (for example, health expenses);
- Fossil fuels are principally not unlimited (life time of Sun 4.5 billions years), they are finite by nature;
- We leave or even "create" problems for our children (new generations) (particularly, burying nuclear wastes);
- Qualitative deterioration fossil resources (for example, growth of gas resources 2–3 times lower than level gas production growth);
- Regions of extraction energy and raw materials move away from regions of their treatment and consumption;
- Fossil fuels technology goes to their efficiency limit, production and treatment will only become complicated;
- Decreasing of competitiveness and impossibility of supply energy to removal areas.

---

* Global dimming is explained first of all by traditional power engineering (we should not forget also about harmful exhausted gases from transport). Human activity is making the planet darker as well as warmer. Tiny particles of soot or chemical compounds like sulphates reflect sunlight and they also promote the formation of bigger, longer lasting clouds. Levels of sunlight reaching Earth's surface have declined by up to 20% in recent years because air pollution. Data from 100 stations around the world show that the amount of black carbon in the atmosphere is twice as big as we assumed.

Climate change and energy security, two challenging global issues for the 21st century, are intimately linked. There will be different sources of energy by the middle of the century.

2.1.2. Can Atomic Energy be Alternative?

Disadvantages of atomic energy are also connected with the high centralization. High concentration of energy (energy flows) and radioactive materials are even more dangerous than in case of traditional power engineering. Consequences of radioactive contaminations and even nuclear explosions are unpredictable and very frightening.

Atomic power stations are excellent targets for terrorists because in case of possible damages of reactors fears of nuclear contaminations can lead to great fears and phobias.

Atomic energy advertised as an ecologically clean energy but the problems with nuclear wastes are still not solved and at any case surplus energy flow leads to global warming.

The measures to stop nuclear terrorism involve political actions: to stop uncontrolled nuclear weapons, to stop new nuclear materials, to stop new nuclear states. Reality is far from these goals but the main responsibilities for their realization are still in the government's hands of the main countries.

What do we have to do in terms of long perspectives of atomic energy development?

Research on nuclear power must be continued but not as a main energy technology.

It will not be possible for the nuclear industry to be developed unless it is guaranteed a sufficient period of stability and solving nuclear waste storage problems.

The statements that atomic energy is only one hope on the way of energy problems solution of mankind is dangerous myth of our era. Atomic energy continues its development because of industrial lobby from the companies and corporations producing equipment for atomic industry and from administrative officials personally connecting with atomic industry.

Official calculations of atomic energy cost take into account only direct costs on construction and management reactor, cost of fuel mining, treatment and transport. They don't include indirect costs of the compensations on damages of nature and health of people, deactivations of radioactive wastes and decommissioning of old atomic power plants. Gas power plant of 1000 MW is 5–7 times cheaper than atomic power plant and can be built in two years. At the same time, building of reactors (from planning to energy production starting) was about 10 years in 70s and this period is doubled in 90s because of many additional problems.

Using low and simple technology is possible to make big harmful damages. Some researchers discuss opportunities and technical assessment of capabilities for terrorists to use small unmanned aerial vehicles (UAV) [3]. Such UAV have relative simplicity of assembling, covertness of preparation and carrying out an attack, high capability to "penetrate" into areas not accessible by land. It is almost impossible to prevent an attack once UAV is launched, long range and high accuracy can be achieved by relative low cost. For atomic power stations and the whole energy infrastructure (as pipelines, electrical grids and so on) such simple means can be very dangerous and can give a strong psychological effect of an attack on population.

How can security and strategic stability be ensured in a globalized world?

2.1.3. Some actions of the energy industry

Energy industry has taken significant action since 9/11 according to Dave Jones, from Argonne National Laboratory. It was increased physical security measures (e.g., staffing, security check points, manned facilities, flyovers, cameras, badge enforcement, escorted visitors), increased employee awareness and training, improved coordination with government (Local/State—law enforcement and National Guard, Federal—threat level conditions, surveys, assessments). Enhanced coordination with stakeholders (e.g., customers, suppliers, infrastructure providers) gave also positive result of these measures. These measures improve reliability of energy supply but still do not cover all problems associated with energy infrastructure.

Many modern energy systems are so complex that their modes of failure often cannot be foreseen. The cyber crimes, the criminal and terrorist use of information technology are significant issues for law enforcement. A sophisticated information infrastructure, a large pool of potential hackers and heavy reliance on computer-based energy infrastructure are all factors in making computer-based crime a serious threat to civilized countries. However, currently there is a limited ability on the part of federal and local government departments and agencies to collect, collate, analyze and synthesize the modest amount of substantive qualitative information on actors, their actual and potential capabilities, intended targets, and recorded attempts to penetrate or attack assets or systems.

3. POLITICAL AND SOCIAL ASPECTS OF ENERGY PROBLEMS

Before 9/11 the term "energy security" was considered mainly as independence of western countries from the oil producing countries i.e., energy security considered as a problem which would appear in near or more distant future [4]. In this sense of term oil security will not be longer an appropriate term of reserves in future.

New realities of terrorist threads give to term "energy security" new dimension which reflects a big gap between North and South.

T. Barnett in his book "The Pentagon's New Map" [5] maps out America's recent military encounters and predicts future ones based on patterns of global economic development. He divided word into two parts. Firstly, the Functioning Core, or Core, where globalization is thick with network connectivity, financial transactions, liberal media flows, and collective security. Here are regions featuring stable governments, rising standards of living, and more deaths by suicide than murder. Secondly, there are regions where globalization is thinning or just plain absent. These regions plagued by politically repressive regimes, widespread poverty and disease, routine mass murder, and—most important—the chronic conflicts that incubate the next generation of global terrorists. He calls these parts of the world as the Non-Integrating Gap, or Gap.

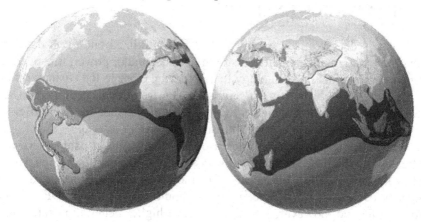

Figure 1. Map by William McNulty [5]

T. Barnett discusses the importance of military activity in Gap and involving these countries into globalization processes.

The economic activity in Gap is not less important. The social and economic gap between the world's richest 1 billion people and its poorest 1 billion is extremely high. The differences between the worlds most rich and its poorest can be seen in the contrasts in nutrition, education, disease patterns, family size, life expectancy and energy supply. Let us remark that the energy as a key economic factor of development can be produced in Gap countries (tropical areas!) with help of new solar energy technologies not introducing environmental burdens and global warming problems. In this case disconnectedness, which T. Barnett defines danger, will shrink.

More than two billion people worldwide have currently no access to grid electricity or other efficient energy supply. This is one third of humanity and the majority live in rural areas. The productivity and health of these people are diminished by reliance on traditional fuels and technologies, with women and children suffering most. Energy is the key element to empower people and ensure water, food and fodder supply as well as rural development. Therefore access to energy should be treated as the fundamental right to everybody. Renewable energy has the potential to bring power, not only in the literal sense, to communities by transforming their prospects.

> *I have no doubt that we will be successful in harnessing the sun's energy. If sunbeams were weapons of war, we would have had solar energy centuries ago.*
>
> — Sir George Porter

4. RENEWABLE ENERGY

What is decentralized energy (DE)? Decentralized energy is defined as the production, management and storage of heat and/or power, irrespective of generator size, fuel or technology that is located close to the customer's load. With respect to electricity, DE complements traditional, centralized, large-scale power generation, which is located at some distance from end-users and connected to customers via bulk transmission system or grid.

Distributed generation can increase system security at competitive costs. Already DE should be as competitive as alternative generation at peak times, a key security period. If the prices for traditional resources reflect their true security enhancement costs, economics should further induce DE selection. To be effective, however, DE must achieve higher penetration rates on the system. It will take a long-term policy commitment on the part of leading nations to capitalize on the potential of DG.

The long discussed, and expected, transition from a central power model to a 'hybrid' central-DE model appears not yet to have started. According to World Alliance for Decentralized Energy latest annual DE market assessment, the World Survey of Decentralized Energy—2004, published recently, the overall share of DE in global power generation remained steady at 7% during the period covered by the survey, January 2001–January 2003 (the share of DE among the countries is shown at Figure 2) [6] .

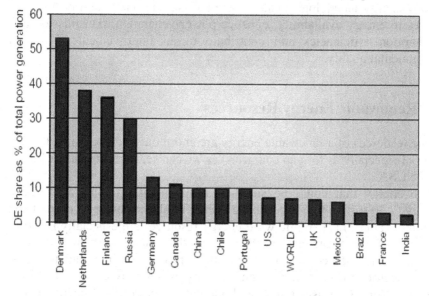

Figure 2. Decentralized Energy on Different Countries

The importance of decentralized energy sources with special stress on renewable energy sources is very high in meeting the needs of remote and difficult terrains besides accent on sustainable energy policy. Renewable energy is decentralized energy by nature.

Renewable energy resources have special attractive attributes. Renewable resources are more modular, even when developed in a centralized situation. Most biomass and geothermal plants are less than 100 MW. Wind turbines are physically separated and thus stand as separate risks. Fifty MW of wind turbines in one wind farm cover a large area. The loss of a single turbine has minimal impact on the system, and there is no fuel supply delivery system risk.

On the other hand, some renewable resources like PV systems remain costly when compared to traditional energy. However, the cost gap is expected to continue to decrease, and, to the extent deployment is accelerated, the gap should close even faster taking into account new approaches as for instance PV/thermal combined systems. Other renewable resources, such as biomass, small hydro, and wind can successfully compete with traditional resources. This is especially true if value (or cost) is assigned to the security attributes.

The benefits provided by renewables enhanced security of energy supply, improved social equity, fueled by locally available resources, can be designed to meet local needs, reduced threat of climate change, stimulation of economic growth, jobs creation (often in rural areas), higher incomes, poverty reduction, and protection of the environment at all levels.

New energy technologies can reduce the nation's vulnerability to major changes in energy availability, enhance power generation, transmission and consumption efficiencies and contribute to an improvement in overall environmental quality.

4.1. Renewable Energy Resources

The resources of a renewable energy are enormous and accessible to each country (especially as for gap countries) as we can see on examples of Russia and the USA.

The energy that could be supplied from sunlight falling on Russian territory (2.30 trillion tce) exceeds the energy of all the country's current and potential (Table 2) [7]. While wind energy resources are especially plentiful along the northern and eastern borders of the country and in the North Caucasus region, the correspondence of these resources with populated areas and/or electric power transmission capacity is less favorable. The high-populated North Caucasus region and populated areas of the Northwest (i.e., Murmansk and Archangelsk) and Far East (Khabarovsk) represent the best potential for either electric-power-grid-connected wind farms or stand-alone wind-diesel systems for electricity supply to small settlements (Table 3).

While year-round solar resources exist only in the most southern regions, summer time-only solar resources for supplemental hot-water heating (potentially an economic addition to existing district heating systems) exist throughout the country. Geothermal resources are concentrated in two small regions, although one of these, the North Caucasus, is heavily populated. There are numerous rapid-current streams, fairly high wind velocity and traditionally high developed electric grid systems in some areas which indicate that the development and introduction of new renewable-based technologies of rural electrification would contribute to the social and economic growth of the rural communities and would serve sustainable progress of the region.

The geographical distribution of renewable energy resources in Russia is shown on the Figure 3.

According to the National Energy Policy the USA will lead the world in the development of clean, natural, renewable and alternative energy supplies [8]. Renewable and alternative energy supplies not only help diversify energy portfolio; they do so with few adverse environmental impacts. While the current contribution of renewable and alternative energy resources to America's total electricity supply is relatively small—only 9 percent— the renewable and alternative energy sectors are among the fastest growing in the United States.

Table 2: Potential Energy Resources in Russia, million ton coil equivalent (tce)

Renewable Energy Resources	
Solar	$2.3 \cdot 10^6$
Wind	$2.6 \cdot 10^4$
Biomass	$1.0 \cdot 10^4$
Mini hydro	360
Geothermal	$115\text{-}20 \cdot 10^6$
Non Renewable Energy Resources	
Coal	$(300\text{-}350) \cdot 10^3$
Petroleum	$(20\text{-}40) \cdot 10^3$
Gas, trillion cub. m	20–40
Primary Energy Production	1500

Renewable energy resources tap naturally occurring flows of energy to produce electricity, fuel, heat, or a combination of these energy types. One type of renewable energy, hydropower, has long provided a significant contribution to the U.S. energy supply and today is competitive with other forms of conventional electricity. However, there is a limited growth of potential for hydropower. Non-hydropower renewable energy is generated from four sources: biomass, geothermal, wind, and solar (Figure 4).

Renewable hydropower has long provided a significant contribution to the U.S. energy supply. Today, hydropower is competitive with other forms of conventionally generated electricity.

Table 3: Renewable Energy Resources over the Russian Regions, million tce

Region	Wind	Mini-hydro	Geothermal
North	11040	-	$9 \cdot 10^6$
North-West	1280	26,5	$0,5 \cdot 10^6$
Central	2560	2,7	—
Central-Chernozem	1040	0,5	—
Volga-Vyatski	2080	—	—
Volga Region	4160	7,0	$4,5 \cdot 10^6$
North Caucasus	2560	12,2	$31,5 \cdot 10^6$
Urals	4880	11,2	$1,8 \cdot 10^6$
West Siberia	12880	24,2	$49,5 \cdot 10^6$
East Siberia	13520	127	$2,2 \cdot 10^6$
Russian Far East	24000	147	$81 \cdot 10^6$
Russia total	80000	359,3	$180 \cdot 10^6$

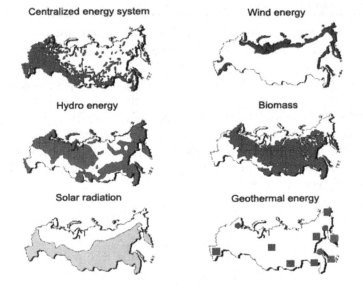

Centralized energy system

Wind energy

Hydro energy

Biomass

Solar radiation

Geothermal energy

Figure 3. Distributing of Russian RE Resources

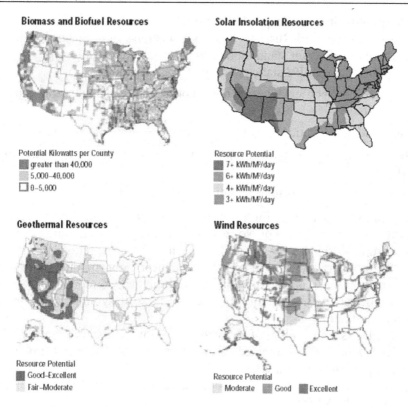

Figure 4. Distributing of U.S.A. RE Resources

4. 2. The VIESH Static Concentrator System Technology

4.2.1. VIESH PV Parabolic Trough Technology

New renewable energy technologies can give netizens the independence of grid problems, the tools to improve local air quality, reduce urban sprawls and so on.

Here we will discuss some concrete technologies based on photovoltaic (PV) effect in solar cells. Actually PV energy systems and computer technology based on the semiconductor p-n junctions that is why energy supply systems based on PV systems are very suitable to computer systems by electrical matching.

The technologies to collect and to generate electricity by solar cells are already in the market. However, competitiveness of PV systems is high only for remote areas, communication and satellite applications. The continued research is needed to reduce costs and improve performance of PV systems.

The photovoltaic static parabolic trough concentrator module has been developed in the All-Russian Research Institute for Electrification of Agriculture (VIESH) for stand-alone and large-scale applications [9].

The advantages of PV static parabolic trough technology:

- the cost of electrical energy does not depend much on the capacity installed;
- static and quasi-static PV parabolic trough concentrators are used;
- the size of PV parabolic trough concentrator can be very large up to 10^{12} m^2;
- up to 25% of diffused solar radiation can be collected.

The ratio concentration for 12 months symmetric static PV concentrator operation is from 3.5–14. For Northern countries application during 9 month of polar summer the static symmetric concentrator has the ratio concentration from 5–20. Quasi-static symmetric PV concentrator module with ratio concentration 7.5–30 needs correction of position every 6 months.

Asymmetric PV trough concentrator has 50% of symmetric PV trough concentration ratio.

Natural (passive) cooling of PV receiver for low ratio concentration 3.5–5 or active cooling with combined electric generation—hot water production for concentration 5–30 is used.

The concentrator system includes three innovative PV technologies developed at the VIESH.

One of the ways to achieve the competitiveness of PV power station is to apply bifacial PV modules originally designed by Prof. D. Strebkov and his colleagues for Russian low orbit satellites in 1970. Today bifacial cells and modules are manufactured in Russia for terrestrial application. In our case bifacial solar cells allow to increase acceptance angle for concentrator system.

The fundamentals of non-image optics are used in the non-tracking concentrator design for bifacial PV module. This innovative concept appears to show significant economic effect compared with the conventional flat plate PV module design. The problems of tracking, large size concentrator field of solar concentrator system can be successfully solved by developing new types of static and quasi-static PV concentrator with bifacial PV modules.

Non-imaging parabolic linear trough, which is finished as spiral trough was used for asymmetric version of concentrator.

Bifacial solar module is designed in such a way that it is capable to receive both direct sunlight and that reflected from the concentrator. The concentrated light spot is directed onto front- and rear-receiving surfaces depending on position of the Sun. The solar module is shorter than the trough intended to focus the light spot at the different hour angles of the Sun. This is important for creation of a uniform strip at each solar cell in working at the different angles of solar rays (see pictures in the next section). When many modules are assembled in line only at the edge modules PV receivers should be shorter in order to be sure to illuminate all solar cells at big hour angular.

Solar module manufacturing companies all over the world use a polymer encapsulant (usually ethylene vinyl acetate—EVA) and/or other plastics for solar module encapsulation. These organic materials are to a substantial extent responsible for relatively low module operation time (about 20–25 years in the best cases) and poor cooling conditions, especially with regard to high solar radiation intensity. We have developed a new plastic-free PV module technology with estimated operating time of 50 years. This new technology uses two sheets of glass with soldered edges and a special liquid inside for solar cell—glass optical and thermal properties matching. Testing of static concentrator module with new bifacial plastic-free module showed that module temperature was about 60°C at ambient temperature 30°C and concentration ratio about four.

4.2.2. The Example of Static Concentrator Systems

Perspective view of vertical asymmetrical concentrator is shown at the Figure 5. Depending on angular position of the Sun light rays 1 form light strip spot which moves at the front and rear surface of the bifacial receiver 2. Mirror reflector should form strip which provides for illumination of each of the bifacial solar cell of the receiver.

An example of a design of the asymmetric module (photo and ray tracing sketch) is shown in Figure 6.

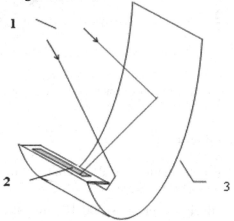

Figure 5. Perspective View of Vertical Asymmetrical Concentrator

Radius of cylinder is equal to the half of the focal length and is equal to the width of solar module. In this case geometric concentration ratio equals:

$$K_{geom} = 1 + 2/(1 \cos 2\delta) = 4.17,$$

where δ is an aperture angle.

The module can be attached to south oriented wall of a building. Additional transparent cover is installed parallel to the facade of the building and used for protection of mirror from the inclement weather conditions.

For symmetrical cylindrical parabolic reflector concentration ratio is even higher:

$$K_{geom} = 1 + 4/(1 \cos 2\delta).$$

An example of electrical power output of PV solar module in concentrator and out of concentrator from 35 bifacial solar cells of 100x33 mm size is shown at Figure 7.

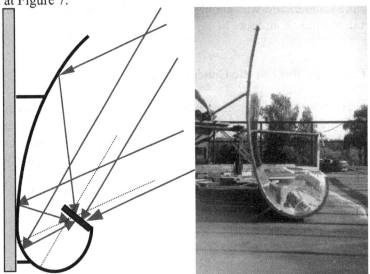

Figure 6. Rays Tracing in Asymmetric Concentrator and Photo of Asymmetric Concentrator

4.2.3. Economic Consideration

For production cost estimation of PV parabolic trough concentrator module several assumptions were made:

- the price of PV bifacial receiver is 500 US\$/m^2 (the price of VIESH production facility);

- the price of Alanod reflector with thickness 0.5 mm is 10 US\$/m^2;

- the price of non-tracking metallic support structure is 40 US\$/m^2 of module aperture (the price of Russian mechanical factory);

- the price of tempered low iron solar glass protective coating is 30 US\$/m^2;

- the peak power output of the concentrator module is 100 W/m^2.

- the results of calculation of technical and cost parameters of symmetrical PV trough concentrator modules are presented in Tables 4 and 5.

The production cost of the PV concentrator module for all aperture angles is less than 2.05 S\$/Wp. At maximum concentration ratio it is close to 1US\$/Wp and weakly depends on aperture angle. For average concentration ratio 7–15 the production cost of the PV concentrator module is less than 1.5US\$/Wp.

Low concentration ratio 3.5–7.5 is attractive due to collection of diffused radiation in the range of aperture angle and possibility of passive cooling. All these costs can be decreased by a factor 1.5 if we apply solar PV receiver with better efficiency and module power output 150 Wp/ m^2.

PV static concentrator module with long lifetime bifacial receivers is a new attractive solar electric conversion technology for stand alone and large-scale application with forthcoming price 1–2 US\$/Wp.

The promising features of this technology are low price for installed kW and possibility to construct large scale concentrator field without tracking system with concentration ration 3.5–30. Demonstration prototypes of the static PV concentrator modules have been tested.

These systems are very suitable for integrating into buildings because of the importance of use simultaneously photoactive and thermal parts of solar radiation. Hence for PV technology the better results can be achieved with concentrating PV/thermal systems.

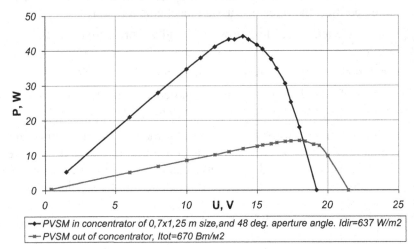

Figure 7. Output Characteristics of PV Module

Table 4. The Basic Material Expenses for Symmetrical PV Concentrator Module of $1m^2$

Aperture angle	Concentration ratio		Area of PV receiver, m^2	Area of mirror receiver, m^2
48°	low	3.5	0.284	1.44
	average	7	0.142	1.89
	max	14	0.071	2.01
36°	low	5	0.2	1.63
	average	10	0.1	1.94
	max	20	0.05	2.1
24°	low	7.5	0.132	2.0
	average	15	0.066	2.21
	max	30	0.033	2.37

One more prototype system was built in Oregon State University and tested in Oregon Institute of Technology [10] (the project was supported by Fulbright program). The awning design was chosen for demonstration concentrator installation because in addition to combined energy supply (photo-electricity and heat) the system can play a role of awning (sun-visor, canopy). Such choice is explained by a number of factors.

Table 5. The Production Cost of Symmetric PV Trough Concentrator
Module of 1m2, US$/Wp

Aperture angle Concentration	48⁰	36⁰	24⁰
low	2.05	1.76	1.46
average	1.49	1.29	1.15
max	1.16	1.06	1.0

In USA many buildings in the form of low (1-2 floors) long parallelepipeds are constructed and such design of installations allows to construct them in existing buildings, creating thus new architectural decisions. Awning above the windows creates additional shading, providing comfortable zones in a hot season. The modular principle (in this case connection of new systems along a building) economically allows to solve problems of connecting installations in a uniform system. The photo of the concentrator prototype for awning applications is shown at Figure 8.

Figure 8. Photo of the Concentrator for Awning Applications

If the industry and PV market analysts were to consider 'security' as an independent market segment it would focus attention on developing PV security applications and products, and on marketing.

Recent publications [11] remark if the industry and PV market analysts were to consider 'security' as an independent market segment it would focus attention on developing PV security applications and products, and on marketing. Power grids, pipeline systems and civilian telecommunications systems can be disrupted—sometimes extensively and for a considerable time—by natural disasters. Yet in these times they also offer inviting targets for 'infrastructure terrorism'. The security response may expand to emphasize the elimination of unmonitored public space (using web-cams, tracking devices and interlinked databases) and the need to power a proliferation of sensors and data transmission devices. More robust and impenetrable supervisory control and data acquisition (SCADA) systems to control and monitor power and natural gas flows will be needed. It is obvious that new security needs will require an increasing reliance on distributed generation of electricity. Renewable energy technologies—particularly when deployed as a distributed energy resource—can play a vital role in securing energy infrastructure [11].

Let us describe one more interesting PV technology which is suitable for portable computers. Flexible solar modules which usually based on thin film technologies have a great potential as stand-alone solar electric power systems for providing electricity beyond power lines. They can be installed easily for all types of standard or remote power needs and with a battery backup for uninterrupted power during utility blackouts or outages. An example of flexible solar cell technology incorporated into a military tent is shown at Figure 9.

The flexible solar module based on monocrystalline silicon cells with higher efficiency than thin film solar cells was developed in the VIESH. For example, the folding solar module 36/1-6-P depicted at Figure10 supplies 10W, output voltage 16V, and short circuit current, 0.7A under standard conditions of measurements. His dimensions are 395 x 370 x 4 mm and in the folded condition practically 6 times less by surface (135 x 185 x 12 mm). This folding solar module can be used for applications which small consuming equipment.

Figure 9. Flexible Solar Cell Technology Incorporated into a Military Tent

5. MEASURES SUGGESTED FOR MOVING TO DECENTRALIZED ENERGY SUPPLY

From general consideration and new technological opportunities it is supposed a number of measures for solving <u>infrastructure issues</u>:

- Identify physical and cyber dependencies on critical infrastructures (e.g., electric power, telecommunications, water, transportation);
- Stimulate collecting and managing information pertaining to research, developments and demonstrations on decentralized renewable energy (DRE);
- Develop small and medium sized energy facilities based on RE for municipal utilities, independent utilities, and rural areas;
- Implement appropriate configuration management across all IT systems;
- Develop fully independent technologies for information, emergency situations, and support (as GPS);
- Implement structured security requirements for critical suppliers and partners;
- Provide innovative means of facilitating acceptance of DRE

For <u>human issues</u> suggested measures are:

- Create senior level security council/committee, corporate/company security officer;
- Conduct special training (see "Big Troubles" by Dave Barry as an introduction);
- Raise employee awareness to be proactive on security matters;
- Periodically review and update emergency plans to include newer threats and vulnerabilities;
- Influence government policies at all level;
- Provide a service that identifies and assesses DRE projects.

Figure 10. Folding of Solar Portable Module in Six Times Less State (by surface)

In conclusion it should be emphasized:

- RE helps to distribute energy generation decreasing risks of big natural and man-caused catastrophes;
- RE mitigates social gaps (North and South, rich & poor) and global warming & dimming);
- RE facilitates to clean & save environment;
- Our energy choices must show more respect to the environment;
- There is only one way forward: the future decentralized energy generation demands joint action of specialists on computer systems and power engineering. The future lies in environmentally sustainable, secure energy sources.

REFERENCES

1. Romm, J., A. Rosenfeld, and S. Herrmann, The Internet economy and global warming: a scenario of the impact of e-commerce on energy and the environment, The Center for Energy and Climate Solutions, Washington, D.C., 2000, available online at **http://www.coolcompanies.com**

2. Hayes B., The computer and the dynamo, *American Scientist*, v. 89, p.131-152.

3. **http://www.armscontrol.ru** "Threat of Terrorist Unmanned Aerial Vehicles: Technical Aspects" by E. Miasnikov Center for Arms Control, Energy and Environmental Studies at MIPT, Dolgoprudny, June 2004, 29 pages.

4. The future for European energy security, edited by Curt Gasteyger, Frances Pinter (Publishers), London, 1985, 178 pp.

5. Barnett T., The Pentagon's New Map: War and Peace in the Twenty-First Century, G.P. Putnam's Sons, 2004, 448 pp.

6. WADE annual decentralized energy survey, Press Release, 26 January 2004, available online.

7. Strebkov D. S., I. I. Tyukhov, Renewable energy for rural electrification in Russia, *7th International Conference on Solar Energy at High Latitudes Proceedings*, 1997, Vol. 2, p. 495–502.

8. National Energy Policy. Report of the National Energy Development Group, May 2001.

9. Strebkov D., I. Tyukhov, E. Tveryanovich, P. Bezrukikh, A. Irodionov, TPV—thermal static concentrator modules, The SOLAR 2002 Conference "Sunrise on the Reliable Energy Economy," *Proceedings of 31th ASES Annual Conference Solar Forum 2002*, edited R. Cambell Howe, Reno/Sparks, Nevada, June 15–20, 2002 p. 47–52.

10. Tyukhov I., D. Strebkov, F. Vignola, S. Clouston, R. Rogers, New solar combined concentrator technology in Oregon, *Proceedings of 33rd ASES Conference* "A Solar Harvest: Growing Opportunities," ed. R. Campbell-Howe, 2004, July 11–14, Portland, Oregon, USA p. 223–227.

11. Braun G., P. Varadi, Renewable Energy World, September–October 2003, available online.

PART 2

DEPENDABILITY

SAFETY ANALYSIS METHODS—SOFTWARE DEVELOPMENT QUESTIONS

Tadeusz Cichocki[1]
Bombardier Transportation Rail Control Solutions

Abstract: This paper is a general overview of current practice regarding safety analysis problem and software safety engineering and assessment process. Generic safety development pattern is shown. Some work in progress is mentioned: OF-FMEA and Safety and Trust Cases development methods and tools.

Keywords: System; Safety; Complexity; Safety Analysis; Software Engineering; Formal Methods; OF-FMEA; Safety Claim Structure; Safety Case; Safety Assessment

1. INTRODUCTION

Software engineering is a relatively new discipline and the technology related to software applications changes very quickly. As a result there is no much understanding of how to engineer software projects with mission-critical requirements, particularly those with safety requirements. In addition an increasingly complex world demands better, faster, smaller and cheaper systems. Mixed in with this is the insistence that we all reason and act with new technology even if it is not fully understood. This further extends uncertainty which concerns the state of the world, the effects of our actions, or others' actions: lives are lost, the environment is damaged and money is wasted (from time to time)[2].

---

[1] The Author is currently an Internal Safety Assessor and a member of Quality and Safety Group of Bombardier. He received a Ph.D. from Electronics, Telecommunication and Informatics Department of the Gdansk University of Technology in Gdansk, Poland. The full paper was prepared in December 2004 (e-mail: anta13@plusnet.pl,
www: **http://www.anta13.neostrada.pl/tadeusz.html**).

[2] According to Dagsavisen, 29 Nov 2004:
"Several members of the Norwegian public transportation committee are of the opinion that the government's decision to expose the rail administration to

J. S. Kowalik et al. (eds.), Cyberspace Security and Defense: Research Issues, 101–124.

Specific development projects concerns are:

- It is always a work on time and budget (while correctness in conflict with cost is considered).

- The development and marketing processes are highly dynamic and unpredictable.

- Fragmentation of rational knowledge (due to time or geographic place of its development) leads people to focus on information that is unaware (separated) of its history and context.

- How can a product of good quality arise in an organizational and information chaos?

- The normalization committees and operators are satisfied with the *low* level of harm on railway networks. Significant failures are a precondition of innovation.

Human expertise in complex systems is constantly changing and a New Paradigm for software safety assurance is considered. As the development of Safety Critical Systems is guided by standards, the standards are to be updated[3]. In what follows we present a general view of how the development of safe software systems is currently practiced and show two specific solutions aimed at efficient support of the efforts. Responsibility of organizations, processes and culture, not just efforts of specific members of the organizations, is emphasized.

2. SAFETY ANALYSIS—GENERIC DEVELOPMENT PATTERN

Complexity is the concept that all things tend to organize themselves into *patterns* [B. Edmonds, (1999)] (e.g., common patterns in accidents [N.G. Leveson, (2004)] or patterns in software design [R. Sanz and J. Zalewski, (2003)]), where pattern is understood as a recurring combination of meaningful units that occurs in some context. An *analysis pattern* is a conceptual model that models the core knowledge of the problem, e.g., a set of classes and associations that have some meaning in the context of an

---

competition will jeopardize the safety. The Minister of transports and communication acknowledges that no risk analyses have been made, but points out such analyses are not required."

[3] A maintenance of EN 50128, the Cenelec norm for dependability of railway applications software, was initiated in September 2004 by SC9XA Cenelec group to start the work on 2005.

application; their semantics describe specific aspects of some domain or application. It is the way the systems (its properties) will be understood.

2.1. The Basic Model Needed

In a specific development project case the assumed patterns' completeness and accuracy is critical for effectiveness of the analysis and engineering based on it. Catastrophic failures usually arise in situations compounded by several rare events. The difficulty in reproducing the operational profile for rare events is to be managed. The actual system/software is to be seen in the context of its actual application and based on clearly defined operational profile (i.e., test scenarios closely approximate in type and frequency the distribution of inputs that will be encountered in operation). All credible failure modes are to be covered, particularly including *accidents*. Accident (as seen by IEEE) is an unplanned event or series of events that results in death, injury, occupational illness, or damage to or loss of equipment, property, or damage to the environment; a mishap. In an engineering context, it is the result of inadequate control actions not enforcing necessary constraints on the system design and operation [N.G. Leveson, (2004)]. The models are to identify *hazards*, i.e., states or interactions of the system components and its environment that can lead to accidents. The goal named *safety* is a property of a system which limits the risk of accident (below some specified acceptable level). Demand for measurability and calculations introduced a notion of *risk*. Risk is a forecast in terms of probability/frequency for a future accident of certain severity. Some hazards are decided to be acceptable due to its possibly minor consequences or rare appearance. Safety then is the freedom from unacceptable risk.

This definition appears to be insufficient. Risk characterization requires selection of appropriate mathematical model to calculate potential risk. The probability used here is a measure of uncertainty which in an engineering context is defined in an intuitive, not being precise, way only as 'the likelihood of an expected event occurring'. Varying concerns including a dissatisfaction with some of the axioms of probability lead to introduction of generalizations and alternatives to probability, such as Bayesian epistemology, Dempster-Shafer belief functions or *plausibility measures*. Even the decision making process relies on the availability of accurate estimates of probabilities of specific events, obtaining such data may be problematic; the use of such quantitative techniques is therefore controversial. Discussions of safety tend to take into consideration other aspects than risk. The two difficult questions are to be answered: how to measure/define the required level of system safety and how to engineer the system with a proven satisfaction of the requirement. Two qualitative ways to define acceptance criteria of the system are:

- The system performs a set of scenarios prescribed only.

- The system performs behaviour which will not induce any specific (prescribed) state of some specific structure.

The traditional German railway signaling guidelines, the Mü 8004 norm, apply a rule-based approach to safety. For each type of safety application a certain set of design rules has been established and if these rules are fulfilled by a particular product, then this product is considered to be safe for operation in Germany. The new Cenelec norms for railway software applications, EN 50126 /-8 and -9, use the risk-based as well as the rule-based approaches in one framework. The assumption is that software developed against the process requirements of higher Safety Integrity Levels (SILs) will be less prone to critical failures and thus have a lower impact on the overall system safety.

An evidence-based approach, without precluding the use of existing standards, is defended by [R. A. Weaver, (2003)], where arguments to reflect the contribution of software to system safety are required. The software safety arguments are based on categorization of evidence, which is largely independent of the development process.

2.2. Safety Analysis Process

Safety analysis is a process of preventing accidents which involve operation of system under development or it is a process of (a post-development) demonstration of the system safety properties. Four major steps of the process are distinguished to identify (understand and model) (compare [N.G. Leveson, (1995)], [N.G. Leveson, (2004)], [J. Zalewski and all, (2003)]):

1. the system hazards,

2. the system safety constraints—solutions necessary to maintain safety and to be introduced during the system design and operation, and

3. the hierarchical control structure in place to enforce the constraints (it is a safety engineering of a consistent interaction model: an analysis of what to do about the hazard—*eliminate it, i.e., make it impossible, reduce the likelihood of its occurrence, or mitigate its effects*), or

4. the role in the accident scenario played by each level of the system's hierarchical control structure by not adequately enforcing its part of the

safety constraint (*are controllers able to ascertain the state of the system from information about the process state provided by feedback?*).

Two sources or causes of hazards are to be considered:

1. The system and its environment component failures,

2. The normal behaviour of the system resulting from the interactions among components and its constraints as defined, possibly in an inadequate way (the system failure).

The four steps shown above apply in parallel both to:

- a structure of the system embedded in its operational environment (which is to be documented and maintained in the *Application Architecture*), as well as to

- an organizational structure, actions and processes of the development project (which is to be documented and maintained in *Safety Plan of the Project*).

Comparing to traditional engineering disciplines, software is considered as distinguished by:

1. complexity of behaviour that is achieved by software, and

2. its lack of continuity.

Complexity of behaviour is a source of design faults. Lack of continuity complicates testing. To find out what constitutes an architecture of software, what are the arrangements of elements and structures, we have to look at the basic principles [J. van Katwijk and all, (2003)] [J. Zalewski, (2003)]. That the results obtained by one risk analyst are unlikely to be obtained by others starting with the same information, is not unusual situation [F. Redmill, (2001)].

3. UNDERLYING ACTIVITIES OF THE ANALYSIS

Traditional accident models were devised to explain losses caused by failures of physical devices (chain or tree of failure events) in relatively simple systems. They are less useful for explaining accidents in software-intensive systems and for non-technical aspects of safety such as organizational culture and human decision-making. Creation of an infrastructure based on which safety analysis can function efficiently and effectively is needed. A so called *safety culture* for a development company and processes associated with routine tasks there, in general, is now identified as an area of root cause of accidents and that there is the greatest and most fundamental potential for improvement [M. D. Cooper, (2000)], [J. N. Sorensen, (2002)], [F. Speirs and C.W. Johnson, (2002)], [J. Braband, (2004)]. Safety culture refers to a shared set of understood knowledge and values in a particular group. It is recognized that the organization's structure may have limitations in providing the 'glue' that holds organizations together and act according to its mission (compare particularly [P.M. Senge, (1990)]).

Safety relevant norms require competence of safety analysis processes participants[4]. To achieve competence, people learn through instruction or experience. Knowledge of (currently) objective part (and related skills) of the activity allows for choice of a plan or perspective. The plan or perspective then determines which elements of the situation are treated as important and which ones are ignored.

Quality of conformance (how well the product conforms to the specifications required) is influenced by a number of factors, including the choice of manufacturing processes, the training and supervision of the workforce, the types of process controls, tests, and inspection activities that are employed, the extent to which these procedures are followed, and the motivation of the workforce to achieve quality.

The rest of this section outlines the core sub-processes to support safety analyses (compare [F. Redmill, (2004)], [N. G. Leveson, (2004)], [Ch. Blechinger, (2004)], [J. Zalewski and all, (2003)]). The processes place techniques, such as Hazard And Operability Studies (HAZOP), Failure Modes and Effects Analysis (FMEA) and Fault Tree Analysis (FTA), into context.

3.1. Appropriate Representation of the Problem (Implicit Assumptions and Requirements)

Whenever a system is described, there are always made assumptions on the context in which that system or its development project will operate.

To minimize subjectivity of safety judgments, information about the required behaviour of the system under construction and the project and its context itself is to be collected. The broad picture should include: designers' competence, tools efficiency, criteria of acceptance of their work, their responsibilities and dependence, or how data about the past are indicative of future trends and what the risks we are willing to accept in the future, agreements on 'best practice' or limitations of knowledge and technology;

---

[4] In the internal safety assessment context the discussions regarding *competence* and *independence* (the attributes which do not contradict each other) are usually related by a policy that "Assessment n eeds competence and independence, but competence weighs more than independence."

accepted patterns to specific problems and discussions concerning overconfidence in specific solutions.

It is to be noted that domain or government committees are source of some of the 'objective' measures used in safety engineering while some of the concepts used are problematic, e.g., risk measures or SIL.

3.2 Traceability Analysis

When an implicit assumption turns out to be wrong, it is potentially very difficult to identify those parts of the system which were dependent on that assumption. A relationship (*trace*) is established between two or more products of the development process, especially products having a predecessor-successor or master-subordinate relationship to one another. *Traceability* information can be used to support:

1. the analysis of the implications and integration of changes requested in the system development process;

2. the maintenance and evolution of software systems and documentation;

3. the reuse of software systems and their components; and

4. the inspection and testing of software systems.

In this context, traceability is used to determine the relationships between aspects of the design and aspects of the requirements. When a requirement changes, traceability information shows which aspects of the design need to be considered during impact analysis.

For assessing *change impact* (to perform *impact analysis*) the identification of the elements of the system which are affected (and how they are affected) by the introduction of a particular change (including failure) is maintained. Given the right information about the interactions between those elements, it should be possible to follow the dependencies from the original location of change to all of the affected parts.

Interaction may be explicit, in which case it is either direct interaction (e.g., a procedure call) or indirect (such as an event broadcast). Interaction may also be implicit, for example, if a resource is being shared between different functions. (The simpler these interactions are, the more likely it is that an analysis technique will be able to find them, and hence the more accurate the results of the analysis will be.) *Change propagation* is a central aspect of software development: as developers modify software entities such as functions or variables to introduce new features or fix bugs, they must ensure that other entities in the software system are updated to be consistent with these new changes[5]. Change introduces new forms of failure. Various approaches to control the amount of change propagation and to avoid hidden dependencies were proposed, e.g., the Object Oriented paradigm.

Causes can apparently contribute to effects in a variety of ways: by triggering events (*the only focus of traditional analyses*), by being background or standing conditions, omissions, factors which enhance or inhibit effects, factors that remove a common preventative of an effect.

To support understanding of an interactive complexity of object-oriented systems, the OF-FMEA method was developed (compare Section 4 of this presentation).

3.3. Slow Variation or Degradation Over Time Analysis

The control structure developed to enforcing the system safety constraints usually presents slow variation or degradation over time, particularly in the physical system, human operator behaviour, or the environment. One should be prepared for unexpected: classifications applied may lead to results one expected.

3.4. Resources Against Goals

Project is a unique, temporary endeavour undertaken to create a unique product, service, or result within clearly specified time, cost and quality constraints (compare [PMI, (2003)]). It is to attain its objective and then terminate. Software applications development usually demands projects which involve creating something that has not been done in exactly the same way before and which is, therefore, unique and distinct.

Project management disciplines like cost estimation, project scheduling, resource planning, configuration management, and proactive risk management to avoid the state of wonder why the project is in constant turmoil. Implementation of a minimal process and reliance on staff expertise is not sufficient.

---

[5] The issue of bugs introduced by developers who did not notice dependencies between entities and failed to propagate changes correctly was named by Parnas and Brooks as 'software aging'.

3.5. Misunderstanding

Techniques which attempt to reduce the potential for misunderstanding (to form a common consensus with agreed terminology, scope and semantics). When there is no common language, there is no communication and common understanding.

Roles and goals give structure and organized direction to our personal mission. Expectations around roles and goals may be conflicting or ambiguous and should be clearly understood and to be shared by other people. Clear identification of areas of activity and strategies give a sense of direction and trust. The paradigm that one person's success is not achieved at the expense or exclusion of the success of others is to be applied [M. Robson, (2002)].

3.6. Independent Assessment of Safety Argumentation

Once the safety argument has been constructed and documented, it is analyzed for flaws according to whatever regulatory or assessment criteria happen to be in place in the application domain (whether the system is suitable for use). To support the assessor's reasoning an Assessment Plan is to be developed and maintained, which includes a Safety Claim Structure to be completed (compare section 5 of this presentation).

4. OF-FMEA METHOD

Software failures are in general the result of flaws possibly introduced in the logic of the software design, or in the code-implementation of that logic. These may produce an actual functional failure, in case they are "performed" on an execution path activated according to the specific inputs to the software. It is known that standard testing approaches are not suitable for determining failure rates in regions defined for safety-critical systems [B. Littlewood, (2004)].

To model and predict the characteristics and properties of these designs accurately new tools and approaches are needed. Consideration of all possible behaviours of the system could be valuable evidence. Since "all possible" behaviours may be too many to examine for traditional techniques, two complementary approaches have evolved that attempt to reduce the number of behaviours that must be considered. One way tries to show that the system always does the right thing (liveness), the other tries to show that it never does a seriously wrong thing (safety).

One of the ideas under investigation concerns a reasonable use of formal methods. Experience of using the "formal" way of systems development, verification and its quality assurance is extending. Formal methods, in general, are used for:

1. terminology clarification (including domain objects and structures: net topology, stations,...),

2. methodology clarification,

3. patterns for technical solutions,

4. development and analysis support (to reason about properties of systems) in the phases of specification, design refinement and verification, software code and tests generation.

The general way followed during a formal system development is to start from a description of some specific domain. Then one is to state the requirements and answer the question: *Can the description tolerate ubnormal situations?* Finally, introduce the tolerance of ubnormal situations and argue on the relation of the description to the reality and accepted models.

In formal verification, we verify that a system is correct with respect to a specification. When verification succeeds and the system is proven to be correct, there is still a question of how complete the specification is, and whether it really covers all the behaviours of the system.

Automated examination of scenarios can be taken still further using model checking. In model checking, the case explosion problem is transformed into one of *state explosion*, meaning that the time and space required to run the model checker grows rapidly and eventually becomes infeasible as the size of the model grows, so that abstraction, or consideration of only limited numbers of fault cases and real-time delays, must be employed.

Beyond being fully-automatic, an additional attraction of model-checking tools is their ability to accompany a negative answer to the correctness query by a counterexample to the satisfaction of the specification in the system. Thus, together with a negative answer, the model checker returns some erroneous execution of the system. These counterexamples are very important and they can be essential in detecting subtle errors in complex designs.

To support understanding an Interactive complexity of the systems, the OF-FMEA method was developed [T. Cichocki and J. Górski, (2000)], [T. Cichocki and J. Górski, (2001)], [T. Cichocki and J. Górski, (2002)]. The UML (*Unified Modeling Language*) and CSP (*Communication Sequential Processes*) specification languages and FDR (*Failures Divergence Refinement*) tool are used. The method may address component failures and system failures (the individual components are operating as planned but the problems arose in the unplanned effects of these component behaviour on the system).

4.1. OF-FMEA Background

Failure Modes and Effects Analysis (FMEA) and its variants have been widely used in safety analyses for more than thirty years. With the increase of application domain of software intensive systems there was a natural tendency to extend the use of (originally developed for hardware systems) safety analysis methods to software based systems.

FMEA is focused on safety consequences of component failures. Identified failure modes of a component are analyzed case by case. The analysis process results in an explicit and documented decisions that take into account the risk associated with a given failure mode. The decision can be just the acceptance (supported by a convincing justification) of the consequences of the failure or it can suggest necessary design changes to remove (or mitigate) the consequences or causes of the failures. Documentation is an important output of FMEA. This documentation can be then referred to by a safety case for the considered system.

The work that aims at extending the FMEA to make it suitable to analyze object-oriented software designs is presented in ([T. Cichocki and J. Górski, (2000)], [T. Cichocki and J. Górski, (2001)], [T. Cichocki and J. Górski, (2002)], compare also [J. Zalewski and all, (2002)]), where relevant references may be found. It is assumed that to analyze failure mode consequences formal methods are being used. The approach called OF-FMEA (*Object-oriented Formal FMEA*) follows the 'classical' FMEA process while analyzing system designs and aims at analysing the dependence of system behaviour on possible failures of its components. OF-FMEA extends FMEA in three aspects:

- assumes that the analyzed system is being developed using the object-oriented approach,

- assumes that the object-oriented models of the system are supplemented with their formal specifications,

- assumes that the analysis of failure consequences is based on the formal specifications and is supported by an automatic tool.

4.2. Overview of OF-FMEA

Object models are general enough to represent systems (people, software and hardware) and can then be specialized towards representation of software components. As the consequence, system development can proceed without a major switch of the modeling approach while changing the attention from the system to software aspects. This is an important advantage during the analysis as we can pass the borders between heterogeneous components of the system (both, hierarchically and horizontally) without being forced to work with heterogeneous models.

In OF-FMEA CSP (*Communication Sequential Processes*) was chosen as a formal base for object-oriented models. The motivation behind this choice was that CSP is well suited to modeling co-operating components that interact by passing messages along communication lines. And it was exactly the situation we were facing during our case studies (related to railway switching). The system we were working with is composed of components with a relatively little state information. The components exchange messages with their environment through defined communication channels. A natural way of specifying such components is by describing their possible interactions with the surrounding world. This way of viewing interfaces is well suited to the way FMEA considers the system components: it concentrates on failures, i.e., on what is visible to the environment and to much extend disregards the mechanism (the component's interior) that led to the failure.

It is assumed that before we start OF-FMEA an adequate environment to support the work has been set up. Part of this environment is object-oriented models of the system of interest. Of particular interest are two categories of models:

- The *object model* that presents the system in terms of its constituent objects and relationships among them; of particular interest is the decomposition relationship as it shows how the system decomposes into its components.

- The *object collaboration diagrams* showing how objects interact through communication channels; the channels may model the actual communication links (if the objects are already designed and implemented) or show the designers' intentions concerning the further development of the system.

We assume that the models have been checked against relevant consistency and correctness criteria (e.g., by checking them against documentation standards and by passing them through an inspection process).

Failure checklists are based on experience, producer recommendations, sectoral norms and engineering judgment and support identification of component failure modes. To support modeling of the identified failure modes we provide a set of patterns. Each pattern suggests how to modify the specification of a "normal" behaviour of the component (and possibly of some co-operating components) in order to model a given failure mode. An application of a pattern to represent a given failure mode in the specification of a component is called *failure mode injection*. The specifications with injected failure modes are then verified against safety properties to check for possible failure consequences.

The OF-FMEA method comprises the following steps:

- Choosing the scope of the analysis.
- Formal modeling of the system.
- Analysis of component failures.
- Failure mode injection campaign.
- Interpretation of the results.

The steps are presented in more detail in the subsequent sections.

4.3. Choosing the Scope of the Analysis

While applying OF-FMEA we concentrate on the decomposition hierarchy of the object model. This hierarchy shows how the higher level components are built out of the lower level ones. On top of this we can see the whole system as a single component. Its required properties specify what is considered important concerning the mutual influence of the system and its environment, e.g., for a critical system we postulate that the system should be safe. The lower level decomposition shows the system components and explains how they interact. In our case study the system of interest is LBS— the Line Block System. It controls the traffic of trains between adjacent railway stations. The related decomposition structure is shown in Figure 2 (see the next page). At Level 0 we have a generic railway system and its only attribute represents our (the public) concern that the system should be safe. Level 1 shows the signaling system and its relevant co-operating components. The next Level 2 shows the place of LBS within the signaling system. This is the level with respect to which we interpret the railway signaling rules derived from the railway regulations. The rules impose safety constraints on the model.

With respect to the hierarchy shown in Figure 2 the rules can be understood as the explanation of what "safe" of Level 0 means in terms of levels 1 and 2 of our decomposition. Levels 3 down to 6 represent design decisions (explain the structure of LBS in terms of its components and their interactions).

We chose Level 2 as the reference level during our analysis that means that by "safe" we understand that the system is compliant with the railway safety regulations. And we chose Level 6 as the lowest component level (we did not consider further decomposition levels). Our goal was to analyse how possible failure modes of the components can affect the safety properties expressed with respect to Level 2.

Object models represent the structural aspects of the system design. Communication among objects is represented by collaboration diagrams that belong to the suite of models recommended by UML [6]. An example collaboration diagram is shown in Figure 1. It explains how components of Level 4 co-operate to implement the i-th Local Control Point object.

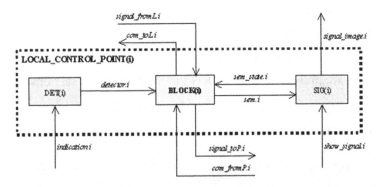

Figure. 1. Collaboration Diagram of the Components
of the i-th Local Control Point Object

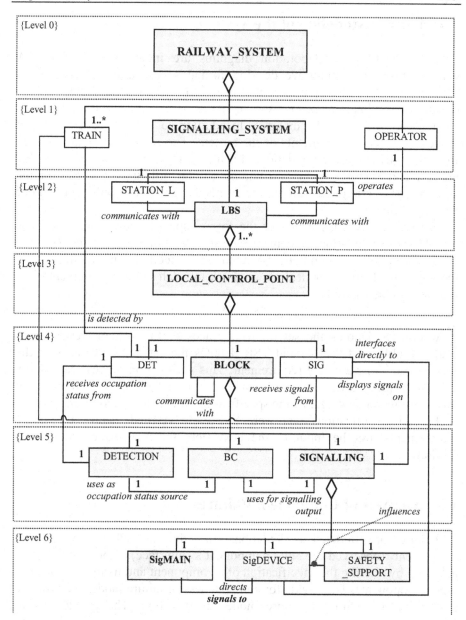

Figure. 2. Object Model of a Railway System. Shadowed blocks show the objects that are subjected to further decomposition. The objects of lower levels were not included in our case study.

4.4. Formal Modeling of the System

The object and collaboration diagrams are input to the OF-FMEA method. From this input we develop formal specification of component interactions. For this purpose we use CSP. Each component of the collaboration diagram becomes a CSP process with input and output channels as shown in the diagram. In addition to this we develop formal models of safety requirements of the system. The requirements are derived from the railway safety regulations. Each requirement is modeled as a CSP process and imposes some restrictions on the ordering of events in the system. The requirements refer to the events that are visible on Level 4 of our decomposition.

We can verify consistency of the formal specifications using the FDR tool. During verification we compare the specification of the system (seen as composition of its components) with the specification of the safety requirements. During verification we check for each safety requirement if the following relation holds:

$$TS \subseteq TSR,$$

where TS denotes the set of event traces of the system (restricted to events visible on Level 4) and TSR denotes the set of event traces of the process modeling a safety requirement. This verification process can follow the design process (in a sense that after we design the next decomposition level we can verify it against the specification of the safety requirements).

Formal specifications that were positively verified against the safety requirements are the input to the next step, the analysis of component failures.

4.5. Analysis of Component Failures

Failures are modeled as deviations from the "normal" behaviour of a component (observed on the component's interface). The modeling is achieved by altering the specification of a component and its interaction with other components. To provide for completeness of failure modes we follow a systematic procedure of failure mode identification. The problem is to formulate hypotheses about potential failure modes of a component X and to decide which of them are included in further analyses (by accepting or rejecting the failure hypotheses). In order to control the completeness of failure hypotheses we apply the following criteria.

C 1.   We look at the domain associated with a given communication channel and admit that the values passed through the channel can be changed.

C 2. We admit that a communication channel can pass values that are beyond the domain of values associated with the channel.

C 3. We admit that after accepting an event a component can switch to a different (defined) state, i.e., there is a faulty transition to the state that is already in the specification.

C 4. We admit that after accepting an event the component can switch to a different (undefined) state, i.e., there is a faulty transition to a state that was not included in the specification of 'normal' behaviours.

The above criteria form a sort of a checklist to be followed while formulating the failure hypotheses for a component. The criteria C1–C4 protect against omissions but cannot be solely used as a tool to identify valid failure hypotheses. Application of C1–C4 can force us to consider a large number of possible failure modes, disregarding their credibility. To provide for a more focused set of failure modes we apply additional criteria that provide for early rejection of incredible failure modes. Those that withstand this selection are passed to the subsequent analysis step.

During validation of the failure mode hypotheses we apply the following criteria:

- Checklists of failure modes of a considered type of component that can be found in sectoral norms and guidelines. For instance, [10] recommends some standard failures of communication channels in railway applications.

- Experience reports provided by users of similar systems.

- Failure profiles of components (e.g., delivered by producers of components).

- Suggestions coming from the project stakeholders (e.g., designers' intentions concerning the components structure and the ways of their interaction).

The above criteria are used to accept/reject failure mode hypotheses. The result of this selection process is a list of credible failure modes that is passed to the subsequent step, the failure mode injection campaign.

4.6. Failure Mode Injection Campaign

The list of selected failure modes is an input to the failure mode injection campaign. The objective of this step is to analyze the consequences of each particular failure mode on the system safety properties. Each failure mode is modeled by altering the CSP specification of the system.

Let assume that a given component X co-operates with another component Y. In terms of CSP, this means that X and Y are connected through a common communication channel as shown in Figure 3.

As X is connected with Y, a failure of X will possibly affect the behaviour of Y. We identified and classified possible patterns of failure related to the co-operation of X and Y and called them *failure modeling patterns*.

Figure. 3. Component X Connected with Component Y
by a Communication Channel Comm.

We apply common techniques used for conditional compilation to control activation and deactivation of those parts of the specification that implement failure modes.

After injecting a failure mode into the system specification we check, using the FDR tool, for its safety consequences.

If the verification confirms that the analyzed failure mode has no negative effects on system safety, the failure mode can be accepted. In the opposite case however we know that the failure mode, if actually occurs, can affect the system safety properties. In such case FDR can provide example event scenarios that lead to a contradiction of safety. Those scenarios can then be very helpful while considering possible redesign of the component objects. The results of the failure mode injection campaign are collected in the OF-FMEA tables (see Table 1).

Table 1. OF-FMEA Table (documentation of specific injection)

Planning part:

SPECIFICATION			
FAULT CODE			
COMPONENT / STATE			
ERROR PATTERN		CRITERIA	COMMENTS
THE FAULT VALIDATION			

Checking part:

Parameters of the specification	Run tine of FDR	Mode (W/I)	Max. number of states checked	Report of FDR	Remarks

EFFECTS PICTURE OF THE FAULT INJECTION		
Test		
Assertion		
Result		

Ad. assertion	Analysis of the FDR report	Assessment and design decision

The results of the fault injection campaign are interpreted by undertaking the following decisions: failure mode acceptance, failure mode handling or failure mode elimination.

The choice between the above interpretations depends on the judgment of the analysts/designer and is beyond the OF-FMEA method. The criteria used to support such decision include availability of the resources for redesign, availability of candidate components to replace a given one, and the assessment of the credibility of the considered failure mode.

5. ASSESSMENT SAFETY CLAIM STRUCTURE

Safety must both be achieved and demonstrated in advance, prior to operation. Many standards require the development of a Safety Case to demonstrate the acceptability of safety critical systems. The Safety Case must provide confidence that the system is deemed safe enough to operate. A state of *belief* or *trust* of the system users must be achieved, that state of the mind by which it assents to propositions because of some qualities of the source. People quite often realize that they know more than they can explain. This is probably the case of Safety Case. It is to represent a clear, comprehensive, definable and auditable argument that a system or installation will be acceptably safe throughout its life (including decommissioning) within a defined environment [P.G. Bishop and R.E. Bloomfield, (1998)], [Ch.B. Weinstock and all, (2004)]. In parallel, an Independent Safety Assessment develops its Safety Assessment Report based on evidence found during the assessment activities, and an independent Safety Claim Structure (where the evidence and assumptions used are linked by the explicit arguments to support a decision) is included there as well. Viewpoints of stakeholders (or safety goals) are proposed as a means of managing the analytical complexity of safety critical systems [J. McDermid,

(2000)]. Each of the viewpoints is a declarative statement of intent to be achieved by the *system* (i.e., the software-to-be together with its environment) under consideration. It is represented by models of the system and its process of development. The representation forms a justified strategy or means of compliance.

The expert judgment must be used in an disciplined way. Too often critical decisions are made in ways that are difficult to justify or even to explain, leaving the doubt (for the decision makers as well as other interested parties) that the decision may be unsound [L. Strigini, (2004)]. A significant amount of practice in developing and maintenance of these structures is still needed. It is already known that relevant tools, based on clearly and consistently defined methodologies, are needed.

Several developments in this direction are known, e.g.,

1. ASCE (Adelard Safety Case Editor) Tool for Safety Case Document Construction—a hypertext tool for constructing and reviewing structured arguments (**http://adelard.com/software/asce/**).

2. Advanced Railway Safety Case Production Tool of Railway Research Centre (**http://www.railway.bham.ac.uk/advanced.htm**)—the research addressed the requirements for a Safety Case Automated Production Tool (SCAPT) environment integrating systems engineering processes and tools, modeling, risk management and domain knowledge.

3. Trust Case development tool by Software Engineering Department of Gdansk University of Technology (a separate presentation on this Workshop).

An independent study is conducted by the author of this presentation in the context of safety assessment of interlocking application development and relevant Cenelec railway norms. A complete Claim Breakdown Structure, the goal decomposition, based on the norms and domain guidelines was represented as a tree. A top level claim is developed on a diagram (compare Figure 4 below). Argumentation tables are developed and maintained for each of the claims to collect argumentation based on sub-claims, facts, assumptions, context information, references, comments, models (see Table 2). The argumentation tables, to be presented in the Safety Assessment Report, are to show the complete information of specific Safety Case modules. The Claim Structure is a part of a overall Safety Assessment Framework[6]. It is still a work in progress.

---

[6] The rule "*If You present a projection of some process, show the models used to develop the projection*" is to be practiced.

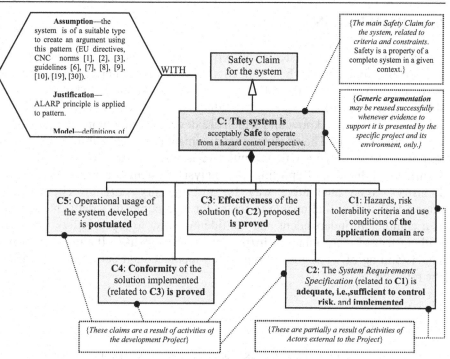

Figure. 4. Top Level Safety Claim Development

Table 2. Argumentation Table: Safety Case Module in a Table Form

Context:	
Code:	**S a f e t y C l a i m :**
Cx.x...	
A r g u m e n t /non-conformity (communication of the relationship between the Evidence and the Claim):	
Code:	**S a f e t y S u b - C l a i m :**
F a c t :	
References:	Trust function: Underlying model:
Assumption:	
References:	Uncertainty: Underlying model:
Comments:	

6. CONCLUSIONS

Identifying whole systems is problematic in general. A system in developers mind may just be a collection of statements intended to describe it sufficiently. This relates the difficulty in formalization of the whole to that of the formalization of its parts. The safety analysis and assurance problem relies on patterns we know and which are developed in a more complete and consistent methods. The process is an organizations responsibility and group activity, where a recent CIRAS initiative is welcome as well. CIRAS—the Confidential Incident Reporting & Analysis System for the UK Railway Industry—is an alternative way for rail industry staff to report safety concerns that they feel unable to report through company safety channels. It is a completely independent and confidential way to report safety concerns without fear of recrimination (**http://www.ciras.org.uk/**). It aims to improve understanding of what goes wrong when incidents and accidents happen on the railways.

7. REFERENCES

BishopP. G. and R.E. Bloomfield, A Methodology for Safety Case Development, Safety-critical Systems Symposium, Birmingham, UK, 1998.

Blechinger, Ch., ProCEN – A tool to manage the CENELEC RAMS Process, SIGNAL + DRAHT (96) 4/2004, p. 15–16.

Braband, J., The importance of a safety culture in railway signaling, SIGNAL + DRAHT (96) 5/2004, p. 33–36.

Cichocki, T. and J. Górski, Failure Mode and Effect Analysis for Safety-Critical Systems with Software Components, in: Floor Koornneef, Meine van der Meulen (eds.) Computer Safety, Reliability and Security, *Proceedings of 19th International Conference SAFECOMP 2000*, Rotterdam (The Netherlands), October 24–27, 2000, Springer Lecture Notes in Computer Science 1943, p. 382–394.

Cichocki, T. and J. Górski, Formal Support for Fault Modeling and Analysis, in: Udo Voges (ed.), *Proceedings of Computer Safety, Reliability and Security, 20th International Conference SAFECOMP 2001*, Budapest (Hungary), September 26–28, 2001, Springer Lecture Notes in Computer Science 2187, p. 190–199.

Cichocki, T. and J. Górski, OF-FMEA—an approach to safety analysis of object oriented software intensive system, *The 9th International Conference on Advanced Computer Systems (ACS'2002)*, Miedzyzdroje (Poland), October 23–25, 2002 (published in The Kuwer International Series in Engineering and Computer Science – 752, ISBN: 1-4020-7396-8, September 2003, p. 271–280).

Cooper, M. D., Towards a Model of Safety Culture, Safety Science (2000): vol. 36, p. 111–136 (**http://behavioural-safety.com/articles/Towards_A_Model_Of_Safety_Culture/**).

Edmonds, B., Syntactic Measures of Complexity, Ph.D. thesis, The University of Manchester, 1999, (245 pp.).

J. van Katwijk, Bo Sandén, and J. Zalewski, An Approach to Evaluate Real-Time Software Architectures for Safety-Critical Systems, 2003, *Proc. Workshop on Critical Systems Development with UML*, San Francisco, Calif., October 21, 2003, 121–128 (**http://www.eg3.com/real/safety.htm**).

Leveson, N. G., Safeware: System Safety and Computers. Addison-Wesley Publishing Company, 1995, ISBN 0-201-11972-2, (680 pp.).

Leveson, N. G., A Systems-Theoretic Approach to Safety in Software-Intensive Systems, to appear in *IEEE Trans. on Dependable and Secure Computing*, 2004.

Littlewood, B., Assessing the dependability of Software-based systems: the importance role of confidence, *KKIO 2004*, Software Engineering Conference, Gdansk, 5–8 October, 2004, p. 13–14.

McDermid, J. A., A.J. Vickers, and S.P. Wilson, Managing Analytical Complexity of Safety Critical Systems using Viewpoints, Department of Computer Science, University of York, UK.

Project Management Institute, A Guide to the Project Management Body of Knowledge (PMBOK® Guide), November 2003, (257 pp.).

Redmill, F., Subjectivity in Risk Analysis. Risk Analysis and Safety Management of Technical Systems, Conference and Workshops, Gdansk- Gdynia, 25–27, June 2001, p. 75–89.

Redmill, F., Risk-based test planning during system development. KKIO 2004, Software Engineering Conference, Gdansk, 5–8 October, 2004, p. 15–29.

Robson, M., Problem-Solving in Groups, Gower Publishing Limited, Gower House, 2002, (185 pp.).

Sanz, R., and J. Zalewski, Pattern-Based Control Systems Engineering, IEEE Control Systems, vol. 23, No. 3, pp. 43–60, July 2003.

Senge, P. M., The Fifth Discipline, The Art and Practice of The Learning Organization, Doubleday, 1990, (389 pp.).

Sorensen, J. N., Safety culture: a survey of the state-of-the-art. Reliability Engineering and System Safety, 76 (2002), p. 189–204.

Speirs, F. and C. W. Johnson, Safety Culture in the face of industrial change: a case study from the UK Rail Industry, University of Glasgow, Scotland, May 29, 2002.

Strigini, L., Formalism and judgment in assurance cases, A position statement for the workshop on "Assurance Cases: Best Practices, Possible Obstacles, and Future Opportunities," held at DSN 2004, International Conference on Dependable Systems and Networks, Florence, Italy, June 2004.

Weaver, R. A., The Safety of Software—Constructing and Assuring Argument, University of York, Department of Computer Science, Ph.D. Thesis, September 2003, (298 pp.).

Weinstock, Ch. B., J. B. Goodenough, and J. J. Hudak, Dependability Cases, May 2004, Technical Note, CMU/SEI-2004-TN-016, (31 pp.).

Zalewski, J., Real-Time Software Architectures and Design Patterns: Fundamental Concepts and Their Consequences, SCR 2003 (also: Annual Reviews in Control, vol. 25, No. 1, p. 133–146, July 2001).

Zalewski, J., W. Ehrenberger, F. Saglietti, J. Górski, and A. Kornecki, Safety of computer control systems: challenges and results in software development, Annual Reviews in Control, vol. 27, No. 1, p. 23–37, 2003.

TRUST CASE—A CASE FOR TRUSTWORTHINESS OF IT INFRASTRUCTURES

Janusz Górski
Gdansk University of Technology, Gdansk, Poland, e-mail: jango@pg.gda.pl
Institute of Protection and Security of Citizen, EU JRC, Ispra, Italy

Abstract: The paper presents an approach to development of trust cases intended to justify and support claims about trustworthiness of IT enabled products and services. It introduces the conceptual framework of a trust case covering its structure and contents, discusses trust case stakeholders and proposes an architecture of a tool supporting the practical application of trust cases. The present status of the tool is briefly summarized. In conclusion, some information about present applications of the approach and about further development plans is given.

Keywords: Trust Case; Safety; Security; Privacy; IT infrastructure; Trust ontology

1. INTRODUCTION

Objectively justified trust is becoming an issue that receives increasing attention as information technologies conquer new application domains and extend the scope of their applications. Intuitively, *trust* is a notion referring to a belief in some postulated property (hereafter called *trust objective*) like honesty, truthfulness, competence, reliability, safety, security, privacy and so on, of a trusted object (the *trustee*) considered in a specific *context*. The object can be any entity perceived as important and interesting from the perspective of the trusting entity (the *trustor*), for instance a person, a concept, a device, a service, an institution. In particular, the trustor can be a part of the context within which the trustee is taken into consideration, for instance we can consider patient's safety (the postulated trust objective) during IT enabled medical procedures (the trustee) within the hospital environment (the context) from the patient's perspective (the trustor).

J. S. Kowalik et al. (eds.), Cyberspace Security and Defense: Research Issues, 125–141.

In most situations trust is not considered as a binary notion (i.e., either we trust in something or not); it is rather represented by some range of *trust levels*. By now, we do not decide which scale is to be used to differentiate between those levels. We do not decide at this point weather this scale is discrete or continuous. We assume that the level of trust is influenced by *trust justification* that refers to the context within which the trustee is being considered. For instance, a patient's level of trust in the therapist's competence depends on the therapist's professional certificates, the recommendations from other patients, the environment within which the therapy is being applied (e.g., hospital, home, casual situation, etc.) and many others. If such justification of trust exists objectively (is explicitly documented) we will call it a *trust case*. Note that we do not postulate that trust justification (the trust case) *determines* the level of trust in the claimed property. Instead, we rather postulate that a trust case *influences* the level of trust of the trustor. This is in recognition of the fact that our understanding of all factors that can affect trust is far from being complete, for instance two different persons can develop different trust levels in the same thing even if they are presented with exactly the same argumentation (take as an example the attitudes to different religions).

We capture the subjectivity that influences the trust level a given trustor has in a specific trustee by distinguishing the trustor's individual *trust profile*. We use this notion to address specific (subjective) differences in the trust levels developed by two different trustors while exposed to the same trust justification.

The model that captures the above concepts is shown in Figure 1.

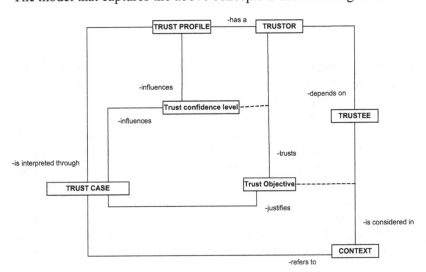

Figure 1. The Ontology of Trust

1.1 Trust Case Definition

We assume the following definition of the trust case:

Trust Case is a documented base that provides a satisfactory (from a given viewpoint) justification for a specified set of claims (regarding system's properties considered for a given application in a given environment) to make a judgment about their trustworthiness.

This definition needs some explanation. The viewpoints mentioned in it represent the stakeholders' concerns about the system (the trustee) under consideration. A viewpoint can represent an individual user who decides about involving herself/himself in the co-operation with the system depending on its trustworthiness (consider for instance e-commerce or e-health applications) or can represent a class of users. An example of a latter is a non-profit institution which assesses a given Web service on behalf of its users (this is what Health On the Net foundation [1] does for the users of e-health services). A viewpoint can be highly formalized, for instance in the situation where the criteria to be met by the trust case (to consider it satisfactory) are documented and supported by regulations (like in the case for safety critical applications [2]) or are documented and widely accepted (which is the case for security critical systems [3]). For some viewpoints 'satisfactory' may mean 'convincing and valid' whereas for some other 'satisfactory' may have more subjective interpretation.

The 'documented base' mentioned in the definition can include any material like: design evidence, assumptions, recommendations, experience. This is further discussed in the next sections.

For comparison we recall two other definitions that are more restrictive than the one proposed above. In [4] we can find the following definition:

Safety case is a documented body of evidence that provides a convincing and valid argument that a system is adequately safe for a given application in a given environment.

This definition is widely accepted within the safety critical systems community. Safety case can be considered as a special case of the trust case where focus is on a specific trust objective, i.e., safety, and highly demanding requirements are needed to be met by the base supporting the case.

Recently the following, more relaxed definition was accepted [5]:

Assurance case is a documented body of evidence that provides a convincing and valid argument that a specified set of critical claims regarding a system's properties are adequately justified for a given application in a given environment.

This definition is becoming presently popular. It provides for covering different aspects of dependability, like safety and security, within a common case. It was used while developing a trust case for the IT infrastructure for distribution and application of drugs in a hospital environment [6].

2. TRUST DRIVERS

We distinguish three 'driving forces' that contribute to the development of trust. This is illustrated in Figure 2.

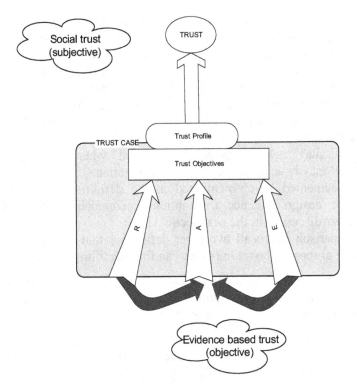

Figure 2. Trust 'Drivers'

- *Assurance* (A)—encompasses 'what you can see and check' type of evidence. This can be in particular:
  - Product (trustee) assurance evidence (facts related to the product);

- Process assurance evidence (facts related to the development process of the product);
- Context of use assurance evidence (facts related to the usage context of the product).

A strong assurance component is typical for safety cases of safety critical systems.

- *Recommendation* (R)—encompasses 'what the others told you' type of evidence. This has a form of recommendations (shared experience, shared attitude) received from other (respected) subjects. Recommendations can be individual or institutional.

- *Experience* (E)—encompasses 'what has been experienced' type of evidence. It can be the own experience (for instance, collected by a given trust case stakeholder) or the system experience (which relates to the trustee's operational profile).

As it is shown in Figure 2, trust is built by interpreting, through the individual trust profile, the assurance, recommendation and experience support for trust objectives. The upper part of the figure represents the 'subjective side' whereas the lower part is where the objective and hard evidence is collected (the assurance base of the trust case).

In the model shown in Figure 2 we admit that the recommendations and experiences supporting trust can eventually be included into the assurance 'pillar' of trust. This is the case when, for instance, the received recommendation is considered as being highly competent and objective and takes a form of 'expert opinion' or 'certificate'. On the experience side, it may relate to the situation where the number of individual experiences provides enough material for some statistical reasoning about the trustee's properties.

The context of a trust case is shown in Figure 3. It shows the three sides contributing to the trust case (assurance, recommendation and experience) together with the 'ontology' component which represents the common conceptual framework supporting the structuring a trust case into trust objectives.

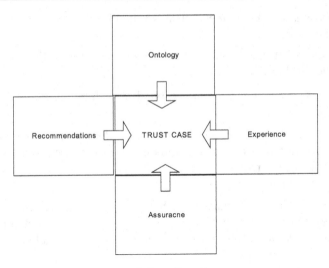

Figure 3. Trust Case Context

3. ONTOLOGIES

Ontology is the description of concepts of a given domain, their meanings and their mutual relationships [7].

3.1 Trust Ontology

The diagram shown in Figure 1 introduces a high level ontology of trust. It can be further specialized by expanding possible trust objectives and showing how they interrelate. Such trust objectives could include: Safety, Honesty, Competence, Security, Privacy, Accountability, Reliability, and so on.

An example decomposition of a safety trust objective is shown in Figure 4. We can notice that the trust objective 'safety' in Figure 4 has still a very general meaning and if considered with respect to a specific application should have been further explained in relation to this context (for instance, the meaning of 'safety' would be different in relation to a hospital system than in relation to say, a breaking system in a car). To provide such an explanation we would have to refer to the *domain ontology* which helps to decompose the generic safety objective into more specialized ones, for instance: *patient's safety requires that he/she does not receive drugs that are conflicting with his/her allergies*. Note that to express such trust objective we have to refer to the notions of: 'patient', 'drug', 'allergy' that clearly belong to the medical domain ontology.

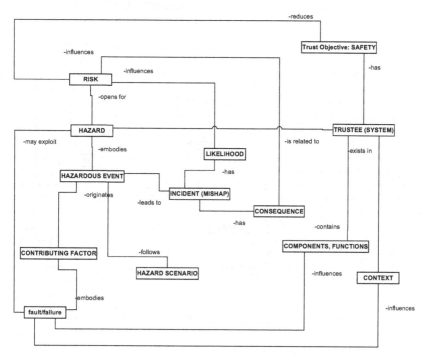

Figure 4. Safety Ontology as an Extension of Trust Ontology

In Figure 5 we show an example decomposition of the security trust objective. We can notice some similarities between the structures presented in figures 4 and 5. This similarity suggests that the two domains (i.e. safety and security) have developed similar conceptual frameworks which possibly could be harmonized into a common one. To illustrate this, compare the notions of 'hazard' and 'vulnerability' or 'mishap' and 'incident' from figures 4 and 5 respectively. In particular, it suggests that the trust cases aiming at safety or security can have similar structures concerning their decomposition into more specific trust objectives. This in particular can lead to the concept of *trust case patterns* which will not be further discussed in this paper.

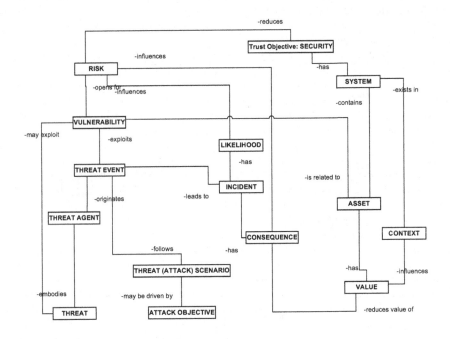

Figure 5. Security Ontology as an Extension of Trust Ontology

3.2 Trust Case Ontology

A trust case is developed by making an explicit set of claims about the system or its environment and then collecting and producing supporting base of facts and assumptions and developing arguments that this evidence justifies the claims. A conceptual model describing the trust case elements and showing their interrelationship is shown in Figure 6 (the arrows show the direction of reading the association names).

The evidence referred to by an argument for a claim can be of the following type:

- *Fact*—a statement or assertion of verified information about something that is the case or has happened. Facts in turn can be:
  - Assurance facts (e.g., a fact documenting demonstrated adherence to established principles, design decisions, results of performed analyses),
  - Experience facts (e.g., a fact documenting observed system property) and

- Recommendation facts (e.g., a fact documenting a recommendation received from other users).
- *Assumption* – a statement assumed to be true for which we do not include any supporting material;
- *Claim* – a (postulated) property that is explicitly justified by giving the argument and evidence that support it.

Note that according to the above definition, claims can be recursively supported by other claims (their sub-claims) to the depth that is arbitrarily chosen by the trust case designer. We also assume that evidence can be linked to references (documents, reports, data, models and so on) that are maintained within the trust case.

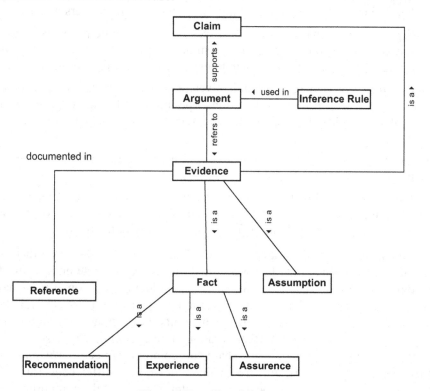

Figure 6. Trust Case Ontology

The inference rules used in arguments are of three basic types:

- *logic* (establishing the validity of a claim from the logical assertions given by the supporting evidence),
- *probabilistic* (e.g., justifying the failure probability postulated by a claim from the probabilities given by the supporting evidence),

- *qualitative* (establishing the validity of a claim by referring to the common acceptance of good practices that were adhered to as demonstrated by the evidence supporting the claim). The qualitative argumentation can in particular refer to accepted standards, guidelines or so called 'engineering judgment'.

4. TRUST CASE STAKEHOLDERS

To understand the context within which a trust case is being used we identify the trust case *stakeholders* who represent different viewpoints at the trust case. This is illustrated in Figure 7.

Particular viewpoints representing the trust case stakeholders include:

- *Supplier*—anticipates trust objectives, identifies/anticipates assessment criteria, contributes to the assurance part of the trust case, collects/produces evidence, maintains the assurance part of the trust case;
- *Operator*—recognizes trust objectives, extends the assurance part of the trust case concerning installation, operation and maintenance of the trustee, enables the experience and recommendation parts of the trust case;
- *Assessor*—selects assessment criteria, assesses the trust case, issues his/her opinion/recommendation;
- *User*—defines his/her own trust profile, collects experience and recommendations and feeds it to the trust case, evaluates own trust, undertake decisions about his/her involvement with the trustee.

The stakeholders illustrated in Figure 7 are generic in the sense that in a specific situation they can be instantiated into more concrete entities. In the picture we also illustrate that the stakeholders can sometimes have conflicting concerns. The generic stakeholders can be further structured to differentiate between more specific viewpoints. For instance, for an e-health application, *User* can be further structured into *Health Professional* and *Patient*. Although both of them share the common concern: *why should I trust this system and get involved?*, their viewpoints differ concerning the trust objectives, their decomposition and interpretation of their importance.

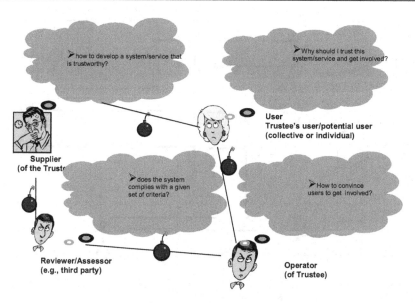

Figure 7. Trust Case Generic Stakeholders

5. PROPOSED ARCHITECTURE

An architecture illustrating how the trust case is integrated with a trustee and offered to its stakeholders is shown in Figure 8.

The architecture distinguishes the following components:

- The Trust Case tool (TC tool) including:
  - The Trust Case (TC) and its base of References (REF);
  - Trust related Ontologies (O) including the Trust Ontology (TO) and the Trust Case Ontology (TCO);
  - Functionalities implementing the Assurance, Recommendation and Experience components of the Trust Case;
  - Trust Profiles of users of the Trustee;
  - Trust Knowledge Base (TKB) including Trust Case patterns and components.
- IT Application (Trustee).
- Trust Case stakeholders (Supplier, Operator, Assessor, User) and their interfaces.

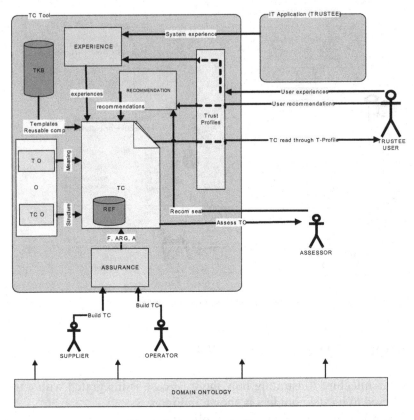

Figure 8. Trust Case Architecture

We assume that Trust Case is developed by the Supplier and Operator with the later contributions by Users (through the recommendation interface). Assessor has access to the Trust Case and can pass recommendations reflecting his/her opinion. Users interpret the Trust Case through their Trust Profiles and in return can pass their experiences and recommendations. The Domain Ontology component represents the influence of the application domain on the content of the trust case (structure of trust objectives, priorities, constraints and so on).

6. COLLABORATIVE DEVELOPMENT

As it has been illustrated in Figures 7 and 8, there can be a number of contributors to the trust case. In some cases the situation may become highly complicated, for instance consider the trust case for an IT infrastructure supporting electricity distribution services with complex ownership structure and distributed responsibilities. In such situation it is not enough to identify the right stakeholders of the trust case and to provide them with effective access channels. In addition to this we have to define and implement an effective co-ordination scheme which would support trust case development and maintenance. This leads to the concept of collaborative development and maintenance of the trust case.

A proposed use case model is shown in Figure 9. The model distinguishes three roles: TC Manager, TC Developer and TC Viewer. The Manager is responsible for planning the development (taking into account the feedback from Viewers) and assigning the tasks to Developers. Developers built parts of the Trust Case and while doing this interpret the feedback from the Viewers. Viewers review the Trust Case and possibly provide their feedback.

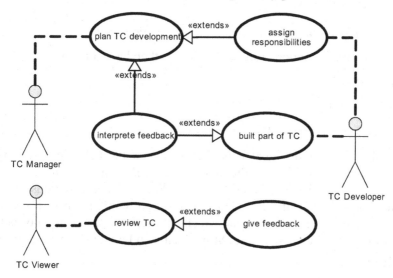

Figure 9. Use Case Model of Trust Case Collaborative Development

7. RECOMMENDATION SCHEME

Recommendations traditionally play an important role in developing trust. As an example take medical services where our decisions concerning the choice of a service provider (doctor, clinic, hospital) are highly influenced by what we hear from the family members, friends or other trusted sources. The trust case architecture shown in Figure 8 provides for a recommendation channel through which recommendations can be fed into the trust case structure.

We presently experiment with different schemes of recommendation based trust development. Some results are presented in [8]. The basic idea is to use Dempster-Shaffer theory of evidence to assign values to trust objectives that represent opinions if a given trust objective is actually met. Those values reflect the belief and plausibility assigned to the trust objective by a recommending subject. In particular this subject can be a user of the trustee or an assessor of the assurance part of the trust case.

To illustrate the idea let us assume a claim CL representing a trust objective in a trust case. For instance, it may postulate that:

> *If a drug is being applied to a patient it is in accordance with the prescription ordered by the doctor who examined the patient.*

Such a claim may result from a decomposition of a more general trust objective:

> *Safety of the patient is continuously maintained.*

The recommendation assigned to CL can then have a form:

$m\,(CL) = f_1$,

$m\,(CL) = f_2$,

$m\,(\{CL, CL\}) = 1 - f_1 - f_2$.

In the above assessment it is expressed that the belief in CL is f_1, the disbelief in CL is f_2 and the uncertainty concerning weather this trust objective is met or not remains $1 - f_1 - f_2$. Such recommendations can result from the assessment of the evidence maintained within the trust case and the application of a reasoning engine which provides for propagation of believes upwards the trust case structure. More details on how this can be done can be found in [8].

8. THE TOOL

The architecture shown in Figure 8 is partially implemented in a tool. The tool covers the Assurance part of the trust case and in particular supports the following functionality:

- Trust case structuring according to the ontology shown in Figure 6 (except recommendation and experience components);
- Maintaining links to the reference documents (both text and graphics);
- Management of trust cases (creating, editing, copying, merging);
- Support for linking claims to the related context models (see [9] for more details);

- Report generation;
- Access control (to support the roles shown in Figure 9).

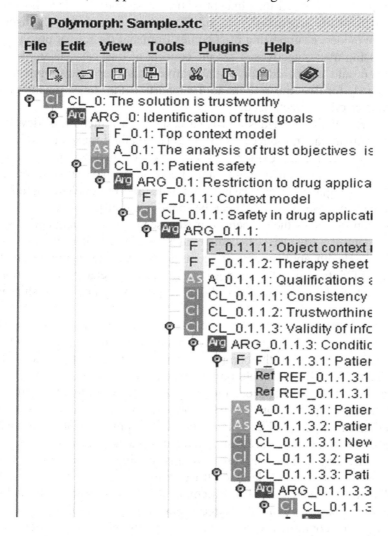

Figure 10. Fragment of a Trust Case for e-Health Application

The tool is implemented in Java and is based on XML. Its architecture provides for high flexibility in changing and extending both, functionality and data formats. An example screen snapshot is shown in Figure 10. It presents a part of the trust case developed for an e-health application. Further details of this trust case can be found in [6].

9. CONCLUSION

The paper introduced the concept of trust case and explained how it can be used to justify trustworthiness of IT systems or services. It discussed where the evidence supporting trust comes from and the role of ontologies in decomposing trust objectives. Then the concept of trust case stakeholder was introduced and the need for collaborative trust case development was emphasized. Finally, the present tool supporting the development of trust cases was briefly characterized.

This presentation provides a broader context for a method of developing trust cases that was introduced in [6], [9]. The method makes use of models which help to define context for trust objectives (claims) within the trust case structure. To support unambiguity and precision we have also introduced a formalized language for expressing arguments and the evidence maintained within the trust case. The details can be found in [6], [9].

The importance of the concept of trust case stakeholder and collaborative development of a trust cases became evident while applying our approach to complex e-Health applications. It seems to be even more important if we consider IT infrastructures supporting for instance electricity distribution where we face the problem of distributed responsibility and ownership of the system.

Further development plans include extending the tool to cover recommendation and experience components of trust (see Figure 8), incorporating to the tool the component implementing trust profiles and the component responsible for ontology management.

We have applied our approach to analyze trustworthiness of a complex IT infrastructure supporting drug distribution and application processes within a hospital environment [10] and presently we are applying it to an innovative system delivering health and lifestyle related services to a citizen [11].

An interesting issue we are presently researching is a possibility of using standards to develop templates of trust cases that would later support the compliance argument. The first attempts to use Common Criteria [3] to define a trust case template delivered promising results in this respect. This work will be continued with respect to a system enabling delivery of electronic signature services.

ACKNOWLEDGEMENT

The work on trust cases reported in this paper is under development in co-operation with my doctoral students: A. Jarzębowicz, R. Leszczyna, J. Miler, M. Olszewski, and M. Zagórski. Valuable input was also received from M

Masera P Chawdhry and M Wilikens. The first version of software tool was developed by M. Jarzebski as a part of his M.Sc. Thesis. The application of this approach to e-Health is supported by the EU 6FR Integrated Project PIPS (Contract 507019) and Polish Committee of Scientific Research (grant 155/E-359/SPB/6,PR UE/DIE 281). The application to public key infrastructure is supported by Polish Committee of Scientific Research (grant 6T112003C/06280).

REFERENCES

[1] Health On The Net Foundation, **http://www.hon.ch/**

[2] Safety Management Requirements for Defense Systems, Defence Standard 00-56, MoD, 1996

[3] Common Criteria for Information Technology Security Evaluation version 2.1, 1999 (Parts 1, 2, 3).

[4] ASCE (Adelard Safety Case Editor) homepage: **http://www.adelard.com/software/asce**

[5] DNS2004 Workshop on Assurance Cases: Best Practices, Possible Obstacles and Future Opportunities, Florence, Italy, 1ˢᵗ July 2004, **http://aitc.aitcnet.org/AssuranceCases/**

[6] Górski J., A. Jarz bowicz, R. Leszczyna, J. Miler, and M. Olszewski, An approach to trust case development, in *Proc. Safecomp Conference*, LNCS 2788, Springer-Verlag, 2003.

[7] **http://www.semanticweb.org**

[9] Górski J., A. Jarz bowicz, R. Leszczyna, J. Miler, and M. Olszewski, Trust case: justifying trust in IT solution, in *Proc. Safecomp Conference, Reliability Engineering and System Safety*, Elsevier, (to be published in Volume 88, Issue 1, 2005).

[10] IST-Drive site: **http://www.sanraffaele.org/Drive/**

[8] Górski J. andM. Zagórski, Using Dempster-Shafer approach to support reasoning about trust in IT infrastructures, in *Proc. 1ˢᵗ Warsaw International Seminar on Intelligent Systems*, May, 2004

[11] **http://www.pips.eu.org/**

DEPENDABILITY, STRUCTURE, AND INFRASTRUCTURE[1]

Brian Randell
School of Computing Science,
University of Newcastle upon Tyne, UK

Abstract: The role that system structuring techniques plays in helping to cope with system complexity and achieve system dependability is analyzed. This leads on to a discussion of (i) the problems of the various kinds of assumptions, both deliberate and unthinking, that are made by system designers, (ii) the increased difficulties regarding such assumptions that can face the designers of complex systems that are intended to function as infrastructures, and (iii) the problems of defending systems and infrastructures against malicious attacks, including those which cause initially-unsuspected structural damage.

Keywords: Dependability; Information Infrastructure; Structure; Failures; Malicious Faults; Systems-of-Systems

1. INTRODUCTION

Governments, industry and the public at large are becoming ever more dependent on a global information infrastructure that is made up of countless inter-linked computer systems. Yet this infrastructure can best be described as fragile, rather than dependable. This is due not just to the immense size and complexity of this information infrastructure and hence the number of faults that occurs almost unavoidably. Rather, it is also due to the damage this infrastructure suffers from the activities of a seemingly ever-increasing number of criminals and hackers.

Unfortunately the current less than satisfactory situation is likely to deteriorate as the global information infrastructure expands to encompass large numbers of huge networked computer systems, perhaps involving

---

[1] This paper draws on material in [Avizienis, et al, 2004], [Jones and Randell, 2004] and [Randell, 2000].

J. S. Kowalik et al. (eds.), Cyberspace Security and Defense: Research Issues, 143–160.
© 2005 *Springer. Printed in the Netherlands.*

everything from super-computers and massive server "farms" to myriads of small mobile computers and tiny embedded devices. Yet in many cases such systems will be expected by the governments and by the large industrial organizations that aim to install them, and indeed by the general public that will have to interact with them, to function highly dependably and essentially continuously. This at any rate would be the consequence should various current industrial and government plans—see for example [European Commission 2002]—come to fruition. Such plans have been formulated despite the fact that the envisaged systems, and hence the information infrastructure that they both rely on and help constitute, seem certain to be far more complex than today's global information infrastructure.

2. SOME STATISTICS

The present situation is perhaps best illustrated by the following sample claims and statistics relating to the (un)dependability of the global information infrastructure:

- The average cost per hour of computer system downtime across thirty domains such as banking, manufacturing, retail, health insurances, securities, reservations, etc., has recently been estimated at nearly $950,000 by the US Association of Contingency Planners[2].

- The French Insurer's Association has estimated that the yearly cost of computer failures is 1.5 – 1.8B Euro (10 – 12B Francs), of which slightly more than half is due to deliberately-induced faults (e.g., by hackers and corrupt insiders) [Laprie 1999].

- The July 2003 report on "Government IT Projects" [Pearce 2003] states that in the UK: "Over the past five years, high profile IT difficulties have affected the Child Support Agency, Passport Office, Criminal Records Bureau, Inland Revenue, National Air Traffic Services and the Department of Work and Pensions, among others."

- Networking dependability is if anything decreasing: "The availability that was typically achievable by (wired) telecommunication services and computer systems in the 90s was 99.999% – 99.9%. Now cellular phone services, and web-based services, typically achieve an availability of only 99% – 90%." [AMSD Roadmap 2003].

- The problem of deliberate attacks on networked computer systems, and potentially via them on other major infrastructures, which is already serious is growing rapidly, as evidenced by SEI/CERT's statistics on

---

[2] **http://www.acp-wa-state.org/Downtime_Costs.doc**

annual numbers of incident reports: 9,859 (1999), 52,568 (2001), 137,529 (2003).

- Price Waterhouse Cooper's "Information Security Breaches Survey 2002" for the UK Dept. of Trade and Industry states that "44% of UK businesses have suffered at least one malicious security breach in the past year, nearly twice as many as in the 2000 survey"[3].

3. DEPENDABILITY

The very concepts of 'dependability' and 'failure' [Avizienis et al. 2004] need careful definition in order to make sense of the problems that can afflict a system whose very complexity is a major cause of difficulties. For our purposes here the following will suffice:

Dependability is the ability to avoid failures that are more frequent and more severe than is acceptable,

where:

A system, operating in some particular environment, may fail in the sense that some other system makes or could, in principle, have made a judgment that the activity or inactivity of the given system constitutes **failure**.

The above definitions are based essentially on just two basic concepts, namely 'system', and 'judgment', for each of which any standard dictionary definition will suffice[4].

The judgmental system is a potential or actual observer of the given system, and may be an automated system, a user or an operator, a relevant judicial authority, or whatever. This judgmental system may or may not have a fully detailed system specification to guide it, though evidently one would expect such a document to be available to guide the system construction task. Ideally such a specification would be complete, consistent, and accurate—in practice there are likely to be many occasions when it is the specification rather than, or as well as, the specified system which is judged as failing.

Different judgmental systems might, of course, come to different decisions regarding whether and how the given system has failed, or might fail in the future, in differing circumstances and from different stakeholders' viewpoints. The crucial issue might, for example, concern the accuracy of

---

[3] **http://www.dti.gov.uk/industry_files/pdf/sbsexecsum_2002.pdf**
[4] Another definition of dependability is "that property of a computer system such that reliance can justifiably be placed on the service it delivers", which though usefully intuitive begs the questions of what is meant by 'reliance', and who or what is providing the 'justification'.

the results that are produced, the continuity or timeliness of service, or the success with which sensitive information is kept private. Indeed, it is likely to concern some balanced combination of such attributes. (Thus, especially with highly complex systems, the notion of what constitutes a failure and whether one has occurred can often be quite subjective.)

Moreover, such a judgemental system might itself fail in the eyes of some other judgemental system, a possibility that is well understood by the legal system, with its hierarchy of courts. So, there is a (recursive) notion of 'failure', which clearly is a relative rather than an absolute notion. So then is the concept of dependability, at any rate when one is dealing with hugely complex systems.

It is in fact necessary to distinguish between three basic concepts—'failure', 'error' and 'fault'.

> An **error** is that part of the system state that is liable to lead to subsequent failure; an error affecting the service that is being provided by a system is an indication that a failure occurs or has occurred. The adjudged or hypothesized cause of an error is a **fault**.

Note (i) that an error may be judged to have multiple causes (for example the occurrence of an attempted attack on the system, and the existence of an exploitable vulnerability within the system, left there by a failing system design and implementation process), and (ii) an error does not necessarily lead to a failure (for example, error recovery might be attempted successfully and failure averted).

Thus a failure occurs when an error 'passes through' the observation interface and affects the service delivered by the system; a system being composed of components that are themselves systems. The manifestation of failures, faults and errors follows a 'fundamental chain':

$$... \rightarrow failure \rightarrow fault \rightarrow error \rightarrow failure\ fault \rightarrow ...$$

Such chains can exist within systems. System failures might be due to faults that exist because, for example, of the failure of a component (i.e., subsystem) to meet its specification.

However, these chains also exist between separate systems. For instance, a failure of a system-design system (constituted by a human design team together with their computer facilities and tools) might result in the wrong choice of component being made in the system that is being designed, resulting in a fault in this latter system that leads eventually to its failure. Also, a system might fail because of the inputs that it receives from some other system with which it is interacting, though ideally it will be capable of checking its inputs thoroughly enough to minimize such failures.

By having separate terms for the three essentially different concepts—'fault', 'error' and 'failure'—one has a chance of dealing properly with the complexities and realities of failure-prone components, being assembled together in possibly incorrect ways, so resulting in systems which in reality will still be somewhat failure-prone.

Note that with highly complex networked systems (i) there are likely to be uncertainties and arguments about system *boundaries*, (ii) the very complexity of the system (and its specification, if it has one) can be a major problem, (iii) judgments as to possible causes or consequences of failure can be subtle and disputable and (iv) any provisions for preventing faults from causing failures are themselves almost certainly fallible.

The above definitions, in clarifying the distinction in particular between fault and failure, lead to the identification of the four basic means of obtaining and establishing high dependability, namely:

- *fault prevention*—prevention of the occurrence or introduction of faults, in particular, via the use of rigorous design methods;

- *fault tolerance*—the means of delivery of correct service in the presence of faults;

- *fault removal*—that is, verification and validation, aimed at reducing the number or severity of faults; and

- *fault forecasting*—system evaluation, via estimation of the present number, the future incidence and the likely consequences of faults.

With less than perfect (i.e., real) systems, in the absence of (successful) fault tolerance, failures may occur and will presumably need to be tolerated somehow by the encompassing (possibly socio-technical) system. However, this notion of 'failure tolerance' is just fault tolerance at the next system level.

Note, however, that one of the most important lessons from work over many years on system dependability is the fact that fault prevention, removal and tolerance should not be regarded as alternatives, but rather as complementary technologies, all of which have a role to play, and whose effective combination is crucial—with fault forecasting being used to evaluate the degree of success that is being achieved.

4. ASSUMPTIONS, ASSUMPTIONS, . . .

System designers always make (possibly arbitrary or unthinking) assumptions concerning, for example: (i) the types and relative frequencies of the faults that might occur, (ii) the effectiveness with which the various dependability means are being deployed, (iii) the relative importance of various (somewhat antagonistic) dependability attributes: reliability, availability, integrity, security, etc., and (iv) the accuracy of any dependability predictions.

The problems of preventing faults in systems from leading to system failures, and of minimizing the severity of failures that do occur, vary greatly in difficulty depending on these assumptions. For example, one might choose to assume that (i) operational hardware faults can be cost-effectively masked

(i.e., hidden) by the use of hardware replication and voting, and (ii) any residual software design faults can be similarly masked by the use of design diversity, i.e., using N-version programming, provided of course that the assumption is correct. In such circumstances error recovery is not needed. In many realistic situations, however, if the likelihood of a failure is to be kept within acceptable bounds, error recovery facilities will have to be provided, in addition to whatever fault prevention and fault masking techniques are used.

The notion of coverage is of relevance to the problem of justifying any such assumptions. In its general sense, **coverage** refers to a measure of the representativeness of the situations to which a system is subjected during its analysis (e.g., in the case of software by means of code inspection, static checking, and program testing) compared to the actual situations that the system will be confronted with during its operational life. This notion of coverage may be made more precise by indicating its range of application, e.g., coverage of a software test with respect to the software text, control graph, etc., coverage of an integrated circuit test with respect to a fault model, coverage of fault tolerance with respect to a class of faults, and, most significantly, coverage of a fault assumption with respect to reality.

By way of an example of the importance of the choice of fault assumptions, consider the problems of error recovery in decentralized systems. If the designer of a distributed database system disallows (i.e., ignores) the possibility of undetected invalid inputs or outputs, the errors that have to be recovered from will essentially all be ones that are wholly within the system. In this situation backward error recovery (i.e., recovery to an earlier, it is hoped error-free, state) will suffice, and be readily implementable, such is the nature of computer storage. If such a system is serving the needs of a set of essentially independent users, competing against each other to access and perhaps update the database, then the now extensive literature on database transaction processing and protocols can provide a fertile source of well-engineered, and mathematically well-founded, solutions to such error recovery problems [Gray and Reuter 1993].

However, the multiple activities in a decentralized system will often not simply be competing against each other for access to some shared internal resource, but rather will on occasion at least be attempting to co-operate with each other, in small or large groups, in pursuit of some common goal. This will make the provision of backward error recovery more complicated than is the case in basic transaction-oriented systems. And the problem of avoiding the "domino effect" [Randell 1975], in which a single fault can lead to a whole sequence of rollbacks, will be much harder if one cannot disallow (i.e., ignore) the possibility of undetected invalid communications between activities.

When a system of interacting threads employs backward recovery, each thread will be continually establishing and discarding checkpoints, and may also on occasion need to restore its state to one given in a previously established and still-retained checkpoint. But if interactions are not controlled, and appropriately coordinated with checkpoint management, then the rollback of one thread to prior to a communication will necessitate that the other thread involved in that communication also rollback, and can possibly result in a cascade of rollbacks that could push all the threads back to their beginnings, i.e., cause the domino effect to occur. (Compare the differing severity of threads T1 and T2, in Figure 1, having to go back to an earlier checkpoint.)

However, the domino effect would not occur if it could safely be assumed that each thread's data was fully validated before it was output, i.e., was transmitted from one thread to another. (Similarly, the effect would be avoided if a thread could validate its inputs fully.) Such an assumption is in effect made in simple transaction-based systems, in which outputs from the database thread to a user thread are allowed to occur only after a transaction has been "committed" in response to a user command. Moreover, in such systems the notion of commitment is regarded as absolute, so that once the commitment has been made, there is no going back, i.e., there is no provision for the possibility that a database output (or a user input) was invalid.

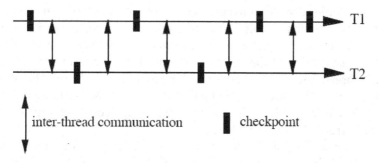

Figure 1. The Domino Effect

The notion of nested transactions can be used to limit the amount of activity that has to be abandoned when backward recovery (of small inner transactions) is invoked. However, this notion typically still assumes that there are absolute "outermost" transactions, and that outputs to the world outside the database system, e.g., to the users, that take place after such outermost transactions end must be presumed to be valid.

Now let us explore the consequences of a less restrictive scenario. The conversation scheme [Campbell and Randell 1986] provides a means of coordinating the recovery provisions of interacting threads so as to avoid the domino effect, without making assumptions regarding inter-thread output or input validation. Figure 2 shows an example where three threads communicate within a conversation and the threads T1 and T2 communicate within a nested conversation. Communication can only take place between threads that are participating in a conversation together, so while T1 and T2 are in their inner conversation they cannot damage or be damaged by T3.

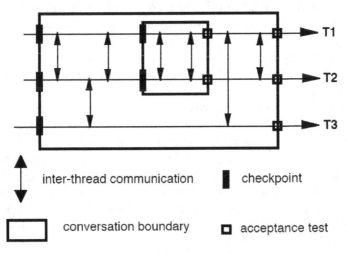

Figure 2. Nested Conversations

The operation of a conversation is as follows: (i) on entry to a conversation a thread establishes a checkpoint; (ii) if an error is detected by any thread then all the participating threads must restore their checkpoints; (iii) after restoration all threads then attempt to make further progress; and (iv) all threads leave the conversation together, only if all pass any acceptance tests that are provided. (If this is not possible, the conversation fails—a situation which causes the enclosing conversation to invoke backward error recovery at its level.)

Both transactions and conversations are examples of atomic actions [Lomet 1977], in that viewed from the outside they appear to perform their activity as a single indivisible action. (In practice transaction-support systems also implement other properties, such as "durability", i.e., a guarantee that the results produced by completed transactions will not be lost as a result of a computer hardware fault.) And both rely on backward error recovery.

However, systems are usually not made up just of computers -rather they will also involve other entities (e.g., devices and humans) which in many cases will not be able to simply forget some of their recent activity, and so simply go straight back to an exact earlier state when told that an error has been detected. Thus forward error recovery (the typical programming mechanism for which is exception handling), rather than backward recovery will have to be used. Each of these complications individually makes the task of error recovery more difficult, and together they make it much more challenging. This in fact is the topic that I and my colleagues have concentrated on these last few years.

Our resulting Coordinated Atomic (CA) Action scheme [Xu et al. 1995] was arrived at as a result of work on extending the conversation concept so as to allow for the use of forward error recovery, and to allow for both co-operative and competitive concurrency, i.e. on relaxing the assumptions even further. CA actions can be regarded as providing a discipline, both for programming computers and for controlling their use within an organization. This discipline is based on nested multi-threaded transactions [Caughey et al. 1998] together with very general exception handling provisions. Within the computer(s), CA actions augment any fault tolerance that is provided by the underlying transaction system by providing means for dealing with (i) unmasked hardware and software faults that have been reported to the application level to deal with, and/or (ii) application-level failure situations that have to be responded to. (However, detailed discussion of this topic is beyond the intended scope of this paper.)

Conversations and CA Actions are methods of structuring the activity of a system, for purposes of error confinement and recovery. The initial issue with regard to system dependability concerns the structuring of the actual system itself.

5. STRUCTURE

A description of a system's *structure* identifies its component systems, their observable boundaries and functions, and their means of interaction. Careful identification of system *boundaries* is fundamental to understanding and distinguishing between failures, faults and errors, so as to analyze possible or actual failure situations and find means of reducing their likelihood, especially in complex systems. System *structuring* thus plays a central role in dependability.

Structure is in effect always "in the eye of the beholder". Having identified a system's boundary, one normally chooses to identify a structuring, in the form of a set of internal boundaries and interactions, which reflects knowledge or assumptions concerning how a system has been or might be constructed, and/or taken apart. Very often the components that are so identified might have had some previous separate existence, and have been chosen from among various possible alternatives. Structuring strategies that facilitate such choices have the additional advantage that they also tend to favor identification of components whose interfaces are seen as relatively simple and/or familiar. However, well-chosen structuring will not only have such characteristics but will also—on grounds of efficiency and effectiveness—identify sets of components that have low coupling and high cohesion. Such well-chosen structuring greatly facilitates understanding of how a complex system functions.

However, for structuring to have some direct relevance to questions of operational dependability, and in particular fault tolerance, it must be what might be described as strong—**strong** structuring actually controls interactions within and between systems, and limits error propagation in both time and space, i.e., constitutes real not just perceived or imagined boundaries.

A well-known form of strong structuring is that provided by the watertight bulkheads in a ship. Clearly, these would do nothing for the ship's seaworthiness, i.e., dependability, if they were constructed merely from cardboard (leave alone if they existed only in the blueprints and not in the actual ship), or if the rules regarding opening and closing of any doors that provided access through them were blithely ignored.

The reality, and hence strength, of physical structure such as provided by bulkheads in ships, or by insulation in electronic systems, can be self-evident. Software structures, as represented by source code constructs such as classes, objects, modules, etc., are more difficult to discern, but nevertheless if retained in some form and used as constraining mechanisms in the operational software can play a similar role in controlling interactions within complex computer systems. (Clearly this involves ensuring that the source code's structuring is not destroyed by, for example, an optimizing compiler.)

All this is assuming that the implemented structuring actually matches the system designers' intentions and assumptions regarding system structuring—something that is by no means certain to be the case with systems that are so large and complex as to be beyond any individual designer's comprehension. Needless to say, inaccurate assumptions about a system's actual structure can invalidate any or all coverage assessments that have been estimated on the basis of these assumptions.

An even worse variant of the problem of inaccurate assumptions about a system's structure arises if the original system structure (which perhaps was put in place at least in part as a defence against malicious faults e.g., due to network hackers) has in fact itself been maliciously subverted. At present, the main defences against malicious faults are structuring mechanisms such as firewalls and intrusion detectors, backed up by manual assessment and system recovery actions—actions that may take hours or even days during which the attacked system may not be operational.

A current research priority therefore is that of finding effective automated means of tolerating malicious faults—this involves (i) defending the critical mechanisms, such as the intrusion detection system, against subversion, e.g., by replicating the services or making them difficult for an attacker to locate, and (ii) finding ways of masking or recovering from any errors caused by malicious faults, in order that system operation can be continued without the need for human intervention.

Progress has been made on means for providing a degree of such intrusion tolerance, for example in the MAFTIA (Malicious-and Accidental-Fault Tolerance in Internet Applications) Project [Powell et al. 2001], and by the DARPA OASIS Program[5]. However, it is an open question as to what extent hackers' inventiveness can be defeated by *pre-designed automated* defensive structuring. And one is always left with the conundrum that structuring is both a means of understanding, and of misunderstanding, systems.

6. COMPUTER-BASED SYSTEMS

Most large networked systems embody human beings as, in effect, system 'components', alongside the hardware and software components, though as indicated above such humans may become actively involved only when things go wrong with the computers and their communication. In other cases, there may be a deliberate decision to sub-divide some overall system task into activities that can be readily automated, and those that are best left to human beings to carry out. Systems that incorporate human 'components' in either of these ways are termed here **computer-based systems**.

The various types of components of such systems have rather different failure characteristics: (i) hardware suffers mainly from ageing and wear, although logical design errors do sometimes persist in deployed hardware (see, for example, [Avizienis and He 1999]), (ii) it is mainly software that suffers from residual design and implementation errors, since this is, quite appropriately, where most of the logical complexity of a typical system resides, and (iii) human beings (users, operators, maintenance personnel and outsiders) can at times, through ignorance, incompetence or malevolence, cause untold damage. (Humans also can, with experience, compensate very effectively for computer system faults and failures.) Malevolent activities

---

[5] http://www.darpa.mil/ipto/Programs/oasis/index.htm

can range from acts of petty vandalism by amateur hackers, through the efforts of expert and highly devious virus creators, to well-resourced and highly sophisticated attacks by terrorists and enemy states. As indicated earlier, these constitute an increasingly serious problem.

The successful design and deployment of any complex system that interacts directly with humans thus calls for socio-technical as well as technical expertise. One particular problem is that of how best to partition an overall task between humans and computers so as (i) to reduce the probability of failures due to misunderstandings across the human-machine interface, and (ii) to make best use of the greatly differing abilities that humans and computers have with respect to following complicated detailed sequences of instructions, and recognizing that a situation is both novel and potentially dangerous.

Achieving *predictable* dependability from sophisticated computer-based systems is therefore a major challenge, and a cynical summary is: if you automate a successful complex human-run system, the best you can possibly achieve is fewer but bigger failures. (An obvious example is a complex payroll system—manual payroll systems produce lots of inaccurate cheques, but none has ever generated one for £999,999,999.99.) Such large failures may be due to careless implementation, but the most difficult to avoid are those that are due to mistaken design assumptions. Yet many of the complex systems that are now being planned are computer-based systems that automate many functions that were previously carried out manually, with all that this implies regarding the difficulty of achieving a high degree of continuity of operation of the global information infrastructure.

7. SYSTEMS OF SYSTEMS

Large systems of any kind are rarely constructed *de novo*, but rather built up from earlier systems. Indeed, they are often actually constructed out of multiple pre-existing operational systems; hence, the term **systems-of-systems**. Moreover, there is almost always a requirement for large systems to be capable of being adapted so as to match changes in requirements—due to changed functionality and changes in system environments—and there is likely to be an increasing need for systems that can themselves evolve. This is needed, for example, in order to serve a dynamic environment constituted by large numbers of mobile devices moving into and out of range.

The typical process of constructing a system-of-systems out of systems that were not designed with this need in mind can best be described as involving "graunching"[6]. This is despite the existence of various more-or-

---

[6] To graunch (v.t.): to make to fit by the use of excessive force [WW2 RAF slang]

less sophisticated tools and techniques, e.g., such software engineering mechanisms as brokerage services and wrappers. But the resulting systems-of-systems, however put together, tend to suffer from their own special dependability problems.

This is particularly the case when the individual systems are separately managed, and continue to function more or less independently, each with its own individual goals. In such circumstances, management decisions (e.g., regarding system shut-downs or changes) can in effect constitute an additional source of faults.

Another new, or at least exacerbated, class of faults is that of mismatches at the interfaces between component systems. These are typically semantic (e.g., confusion between Fahrenheit and Celsius) not just syntactic, or due to fundamental policy incompatibilities. (There is in many quarters a present assumption that a middleware infrastructure facilitating the use of Web Services, XML, etc., will largely solve the problems of creating systems-of-systems, but such facilities mainly help deal with syntax issues.)

But there is also a totally insidious dependability problem caused by the fact that systems-of-systems may come into existence essentially accidentally. Interconnections may be made between systems, without due regard for the consequences, and have the result of creating an accidental system-of-systems, indeed one of such utility it comes to be depended upon, even though there is no-one responsible for ensuring its dependability. And indeed this in part is exactly what has happened on a massive scale, as various separate critical national infrastructures (e.g., for energy, water, transportation, finance, information, etc.) have become much more inter-dependent than anyone had planned—hence the setting up of various national and international investigations into critical infrastructure interdependencies.

8. INFRASTRUCTURE DEPENDABILITY

The term **infrastructure** in general refers to an *underlying* set of *general purpose* facilities. It is a matter of viewpoint whether these facilities are regarded as a system or an infrastructure, since one organization's *system* often becomes another organization's *infrastructure*.

An infrastructure has connotations of being reusable by different individuals/organizations for different purposes on different occasions. Typically, not all of these uses are known to, or even the concern of, the designer(s) of the infrastructure, who therefore must create something that will respond to and support types of use that have not yet been conceived. Moreover, infrastructures typically need to be *capacity engineered*—so that the amount of resource can be changed to meet current and expected demand. (Over-deployment endangers the supplier, under-deployment frustrates the user.)

All these uncertainties about the uses to be made of, and the demands to be placed on, an infrastructure exacerbate the problems of designing for dependability. Design decision-making often has to be based on very vague evidence and statistics, and very suspect assumptions, much more than is the case with systems that are designed for an identified owner and set of users.

Evolvability and adaptability are usually crucial, but an additional dependability challenge. A particular problem is that, just as with ordinary systems, whatever analysis was undertaken in order to establish that an infrastructure is likely to be adequately dependable, may have to be redone virtually from scratch for a modified version of the infrastructure. (Ideally the amount of reworking of the dependability analysis would be commensurate with the extent of the change.)

Given the uncertainties as to the amounts and types of demand that an infrastructure may have to face, decisions involving trade-offs between the various attributes of dependability (e.g., between security and availability) are likely to be uninformed initially. In essence the problem is that infrastructure dependability also needs to be capacity engineered—and means provided of making effective trade-offs between the various dependability attributes, as their relative importance changes. This can be a major challenge.

9. INFRASTRUCTURE AND STRUCTURE

The 'Idealized Fault-Tolerant Component' diagram (see Figure 3) is a simple, indeed simplistic, structuring technique that shows one approach to distinguishing between various sorts of system interactions, in particular identifying and classifying those that relate to system activity aimed at error recovery.

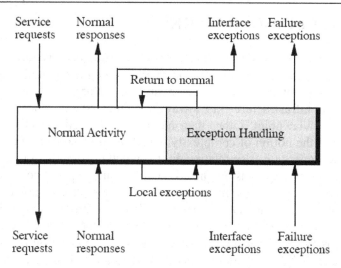

Figure 3. Ideal Fault-Tolerant Component

In fact the diagram relates to the "failure → fault → error" causal chains that can occur, either between systems and their components, or between interacting (though otherwise separate) systems. The terminology used is that of programmed exception handling, even though it can equally well relate to inter-system interaction protocols. It implies that is useful to distinguish carefully between normal processing, and that involved in error recovery, and between normal and erroneous activations and activities of systems or system components.

Given that an infrastructure is just a special kind of system, or rather a system viewed from a particular vantage point, the diagram can be used in connection with certain types of "failure → fault → error" chain between an infrastructure and the systems the infrastructure is supporting, namely chains related to failures in the systems being supported, or by infrastructure *service* failures.

But we typically use the term 'infrastructure' for a system that is *supporting,* in the sense of initiating and/or enabling the continued effective existence of, some other system, not just interacting with it. This being the case, one can envisage a class of infrastructure failures that in effect destroy the supported systems or their means of communication (e.g., an electrical power blackout, a network outage, or a middleware crash). This class, which includes the case of one system being used to design or construct another, forms the third type of relationship across which "failure → fault → error" chains can operate (the others being system interaction relationships system and composition relationships)—and is one for which a richer more dynamic structuring concept diagram still has to be developed.

10. CONCLUDING REMARKS

The main message of this paper is that when one is considering complex systems (and infrastructures), it is important to recognize that all the relevant concepts and entities—system, dependability, failure, fault, error, failure, structure, and infrastructure—are always to be understood as being relative to some current viewpoint, rather than having some fixed objective meaning. (Indeed even the notion of complexity, which is often spoken of as though it is a system property, in also relative, in that whether something is regarded as complex or simple depends on one's knowledge and experience.)

Moreover, every viewpoint implies a set of assumptions—not all of which will be recognized as such, despite efforts to provide high levels of assumption coverage. During system design, there may be differing assumptions as to the types of demand that will be placed on a system, and the value that will be placed on different system attributes, e.g., usability and security. The whole process of debugging a complex system involves the difficult task of identifying and often repeatedly modifying one's assumptions as to how the system actually works and what possible faults would explain the failure symptoms, etc. And in complex situations different people may, quite understandably, come to different (equally defensible) conclusions, and hence propose alternative ways of repairing the system.

In particular, there will be assumptions about system structure, and these can be the most difficult ones to recognize and allow for. For example, a hacker who is trying to penetrate a system and obtain confidential data will by means of probes and experiments be building up one body of knowledge and assumptions about how the system is structured, in particular how its defenses are organized. A system administrator will, through experience of the system, access to its documentation, etc., have a perhaps very different and much more detailed set of information about how the system is (assumed to be) structured. (And the hacker may well have found, or indeed managed to insert, vulnerabilities (i.e., faults) into the system, which in effect—did he or she but know it—completely invalidate the system administrator's information and assumptions!)

Complexity is the main enemy with regard to achieving dependable systems and infrastructures, and structure is one of the main means of mastering this complexity. In particular, good system structuring helps one to deal with the unavoidable additional complexity that results from adequately realistic fault assumptions.

But it would seem that, particularly when one has to allow for malicious attacks by intelligent adversaries on a system's or an infrastructure's protective structuring, there are at least in principle some fundamental limitations as to what can be achieved solely by automated defenses—

assuming, surely rather reasonably, that these automated defenses cannot be made to function with a level of intelligence (and deviousness) comparable to that of their human adversaries.

11. ACKNOWLEDGMENTS

The material in this paper has benefited from numerous discussions with many colleagues, both at Newcastle and in IFIP Working Group 10.4. This particular text has been very helpfully commented on by Peter Andras.

12. REFERENCES

[AMSD Roadmap 2003] AMSD Roadmap, *A Dependability Roadmap for the Information Society in Europe*, Accompanying Measure on System Dependability (AMSD) IST-2001-37553 —Work-package 1: Overall Dependability Road-mapping, deliverable D1.1, 2003.

[Avizienis and He 1999] A. Avizienis and Y. He. "Microprocessor Entomology: A Taxonomy of Design Faults in COTS Microprocessors," in *Proc. Dependable Computing for Critical Applications (DCCA '99)*, pp. 3–23, San Jose, CA, 1999.

[Avizienis et al. 2004] A. Avizienis, J.-C. Laprie, B. Randell and C. Landwehr, "Basic Concepts and Taxonomy of Dependable and Secure Computing," *IEEE Transactions on Dependable and Secure Computing*, vol. 1, no. 1, pp.11–33, 2004.

[Campbell and Randell 1986] R.H. Campbell and B. Randell, "Error Recovery in Asynchronous Systems," *IEEE Trans. Software Engineering*, vol. SE-12, no. 8, pp.811–826, 1986.

[Caughey et al. 1998] S.J. Caughey, M.C. Little and S.K. Shrivastava. "Checked Transactions in an Asynchronous Message Passing Environment," in *1st IEEE International Symposium on Object-Oriented Real-time Distributed Computing*, pp. 222–229, Kyoto, 1998.

[European Commission 2002] European Commission. *e-Europe 2005 Action Plan: An Information Society for All*, COM(2002) 263 final, European Commission, 2002.

[Gray and Reuter 1993] J. Gray and A. Reuter, *Transaction Processing: Concepts and techniques*, Morgan Kaufmann, 1993.

[Jones and Randell 2004] C. Jones and B. Randell. *Dependable Pervasive Systems*, Technical Report No. 839, School of Computing Science, University of Newcastle upon Tyne, 2004.

[Laprie 1999] J.-C. Laprie. "Dependability of Software-Based Critical Systems," in *Dependable Network Computing*, ed. D. R. Avresky, Kluwer Academic Publishers, 1999.

[Lomet 1977] D.B. Lomet, "Process Structuring, Synchronization, and Recovery Using Atomic Actions," *ACM SIGPLAN Notices*, vol. 12, no. 3, pp.128–137, 1977.

[Pearce 2003] S. Pearce. *Government IT Projects*, Report 200, Parliamentary Office of Science and Technology, 7 Millbank, London, 2003.

[Powell et al. 2001] D. Powell, A. Adelsbach, C. Cachin, S. Creese, M. Dacier, Y. Deswarte, T. McCutcheon, N. Neves, B. Pfitzmann, B. Randell, R. Stroud, P. Veríssimo and M. Waidner. "MAFTIA (Malicious-and Accidental-Fault Tolerance for Internet Applications)," in *Supplement of the 2001 Int. Conf. on Dependable Systems and Networks*, pp. D32–D35, Göteborg, Sweden, IEEE Computer Society Press, 2001.

[Randell 1975] B. Randell, "System Structure for Software Fault Tolerance," *IEEE Trans. on Software Engineering*, vol. SE-1, no. 2, pp.220–232, 1975.

[Randell 2000] B. Randell, "Facing up to Faults (Turing Memorial Lecture)," *Computer Journal*, vol. 43, no. 2, pp.95–106, 2000.

[Xu et al. 1995] J. Xu, B. Randell, A. Romanovsky, R.J. Stroud and Z. Wu. "Fault Tolerance in Concurrent Object-Oriented Software through Coordinated Error Recovery," in *Proceedings 25th Int. Symp. Fault-Tolerant Computing (FTCS-25)*, Los Angeles, IEEE Computer Society Press, 1995.

DESIGN FOR SAFETY AND SECURITY OF COMPLEX EMBEDDED SYSTEMS: A UNIFIED APPROACH

Erwin Schoitsch
ARC Seibersdorf research, A-2444 Seibersdorf, Austria

Abstract: Safety has a long tradition in many engineering disciplines. Standards (e.g., IEC 61508), methods of risk and hazard analysis, and certification methods have evolved long before IT. Security has evolved quite recently with networked IT-systems and concerns about privacy, data integrity, authenticity and protection. Both communities have developed their own standards, methods and system views—and neither in standardization nor in application areas they cooperate well. The paper takes a holistic view of critical systems and proposes a unified approach to system dependability, integrating both safety and security, arguing that in case of massively deployed embedded systems security issues have severe safety impact and vice versa.

Keywords: safety; security; dependability; safety-critical systems; functional safety; embedded systems; critical control systems; fault tolerance; connectivity; distributed systems; standards; IEC 61508; System Life Cycle; Safety Life Cycle; Security Management; Risk; Hazard Analysis

1. INTRODUCTION

Safety engineering has a long tradition in most engineering disciplines. This has nothing to do with IT and "modern times," it started long ago with construction engineering (buildings, machines), and at least since the first steam vessels exploded, safety became a legal issues, requiring safety assessment, evaluation and certification by independent bodies—in Central Europe e.g., the TÜVs (Technical Test and Certification Associations) were founded and are operational until today. The next major technology was electricity—because of new hazards, electro-technical organizations were

J. S. Kowalik et al. (eds.), Cyberspace Security and Defense: Research Issues, 161–174.

founded to set standards, do evaluations and certifications. On international scale, IEC became the recognized standardization organization in the area of electrical equipment. The next type of hazard evolved with the age of programmable electronics (PE) computers and software. Risk analysis and evaluation methods, based mainly on probabilistic for hardware, were no longer directly applicable to complex systems. The problem was somehow resolved for isolated PE Systems, an example are the standards around IEC 61508 for safety critical systems. Again, a community was established—the safety-critical systems community.

With increasingly networked, distributed computer systems the risk of deliberate malicious interactions, using software-based tools, became a serious threat. Many-fold related issues like data protection, privacy, integrity, authenticity, and denial of service attacks, viruses, worms etc. lead to a separate community to be established, which is nowadays in the main focus of the public as was safety some time ago (and still is—but only after catastrophic events). This community developed separate standards, methods, taxonomy and ways of thinking.

The missing interaction of both communities did not matter so much as long as safety-critical systems were mainly proprietary, isolated from the environment and only loosely or not at all coupled with other systems were a larger public has access to. With ubiquitous computing, seamless connectivity, massively deployed networked embedded systems (1), use of public networks for critical controls, maintenance access from outside to critical systems, or even interaction between critical components or subsystems via public networks or wireless, the situation has changed dramatically: Security breaches may become safety critical, and safety problems or measures to maintain safety integrity levels may open loopholes for security attacks. Now it becomes necessary, that both communities co-operate to be able to take a unified approach to system dependability taking into account both—safety and security (6). We have to take a holistic view of critical systems—unfortunately, the author has already experienced, that integration of both views has been refused by both communities in some cases already e.g., in standardization or projects.

2. DEPENDABILITY—A HOLISTIC APPROACH

As already outlined in (4), used in (1), (2), or in the multilingual book "Dependability—Basic Concepts and Terminology" (J.-C. Lapries, A. Avizienis, H. Kopetz, U. Voges, T. Anderson, Springer Verlag), a set of basic definitions on dependability as an umbrella term of various system attributes (Figure 1) (not necessarily complementary, but in certain cases (application dependent) even contradicting) is provided, which fits best the goal of a "holistic system view." In short, the most important ones are

Dependability: Trustworthiness of a computer system such that reliance can be justifiable placed on the service it delivers.

Safety: Dependability with respect to non-occurrence of catastrophic failures (freedom from unacceptable risk, based on un-deliberate actions or events, "risk to life and limb")

Security: Dependability with respect to unauthorized access or information handling (deliberate action!).

Reliability: Dependability with respect to continuity of service ("time to failure," probability)

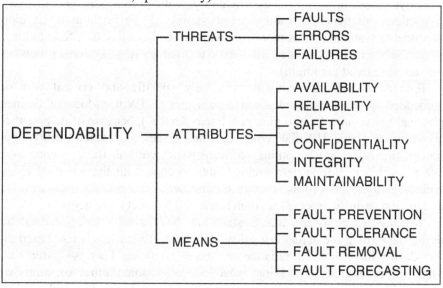

Figure 1. Dependability—Basic Concepts and Terminology

Although this very clear terminology does exist since many years, the use of the terms is imprecise. Very often, the term "Dependability" is now used more or less as synonym for "Security," even in EU-publications or standards.

Another important contribution of the referenced terminology was the "fault – error – failure – ..." chain, which provides a deeper understanding of fault propagation, fault containment and fault consequences in critical systems: A fault in a hardware part, component or subsystem may lead to an erroneous state of this element of the system, which may lead to a failure of this element (the fault is the cause of the error respectively failure, the failure the consequence of the fault respectively error). The failing component constitutes a fault of the subsystem where it is embedded, and so on. This is important especially in case of security breaches: then a fault is inserted into the system (deliberately) to lead to a failure, which may impact safety of the system.

3. CHARACTERISTICS OF EMBEDDED SYSTEMS

There are many definitions of Embedded Systems around. Generally speaking (5), embedded systems are a combination of processors, sensors, actuators, "intelligence," "hidden computers" and massive deployment, with intensive interaction with an uncertain environment: "A physical process with dynamics, fault, noise, dependability, with power, size and memory restrictions (in general: resource restrictions)...." To be able to develop dependable systems with components with these characteristics, foundational system infrastructures are needed as core technology (e.g., systems following the time-triggered paradigm).

Embedded Software constitutes a very specific and critical part of embedded systems. It provides new capabilities to HW transducers ("defines physical behaviour of a complex non-linear device"), because of its potential criticality we need HW/SW co-design, and issues like dependability, low power, timeliness are becoming software issues with all the consequences. We need dependable system architectures to cope with the potential risks, including safety as well as security requirements and counter measures. Be aware, that security aspects are often neglected by safety engineers!

We have to be aware, that Systems are NOT always safety-critical by definition—often the actual criticality and dependability levels rise based on our desire for enhanced reliance on them!! (Human Factors—safer cars imply more aggressive driving behaviour after some time; or: (almost) perfect driver assistance systems may lead to too much reliance on them thus becoming safety critical). On the other hand, sometimes system evaluation was not done properly, and severe impacts have been overlooked—one example is the London Ambulance System Disaster: The ambulance car emergency management system was not considered safety critical—but because of ambulances not arriving in time or at all at the required location several people died ! The same would be the case if security breaches, e.g., by inserting wrong data or commands in a control loop, could cause dangerous situations (chemical reactor explosion, traffic jam, air traffic control, ...), and nobody has thought it likely that someone could have interest in such an incident. After 9/11, we have to take into account malicious actions by intrusion into communications or computer control systems and consider this type of security risks in our safety analysis.

4. APPLICATION TRENDS: AUTOMOTIVE SYSTEMS

The AMSD Roadmap for Dependable Embedded Systems (1) has taken into account several application areas, where mass deployment of embedded systems will become critical:

- Automotive
- Aerospace/Avionics
- Railways
- Medical Devices/Systems
- Industrial Automation and Control

  Typical for all of these applications, there are certain trends:

  - a shift from electro-mechanical to programmable electronics in the systems
  - connectivity between systems on a local and global basis (no longer isolated), integration of systems on several levels
  - a shift from purely human responsibility and activity to more automation with goals such as more safety, more efficiency, more comfort and services, new functionality and devices (vision driven).

Initially, safety was the only critical issue to be looked at (safety-driven visions), but increased connectivity and interaction with higher layers of overall "systems of systems" (e.g., traffic/transport) and more access points (e.g., for diagnosis and maintenance, error correction and upgrading) enforce a more security-driven approach: Security has severe safety impact!

Since automotive industry is the driver for safety-critical, advanced application of embedded systems with extremely high impact on the public and economy (mass deployment, cost driven), this sector is chosen as an example.

Already now, in cars of the upper class, there are about 80 ECUs (Embedded Computing Units) and five or more bus systems, controlling comfort as well as safety critical functions. Most of the innovations (80–90%) in cars are ICT-driven, especially product individualization and differentiation are based on ICT. The cost of electronics and software in such a car will rise from 25% to more than 40%. On the other hand, according to reports at the 2003 informatics conference in Germany, 55% of car failures are caused by electronics and software, and the "X-by-wire" implementation plans had to be delayed by major players in the field by years. Diagnosis and maintenance in the field are again a challenge—because of complex electronic systems.

Automotive is clearly the "driver" in this area:

- cost-driven (clear goal: "from supply chain to design chain," to build consistent dependable systems from components of many different suppliers) and

- requiring mass-deployment capabilities for critical (sub-) systems composition ("aerospace safety at automotive cost"), and

- with a clear overall vision: "accident-free driving," and as

- ultimate goal: "Autonomous Driving" (at least on specialized highways and lanes)

Automotive is an exquisite example for a long term vision in the area of critical applications, because the potential for networking to build adaptive systems on several levels of connectivity, which requires the full set of dependability attributes to be fulfilled (safety, security, reliability, availability, maintainability) in a holistic manner, is already there, although the gaps are at the moment bridged by human interaction only:

- on-board embedded systems, vehicle-bound connectivity
  - advanced comfort functions (car body electronics, noise suppression, configurable cockpit, navigation, communication, information)
  - Safety Enhancement
    - Vehicle dynamics (ABS, ASR, ABC, ESP (Electronic stability program), AAS (Active additional steering), adaptive cruise control road tire friction control),
    - Advanced Warning and Control (pedestrian protection, crash avoidance, lane support, track control)
    - Driver Monitoring, predictive driver assistance, emergency call system

- extending autonomous on-board functions with interactive and co-operative systems (7)
  - roadside embedded systems and interaction (e.g., intersection control, speed control, automatic advanced emergency call systems)
  - Vehicle-to-vehicle communication (advanced adaptive cruise control, traffic throughput optimization)

- Global connectivity: Integration into regional traffic navigation and control, satellite bound global connectivity

A simple example will highlight the security issue (from a presentation of DaimlerChrysler at SAFECOMP 2004 in Potsdam): Wireless communication between cars on a highway enables early warning if the first one in a long column of cars is braking so that all following cars can easily adapt. This makes higher throughput, shorter distances between cars and fewer accidents possible at the same time. Imagine now someone fakes such messages, resulting in an uncoordinated jam on the highway, i.e., may be in a catastrophic event. There are of course considerations how to avoid such problems—but all countermeasures have to take into account real-time and long-term usage (20 years!) requirements as boundary conditions so that simple encryption does not work.

Cost-effectiveness and mass deployment of critical systems in combination with non-critical systems is a trend, where many other application areas will benefit from, so that there is a clear need not only for application-specific ICT-technology, but for generic dependable ICT-technology (hardware, software, SoC (Systems-on-Chip), building blocks, communication) which fulfils the requirements of generic functional safety and security standards as well as of sector-specific ones (certification to create trust in these systems!).

5. SAFETY & SECURITY: DIFFERENT VIEWS?

As already stated, security very often has safety impact, and vice versa. But there exist two separated communities at the moment, with different traditions, standards, methods, almost ignoring each other.

The generic standard of the safety community is IEC 61508, Functional Safety of E/E/PE safety-related Systems. The engineering community has built a set of standards based on IEC 61508 for specific sectors, taking into account the experiences, background knowledge and requirements: the process control sector, medical sector, nuclear, railways, and is still continuing (e.g., automotive in progress). But this standard takes only the safety view, security is not even mentioned!

IEC 61508 is already in the maintenance phase, working groups MT12 (software) and MT13 (systems) are working closely together. In MT12, a task group JTT4, Remote Access and Security (8), tried to integrate the security issue into IEC 61508, giving advice on how to include security issues into the IEC 61508 life cycle, especially on the analysis and functional allocation level. IEC 61508 defines so-called SILs (Safety Integrity Levels), for complex systems "Criticality Levels." On the other hand, the relevant Security Standard ISO 15508 (Common Criteria) uses so-called EALs (Evaluation Assurance Levels). The task group did not succeed to define a consolidated view on these different approaches to define system dependability.

The conclusion was to add separate clauses into IEC 61508 everywhere where security could have an impact on safety giving advice on how to integrate the security aspect as an additional hazard (risk) for the safety-critical system, i.e., to look at the safety impact of security breaches and then derive requirements for the safety critical system, based on a joint hazard and risk analysis.

Unfortunately, the committee decided not to take into account in-depth considerations on security in the new standard draft. The security issue was delegated to another committee of SC65, to SC65C, WG 13, Digital Communications, Cyber Security (9), and the chairman of JTT4 became member of this committee. Unfortunately, this committee was not at all interested in safety, only in communications and cyber security. Here again, both "worlds" kept themselves separated!

On the other hand, we have ISO 15508 (Common Criteria, focusing on component evaluation) and ISO 17799 (system guidelines on security, holistic, not only IT), for Security. They have even another "language" than the safety community, and another view what levels of protection mean (EALs vs. SILs). From the dependability point of view, requirements could be derived for security features and profiles depending on the SILs required for safety. Allocations could be done not only between HW, SW and components on functional level with respect to safety but with respect to security also. But interaction and discussion would be necessary! (Note: The aspects of "multilateral security" could be correlated to SILs according to (7)).

In industry, independent work was started in the meantime to define "Security Profiles" for Avionics by CAA (Civil Aviation Authority) (14) and the US Industrial Automation Group PCSRF—Process Control Security Requirements Forum (10)(11)(12)(13), very much triggered by ISO 15508. On the other hand, the maturity and process assessment models of CMMI and SPICE (ISO 15504), where the maturity of processes within companies with respect to IT-development are assessed and made comparable, have found their counterparts already in the security world (15).

Unfortunately, the gap has not been spanned by these approaches. As far as I know, only JRC Ispra has once financed a project of EWICS TC7 (European Workshop on Industrial Computer Systems, TC7, Safety, Reliability and Security, an expert group in this area), on "Study of the Applicability of ISO/IEC 17799 and the German Baseline Protection Manual to the needs of safety critical systems (March 2003)(**www.ewics.org**)" (3), where the gaps between the security standards and the safety-related system evaluation requirements have been analyzed for several sectors (medical, railways, nuclear, electric power networks) and in general.

The author was member of JTT4, and has similar experiences from research projects in the area of dependable systems, where it was either very difficult, under cost-pressure and funding priorities, to include certain security aspects besides the safety related issues, or, after reduction of funds, the work package was deleted where the security modeling aspect should have been added to the safety-related part.

6. A PROPOSAL FOR A UNIFIED APPROACH

6.1. The Approach of IEC 61508—the Safety View

To understand the underlying principles of IEC 61508, Figure 2 explains the safety-view and basic assumptions:

There is equipment under control (EUC), which, with its control system (which is the safety-related PE System) poses a (potential) threat to its environment (in case of security, the system is threatened by its (may be far remote) environment, what, in turn, might pose a threat to its close environment).

- Safety functions are performed by the E/E/PE Systems
- Steps are to be taken to understand the risks involved and reduce them to a tolerable level

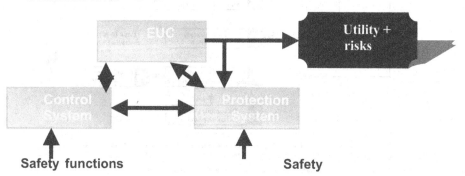

Figure 2. IEC 61508—Equipment Under Control

To fulfill these goals, the standard requires:

- Assessment of the risks posed by the EUC
- Decision on what level of risk is tolerable
- Decision on which risks should be reduced
- Determination how the risks could be reduced best

Applied is the ALARP-principle—risk should be as low as reasonably possible.

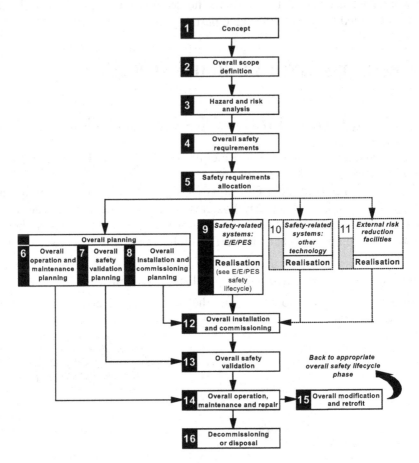

NOTE 1 Activities relating to **verification, management of functional safety** and **functional safety assessment** are not shown for reasons of clarity but are relevent to all overall, E/E/PES and software safety lifecycle phases.

NOTE 2 The phases represented by boxes 10 and 11 are outside the scope of this standard.

NOTE 3 Parts 2 and 3 deal with box 9 (realisation) but they also deal, where relevant, with the programmable electronic (hardware and software) aspects of boxes 13, 14 and 15.

Figure 3. IEC 61508—the IT/DES Safety Life Cycle (from the IEC 61508 Standard)

The standard gives guidance on E/E/PE Systems. The goal may be achieved by more than one safety-related system and by a bundle of measures, but always based on hazard and risk analysis, on getting the overall safety requirements right, and by developing a concept for proper safety requirements allocation.

To structure guidance, IEC 61508 proposes a well defined safety life cycle (Figure 3).

The principles involved are:

- The safety lifecycle is a model for identifying the activities appropriate to safety-related systems
- A risk based approach means not merely following a procedure and assuming that "safety" will result, but: Identifying the risks and reducing them appropriately
- Safety integrity levels (SILs) provide targets for risk reduction (Security: EAL-Evaluation Assurance Level? Correlation to SIL?)
- The safety requirements specification defines the safety requirements necessary for risk education
- Carrying out safety planning ensures a methodical and auditable approach

Is this a safety view only? The following chapter will provide some insight in the proposed unified approach to dependability of safety – critical systems, taking security into account.

6.2. The Unified Approach to IEC 61508—the Security View

The important step to safety as well as security is hazard and risk analysis beforehand—and based on these, safety requirements may be defined and allocated as well as security requirements.

To identify the hazards of the EUC in all modes of operation, the event sequences leading to the hazards, and the EUC risks associated with the hazards have to be analyzed (methods are well known like FTA, FMEA, FMECA, etc.)

⇨ What hazards does the system pose?
⇨ What are their possible causes and consequences?
⇨ What is the likelihood of their occurrence?
⇨ What are the risks associated with each of the hazards?
⇨ By how much do we need to reduce the risks

This is achieved through a sequence of three activities (may be iterated if required):

- Hazard identification
  - Define hazards and hazardous of EUC and EUC control system for all reasonably foreseeable circumstances
    - Fault conditions
    - Reasonably foreseeable misuse
    - Human factors (not sufficient to confirm that normal operation is safe)
- Hazard analysis

- Determine the event sequences leading to each hazardous event
- Identify the causes of hazards and assess the consequences of hazardous event
- Risk analysis
  - Determine the risks associated with the hazardous events

The result of the consideration that there are similar activities in both the security and safety life cycle, a unified approach is proposed:

Step 1: System requirements (Figure 4)

System Requirements—Unified Approach

Security	Safety
|	|
|	|
Security Analysis	**Risk/Hazard Analysis**
(Environment, Risks,	(System Boundary, Probabilities,
Threats, Counter Measures, ...)	Effects, Mitigation)
|	|
Security Requirements	**Safety Requirements**
|	|
Security Design	**Safety Design**
(Secure components,	(Safe Components,
Interaction, Procedures)	Interaction, Procedures)

Figure 4. System Safety & Security Life Cycle—Unified Approach

Activities may differ very much between Safety and Security depending on requirements. As an example, the Decommissioning and Disposal phase can be discussed briefly (Life Cycle Phase 16):

Security: Secure management of data, i.e., un-retrievably destroyed or secure archiving of preserved integrity, depending on application)

Safety: Safe management of shut down or continued (degraded) operation

The unified approached, which could be a proposal for a new version of IEC 61508 (with focus still on safety), requires analysis and evaluation as well as requirements definition and allocation with both, safety and security in mind. For details, how to handle the security issues, the security standards and the relevant chapters should be referenced (not to re-invent the wheel!).

The security life cycle of safety-related systems has to take into account the complete IT-security management life cycle as addressed in ISO 17799 and many national IT Security Handbooks, equivalent to the safety life cycle of IEC 61508. IT-Security Management is a continuous process of

- Development of IT-Security Policy

- Implementation of IT-Security Policy
- IT-Security during Operation

IT-Security includes the following processes, which are related to the corresponding phases of the IEC Life Cycle Model (in [nn], Figure 3). Following this concept, the complete security management life cycle can be considered and integrated in a holistic, unified model of parallel, equivalent activities:

- Definition and Implementation of Security Policy ([1]–[5], from „Concept" to „Security Requirements Allocation")
- Security during System Development (includes Security during the whole lifecycle of the system ([6]–[11]), Documentation, Evaluation and Certification ([12], [13])
- Maintaining Security Level during Operations [14] (includes Maintenance, Change Management and Incident Handling), Disaster Recovery ([14], [15])and Business Continuity Planning ([15], [16])

7. CONCLUSIONS

It has been demonstrated, that mass deployment of networked, dependable embedded systems with critical control functions require a new, holistic system view on safety critical and security critical systems. Both communities have to interact, communicate and integrate at the end. A unified approach to address the safety AND security requirements of safety related systems is proposed, based on the functional safety standard IEC 61508 and IT-Security management standards, handbooks and guidelines.

8. REFERENCES

(1) E. Schoitsch, G. Sonneck, G. Zoffmann, AMSD-Project: IST-2001-37553, Dependable Embeddded Systems Roadmap, Part I and II – Final deliverable V5.0 (**www.am-sd.org**)

(2) M. Masera, R. Bloomfield (ed.), AMSD-Project IST-2001-37553, A Dependability Roadmap for the Information Society in Europe, Part I, II, III (**www.am-sd.org**)

(3) E. Schoitsch, Ian Smith, U. Voges, P. Daniel, H.R. Fankhauser, F. Koornneef, Z. Zurakowski, A Study of the Applicability of ISO/IEC 17799 and the German Baseline Protection Manual to the Needs of Safety Critical Systems, Final Report, March 2003, on work carried out for JRC ISPRA under contract N° 20215-2002-12 F1EI ISP GB., 268 pages. (**www.ewics.org**)

(4) Avizienis, A., J.-C. Laprie, and B. Randell, "Fundamental Concepts of Dependability," Technical Report 739, pp. 1–21,, Department of Computing Science, University of

Newcastle upon Tyne, 2001, [**http://www.cs.ncl.ac.uk/research/trs/papers/739.pdf**] [also UCLA CSD Report no. 010028, LAAS Report no. 01-145]

(5) D. Donhoffer and E. Schoitsch, (ed.), *Proceedings of the Joint EU Workshop* "Advanced Real Time Systems." Vienna, March 26, 2001, 2001.

(6) Pfitzmann, Why Safety and Security should and will merge, invited talk at the 23rd International Conference SAFECOMP 2004, Potsdam, September 2004, *Proceedings of SAFECOMP 2004*, LNCS 3219, Springer Heidelberg 2004.

(7) European study, "eSaftey – Final report of the eSaftey working group on Road Safety," EC-IST DG, Nov. 2002, **http://www.europa.eu.int/information_society/programmes/esafety/index_en.htm**)

(8) IEC 61508, "Functional Safety of E/E/PE safety-related Systems," Maintenance Group MT12, JTT4, "Remote Access and Security"

(9) IEC SC65C/307/NP: New Work Item on Communications Profiles for Safety and Security

(10) Process Control Security Requirements Forum (PCSRF)—Security Capabilities Profile for Industrial Control Systems, June 13, 2003; Aug. 8, 2003.

(11) PCSRF—Security Profile Specifications (SPS), Aug. 26, 2002, applying CC

(12) Falco, Joe, Keith Stouffer, Albert Wavering, and G. Frederic Proctor, Intelligent Systems Division, NIST, USA: "IT Security for Industrial Control Systems"

(13) Beaver, C. L., D.R. Gallup, W.D. NeuMann, and M.D. Torgerson, Key management for SCADA, Scandia National Laboratories, March 2002, Security Aspects and requirements of the Supervisory Control and data Acquisition System, for the Electric Power Grid

(14) CAA: Report on the development of security requirements for CAA safety related software

(15) SSE-CMM—System Security Engineering Capability Maturity Model, June 15, 2003, in line with ISO 15504-2 (SPICE) and CMM-I (following the processes and maturity level concept, but for security engineering instead of software development) (not safety application-specific)

(16) EWICS TC7—Study of the Applicability of ISO/IEC 17799 and the German Baseline Protection Manual to the needs of safety critical systems (March 2003)(**www.ewics.org**)

PART 3

NETWORKS

DESIGN OF DISTRIBUTED SENSOR NETWORKS FOR SECURITY AND DEFENSE

Zdravko Karakehayov
Technical University of Sofia

Abstract: Distributed sensor networks are a new wireless networking paradigm suitable for security and defense applications. Attacks on an ad-hoc mobile network disrupt its ability to sense the environment and forward traffic. The capacity of a distributed sensor network for corrective actions in face of attacks depends of the energy available in the batteries. The analysis shows that low-power design at all phases, from nodes location through computation and communication, is crucial for reliable operation and sufficient lifetime.

Keywords: Mobile ad-hoc networks; Distributed sensor networks; Secure routing; Vulnerability; Embedded systems; Low-power design

1. INTRODUCTION

The transition from desktop computing to embedded systems is associated with price, power and timing constrains. A special class embedded systems, termed distributed sensor networks (DSN), are characterized by extra requirements: small size and sufficient battery lifetime. Distributed sensor networks can be alternatively labeled mobile ad-hoc networks (MANET). While the term DSN is associated with data acquisition applications, MANET emphasizes mobility and the lack of infrastructure. Distributed sensor networks can be scalable to thousands of nodes that cooperatively perform complex tasks. The interaction between the nodes is based on wireless communication [Kah 00, War 01, Hil 02]. Wireless sensor networks (WSN) is yet another synonym.

There are several, fairly common, security and defense applications based on distributed sensor networks.

- *Monitoring and management.* Commanders can monitor the status and locations of troops, weapons and supplies to improve military command, control, communications, and computing (C4) [Hae 05].

J. S. Kowalik et al. (eds.), Cyberspace Security and Defense: Research Issues, 177–192.
© 2005 *Springer. Printed in the Netherlands.*

- *Surveillance.* Vibration and magnetic sensors can detect vehicle and personnel movement.

- *Protection.* Industrial and military objects such as nuclear power-stations, oil pipelines, ammunition depots and headquarters can be protected by distributed sensor networks. The sensors should be able to distinguish between different classes of intruders.

- *Urban warfare.* Sensor networks are deployed in buildings and open air urban areas. Snipers can be localized by comparing the samples from multiple acoustic sensors.

- *Rescue missions.* Buildings razed by an earthquake may be sensed to locate signs of life. Event tracking in case of disasters can be used to guide rescue teams.

Availability emerges as a top-priority security requirement. A proper implementation has two parts: a prompt deployment and a constant ability to sense the environment and forward traffic. In the traditional computer security, secrecy is associated with controlling who gets to read information. In the field of distributed sensor networks, the situation is different. The network itself may act as an intruder. In this case, the size of the nodes becomes an important design metric. Short range, multihop communication is also the prudent course of action.

Security requires additional processing. Likewise, communication has a security overhead. Routing utilizes longer paths in an attempt to work around compromised nodes. As a result, the energy drawn from the batteries is increased and low-power design becomes a vital issue [Doh 01, Swa 05, Kar 05]. Battery attacks emerge as a significant threat. There are two typical cases of battery attacks: redundant communication and false alarms.

Every aspect of distributed sensor networks, from nodes location through computation and communication, must be viewed from the low-power perspective.

2. LOCATION

An example of event tracking can be used to introduce a false alarm battery attack. While for some cases it is sufficient sensor readings to be bound to known locations, this application requires each node to be aware of a set of neighbor locations. The location data base allows all nodes to be turned off, but the nodes in the close vicinity of the event. Assume that the event is a moving light shadow edge. Figure 1 shows an example deployment of four nodes and the current position of the shadow edge, *E*.

A method has been developed to identify the nodes which will not be immediately approached by the event and can be turned off to save energy [Liu 02]. The method is based on the dual space transformation [O'R 98]. Figure 2 shows the dual space. Points from the primal space are transformed into lines in the dual space. Lines from the primal space are transformed into points in the dual space. As a result, the dual space is partitioned into cells. The *e* point, the shadow edge, is contained in the shaded cell. Since the *e* point can not intersect the *n2* line, before it crosses one of the cell boundaries, the N2 node can stay turned off as long as none of N1, N3 and N4 senses a transition. This method may provide a substantial power reduction for a large sensor field. However, if nodes that line the perimeter around the event misbehave and declare a transition, it will force several other nodes to wake up and waste energy.

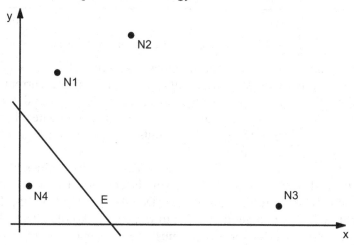

Figure 1. Four Nodes Sense the Moving Light Shadow Edge

3. AGGREGATION

When data is collected from numerous sensors in a dense network, there is a high probability for redundancy. Data redundancy will result in unnecessary and replicated transmissions. Aggregation, based on correlated data of neighboring nodes, helps to reduce the total volume to be routed.

The nodes of a wireless sensor network can be broken down into two types: energy unconstrained network stations and energy constrained sensor nodes. While many applications will only need one network station, the demand for sensor nodes may reach thousands [Bha 02].

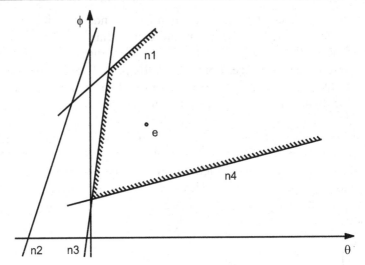

Figure 2. Dual Space Indicates the Sequence of Transitions

Figure 3 shows the locations of the nodes in a sensor field. Also, Figure 3 shows how the network station is gathering data from the current area of observation. Nodes 1 and 4 sense the environment. Nodes 2 and 5 relay the data. Node 3 receives two raw data streams and then aggregates them into a single stream. Furthermore, node 3 transmits the aggregated data to node 6. Nodes 6 and 7 relay the data onward without any processing.

This approach, however, makes the network more vulnerable. If the packets through a malicious node are simply consumed or lost, the attack against the network is termed black hole [Den 02, Hu 04, Woo 05]. Figure 3 shows that node 6 is in a good position to wage a black hole attack. To work around this problem longer routes must be employed or perhaps more streams. Inevitably, the corrective actions will increase the power consumption.

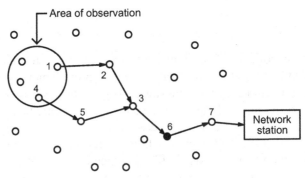

Figure 3. Data Gathering and Aggregation

4. ROUTING

The routing protocols for wireless ad hoc networks must have a sufficient capacity to adapt to changing conditions [Roy 99, Gao 00, Mau 01, Hon 02, Sch 03]. The free movement of network nodes results in a dynamic topology. Moreover, the environment may influence the radio propagation. Important internal factors must also be taken into account. Depletion of batteries and congestion impact the routing performance. Figure 4 shows a taxonomy of routing protocols. The protocols can be broken down into three styles: topology-based, position-based and hybrid. The topology-based algorithms can be further split into table-driven and demand-driven.

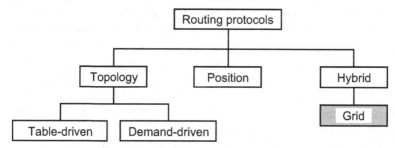

Figure 4. Routing Protocols for Wireless Ad Hoc Networks

The table-driven protocols are alternatively labeled proactive [Mau 01]. The main idea behind the table-driven routing protocols is to create a clear picture of all available routes from each node to every other node in the network. As a result, each node has to maintain tables with routing information. Due to the dynamic nature of the wireless ad hoc networks, updates travel over the network to maintain a consistent topology scheme.

In contrast to the table-driven protocols, the demand-driven algorithms create routes only when a necessity arises. The demand-driven protocols are also named reactive protocols [Mau 01]. When a node has to send a packet to a destination, it initiates a route discovery procedure. Once the route has been found, it is maintained by a route maintenance procedure as long as necessary.

Another axis along which we can organize routing protocols relates to node positions [Mau 01]. While in this case we may need additional information, the physical position of the participating nodes, on the positive side is the possibility to forward packets without pre-established routes. As an additional benefit, position-based routing allows communication with all nodes in a given geographical region in a natural way [Nav 97].

Grid is a hybrid scheme where each node is characterized by its ID and geographic position: latitude and longitude [Li 00, Che 02]. Grid employs geographic routing, selecting for the next hop the neighbour that is closest to the destination. Grid's functionality includes three major tasks:

- Selecting location servers
- Providing geographic positions
- Actual routing.

Each node recruits a small set of nodes to keep track of its location. These nodes are called location servers. The density of location servers is decreased with the distance. To achieve this, the algorithm selects a server from squares of increasing size. When a node must be accessed, it will be sufficient to reach one of its location servers and to obtain the required geographic position. Figure 5 shows an example for selecting location servers. The node's ID is 11. To support the idea of decreasing with distance density of location servers, the network field is partitioned into a hierarchy of grids with squares of increasing size. The smallest square is referred to as an order-1 square. The order-1 square for the 11 node can be seen on the top of Figure 5. Four order-1 squares make up an order-2 square. Node 11 recruits nodes in the three neighboring squares to serve as location servers. Node 45 is the only node in the corresponding square and is selected to know the position of node 11. If there are more than one node in a square, the node with the least ID greater than 11 is selected. For the current example, these are 22 and 13. The location servers selected by node 11 are shown in bold. The selection process goes on with the higher order squares. The new-elected servers in the order-3 square are 20, 18 and 48.

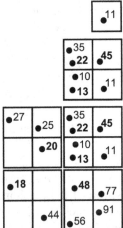

Figure 5. Location Servers

The next task is to provide geographic positions. According to the Grid's terminology, this task is labeled Grid's Location Service (GLS). Assume that 81 wants to send a packet to 11. Figure 6 provides an illustration for this example. The location of 11 is not available in the 81's data base. It is not possible to start routing in the physical space (geographic routing). The 81 node begins routing in the ID space. Since 37 is the least ID greater than 11 whose location is available in 81, the query is past to 37. Likewise, 37 forwards the query to 18. 18 happens to be a location server of 11 and employs geographic routing. The destination, 11, receives the query and sends its location to 81.

The third major task is actual routing. 81 knows the position of 11 and applies routing in the physical space (geographic routing). Each intermediate node takes a decision for the next hop on the base of the destination location and the locations of the neighbors.

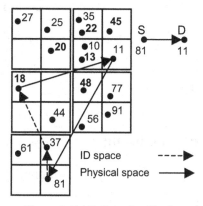

Figure 6. Grid's Location Service

Again, any intermediate node is in position to wage a black hole attack. One way to detect black hole attacks is to use feedback. When the destination node receives the packet it sends out an acknowledgement. The replay routing must replace some intermediate nodes from the actual routing. Each intermediate node adds its ID and position to the packet.

Figure 7 illustrates how a source evaluates the chance a malicious node to fabricate an acknowledgement on behalf of the destination node. The shaded area indicates a subset of nodes. The locations of the nodes are available in the sender's database, however they are unknown to the malicious node. A test for inconsistency may reveal a false acknowledgement.

While the location servers in Grid networks are organized only to help the routing, there are other network architectures, where the nodes are split into two sets: nodes that sense the environment and nodes that form the communication backbone topology. Hierarchical or cluster-based routing protocols are beneficial in terms of scalability and power efficiency. A dynamical organization for the clusters is employed to distribute the energy load evenly among the nodes. As a result, different nodes will play the role of a cluster head. In principle, hierarchical approaches are more vulnerable.

A malicious node elected as a cluster head may easily inject a black hole in the network. The rotation of the nodes is not only beneficial for the lifetime of the network, but also helps to temporary avoid blackholes.

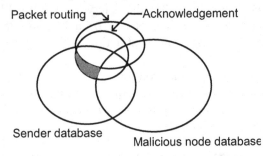

Figure 7. The Shaded Area Provides Potential to Detect False Acknowledgements

4. COMPUTATION

4.1 Compile-Time Scheduling

Assume that the node's functionality is partitioned into a set of tasks

$$T = \left\{ T_1, T_2, \dots T_{n(T)} \right\}$$

The tasks cannot be pre-empted. Each task is characterized by its execution time and deadline. The execution time is measured in number of clock cycles, NC. Assume that the processor has two modes: an active mode and a power saving mode [Kar 99]. The task deadline T_{DL} accommodates both the active period T_{ACT} and the power-saving period T_{PS}

$$T_{DL} = T_{ACT} + T_{PS}$$

In both CPU modes the power consumption scales linearly with the clock frequency.

$$P_{ACT} = k_{ACT} \times f^{CLK} + n_{ACT}$$

$$P_{PS} = k_{PS} \times f^{CLK} + n_{PS}$$

If $n_{ACT} > n_{PS}$, the energy per task has a minimum for

$$f^{CLK,OPT} = \sqrt{\frac{n_{ACT} - n_{PS}}{k_{PS}}} \sqrt{\frac{NC}{T_{DL}}}$$

If $n_{ACT} \leq n_{PS}$, the clock frequency must be selected as low as possible.

Due to the quadratic relationship a reduction of the supply voltage has a significant effect on the power consumption [Bro 03]. Best results can be achieved if the Dynamic Voltage Scaling (DVS) is combined with clock frequency scaling. When the performance requirements decline, the power manager slows down the clock frequency. After that the power manager decreases the supply voltage accordingly.

4.2 Run-Time Scheduling

While the compile-time scheduling does not fully exploit the potential for power reduction under changing conditions, a run-time scheduling would provide adaptability. An operating system will be responsible for the dynamic scheduling. Moreover, the operating system will act as a power manager, adjusting the supply voltage and the clock frequency.

An algorithm has been developed for low-power, run-time scheduling [Swa 05]. The algorithm, named LEDF, maintains a list of all ready for execution tasks. Again, the tasks cannot be pre-empted. The CPU is capable of operating at different voltages and clock frequencies. The supply voltage and the clock rate are controlled by the operating system. The LEDF algorithm is an integrated part of the operating system. On the top of the ready list is the task with the earliest deadline. The first step is to test if this task can meet its deadline at the lowest clock rate (lowest voltage). If this clock rate is too low, the next higher possible value is considered. When the current task deadline is met, an additional test is performed. The algorithm checks if the other tasks from the ready list can meet their deadlines at the highest clock rate. If any task will miss its deadline, the rate in focus is insufficient and the next higher speed for the current task is considered. As soon as the deadlines of all other tasks in the ready list can be met at the highest speed, the clock rate (voltage) is accepted and the task begins execution. When the task completes execution, the algorithm again selects the task with the nearest deadline to be off and running.

Inevitably, the CPU must spend energy to sort the tasks in the ready list and verify both tests. The LEDF algorithm has a computational complexity of $O(n \log n)$ for n tasks and a processor with two clock rates [Swa 05]. For k different clock rates the complexity of LEDF emerges as $O(n \log n + kn)$.

The scheduling has a subtle effect on the lifetime of the sensor network. The lifetime depends on the actual amount of charge that can be drawn from the battery. The effective amount of charge is a result not only of battery's capacity, but also of the temperature and the rate of discharge [Ben 00, Ben 01]. Furthermore, a battery can recover some of its deliverable charge when its discharge periods are interleaved with rest periods. Battery-driven designs can be built up on slack-based list scheduling schemes by optimizing the discharge power profile [Luo 01] similarly to the way incremental design methods deal with the slack distribution [Pop 01]. Also, battery-driven dynamic power management can be implemented by tracking the battery's charge state to provide graceful degradation of system performance [Ben 01].

5. STORAGE

The memory power consumption emerges as a key challenge in the embedded systems design. There are two approaches that improve the power budget. Using the results of computation as soon as possible reduces the memory requirements [Ben 00]. Another approach is to apply data compression. Compressed memory content declines the storage requirements. Breaking down the memory content into code and data, it will be easier to apply compression techniques for the code component [Lek 00]. Since no modification of the code is required, it is possible to keep compression and decompression asymmetric. There is no need the compression to be done real time. However, if the compression and decompression are extended to data, both transformations must be processed real time.

The hardware implementations can be split according to the availability and location of the cache memory. Figure 8 shows different implementations of the decompression engine. Architectures which lack cache memory are classified as direct decompression machines. A decompression engine translates the instructions on-the-fly. If a cache memory unit is available in the system, we distinguish between pre-cache architectures and post-cache architectures. An advantage of the post-cache architectures is that the instruction cache is effectively larger since it contains compressed code [Lek 00]. Regardless of the engine delay, the overall performance of the post-cache architecture can be improved due to the increased number of cache hits.

ARM Thumb processor is an example of a commercial processor with code compression [Atm 99]. The Thumb instruction set is a subset drawn from the ARM instruction set. All Thumb instructions are 16-bit long. Upon execution, the 16-bit Thumb instructions are decompressed into their 32-bit ARM equivalents in real time. The transition to the Thumb instruction set reduces the code size typically by 30 percent [Fur 00]. An additional advantage is the power-efficient access to the external memory. A disadvantage of the Thumb instruction set is a certain decline in performance due to the increased number of instructions.

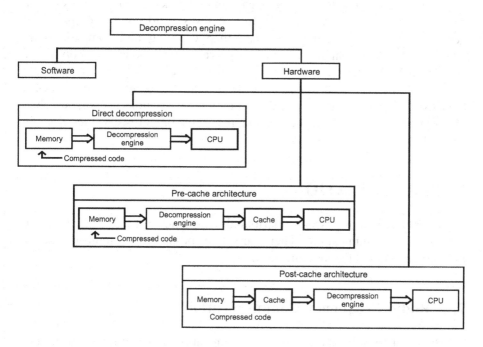

Figure 8. Decompression Engine Alternatives

6. INPUT/OUTPUT

The node sensors convert physical variables into electrical signals. Input signal conditioners are used to filter and amplify the signals. Energy is consumed in the sensor, amplifier and Analog-to-Digital Converter (ADC). The ADC's resolution has a significant impact on the energy budget. For example, if the ADC's resolution is increased from 15 to 16 bits while keeping the other parameters unchanged, the power consumption is increased from 100 mW to 400 mW [Doh 01]. Many designs allocate microcontrollers for network nodes. Commercial microcontrollers frequently have two types of resolution: high and low. This degree of freedom can be used in trading-off quality of service for energy efficiency. Using the low resolution we can achieve a certain reduction for the energy cost. Another degree of freedom is associated with the counters clock rate. The highest possible frequency provides the highest accuracy [Kar 05].

Using microcontrollers we can easily map chunks of functionality to the hardware subsystems. A typical chain of tasks is to count, compare and generate an output reaction. We can map counting and compare to an embedded counter channel and enter a power saving mode. As soon as the counter reaches the limit, a comparator will set a flag and awake the processor. Then the processor generates the required output reaction. Modern microcontrollers are capable of performing simple reactions such as set, clear or toggle an output, when the counter reaches a predefined value [Kar 99, Atm 02].

7. COMMUNICATION

Another axis along which distributed sensor networks can be classified relates to communication. There are two possibilities: radio-frequency radiation and optical communication.

7.1 Radio-Frequency Communication

The essential advantage of RF communication is that it does not require line of sight. However, many security and defense applications demand tiny nodes and the antenna size may be prohibitive for this domain. Another drawback associated with RF communication is the power efficiency.

The energy used to send a bit over a distance d may be written as

$$E = A \times d^n$$

Where A is a proportionality constant and n depends on the environment [Soh 00, Rab 00, Aky 02]. The greater than linear relationship between energy and distance promises to reduce the energy cost when the link is partitioned into several short intermediate hops. If we take into account the energy for receiving E_R, the energy for computation E_C and assume equal distances for each hop, the optimal number of hops (NH) is defined by the following equation [Kar 05].

$$NH_{OPT} = d \times \sqrt[n]{\frac{A(n-1)}{E_R + E_C}}$$

An additional benefit of the multihop communication is that the energy consumption is distributed over the nodes fairly.

7.2   Optical Communication

Optical communication may give the design power efficiency that we would not otherwise be able to obtain. Optical transmission provides extremely high antenna gain and the received power only decays as the inverse of the distance squared [War 01, War 05]. Optical systems can be made extremely tiny. Finally, it is very difficult to eavesdrop on collimated optical communication, which is a significant advantage for security and defense applications [War 05].

There are two types of optical communication systems: passive reflective systems and active-steered laser systems [War 01, War 05]. A passive reflective system, such as a corner-cube retroreflector (CCR), consists of three mutually orthogonal mirrors that form the corner of a cube. Light entering the cube bounces off the mirrors and is reflected back to the sender. By electrostatically actuating the bottom mirror, the orthogonalty can be disturbed and the reflection is no longer returned to the sender.

Active-steered communication systems include a small laser diode, a collimating lens and beam-steering optics.

8. ORIENTATION

The narrow beams used for optical communication require accurate pointing. Many applications will deploy nodes in random orientation. As a result, it will not be possible for all CCRs to return light to the network station. At the same time, there might be a need to avoid some directions. In particular, security and defense applications may require the network to be invisible from a certain area.

It is proposed that the nodes be magnetized and the CCR oriented to a predefined direction [Kar 02, Kar 05]. When the nodes fall through the air after being deployed, they will orient themselves. If the network has a sufficient density of nodes, it may not need the nodes, which change orientation upon landing. This approach for zero-power orientation is even more efficient for nodes floating on the water. They could freely rotate to orient themselves.

9. CONCLUSION

The capacity of a wireless ad-hoc network for corrective actions in face of malicious attacks is defined by its energy signature. The energy spent for communication has a significant impact on the overall energy budget. Multihop communication not only brings down the power consumption, but also helps to avoid obstacles. A subtle effect of the multihop transmission is that the energy demand is distributed over the nodes fairly.

Optical communication is associated with pointing and orientation. A deployment characterized by a predefined orientation of the nodes simultaneously improves the accessibility of the network and declines the vulnerability.

10. REFERENCES

[Aky 02] Akyildiz, Ian F., Weilian Su, Yogesh Sankarasubramaniam, and Erdal Cayirci, "A survey on sensor networks," *IEEE Communications Magazine*, vol. 40, August, 2002, pp. 102–114.

[Atm 02] Atmel Corporation, *AT91 ARM Thumb Microcontrollers, AT91M55800A*, 2002, available at **http://www.atmel.com**

[Atm 99] Atmel Corporation, ARM7TDMI (Thumb) Datasheet, 1999, available at **http://www.atmel.com**

[Ben 00] Benini, Luca and Giovanni De Micheli, "System-level power optimization: techniques and tools," *ACM Transactions on Design Automation of Electronic Systems*, vol. 5, No. 2, pp. 115–192, April 2000.

[Ben 01] Benini, Luca, Giuliano Castelli, Alberto Macii, and Riccardo Scarsi, "Battery-driven dynamic power management," *IEEE Design & Test of Computers*, pp. 53–60, March–April 2001.

[Bha 02] Bhardwaj, Manish and Anantha P. Chandrakasan, "Bounding the lifetime of sensor networks via optimal role assignments," *IEEE INFOCOM*, 2002, pp. 1587–1596.

[Bro 03] Brock, Bishop and Karthick Rajamani, "Dynamic power management for embedded systems," *Proceedings of the IEEE International SOC Conference*, pp. 416–419, September 2003.

[Che 02] Chen, Benjie, Kyle Jamieson, Hari Balakrishnan, and Robert Morris, "An energy-efficient coordination algorithm for topology maintenance in ad hoc wireless networks, *ACM Wireless Networks Journal*, vol. 8, Number 5, 2002, pp. 481–494.

[Den 02] Deng, Hongmei, Wei Li, and Dharma P. Agrawal, "Routing security in wireless ad hoc networks," *IEEE Communications Magazine*, October, 2002, pp. 70–75.

[Doh 01] Doherly, Lance, Brett Warneke, Bernhard Boser, and Kristofer Pister, "Energy and performance considerations for smart dust," *International Journal of Parallel and Distributed Systems and Networks*, vol. 4, no 3, 2001, pp. 121–133.

[Fur 00] Furber, Steve, *ARM System-on-Chip Architecture*, Addison-Wesley, 2000.

[Gao 00] Gao, Jay Lin, *Energy Efficient Routing for Wireless Sensor Networks*, Ph.D. theses, University of California, Los Angeles, 2000.

[Hae 05] Haenggi, Martin "Opportunities and challenges in wireless sensor networks," in *Handbook of Sensor Networks: Compact Wireless and Wired Sensing Systems*, edited by Mohammad Ilyas and Imad Mahgoub, CRC Press LLC, 2005.

[Hil 02] Hill, Jason L. and David E. Culler, "Mica: a wireless platform for deeply embedded networks," *IEEE MICRO*, November–December, 2002, pp. 12–23.

[Hon 02] Hong, Xiaoyan, Kaixin Xu, and Mario Gerla, "Scalable routing protocols for mobile ad hoc networks," *IEEE Network*, July/August, 2002, pp. 11–21.

[Hu 04] Hu, Yih-Chun and Adrian Perrig, "A survey of secure wireless ad hoc routing," *IEEE Security & Privacy*, May/June, 2004, pp. 28–39.

[Kah 00] Kahn, Joseph, R.H. Katz, and Kristofer Pister, "Next century challenges: mobile networking for "Smart Dust," *Journal of Communication and Networks*, no. 3, September 2000, pp. 188–196.

[Kar 02] Karakehayov, Zdravko, "Zero-power design for Smart Dust networks," *Proceedings 1st IEEE International Conference on Intelligent Systems*, Varna, 2002, pp. 302–305.

[Kar 05] Karakehayov, Zdravko, "Low-power design for Smart Dust networks," in *Handbook of Sensor Networks: Compact Wireless and Wired Sensing Systems*, edited by Mohammad Ilyas and Imad Mahgoub, CRC Press LLC, 2005.

[Kar 99] Karakehayov, Zdravko, Knud Smed Christensen and Ole Winther, *Embedded Systems Design with 8051 Microcontrollers*, Dekker, 1999.

[Lek 00] Lekatsas, H., J. Henkel, and W. Wolf, "Code compression as a variable in hardware/software co-design," *Proceedings International Workshop on Hardware/Software Codesign*, 2000, pp. 120–124.

[Li 00] Li, Jinyang, John Jannotti, Douglas S. J. De Couto, David R. Karger, and Robert Morris, "A scalable location service for geographic ad hoc routing," *Proceedings ACM/IEEE MobiCom*, August 2000.

[Liu 02] Liu, Jie, Patrick Cheung, Leonidas Guibas, and Feng Zhao, "A dual-space approach to tracking and sensor management in wireless sensor networks," Palo Alto Research Center Technical Report P2002-10077, 2002. Available at **http://www2.parc.com/spl/projects/cosense/pub/dualspace.pdf**

[Luo 01] Luo, Jiong and Niraj K. Jha, "Battery-aware static scheduling for distributed real-time embedded systems," *Proceedings 38th Design Automation Conference*, ACM Press, pp. 444–449, 2001.

[Mau 01] Mauve, Martin and Jorg Widmer, "A survey on position-based routing in mobile ad hoc networks," *IEEE Network*, November/December, 2001, pp. 30–39.

[Nav 97] Navas, J. C. and T. Imielinski, "Geographic addressing and routing," *Proceedings 3rd ACM/IEEE International Conference Mobile Computing Networks*, MobiCom'97, September, 1997.

[O'R 98] O'Rourke, Joseph, *Computational Geometry in C*, Cambridge University Press, 1998.

[Pop 01] Pop, Paul, Petru Eles, Traian Pop, and Zebo Peng, "An approach to incremental design of distributed embedded systems," *Proceedings 38th Design Automation Conference*, pp. 450–455, 2001.

[Rab 00] Rabaey, Jan, M. Josie Ammer, Julio L.da Silva Jr., Danny Patel, and Shad Roundy, "PicoRadio supports ad hoc ultra-low power wireless networking," *IEEE Computer*, vol. 33, July 2000, pp. 42–48.

[Roy 99] Royer, Elizabeth M. and Chai-Keong Toh, "A review of current routing protocols for ad hoc mobile wireless networks," *IEEE Personal Communications*, April, 1999, pp. 46–55.

[Sch 03] Schiller, Jochen H., *Mobile Communications*, Addison-Wesley, 2003.

[Soh 00] Sohrabi, Katayou, *On Low Power Self Organizing Sensor Networks*, Ph.D. theses, University of California, Los Angeles, 2000.

[Swa 05] Swaminathan, Vishnu, Yi Zou, and Krishnendu Chakrabarty, "Techniques to reduce communication and computation energy in wireless sensor networks," in *Handbook of Sensor Networks: Compact Wireless and Wired Sensing Systems*, edited by Mohammad Ilyas and Imad Mahgoub, CRC Press LLC, 2005.

[War 01] Warneke, Brett, Matt Last, Brian Liebowitz, and Kristofer S. J. Pister, "Smart Dust: communicating with a cubic-millimeter computer," *IEEE Computer*, vol. 34, January, 2001, pp. 44–51.

[War 05] Warneke, Brett, "Miniaturizing sensor networks with MEMS," in *Handbook of Sensor Networks: Compact Wireless and Wired Sensing Systems*, edited by Mohammad Ilyas and Imad Mahgoub, CRC Press LLC, 2005.

[Woo 05] Wood, Anthony D. and John A. Stankovic, "A taxonomy for denial-of-service attacks in wireless sensor networks," in *Handbook of Sensor Networks: Compact Wireless and Wired Sensing Systems*, edited by Mohammad Ilyas and Imad Mahgoub, CRC Press LLC, 2005.

A DISTRIBUTED APPROACH TO THE RECOGNITION OF GEOGRAPHICALLY LOCATED IP DEVICES

George Markowsky
Professor, Department of Computer Science, University of Maine
5752 Neville Hall, Orono, ME 04469-5752, USA,
Phone: +1-207-581-3940 CS, Fax: +1-207-581-4977 CS
markov@cs.umaine.edu

President, Trefoil Corporation
P.O. Box 127, One Ayers Island, Orono, ME 04473-0127
Phone: +1-207-866-2619 x15, Fax: +1-207-866-0362
markov@turing.trefoil.com

Roman Romanyak,
Anatoly Sachenko
Department of Information Computing Systems and Control
Institute of Computer Information Technologies
Ternopil Academy of National Economy
3 Peremoga Square, Ternopil, 46004, UKRAINE
rrm@tanet.edu.te.ua, as@tanet.edu.te.ua

Abstract: We introduce a method based on time delays between among Internet protocol packages is proposed and software for determination of attacking computer status is developed within its virtual connection with a victim computer. An attacking computer functioning in two modes is considered: direct connecting to the victim computer and connecting through the chains of intermediate computers.

Keywords: Internet protocol; time delay; attacking computer; victim computer; remote computer; virtual connection

INTRODUCTION

An Internet user with the appropriate knowledge can create considerable damage. The "I love you" computer virus created an estimated $6.7 billion of

J. S. Kowalik et al. (eds.), Cyberspace Security and Defense: Research Issues, 193–207.
© 2005 *Springer. Printed in the Netherlands.*

damage [1]. It is difficult to get accurate estimates of damage caused by computer viruses and other cyberattacks.

The Internet and the global information society are all targets of attacks that can come from any point in the global computer network. Nowadays, terrorists and cyber-criminals use the speed and global connectivity of the Internet for making attacks.

An importance step in preventing future attacks is being able to identify the source of an attack. The ability to identify the source of an attack provides a powerful disincentive for potential cyber-criminals and terrorists, since it can provide evidence that can be used in court actions to deliver economic sanctions against transgressors [2]. Being able to identify the source of a cyber-attack can also provide technical details that can be used to prevent such attacks in the future. Tracing cyber-attacks can disrupt computer attacks in real time. In many cases it is impossible to obtain sufficient compensation from cyber-criminals to cover the damage that they inflict. Consequently, it is much better to prevent or disrupt such attacks before they can cause much damage [3].

One way to detect computer attacks is via an intrusion detection system (IDS). Such systems are characterized by two basic functions including the automatic detection of attacks, and the reporting of information about attacks to the administrator. An IDS works in real-time and monitors network traffic comparing it with templates from a database. If some template coincides with a template from a database, it means that the system has been attacked.

Some people use honeynets to investigate cyber-criminal behavior and to discover new types of cyber-attacks. We should mention that a honeynet is a computer network created especially to attract cyber-attacks. Whenever a honeynet is attacked, lots of information is collected and then analyzed in order to better understand the cyber-criminals activity. A key step in protecting a network is to detect defects in the defense systems and removing them immediately.

Most contemporary computer environments have very primitive facilities for localizing and tracing sources of cyber-attacks [2]. Contemporary tools are incapable of effectively identifying the source of cyber-attacks. Nowadays computer criminals are very good in staying anonymous while committing criminal activities during unauthorized access to networks [4].

1. THE KNOWN METHODS OF REMOTE COMPUTER LOCALIZATION

In contrast to telephone systems, which have effective methods for tracing phone calls, there is a shortage of effective tools that can trace cyber-attacks. A key reason for this is that computer network protocols were designed on the assumption that all users should be trusted. As a result we do not have any reliable identification of the information located in an IP-packet. Thus, any user can change the information in an IP-packet, effectively hiding its real source. A cyber-criminal can insert an incorrect address into the source field of an IP-packet if he is only interested in a one-way connection. Source falsification is more complicated if the cyber-attacker is interested in two-way connections.

There are three basic methods to determine the geographical location of a cyber-attacker: using the WHOIS service, using the *traceroute* utility and using a distributed *traceroute* approach.

The WHOIS service searches a database of domain names and provides email addresses, mailing addresses and telephone numbers of people responsible for a particular domain [5]. This information is provided by the Internet Registration service (InterNic). The WHOIS service is accessible by Internet users using *telnet*, via e-mail, and by the whois command. A limitation of this service is that it only contains information about the top-level domains, but no information about subdomains and individual computers. Moreover there is no cooperation between the distributed WHOIS databases [4].

The *traceroute* utility is a debugging tool that allows tracing the route of IP-packets from one computer to another [6]. *traceroute's* works as follows:

1. A computer-source send IP-datagram with TTL=1 (it is field of IP-packet "Time To Live") to destination computer;

2. First router process the datagram, delete it and sends it back an ICMP (Internet Control Message Protocol) message reporting that packet lifetime has been exceeded. This is way to determine an address of the first router;

3. Then *traceroute* sends datagram with TTL=2 that allows determine an IP-address of the next router;

4. The increasing of TTL value is continuing while the datagram will arrive to the destination computer [6].

Traceroute is effective for analysis of packets' route and for determination of the host domain name. However its application for geographical localization of remote host has some limitations because it is based on determination of the packets' route but not determination of destination computer [7]. Therefore in [8] is shown that using the *traceroute* can give an ambiguous results.

The limitations described above can be taken into account in a case when *traceroute* is running from different geographical points connecting to the same destination computer. The proposed approach considered in [8] allows comparing many routes. Application of the proposed approach together with WHOIS database gives better possibility to define geographical location of the destination computer. Although such method is one of the most accurate, it has the following disadvantages:

- The results are not exact sometimes because they show an approximating location of the attacking computer (AC) [8];

- this approach should not be applied in a case, when intermediate computers (redirectors) are used for the attack.

The method of AC status determination without listed disadvantages is considered below.

2. METHOD OF TIME DELAYS ANALYSIS

One of widespread ways of AC address hiding is taking a few intermediate computers for the communication with a victim computer (VC) [2]. If many intermediate computers are used for the attack then VC can detect only last computer with unknown status from the chain of intermediate computers.

Such technique of attack is very effective and very hard for tracing of AC address. Especially, if there are large time-delays on intermediate computers which connecting to the attack (a hacker can send the special signals to the intermediate computers for the beginning of the attack). AC creates the connection with VC through the intermediate computers using redirectors (Figure 1). Redirector is a part of network software, which receives the I/O queries for the remote files and services and redirects them to other computer [9]. This software should be code and should be constantly placed in the memory. Therefore it is hardly to detect an AC address in the attacks of the given type.

It is more reliable to calculate the time-delays between the IP-packets during open session between AC and VC. In this case after session closing we will get two arrays of time-delays values: time-delays between AC and VC (M_1) in forward direction and time-delays between VC and AC (M_2) in back direction. Thus VC can receive the information about AC address or the address of the last intermediate computer. If the attack is carried out with direct connection to VC (Figure 1) then the values of time delays between the packets which goes from AC to VC will be approximately equal to the values of time delays between the packets that goes from VC to AC.

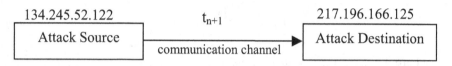

Figure 1. Scheme of Direct Attack

At the attack goes using intermediate computers, VC is directly connected with the last intermediate computer (Figure 2) and its status is still unknown. If value of time delays between the packets sending by ACE is much greater than value of time delays between packages that comes from VC to AC then the attack executing using by intermediate computers. Time of IP-package delivering from ACE to VC can be calculated as

$$T_{sum} = \sum_{i=1}^{n+1} t_i \, ,$$

where t_1 ., t_{i+1} are the values of time delays between the intermediate computers.

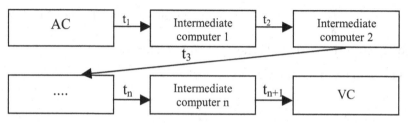

Figure 2. Scheme of Attack Using Intermediate Computers

It is obviously, that total time of packet delivering from AC to VC will be greater than time of package delivering from VC to the last intermediate computer

$$T_{sum} > t_{n+1}$$

If we suppose that two arrays of time delays M_1 and M_2 correspond to the normal distribution law and they are not homogeneous then the attack is carried out using intermediate computers [12]. Therefore, it is necessary to fulfill the appropriate analysis in order to determine the attack source status. For this purpose it is necessary to calculate mathematical expectations x_v for an array $M_1(t)$ and y_v for an array $M_2(t)$, dispersions D_{vx}, D_{vy} and mean-square errors σ_{vx} and σ_{vy} respectively [13].

In our case we have small data samples, therefore it is expediently to use the average absolute deviation (AAD) from the mean value as dispersion measure [14], which is also named as "mean deviation from the mean value"

$$AAD = \frac{\sum |x_i - \bar{x}|}{n},\tag{1}$$

where n is a quantity of array cells,
x_i is i - cell of the array.

For verification of one-dimensional data arrays with normal distribution law, it is necessary to find the relation [15]

$$k = AAD/\sigma,\tag{2}$$

where $k = \sqrt{2\pi} = 0.79788$ for the normal law of distribution [15].

For determination of two independent sets belonging to the same general aggregate, it is needed first to check up a necessary condition [16]

$$\hat{F} > \mathrm{Ft}\tag{3}$$

where $\hat{F} = \dfrac{s_1^2}{s_2^2}$ (s_1^2 is a large selective dispersion of array M_1, s_2^2 is a large selective dispersion of array M_2), F_t is a table value.

If (3) will be true, then we should find

$$\hat{t} = \frac{\sqrt{n-1}(s_1^2 - s_2^2)}{2\sqrt{s_1^2 s_2^2}}$$

and check up a sufficient condition

$$\hat{t} > t_t\tag{4}$$

where, t_t is the tabular value.

If condition 4 is satisfying then these two arrays do not belong to the same universal set and they are heterogeneous.

Consequently, for defining AC status it is necessary to provide the following actions:

- to form two time delays arrays between AC and VC and between VC and AC,
- to find the basic statistical-probabilistic descriptions and check up the sufficient and necessary conditions to belong the arrays to the same universal set.

If data are distributed in arrays on the normal distributed law and they are not homogeneous, it is possible to make a conclusion that attack was done by using the intermediate computers (redirectors). In other case, if (i) necessary condition (3) is not executed or (ii) necessary condition is executed but a sufficient condition (4) is not executed, then the attack take place without intermediate computers.

3. ALGORITHM FOR DETERMINATION OF REMOTE COMPUTER STATUS

The algorithm is based on the above-described method of comparative analysis of time delays between VC and AC from one side, and AC and VC time delays from another side. There is introduced the necessary initial information at the beginning (Figure 3):

- IP-address of AC and a port number which is attacked;
- IP-address and port number of computer, where the VC will be send its packages.

It should be noted that the IP-address of attack source, and the coordinates of the attacked port can be detected by the user applying the standard operating system Unix or the Windows utilities, the net stat, the sock list for example or any IDS.

Network adapter establishment in the listening mode of all packages received by VC on the proper port is a next step, the promiscuous mode. Then there are selecting the network packages which are arrived from the AC on the proper number of the VC port. The special filter is installed for this purpose, it contains the data entered by user during module initialization. Every package is checked up, and if it corresponds to the set filter, the current time is written in Unix-format in the proper cells. The selection of network information is executed using the standard pcap library, the well-known utility tcpdump is made on its basis.

After collection of time delays packages from the AC to the VC there is a processing of the received time values and the statistical analysis is executed. The delays values between packages are saved in two arrays [18], the first array includes the microseconds, the second one includes the seconds. The difference between any two neighboring pairs of time delays is calculated in the cycle, then it is saved in other array and calculated the arithmetic mean. Really the received array of time delays differences and the calculated arithmetic mean form the first half of general result which the module gives.

The establishment of a new package filter, which also takes the information from the data entered by user, is a next step, namely the IP-address and the number of computer port, where VC will trace the packages. Then a cycle is declared where the VC packages are sent on the proper port refer in, this cycle is executed many times, as was set in a parameter, which is responsible for calculation process. There is carried out the selection of the packages which satisfy the conditions of the installed, this selection is made simultaneously with sending of the AC packages. As a result, we get the two arrays of time delays which are needed to be analyzed on belonging to the same universal set.

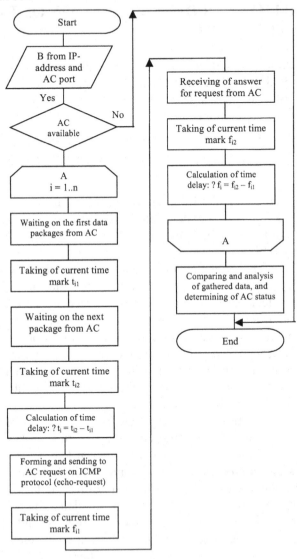

Figure 3. General Algorithm of Remote computer Status Determination

4. THE CHARACTERISTICS OF SOFTWARE MODULE

Software that implements the algorithm described above must be high-speed because it should process IP-packets and the delays between them [9]. The speed of the software depends on programming language and therefore it is expediently to choose C++.

The developed software module consists of the following components:

- The procedure, which executes verification of remote computer presence in the network. This computer is recognized as computer of potential hacker. This function is executed by the standard instrument of C language namely by using a function *connect()*. If communication with a remote computer does not exist the procedure must finish its operation;

- The procedure that executes listening the network channel and choosing the packets corresponding to the set of filter conditions. The *pcap* library carries out listening the network channel. For listening the network channel a network adapter is turned to the special mode for listening only those frames, that deal with the attacked computer;

- The procedure, which calculates the time delays between IP-packets, that arrived from the attack source to the object, and also carries out their analysis and calculates the average mean value of these time delays. Every IP-packet has the special header, which contains a time stamp showing time of the packet forming. We do not need to create own times and therefore we have not any time loosing, which may affect on the accuracy of time calculation. When the procedure gets a next packet, the value between its time and time stamp of the previous packet should be considered as the time delay between passing of two IP-packets;

- The procedure, that executes one TCP-packet sending to the remote computer for the proper port. The IP-address and port number are used as input of this procedure. Then IP-package which goes to the remote computer and comes back the time delay is calculated similarly;

- The procedure, that executes processing and analysis of time delays between packages, that arrived from the object of attack to the computer of potential hacker. On this stage there are formed two arrays of time delays between IP-packets of remote computers. The analysis of these arrays done by the mathematical approach described in Section 2. If these two arrays of time delays do not belong to the same universal set, the attack is carried out using redirectors.

The developed software module works under Linux operating systems. This software module can be used in the Windows operating systems by simple source code recompiling. A user dialogue is implemented in the text (console) mode. For the correct and safe functioning of the given software module, it must be started with administrator (root) privileges. It is caused by the facts that a network adapter tracing all frames, despite their destination addresses (promiscuous mode). Administrator privileges are needed also in order to create a network socket for getting of all frames, that arrived to network card.

5. EXPERIMENTAL RESULTS

For the verification of the implemented software module the experiments were conducted between the following three servers:

- Ternopil Academy of National Economy, Ukraine (IP:217.196.166.105 – TANE-srv)
- University of Kiel, Germany (IP:134.245.52.122 – Kiel-srv);
- HTTL Company – London, Great Britain (IP: 217.34.204.1 – HTTL-srv);

The graphs of time delays between IP-packages HTTL-srv and TANE-srv at direct connection are shown in Figures 4 and 5 respectively. Figure 6 shows the time delays between the servers HTTL-srv and TANE-srv when the Kiel-srv redirector is used. The values of time delays shown in Figures 4 and 5 are significantly different from the values in Figure 6, so the presence of the redirector has been determined.

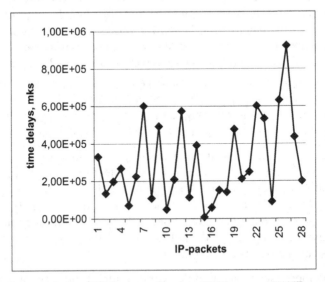

Figure 4. Delay of IP-Packages Between HTTL-srv and TANE-srv

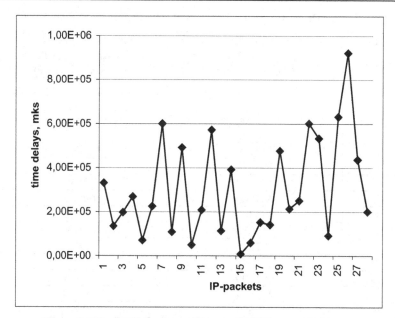

Figure 5. Delay of IP-Packages Between TANE-srv and HTTL-srv

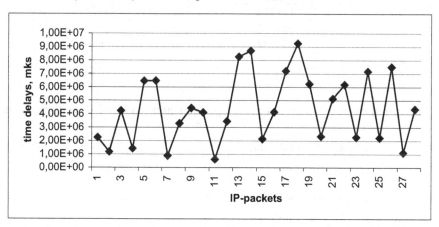

Figure 6. Delays Between IP-Packages of HTTL-srv and TANE-srv Using Kiel-Redirector

The results of these experiments are reprinted in Table 1. We used this data to conduct an analysis of the time delays using the normal distribution and homogeneity.

Table 1. Time Delays Between   -Packages of HTTL-srv and TANE-srv Servers

№	Time delays between HTTL-srv and TANE-srv (the first array)	Time delays between TANE-srv and HTTL-srv (the second array)
	X	IN
1.	249442	33037
2.	155904	13430
3.	298592	19785
4.	422179	26893
5.	406248	7073
6.	479732	22538
7.	99082	60083
8.	294380	49173
9.	408088	4913
10.	107695	20854
11.	21520	57290
12.	481499	11333
13.	269504	39170
14.	269504	20005
15.	143056	5898
16.	135539	55170
17.	200162	14134
18.	253494	47681
19.	247231	31337
20.	330370	65040

The mathematical expectation, dispersion and standard deviation are as follows:

$$x_v := 2{,}57*105;$$
$$y_v := 3{,}186*104;$$
$$D_{vx} := 2{,}079*1010;$$
$$D_{vy} := 3{,}663*108;$$
$$\sigma_{vx} := 1{,}442*105;$$
$$\sigma_{vy} := 1{,}914*104.$$

According equation (1) the mean of absolute deviation was calculated:

$$AAD_X = 1{,}167*105,$$
$$SAV_Y = 1{,}47*104.$$

Having the mean of absolute deviation for two arrays of time delays we may define according equation (2) their belonging to the normal distributive law:

$$k_x = 0,809,$$

$$k_y = 0,79.$$

As the value of $k_x \approx k_y \approx \sqrt{2\pi} = 0.79788$, the values of time delays belong to the sample, which has the normal distributive law.

For determination of two independent samples belonging to the same universal set we check up the requirement and sufficient condition after equations (3) and (4) accordingly:

Requirement:

$$\hat{F} = 60,632;$$

$$F_t = 2,12.$$

$\hat{F} > F_t$, —a requirement is satisfied.

Sufficient condition:

$$\hat{t} = 16,691;$$

$$t_t = 1,729;$$

$\hat{t} > t_t$, —a sufficient condition is satisfied as well.

Consequently, the arrays of numerical delays given in Table 1 have the normal distributive law. However they do not belong to the same universal sample, and it means that time delays between HTTL-srv and TANE-srv, the first array, and time delays between TANE-srv and HTTL-srv, the second array are heterogeneous. So we may conclude the attack in this case takes place using of intermediate computers.

6. THE POTENTIAL AREAS OF METHOD APPLICATION

The developed program module can work on the servers as well as workstations, and it's designed for determination of remote computer status during network attack.

Software can not be used for the detection of network attack and correspondent reaction. This function must be fulfilled by the system of intrusion (attacks) detection. Meantime the IDS has to push the software module for detection of attacking computer status after execution of IDS' proper functions, preventing of attack making and notification of administrator. Software module determines a status of this AC, and if the attack is fulfilled using of intermediate computers, notifies the administrator. In other case, the attack is direct the software module passes the control to the other software module [8] for geographical localization of attacking computer.

Hence, the presence of installed IDS is the necessary requirement , such IDS allows to detect the unauthorized access to the network resources. The developed software module can be used as one of components which are implemented for creation of corporate network defense system, and the output result of this software module can be applied by the utility of remote IP-devices localization.

CONCLUSIONS

There is proposed the method of remote computer status determination allows to determine the remote computer status with potential terrorist on the basis of time delays between IP-packages, and developed algorithm, and implemented software module which can be used as one of components of remote network attacks detecting system in a combination with other known methods.

In the result of experiments the values of time delays were obtained and analyzed by the tools of mathematical statistics on accordance to the normal distributive law, they were tested on homogeneity and their belonging to the same universal set.

The proposed method is universal to different attack types, and it enables to detect the status of remote attacking computer in the real time. The software module allows to promote the efficiency of corporate networks defense systems functioning, using its aggregation with the program complexes of the Intrusion Detection System.

REFERENCES

1. "Love Bug Damage costs Rise to 6.7 Billion" available at
   http://www.businesseconomic.com/cei/press.index.html

2. Lee, H., K. Park, "On the Effectiveness of Probabilistic Packet Marking for IP Traceback Under Denial of Service Attack," *Proceedings of IEEE INFOCOM 2001*, Anchorage, Alaska, April 22–26, 2001, New York: IEEE Computer Society Press, 338–347.

3. Lipson, Howard & Fisher, David. "Survivability—A New Technical and Business Perspective on Security," 33–39. *Proceedings of the 1999 New Security Paradigms*

Workshop, Caledon Hills, Ontario, Canada, Sept. 22–24, New York: Association for Computing Machinery.

4. Savage, Stefan; David Wetherall, Anna R. Karlin, and Tom Anderson, "Practical Network Support for IP Traceback," 295–306, *Proceedings of ACM SIGCOMM 2000*, Stockholm, Sweden, Aug. 28–Sept. 1, 2000, New York: Association for Computing Machinery.

5. Fadia A, and P. Ankit, Getting geographical Information using an IP Address, New York: Association for Computing Machinery, 2000.

6. **http://www.sarangworld.com/TRACEROUTE/**

7. Nemeth C., D. Evi, and P. Ram, "GTrace – A Graphical Traceroute Tool," Boston: Addison-Wesley, 2003.

8. Connolly, Gene M., George Markowsky, and Anatoly Sachenko, "Distributed Traceroute Approach to Geographically Locating IP Devices" *Proceedings of 2003 Spring IEEE Conference on Technologies for Homeland Security*, Boston, USA, May 7–8, 2003.

10. Meadows, Catherine, "A Formal Framework and Evaluation Method for Network Denial of Service," 4–13, *Proceedings of the 12th IEEE Computer Security Foundations Workshop*, Mordano, Italy, June 28–30, 1999. New York: IEEE Computer Society Press, 1999.

12. L. Zaks, Statistical Evaluation, Translated from German by N.N. Varygin, under edition of Y.P. Adler, V.G. Gorsky. – Moscow: Statistics, 1976, 598 p.

13. Rao S.P., Linear Statistical Methods and Their Using, Moscow: Nauka, 1968, 548 p.

14. Leman E., Verification of Statistical Hypothesis, Moscow: Nauka, 1979, 408 p.

15. Bolshev L.N. and N. V. Smirnov, Tables of Mathematical Statistics, Moscow: Nauka, 1983.

16. Kozlov M.V. and Z. V. Prokhorov, Introduction to Mathematical Statistics, Moscow: MSU publisher, 1987.

17. Krammer G., Mathematical Methods of Statistics, Moscow: Gosinoizdat, 1948.

18. R. Romanyak, A. Sachenko, S. Voznyak, G. Connolly, and G. Markowsky, "Detecting a Cyber-Attack Source in Real Time," *Proceedings of 2004 Spring IEEE Conference on Technologies for Homeland Security*, Boston, USA, April 21–22, 2004.

19. **http://cpp.samara.ws/articles/kir/intro.shtml**

SITUATIONAL AWARENESS AND NETWORK TRAFFIC ANALYSIS[*]

John McHugh,
CyLab and CERT Network Situational Awareness Center, Carnegie Mellon University, Pittsburgh, PA 15313, USA
jmchugh@cert.org

Carrie Gates
2CERT Network Situational Awareness Center,
Carnegie Mellon University, Pittsburgh, PA 15313, USA, and
Department of Computer Science, Dalhousie University, Halifax, NS, CA
gates@cs.dal.ca

Damon Becknel
United States Military Academy, West Point, NY
damon.becknel@usma.edu

Abstract: As network traffic increases, the problems associated with monitoring and analyzing the traffic on high speed networks become increasingly difficult. In this paper, we consider a variety of techniques for analyzing such data and using it to develop a variety of network views that reflect the status of the monitored environment. The powers of the monitoring approach and the analysis techniques is such that it is possible, on one hand, to identify network wide phenomena, and, on the other, to look at the behavior of individual network hosts.

Keywords: Situational Awareness; Cyber Defense; NetFlow; Network Measurement

---

[*] This material is based upon work partially supported by the National Science Foundation under Grant No. 0326472. Any opinions, findings, and conclusions or recommendations expressed in this material are those of the author(s) and do not necessarily reflect the views of the National Science Foundation. This work is also supported by the Army Research Office through grant number DAAD190210389 ("Perpetually Available and Secure Information Systems") to CyLab at Carnegie Mellon University. The first author's participation in the workshop where the material on which this paper is based was presented was partially supported by NATO.

J. S. Kowalik et al. (eds.), Cyberspace Security and Defense: Research Issues, 209–228.
© 2005 *Springer. Printed in the Netherlands.*

1. INTRODUCTION

Situational Awareness involves taking a broad view of a given situation that puts local or detailed observations into perspective. CERT is fortunate to have access to network flow data from the border of a large customer network. The network in question can be viewed as larger than a /8 comprising several million active hosts. It is geographically distributed, with multiple border routers that serve as connections to the internet. Some of the border routers define isolated stub networks while others serve to route traffic among portions of the monitored network, as well. We see the vast majority of the traffic that passes between the monitored network and the internet in general as well that portion of the traffic between internal hosts that passes through the border routers. This allows us to consider both the similarities and differences among traffic intended for various subcomponents of the enterprise.

Data from the internet border allows us to develop a unified view of the overall posture of the enterprise, e.g., is it under constant probing, what is the general mix of traffic traveling between the internet and the monitored network, are there significant numbers of internal hosts exhibiting behaviors that are consistent with infection by the *worm du jour*, etc. In addition to global views, it is possible to consider the externally visible behavior of small subnets or of individual hosts. In this paper, we will try to sketch a variety of analyses that can be performed when such data is available

We note that our data is composed from observations made at a variety of individual connection points. In principle, similar, aggregated networks can be constructed by aggregating border data from a variety of smaller enterprises, assuming that political obstacles can be overcome. Similar collection and analysis facilities, albeit on a smaller scale, are described by Fullmer and Romig, 2000.

2. NETWORK DATA COLLECTION APPROACH

The data that we collect is primarily unsampled NetFlow V5Cisco Systems, 1999 that originates at the routers defining the border of the customer network. In addition to Cisco routers, the border deploys additional NetFlow capable sources including Juniper routers and specialized collection hardware. Collection is trending towards the latter due to performance considerations and lack of support for TCP flag capture on recent Cisco 7800 series routers. NetFlow is an abstraction that provides a level of detail that is less than that from packet headers, but greater than session summaries. Flow records capture source and destination addresses, protocol, ports (for TCP and UDP), traffic volumes (packets and bytes), and start and end times. Most V5 implementations also capture the "or" of the TCP flags for TCP flows. Flows are unidirectional, so the two sides of a TCP connection will be captured separately. A flow record is started when a new connection (Unique source, destination IP pair, protocol, and ports (if appropriate)) is recognized. The flow is terminated if it is closed by a TCP FIN or RST, if it is idle for too long (typically 15 seconds) or if it persists for longer than a time limit (typically 30 minutes). These constraints may result in a TCP connection being spread over many flow records. Individual flow records are aggregated into large UDP packets and sent to a central collection point for aggregation and analysis. In our case, we have build a high performance collection and file system for this purpose.

The collection system provides comprehensive coverage of the customer network. We estimate that more than 95% of the traffic that flows between the customer network and the internet is captured, however, we are aware of a small number of uninstrumented routers and occasional failures of parts of the collection system. The volume of traffic captured is some tens of gigabytes per day with some tens of terabytes currently available for analysis. This requires a large computational and storage facility to support historical analysis. Note that there are a number of sources of delay in the collection process and flow records do not arrive at the collection facility in temporal order. The data set consists of hourly files as described in the next section. In general, the data for one hour may not be complete until well into the next hour and "real time" analysis is not feasible.

Figure 1 shows the general collection setup at a typical border location. Note that inbound and outbound traffic is handled by separate routers. Access Control Lists (ACLs) are routinely used at the border to block sources or protocols deemed malicious by the customer. This data is also captured, but is segregated from the data that is routed.

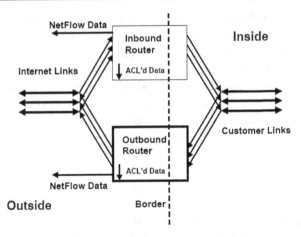

Figure 1. Data Collection at a Border

3. ANALYSIS FOR SITUATIONAL AWARENESS

The NetFlow data is organized into a series of flat files on an hourly basis. Several files are provided for each sensor (router) with web traffic being segregated into its own set of hourly files. The data is also partitioned by direction (inside to outside and outside to inside), ACL data, etc. with the objective of minimizing the amount of data that must be processed for the most common routine analyses. The data is packed in a format that is designed to minimize the disk space required to store it, which minimizes the read time, the dominating factor in much of the initial processing. Creating files by sensor, type, date and hour, etc. reduces the size further since these values are implicit for all of the data in a given file. In general, the packed format supports efficient linear searches of the data.

A variety of programs are available that access the file system as though it were a single unified entity. The flat file format used is packed into minimum length bit fields, with certain fields (hour, sensor, direction, etc.) being implicit in the file structure. This minimizes file reading during the search process. The primary search operation is selection based on time, IP, flow characteristics (protocol, volume, etc.) which creates files of raw data satisfying selection criteria. In addition, statistics files can be produced either directly from the flat file system, selecting on time, sensor, type, etc. or from the files produced by the selection process. A powerful analysis capability is based on the ability to create sets or bags (multisets, counted sets) of IPs with selection characteristics. These can be used for further selection / filtering, displayed in ways that reflect network structure or connections, and manipulated using the usual set primitives. This is described in detail in McHugh, 2004.

4. A FEW QUICK EXAMPLES

The next few figures show some typical samples of the kinds of information that can be derived from the flow data. They range from network wide analyses to examinations of the characteristics of specific subnets and even of specific hosts. The analysis system can be viewed as a powerful zoom lens. It is capable at looking at the overall traffic on a few percent of the internet at its widest angle, or at a single host at its highest magnification.

Characteristics of Small Sample

We looked at 1 minute of data from the monitored network. We estimated the set of hosts in the monitored network by creating the set of source IP addresses appearing on outgoing traffic during that period. While this is not perfect (spoofing of source addresses is possible), it provides a reasonable estimate of the currently active hosts. This set is used by the filter program to partition incoming traffic into that which is addressed to hosts that might possibly respond (the hit partition) and that which is addressed to apparently nonexistent hosts (the miss partition). The miss data appears to be largely a mix of scans (many of them blatant), and noise. The hit data also contains a mix of noise and scans addressed at active machines, but, most of it appears to be intentional communication between hosts. In terms of flows per destination and flows per source, the partitions have very different characteristics.

Figure 2 shows the flows per destination for the two partitions. In the miss partition, only about 0.1% of the destinations receive more than 9 flows while the corresponding figure for the hit partition is 2.4%. This probably is a consequence of multiple connections made to servers or from clients among the active hosts during the sample period. Figure 3 shows the flows per source for the two partitions. Again, the differences are striking. In the miss partition, more than 36% of the sources generate more than 9 flows while only 4% of the sources do so. This is evidence that many of the sources that appear in the miss partition are conducting high volume scans. Examples are shown in Figure 4.

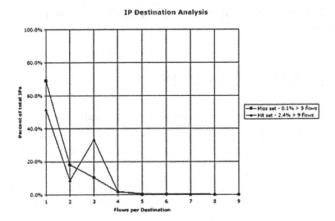

Figure 2. Reduction in Incoming IP Destination Set Sizes
as a Function of Number of Flows

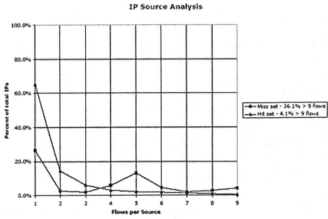

Figure 3. Reduction in Incoming IP Source and Destination Set Sizes
as a Function of Number of Flows

Figure 4 shows some of the results of this analysis. The destination set for this contains 12994 hosts, all from XXX.YYY.0.0/16 The hit set also contains entries from this network, 7 in all. All the flows sent to these addresses are 48 byte SYN packets addressed to port 4899 (listed as a "radmin" port by IANA, with other possible usages reported as ChiliASP and iMesh). An inspection of the outgoing traffic from this network indicates no responses to the connection attempts.

```
(39) lip$readbagcountprintjcmtcps10+.bag|sortrn|head
     12994 AAA.BBB.068.218
      6598 CCC.DDD.209.215
      5944 EEE.FFF.125.117
      5465 GGG.HHH.114.052
      5303 III.JJJ.164.126
```

Figure 4. The Top Five Sources in the Small Sample

The second entry is somewhat different. The traffic from this address scans a different /16. looking for responses on port 7100[1] (X Font service according to IANA). Some 112 responses are seen from hosts SSS.RRR.QQQ.178,120131,224254. The contiguous ranges and the consistency of responses on a relatively obscure port may indicate the presence of a honey pot or a similar decoy. In all cases, the connection seems to have been broken after the probed host's SYN/ACK reply.

The third and fourth entries are scans of portions of other /16s, this time looking for service on port 20168. This appears to be associated with the "Lovegate" worm which binds a shell to this port on infected machines.

The fifth entry is a scan of a portion of yet another /16, this time looking for service on port 3127. This port is currently being used by the "MyDoom.C" worm on Linux[2].

At the other end of the spectrum, there are 3335 external hosts that sent exactly one TCP flow into the monitored network during the analyzed time interval. Of these, only two port and flag combinations appear more than 100 times. SYN probes for port 8866[3] are seen 449 times. SYN probes for port 25 (SMTP email) are seen 271 times. The vast majority of the remainder are SYNs to a variety of ports, mostly with high port numbers. There are a number of ACK/RST packets which are probably associated with responses to spoofed DDoS attacks.

Massive Scanning: One Week on Another /16

Figure 5 shows evidence of massive scanning. In this case, we conservatively approximated the active population of the subnet by counting as a valid destination address any host that emitted traffic during the week. The solid line shows traffic directed to such hosts while the higher, dashed line shows traffic to vacant addresses. The highest peaks represent two scans of the entire subnet during a one hour period. Lower peaks represent scans of 40,00 to 65,000 hosts per hour. The investigated scans consist mostly of SYN packets to a variety of ports. Most of the target ports are used by Trojans or back doors.

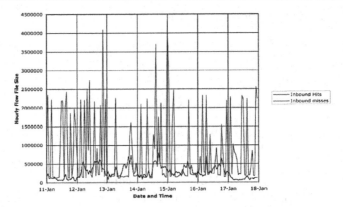

Figure 5. Evidence of Massive scanning on a /16

Subnet Characterization

It is possible to focus the analysis on the behavior of individual domains. Figures 6–8 show several aspects that can help to characterize a network, in this case a /16 with 2^{16} possible addresses. Figure 6 shows the active host population of the subnet as seen from the network border. Several things are immediately obvious. The most striking aspects of the network are the sparseness of the population and the weekly cycle of activity. Of the 256 possible /24 subnetworks only a handful appear to be populated. This is typical of many of the networks used by our customer. In addition, the activity level varies by day of the week. Note that April 4 and 11 are Sundays. There is a definite lull in the level of activity on those days as well as on April 10, a Saturday. On the other hand, April 3, another Saturday, shows activity peaks. This probably deserves further investigation. Note also that one small subnet has no weekly pattern and a very small population, but none of the active subnets is as much as 50% populated at its peak.

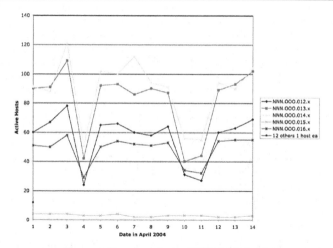

Figure 6. Host Activity on NNN.OOO.0.0/16

When we look at the hourly distribution of port activities, we see additional patterns. The system activity is consistent with an activity that operates 8 hours per day, 5 or 6 days per week. Looking at the top ten destination ports in Figure 7, we see evidence of a lot of web browsing combined with some email. The remaining ports in the top 10 list do not appear frequently enough to be visible on the chart. Source port activity as seen in Figure 8 is consistent with a substantial web secure web service with small amounts of normal web and email service. It would be possible to drill down further, looking at individual host activity, but we have not done so for this data.

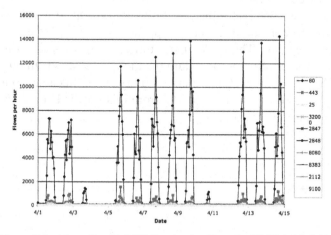

Figure 7. Inside to Outside TCP Destination Ports for NNN.OOO.0.0/16

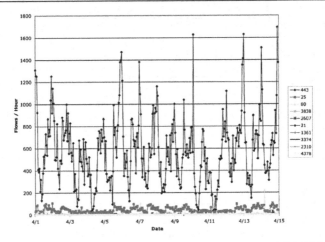

Figure 8. Inside to Outside TCP Source Ports for NNN.OOO.0.0/16

Host Characterization

One of the authors (Becknel) looked at host characterization based on port mixes. We developed the following visualizations to help in the process. The log scale on flows helps when there are large differences in flow volumes among ports. The data was NOT filtered by protocol and there is "noise" in the port fields for some protocols, especially ICMP and possibly others. Figures 9–11 show apparently normal behaviors for a workstation, a mail server, and a web server.

Figure 9 shows behaviors that are probably typical of a workstation. As seen from the border, the workstation appears to be used 7 days a week, but not 24 hours per day. The bulk of the traffic is web based with a mix of normal and secure services. In addition, there is a small amount of TCP activity. The lack of visible email activity is noticeable, but not too surprising. It is likely that email to and from this host is handled by a server inside the monitored network.

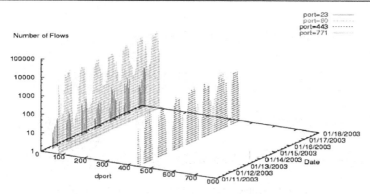

Figure 9. Apparently Normal Workstation Behavior

Figure 10 shows behavior that is consistent with that of a mail server. Note that SMTP and DNS activities occur at similar levels. This is consistent with the mail transmission process in which the host portion of the address must be converted to an IP address before the mail can be sent.

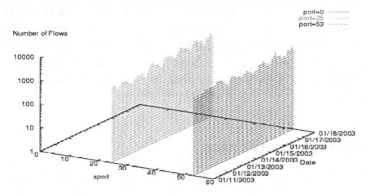

Figure 10. Apparently Normal Mail Server Behavior

Figure 11 shows traffic from a web server. Looking at the source port distribution shown in the figure, the bulk of the traffic appears to be normal HTTP with a small proportion of HTTPS.

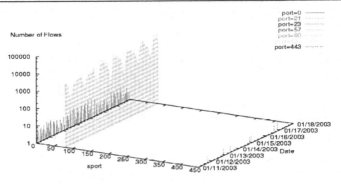

Figure 11. Outgoing Web Server Traffic by Source Port

5. ANALYSIS OF MISCONFIGURATIONS AND MALICIOUS ACTIVITY

Having given some consideration to various kinds of normal activity, we continue the exposition by considering a variety of situations in which undesirable activities become manifest. These cover a variety of levels of detail, ranging from individual host behaviors to examples of network attacks such as worm and DDoS attacks that are visible at the border of the monitored network to persistent global phenomena.

Questionable Host Behavior

The source port distribution of the traffic originating at the web server shown in Figure 11 appears to be normal, but the destination port distribution as shown in Figure 12 is distinctly peculiar. The web server is originating a substantial quantity of port 80 traffic, uncommon for a pure server (which this appears to be). Examining the traffic in detail is interesting. Each port 80 flow starts with a flow of several packets with a total volume of a few hundred bytes. Since the flow contains both SYN and ACK flags, we infer that a TCP handshake has occurred, but the absence of a FIN or RST flag implies an open connection with the flow closed by an inactivity timeout. Two minutes later, another flow on the connection occurs, this one with a single packet of about 50 bytes and an ACK flag. This repeats every two minutes, sometimes for hours at a time until the connection is closed. The high flow volumes shown in the figure result from many simultaneous similar connections. A search for the other side of the connections shows no traffic, but we may be dealing with an uninstrumented router or a collection failure as the data originated early in the collection effort. The destinations of the connections are in address spaces that are associated with individual customers of several national ISPs. Attempts to contact several of the target addresses produced mixed results, but none of the addresses contacted were running generally accessible web servers. Since the contact attempts were made months after the original observations, this may not be significant.

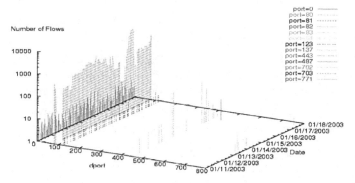

Figure 12. Outgoing Web Server Traffic Destination Port

Figure 13 shows the activity of a very active scanner. Examination of the outgoing traffic depicted in the figure shows a combined vertical (port) and horizontal (address) scan in which every port up to 1024 is being scanned. The scan rate is in excess of 100,000 per hour or about 30 per second. The target of the scan is another subnetwork in the monitored network, albeit one with a different point of attachment to the internet, so that we may be observing a routine, but sustained, legitimate mapping effort.

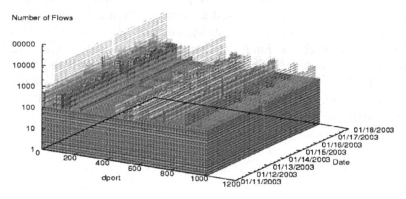

Figure 13. A Very Active Scanner

Routing Anomalies and Back Doors

We are able to detect a variety of routing anomalies through examination of the flow data. Figure 14 shows a case where increasing amounts of foreign traffic was being routed through the client network. At one point, this came to the attention of a network operator and much of the traffic was blocked, only to slowly reappear over time as the operator's attention was concentrated elsewhere.

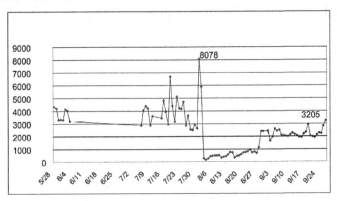

Figure 14. A Routing Anomaly

Examining Denial of Service Attacks

Address spoofing during a Distributed Denial of Service (DDoS) attack can drastically change the observed address distributions. This is shown strikingly in Figure 15. Under "normal" circumstances, only a relatively small number (on the order of 50) of /8 prefixes (the value of the high order octet of the IP address) are observed as sources entering a monitored subnet during a typical hour of operation. At the onset of a large scale DDoS attack the number of prefixes jumps to almost 250 (of 255). When various unroutable or unrouted prefixes are taken into account, this is the maximum that are likely to be observed originating on the internet backbone. The intervals when the number of prefixes drops to 0 are the result of collector failure due to traffic overload.

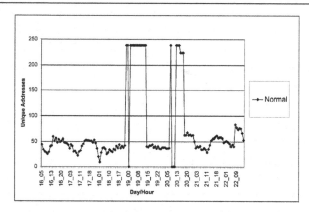

Figure 15. DDoS Address Distribution

Examining Worms in Action

The presence of active worms is indicated by a variety of observable phenomena. Scanning worms are particularly obvious as can be seen in Figure 16 which shows UDP activity from roughly 1 May 2002 through the end of February 2003. A dramatic increase in activity is clearly visible near the center of the figure at the end of August 2002. This is attributed to the release of the Opaserv worm which causes massive scanning on UDP port 137.

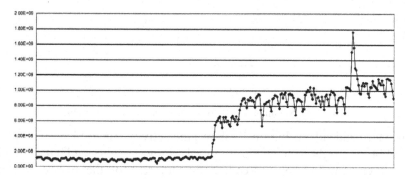

Figure 16. Opaserv Worm Behavior

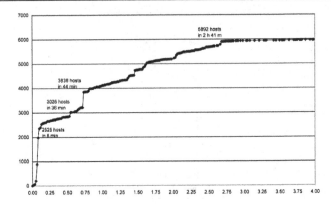

Figure 17. Slammer Worm Behavior

Slammer was a very rapidly spreading UDP worm. It infected over 6000 machines in the monitored network. Figure 17 shows the growth of the infection within the network. The exponential growth phase lasts only about 8 minutes with 2525 hosts being infected in that period. Half of the hosts eventually infected were compromised with the first 36 minutes. A large jump in infected machines occurred during minute 43. The linear growth phase tapered off after 2 h 41 m, by which time 97.5% of the hosts eventually infected had been compromised.

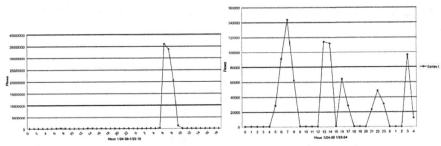

Figure 18. Slammer Traffic (left), Slammer Precursor (right)

The lefthand side of Figure 18 shows the activity due to Slammer on UDP port 1434. The right hand side of Figure 18 shows activity on UDP port 1434 in the hours immediately preceding the outbreak of the worm. Note the differences in scale. The precursor traffic is lost in the baseline of the Slammer Attack. Our analysis focused on hours 6, 7, 8, 13, and 14. We identified three primary sources of the activity, all from sources that were known as adversaries by the analyst. All 3 used a fixed pattern of scanning. We identified four machines that responded to the initial probing. Two of the responders were subsequently compromised.

MISSILE—Scan Detection

The MISSILE scan detection system, which is being deployed operationally, examines characteristics of all TCP flows from each source, looking for activity that indicates a scan. If also looks at "event level" data for scans (e.g., majority of flows consisting only of just SYN packets, malformed packets designed to provoke specific responses from certain TCP implementations, etc.)

As an example, we analyzed one /16 in the monitored network for one week. During this period, we examined 24,114,559 flows consuming 3 hours of processing time on a well provisioned Linux workstation. The analysis identified 7481 unique source IP address as scanning. Of these, 1436 attempted to exploit target hosts during the scanning process. 5667 sources were identified as performing SYN scanning. The identified scanning is fairly high volume with an average of 452 destinations/source. The most prolific scanner seen during this period attempted 196073 contacts (3 ports (1080, 3128 and 10080) on 65469 IPs) in a period of about 8 hours.

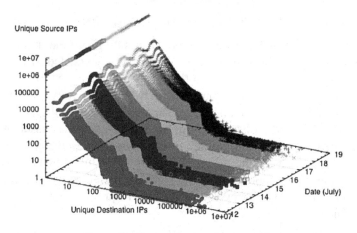

Figure 19. Contact Surface for July 2003

Scan Detection and the Contact Surface

Scanners typically probe a network attempting to determine the addresses of hosts within the network and to discover whether the discovered hosts are running vulnerable services. For a sparsely populated network, a scanner without prior knowledge of the host distribution might be expected to attempt a large number of contacts with a relatively small success rate. One of us (Gates) has been working on the problem of identifying subtle scanners, i.e., those who do not launch large numbers of probes such as those seen in Figure 5 above. In an attempt to discover the nature of "normal" contact behavior in the monitored network, she developed the graphical "contact surface" shown in Figures 19 and 20 These show that the contract distribution when described as the number of outside hosts seen in a given hour who contact a specific number of inside hosts during that hour approximately follows a power law distribution.

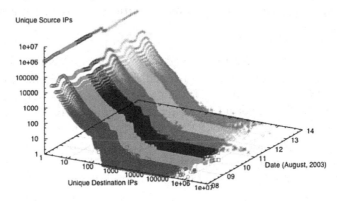

Figure 20. Contact Surface for August 2003

The power law distribution is not too surprising given that many network connection patterns follow such laws. What was unexpected, however, was the persistent wave structure seen in the left hand side of the Figure 19. This surface is for a week in July, but a similar surface persists from January through mid August where it abruptly disappears as seen in Figure 20.

Figure 21 shows the distribution of source IP addresses associated with the wave phenomenon. Each "spike" in the figure represents activity from a given /8 prefix. The left hand side of the figure is for July when the wave was present for the whole month while the right hand side shows the changes in distribution as the wave disappears in August. Figure 22 shows details of the disappearance over several days.

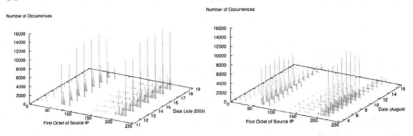

Figure 21. Wave Address Prefix Distributions(July–left and August–right)

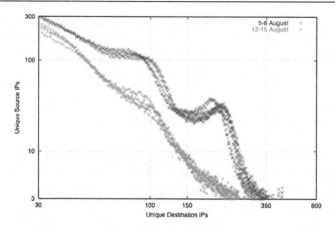

Figure 22. The Disappearing Wave

Phase 1 of the activity persisted from January–August; the following are details for 1 week in July.

- 91% port 80, 87% SYN, 96% unique sIP/dIP pairs
- 49% to 60 /16s in 1 /8, 50% of the 49% to 5 /16s 14% to 1 /16, 48 /24s with less than 3.2% each, no specific target
- 14% to another /8
- 3 /8 sources 46%, 34%, 20% respectively (2–Asia Pacific, 1–South American)
- Too slow to be DoS. Too persistent for scan?

Blaster was released on August 11. Could this be the related? Phase 2 occurred from mid February– early June, 2004 with similar characteristics and sources, but with 23% of the traffic to a now /8. This appears to be well coordinated activity, but what, or why?

6. SUMMARY, CONCLUSIONS AND FUTURE DIRECTIONS

We have an unprecedented ability to examine network traffic for long periods of time and at large volumes. We are investigating a number of techniques for analyzing it. One of the current tasks is the identification of low rate and distributed scans. Another is characterization of denials of service attacks and the investigation of countermeasures. We are also trying to develop general techniques for identifying machines that have been compromised. In the future, we hope to acquire data from additional sources and to look at different network topologies. In particular, we would like to look at interior nodes and subnets as well as border traffic. Much of our original work has been of direct benefit to our customers and we hope to continue in that tradition.

CREDIT WHERE CREDIT IS DUE

The work represented in this paper is the result of efforts by the entire Situational Awareness team at CERT. The late Suresh L. Konda was, and remains, the inspiration for this program. His vision is largely responsible for the current shape of the program. Mike Collins, Andrew Kompanek, and the SiLKtools developers especially Mark Thomas and Mike Duggan continue to carry the program forward, supporting additional analyses and viewpoints. CERT analysts and users of the data have contributed to many of the results that have been presented in the paper. These include Marc Kellner, Mike Collins, and Jim McCurley. Finally, Tom Longstaff has made the whole effort possible by managing the unmanageable.

NOTES

1. **http://www.cert.org/advisories/CA200234.html**d describes a vulnerability in the X font service on Solaris. It is likely that the scanner was looking for machines that could be attacked.

2. **http://www.linuxworld.com/story/43628.htm**

3. "W32.Beagle.B@mm is a massmailing worm that opens a back door on TCP port 8866. The worm uses its own SMTP engine for email propagation. It can also send to the attacker the port on which the back door listens, as well as a randomized ID number." according to
    http://securityresponse.symantec.com/avcenter/venc/data/w32.beagle.b@mm.html

REFERENCES

Cisco Systems (1999), Flow collector overview, found on web at
   http://www.cisco.com/univercd/cc/td/doc/product/rtrmgmt/nfc/nfc_3_0/nfc%_ug/nfco ver.htm

Fullmer, M. and S. Romig, (2000), The OSU flowtools package and Cisco NetFlow logs, in *LISA XIV*, pages 291–303, New Orleans.

McHugh, J. (2004). Sets, bags, and rock and roll: Analysis of large sets of network data, in *Proceedings of ESORICS 2004*, volume 3193 of *LNCS*, Springer.

PART 4

EARLY WARNING INFORMATION SYSTEMS AND SECURE ACCESS CONTROL

HONEYNETS: FOUNDATIONS FOR THE DEVELOPMENT OF EARLY WARNING INFORMATION SYSTEMS

F. Pouget, M. Dacier, V.H. Pham
Institut Eurecom
2229, route des Crêtes ; BP193
06904 Sophia-Antipolis Cedex ; France
pouget,dacier,pham} @eurecom.fr

H. Debar
France Telecom R&D[1]
42, rue des Coutures; BP 6243
14066 Caen Cedex 4 ; France
herve.debar@francetelecom.com

Abstract: This paper aims at presenting in some depth the "Leurré.com" project and its first results. The project aims at deploying so-called low level interaction honeypot platforms all over the world to collect in a centralized database a set of information amenable to the analysis of today's Internet threats. At the time of this writing, around two dozens platforms have been deployed in the five continents. The paper offers some insight into the findings that can be derived from such data set. More importantly, the design and the structure of the repository are presented and justified by means of several examples that highlight the simplicity and efficiency of extracting useful information out of it. We explain why such low cost, largely distributed system represents an important, foundational element, towards the building of early warning information systems.

Keywords: Honeynet; Internet Attacks; Database; Malware; Cybercrime

---

[1] This research is supported by a research contract with France Telecom R&D, Contract Number 46127561

J. S. Kowalik et al. (eds.), Cyberspace Security and Defense: Research Issues, 231–257.
© 2005 *Springer. Printed in the Netherlands.*

1. INTRODUCTION

The mere existence and success of workshops such as WORM, DIMVA and SRUTI ([1], [2], [3]) indicate that Internet-wide infectious epidemics have emerged as one of the leading threats to information security and service availability. Important contributions have been made in the past that have proposed propagation models ([4], [5], [6]) or that have analyzed, usually by reverse engineering specific worms, their modus operandi [7], [8], [9], [10]. Several initiatives exist to monitor real world data related to worms and attacks propagation. The Internet telescopes, the DShield web site, the work reported by John McHugh in [11] are among them. These approaches are extremely valuable and have in common the wish to collect very large amount of data collected thanks to a large amount of monitored addresses.

By launching the Leurré.com project in the course of 2004, we have decided to take a different, yet complimentary, approach. Instead of collecting aggregated information, such as Netflow records, about a very large number of connections and hosts, we have decided to keep in one centralized database very precise information concerning a very limited number of nodes under close scrutiny. Furthermore, we have proposed to several partners to join the project by hosting such data collection platform. Concretely speaking, we do use low interaction honeypots, based on the honeyd software [12], emulating 3 vulnerable machines on a single home computer. We do record all packets sent to or from these machines, on all platforms, and we store the whole content of all the packets into a database. Special care must be taken in the design of the database to offer an easy and intuitive way to retrieve interesting information.

Before launching the Leurré.com project, we have investigated the usefulness of honeypots to analyze Internet threats. Therefore, a first platform has been deployed for almost two years and its results analyzed. Experience gained led to the publications of several papers and to several iterations in the design of the database used to store the information. The most important results can be summarized as follows:

- In [13], we present early results based on a couple of months of data highlighting the potential of the data set we were in the process of building. The apparent limited number of attacks as well as the regularity of their origins is presented and explained.

- In [14], we introduce a clustering algorithm to group together traces of attacks likely due to the same attack tool. The method is presented, a technique to test the consistency of the obtained clusters is offered and experimental results, based on 16 months of data are detailed.

- In [15] we highlight, based on concrete cases, the limitations of the other approaches such as the internet telescopes or Dshield. We discuss the aftermath of a very atypical worm, the Deloder one, as we see it from our honeypot point of view. We also describe an experimentation protocol, as well as its results, aiming at validating the assumption that several groups of attackers are exchanging information on the Internet in a non trivial way.

All these results have been obtained thanks to a single platform collecting data from one environment only. Encouraged by these results, we have decided to collect the very same kind of data from a diversity of places. This led to the creation of the Leurré.com project. A key element for the success of such project is its ability to store large amount of data and, more importantly, to offer its users a simple way to retrieve meaningful pieces of it efficiently. This is where the design of the centralized database plays a key role. In the next Sections, we will present not only the structure of this database but also how it can be used to bring to light some ongoing attack processes in the Internet. Using several examples, we will present in parallel the structure of the database and the results it delivers to us.

The structure of the paper is as follows. Section 2 introduces the design of the platform we are using. Section 3 details the raw data we can get from the platforms we monitor and how this information can be stored in and retrieved from the database. Section 4 explains the need for enriching this data set with several kinds of external related information such as, for instance, the geographical locations of the attacking sources. For each new type of added attribute, we explain how it fits into the general database structure and, by means of examples, how one can take advantage of it. Section 5 explains why, from a usability point of view, it is also important to build what we call meta-data tables. These are tables that contain redundant information that could be retrieved by means of SQL queries on the database but that, for some efficiency reasons, we explicitly include as part of its design. Examples are given. Section 6 concludes the paper.

2. HONEYPOTS

2.1 Initial Set Up

Table 1. VMWare-Based Environment, a Big Picture

Average daily tcpdump file size	1.5 Mbytes
Maximum file size	9.6 Mbytes
Number of files collected	516 days
Average number of packets per tcpdump file	13600 packets

A detailed description of our initial platform as well as a thorough treatment of the state of the art in honeypots is given in [16]. This first platform is a so-called high interaction honeypot. It consists in a VMWare virtual environment with three virtual machines running various Operating systems (Linux RedHat, Windows 98, and Windows NT) and services (ftp server, web server, etc.). Virtual machines are built on non-persistent disks [17] which means that changes are lost when machines are powered off or reset. In other words, rebooting a compromised machine offers us a new, clean, environment. This platform has been deployed in February 2003. We collect every day all traffic coming from or to the three virtual machines in tcpdump pcap files [18]. Table 1 summarizes the files characteristics we have obtained from February 2003 until now. The total number of collected files represents the amount of days during which the platform was up and running.

2.1.1 Distributed Honeypots

The results obtained with this initial platform and summarized here above have shown that most of the attacks are caused by a few numbers of attack tools and that there are very stable processes occurring in the wild. Furthermore, as discussed in [15], the fingerprinting capability of the attack tools appears to be very limited. Therefore, one can reasonably decides to use low, instead of high, interaction honeypots despite the fact that they can be easily identified by a remote attacker. A low interaction honeypot being much cheaper to implement in terms of software and hardware, our hope is to see many institutions volunteering to deploy such a platform on their premises, whereas they wouldn't have been eager to pay the price of a full fledged high interaction honeypot.

As a consequence, we have implemented a new platform similar to the one presented before, but with emulated operating systems and services. We have developed such a platform based on open source software[2]: it emulates three different Operating Systems, Windows 98, Windows NT Server and Red Hat 7.3 respectively. The platform only needs a single host station, which is carefully secured by means of access controls and integrity checks. Every day, we connect to the host station machine to retrieve traffic logs and to check its security logs.

In the context of the Leurré.com project, we have started deploying these platforms all over the world [19]. At the time of this writing, we have deployed 25 platforms, in 5 continents and 12 different countries. We invite the interested reader to look at [20] for a first analysis of this distributed honeypot architecture.

Table 2 gives an overview of the data which is collected every day for these 25 platforms. We only consider here the tcpdump pcap files. Volumes vary greatly between platforms. For instance, log files collected on one German platform can be as twenty times bigger than those of one Lithuanian platform, whereas the number of collected packets can be almost thirty times higher. Therefore, this Table does not fairly represent any of the platforms but gives a rough idea of the amount of data we deal with.

Table 2. LEURRE.COM Project, the Big Picture

Average daily dump file size	114 Kbytes
Maximum file size	13 Mbytes
Number of collected files	1492 files

3. RAW COLLECTED DATA

3.1 Raw Data

As explained in Section 2, we collect from the different honeypot platforms tcpdump files which contain observed suspicious packets. We also collect other information, such as application log files to verify the integrity of the platforms but these lie outside the scope of the paper as they are not used to analyze the attacks we face. It is worth noting that broadcast and multicast traffic is filtered out from the tcpdump files we collect (e.g., arp traffic, Cisco Discovery Protocol CDP, Spanning-Tree Protocol STP, etc.). In other words, we only are interested in packets from/to the honeypot virtual machines specifically. At the network level, these are mainly IP and ICMP packets. At the transport protocol, they are mainly UDP and TCP ones.

---

[2] The platform implements a modified version of Honeyd at this time.

3.2 New Definitions

This data needs to be properly organized as it will be used for further analysis and experiments. One major remark is that it is not obvious, *a priori*, to define what the best structure of the database could be as we do not know the most frequent queries that we will have to run on the dataset. As explained before, this is the reason why we went through several iterations in its design, as we were progressing with our research. The result presented here appears to have reached a relative stability, based on several months of work with it.

In theory, no traffic should be observed to or from the machines we have set up. As a matter of fact, many packets hit the different virtual machines, coming from different IP addresses. Typically, if an attacker decides to choose one of our honeypots as his next victim, he tries to establish direct TCP connections or to send UDP packets against it. We group all these attempts into what we call a *"Tiny Session"* by contrast to the notion of *"Large Session"* which includes all *Tiny Sessions* that a given attacker might have launched against a given platform. In our setup, as we have three honeypots, a *Large Session* can be made of 1 to 3 *Tiny Sessions*. This idea of *Tiny* and *Large Sessions* is at the core of the design of the database. Therefore, the five most important tables in the database are the following ones:

- *Host:* this table contains all attributes (or links to other tables containing attributes) required to characterize one honeypot virtual machine.
- *Environment:* this table contains all attributes (or links to other tables containing attributes) required to characterize one honeypot platform, i.e., a group of three *hosts*.
- *Source:* this table gathers all attributes (or links to other tables containing attributes) required to characterize one attacking IP within one day.
- *Large_Session:* this table contains all attributes (or links to other tables containing attributes) required to characterize the activity of one *Source* observed against one *Environment*.
- *Tiny_Session:* this table contains all attributes (or links to other tables containing attributes) required to characterize the activity of one *Source* observed against one *Host*.

It is worth noting that, according to these definitions, we consider that we have two distinct *Sources* of attacks when a given attacking IP address is observed twice on the same Environment with more than 24 hours between the two observations. The reason for this doing is experimental. We have found out that it was extremely rare, not to say impossible, to see Large

Session lasting more than a couple of seconds. It is also extremely rare to observe the same IP address in multiple days. Last but not least, we do know that most of the attacks come from personal PCs which, usually, use temporary addresses [15], [16]. For all these reasons, it is quite likely that the same IP address observed in two different days is not linked to a single physical machine. Therefore, it makes sense to separate, in the database, the activities of the first from the activities of the second one by giving them distinct Source identifiers.

The Entity-Relationship diagram presented in Figure 1 exhibits the respective roles of these tables. The relationship between *Source* and *Environment* is called *Large_Session*. The relationship between one *Source* and one *Host* is called a *Tiny_Session*.

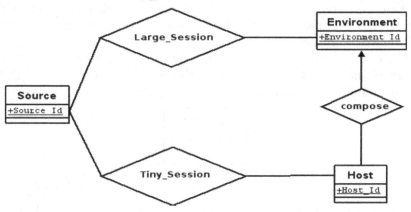

Figure 1. Entity Relationship Diagram

3.3 Database Construction

The purpose of the Entity-Relationship model is to allow the description of the conceptual scheme. It is normal to turn it into a practical relational model upon which the real database is built. There exists a vast amount of knowledge and a rich literature explaining how to optimize this process, with respect to various types of constraints (speed, memory consumption, table sizes, number of indices, etc.). We invite the interested reader to see [21], [22], for instance, for more on this topic.

Typically, the theory on the 'good' design of relational databases has been looking at problems such as: data redundancy in the tables, *update and insertion* anomaly issues. These problems are classically solved by transforming non optimal entity relationships models into their so-called "normal forms" (*Third Normal Form, Boyce-Codd Normal Form*). In our case though, the problem is slightly different and offers us the freedom not to follow that path. There are two important reasons for that. Firstly, we do not care about update and insertion anomaly issues as we do not touch to the data once they are inserted into the database. Indeed, the stored information is something that we have no reason to modify as it represents a fact of the past. Secondly, we do care a lot about the efficiency of querying the database and are not too concerned by space efficiency (be it on disk or in memory) as the total amount of data we deal with remains rather modest, compared to what existing database systems can handle. Therefore, we do have consciously decided to introduce in our design tables that contain redundant information. In other words, these tables contain information that could be retrieved by querying other tables. However, having the results of such queries available at hand in ad-hoc tables proves to be extremely useful when using the database. As a consequence, we decide to keep them, acknowledging the fact that, without their presence, the database would be more 'optimal' according to the classical criteria.

These remarks have been carefully taken into account for the database implementation. Figure 2 represents the Unified Modeling Language (UML) class diagram we have chosen corresponding to the ER diagram in Figure 1.

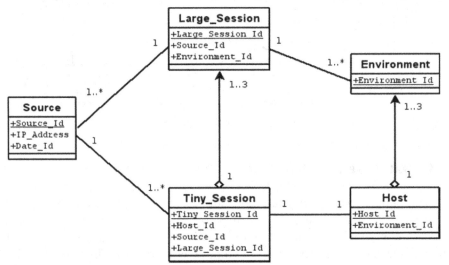

Figure 2. UML Class Diagram

Primary keys are underlined in Figure 2. For the *Source* table, the key *Source_Id* is equivalent to the expected double key (*IP_Address,Date_Id*). For the *Large_Session* table, the primary key *Large_Session_Id* is equivalent to the expected double key (*Source_Id,Environment_Id*). Finally, similarly to the two last cases, the primary key *Tiny_Session_Id* from table *Tiny_Session* is equivalent to the expected key pair (*Source_Id, Host_Id*). Some redundancies have also been introduced on purpose: as an illustration, the

Large_Session_Id attribute in the *Tiny_Session* table can be potentially removed. Indeed, it is always possible to identify the Large Session a given Tiny Session belongs just by knowing its Host_Id and Source_Id. We show in the following that this redundancy is however beneficial for performance improvements. Moreover, it greatly simplifies the process of writing new queries.

Raw packets were not presented in the previous figure for clarity concerns, but they are definitely stored. They are parsed and stored in tables similar to those used by the Snort Intrusion Detection System [23]. Packets are either coming from a Host or from a Source. They are linked to a given Tiny Session. Figure 3 presents the resulting new tables. Each packet has its unique identifier, called *cid*. The reader can easily deduce the global graph from the two Figures 2 and 3. In the following, we will keep introducing new tables, in an incremental way. We will represent only the relevant information as the representation of the whole schema appears to be rather difficult. We invite the interested reader to contact us if he wants to obtain the whole diagram.

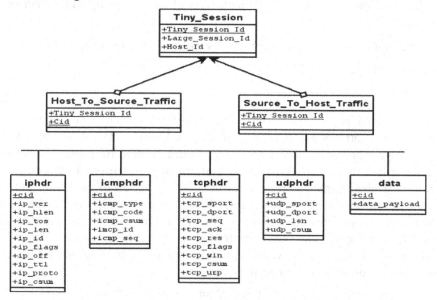

Figure 3. Raw Packet Storage

3.4 Illustrative Examples

At the end of 2004, the database contains 17 Gbytes. The tables presented in Section 3.3 have been implemented in a MySQL [24] database running on a RedHat 9.0 server, with 2GHz, 80 GB ROM and 1GB RAM. The entries for the previously introduced tables are given in Table 3.

Table 3. Number of Table Entries in 11/04

Table names	Number of entries
Source	511 415
Large Session	525 152
Tiny Session	933 536
Environment	25
Host	75

From these tables, it is now very simple to answer questions like the four following ones:

1. How many *Sources* have been observed per *Environment*?

2. How many *Hosts* have been targeted by each *Source*?

3. How many *Sources* have been observed from multiple *Environments*?

4. What is the percentage of IP addresses observed during more than one day?

The first question can be answered by means of the following SQL query:

```
➢ SELECT Environment_Id, count(Source_Id) FROM Large_Session
  GROUP BY Environment_Id
```

The output is a two-column table. It gives for each environment (left column) the corresponding number of observed Sources (right column). This is partially-represented in the second and third column of Table 4 in which we see a large diversity in the number of hits against various Environments. Of course, this number is relative to the activity period of each platform as they did not start at the same time. A better output consists in dividing the total number of observed Sources by the number of active days. This provides the average number of Sources observed each day on each platform. Even in this case, we observe on some platforms twenty times more Sources per day than on some others, in the average.

Table 4. Number of Observed Attack Sources per Platform

Platforms	Number of Observed Sources	Number of days the platform has been active	Average number of Source observed each day
Platform 1 (France, industry)	58791	70	840
Platform 2 (France, academy)	21781	121	180

Platforms	Number of Observed Sources	Number of days the platform has been active	Average number of Source observed each day
Platform3 (Germany, academy)	109426	105	1042
Platform 4 (Lithuania, academy)	7841	156	50
Platform 5 (USA, industry)	22784	79	285

The clear difference between Large_Session entries and Tiny_Session entries in Table 3 indicates that many attacks target more than one virtual machine. This is verified when answering to our second question by means of the following SQL query:

➢ SELECT Source_Id, count(Tiny_Session_Id) FROM Tiny_Session
  GROUP BY Source_Id

The output is a two-column table which provides for each Source_Id (left column) the associated number of *Tiny_Sessions* (right column). As a reminder, all the exchanges of packets between one Source and one Host are part of a single *Tiny_Session*. We find out with this request that in average, 54% of the Sources have targeted the three virtual machines. A closer look also indicates that they always have targeted the three virtual machines in the same order, the sequential order. 40% of the observed *Sources* have targeted one and only one virtual machine. The remaining 6% *Sources* have targeted two out of the three honeypots.

The answer to the third question tells us if some IP addresses have been observed on multiple platforms the very same day. This is given by the following query:

➢ SELECT Source_Id, count(Large_Session_Id) FROM Large_Session
  GROUP BY Source_Id

This request reveals that 9995 out of the 511415 *Sources* (i.e., less than 2% of the *Sources*) have been observed on more than one platform the very same day, by definition of the notions of *Source* and *Large Session*.

The fourth question goes one step further than the previous one by looking at the percentage of IP addresses that have been observed on two different days. In other words, how many IP addresses are found under more than one *Source* identifier? This number can be found by dividing the result of this query:

➢ SELECT count(distinct(IP_Address)) FROM Source

By the result of this other one:

➤ `SELECT count(Source_Id) FROM Source`

The result is around 91%. This simply means that it is unlikely to observe the same attacking IP address twice on the same platform. The last two questions highlight the fact that, first, attacks are issued from a very large pool of IP addresses and, second, that it might not be worth the effort of implementing the notion of blacklists [25] since, apparently, a few of them are observed more than once.

4. ADDITIONAL INFORMATION

4.1 IP Geographical Location

4.1.1 Various Information

The geographical location of IPs can represent interesting information to better understand where the attacks are coming from. We initially used one utility called Netgeo, developed in the context of the CAIDA project [26]. NetGeo is made of a collection of Perl scripts that map IP addresses to geographical locations. This software is open source and has been applied in several research papers, among which [27], [28], [29], [30]. However, as we show in [15], there are some differences with other tools like MaxMind, IP2location or GeoBytes [31], [32], [33]. The reason is that Netgeo returns in many cases the geographical location of the Autonomous System (AS) instead of the real location of the IP itself. Thus, we have decided to include into our database the geographical information provided by several tools and leave it up to the user to choose the one whom he felt more comfortable with. This offers us as well the opportunity to test and compare the results of these tools. We have subscribed to a commercial solution called MaxMind, and have made some comparisons with demo versions of commercial tools like IP2location and GeoBytes [32], [33].

4.1.2 Database Modifications

The geographical information has to be considered for one IP at a given point in time. Indeed, the location can change over months (see Maxmind updates presented in [31] for instance). For this reason, the geographical location is linked to the notion of *Source*. Two choices are possible here. The first solution consists in adding into the *Source* table one attribute for each utility which will be a pointer to its output. This method is not practical, as it requires modifying permanently the Source table for each tool application. On the other hand, the second solution considers that the geographical location characterizes a *Source* but also represents a new and important information type. Thus a new table called Geographical_Information is introduced. This enables us to leave the important *Source* table unchanged. Details are presented in Figure 4.

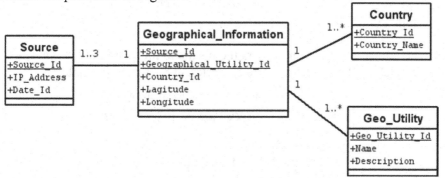

Figure 4. Geographical Information on the Attacks

One *Geographical_Information* entry is defined by the primary key pair (*Source_Id, Geographical_Utility_Id*).   It   returns   the   corresponding *Country_Id* provided by the *Geo_Utility* whose identifier is *Geo_Utility_Id*. The table *Country* maps the full country name associated to the Country_Id. Luckily enough, all tools are using the same Country_Id. It consists in 2 letters, as specified in the ISO 3166-1 alpha-2Code [34]. Thus, it is very easy to directly work on the *Country_Id* attribute, as shown with the examples given below.

4.1.3 Examples

A very simple SQL request enables us to get an idea of the amount of differences between the outputs provided by the various tools.

```
➢ SELECT Source_Id, count(distinct(Country_Id)) FROM
   Geographical_Information GROUP BY Source_Id
```

This gives a two-column output. If the values in the second column are strictly higher than one, it means that the same *Source* is seen as belonging to different countries by the various tools. As a matter of fact, we find out that Maxmind and Netgeo give a different result for 65% of the *Sources*. This result is obtained by looking at the number of cases where two different countries are assigned to the very same *Source*. The comparison with another tool called IP2location ([32]) confirms Maxmind results.

It is usually said that most of the attacks originate from China and the United States of America. This is confirmed by the following request which focuses on the results provided by Maxmind (identified by *Geographical_Utility_Id* = 2)

```
➢ SELECT Country_Id, count(Source_Id) n FROM
  Geographical_Information WHERE Geographical_Utility_Id = 2
  GROUP BY Country_Id ORDER BY n
```

The ORDER BY command orders the results in increasing order. Thus, it is easy to pick up the ten most active countries, as presented in Table 5.

Table 5. Top 10 Attacking Countries for all Sources

Top Ten attacking Countries for all Sources (given in decreasing number of importance)	Number of Observed Sources
US – The USA	77621
TW – Taiwan	48440
CN – China	40046
DE – Germany	34348
FR – France	26911
KR – Republic of Korea	24496
ES – Spain	22756
JP – Japan	20602
GB – The United Kingdom	19771
CA – Canada	18286

More generally, 185 distinct countries have been observed since the beginning of this experiment. It is worth noting that there are 191 countries members of the United Nations and 192 countries are recognized by the United States State Department.

We also note that 10 countries are responsible for more than 66% of the attacks while 175 countries are for the remaining 34%. This analysis can also be performed per platform. This is done by introducing the notion of *Environment* into the previous request:

```
➢ SELECT Country_Id, count(Source_Id) n FROM
  Geographical_Information, Large_Session WHERE
  Geographical_Utility_Id = 2 AND Large_Session.Source_Id =
  Geographical_Information.Source_Id AND
```

```
Large_Session.Environment_Id = 21 GROUP BY Country_Id ORDER
BY n
```

We apply the same request than previously, but we only consider here Sources having targeted the Environment 21. An analysis of the evolution of the attacks per country has been performed in [20]. We refer the interested reader to this paper for more results on the analysis of the attacks based on geographical information.

4.2 Passive OS Fingerprinting

4.2.1 Various Utilities

Many worms propagate through Windows machines [9], [10], [35]. Others target specific Linux services [36], [37]. In all cases, it seems that there exists some correlation between the Operating System of the attacker and the attack type it is performing. Many techniques exist to determine/fingerprint the operating system of machines, even if they are not all perfect. They are often classified as *active* when they send specific traffic to the machine to probe its OS. On the contrary, so-called *passive* fingerprinting methods rely on the observation of packets without interacting with the machine. This last approach is far more interesting in our case. Indeed, we want our honeypot machines to remain passive. Indeed, we do not want to show to the attacker that his activities are under observation.

A dozen of utilities implements passive fingerprinting techniques. Most of them compare packet fields to a given fingerprints database. A match means that the OS has been determined. Some tools differ by the answer provided in the case of uncertainty, others by their fingerprinting tables. As a consequence, we have decided to use three different passive fingerprinting utilities, with the possibility to add new ones later on if needed. They are respectively called Disco, p0f and ettercap [38], [39], [40]. They all use tcpdump pcap files as input. Their output is in text format which we parse to store the information into the database. Details of the tables are provided in the next Section.

4.2.2 Database Modifications

Supposedly, the OS fingerprinting qualifies a given attack *Source*. However, for practical reasons, we have decided to run the OS fingerprinting process on a per platform basis. As a consequence, we consider that the OS fingerprinting information is related to a given *Large_Session* and not to a given *Source*. Details on the database architecture are presented in Figure 5.

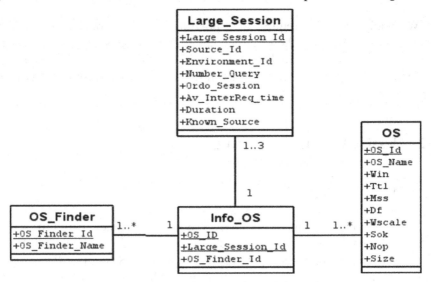

Figure 5. Passive OS Fingerprinting Information

There are two options here, as with the geographical location information. The first solution consists in introducing a new attribute in the *Large_Session* table for each fingerprinting tool. The second solution consists in having the OS information in a new table called *Info_OS*. Using a similar reasoning as before, we decide to use the second option. Each entry is totally determined by the triple key (*Large_Session_Id*, *OS_Finder_Id*, *OS_Id*). The OS table contains all fingerprints, even those which are not currently determined.

4.2.3 Some Applications

It appears that a comparison between fingerprinting tools is not straightforward. Indeed, the tools rely on different fingerprints database. As a consequence, two same signatures might not be associated exactly to the same OS(s). For instance, the very same signature will be detected as "*Windows 2000 SP2+, XP SP1 (seldom 98 4.10.2222)*" by p0f and as "*Windows XP Pro,S*" by Disco. A naive comparison will claim that these are two different operating systems. On the other hand, they both point out that the attack *Source* runs on a Windows machine. This can be an interesting hint to better characterize the *Source* profile.

To avoid such a problem, we make use of regular expressions. They can also be easily implemented with MySQL. Thus, if we are interested in looking at the number of attacking *Sources* considered to be Windows machines by p0f (OS_Finder=2), we write the following request:

```
➤ SELECT count(distinct(Source_Id)) FROM Large_Session,
  Info_OS, OS WHERE Large_Session.Large_Session_Id =
  Info_OS.Large_Session_Id AND Info_OS.OS_Id = OS.OS_Id AND
  OS.Name REGEXP "Windows"
```

We count all the distinct sources to avoid counting multiple times all sources having targeted multiples platforms. By repeating this query with various parameters, we obtain the comparison proposed in Table 6:

Table 6. Comparison Between Three Passive OS Fingerprinting Tools

Passive Fingerprinting Tools	Detected "Windows" Machines	Detected "linux/unix/solaris" machines	Number of returned undetermined values
Disco	66%	0.3%	33.7%
P0f	81.8%	0.5%	17.7%
Ettercap	77,6%	0.4%	22%

All tools agree that the majority of attacks are coming from Windows machines. P0f and Ettercap give very high percentage values for these machines. We also notice that Disco has a high rate of undetermined fingerprints. This is the less elaborated tool. It bases its fingerprints on TCP SYN and TCP SYN/ACK packets only. If we now compare how many Sources differ between Disco and p0f, we find out that Disco does not return any result when there is an ambiguity. Ettercap and p0f, however, tend to assign a default Windows value in many cases. This is all the more confirmed that we have learnt recently that Ettercap passive fingerprinting functionality is apparently based on the p0f_v1 (p0f first version) code. As a consequence, we have decided to use p0f as our default OS fingerprinting tool.

4.3 Domain Name Resolution

4.3.1 DNS and Other Network Features

It is interesting to analyze the geographical location of the attack sources, as we have shown in Section 4.1. Other potentially interesting information can be the machine name resolution. The Domain Name Resolution (DNS) associates one name to one IP. It is based on a distributed database containing all name/address pairs. This database is organized in domains that form a hierarchy. The nslookup tool enables us to query a NS to find (among other information) the IP address corresponding to a host name. It is also possible to obtain the name corresponding to an IP address. The reason is that NS manages two databases: the direct zone and the inverse zone. We have implemented a simple Perl script based on the Perl Net-DNS library that recursively performs the reverse DNS request.

The network from which the attack occurs can also be of interest. This information can be retrieved with *Whois* queries. A Whois query against a registry's database identifies the registrar and the name servers for the domain name given in the query. A query against a registrar's database identifies the owner of the domain name, and the contacts associated with it. Some simple Perl scripts exist to directly perform WHOIS lookups automatically [41]. These lookups provide various information on the domain, such as its registration ID, its creation date, its expiration date, etc.

Finally, each IP belongs to a given network. A network can be defined as an IP address with a Classless Inter-Domain Routing (CIDR) mask. The method is precisely described in RFC 1520 ([42]). The CIDR notation specifies an IP address range by the combination of an IP address and its associated network mask. CIDR notation uses the following format xxx.xxx.xxx.xxx/n where n is the number of (leftmost) bits in the mask. For example, 192.168.12.0/23 applies the network mask 255.255.254.0 to the 192.168 network, starting at 192.168.12.0. This notation represents the address range 192.168.12.0–192.168.13.255. We have decided for each *Source* to store its corresponding CIDR mask in the database. Both Netgeo and Maxmind provide information on the network the *Source* is coming from. We derive from the IP-range network values the CIDR network mask.

To summarize, we thus introduce into the database three new external important information types: the domain reverse resolution, the result of *Whois* queries and the network parameters. As a follow up, since these information characterize uniquely a given *Source*, we have decided to enrich the corresponding table with this information by adding attributes, the value of which point to new tables providing the imported information. This is represented in Figure 6. For instance, *Network_Id* is a pointer to an entry in the table *Network* where a network address can be found together with an estimated CIDR value.

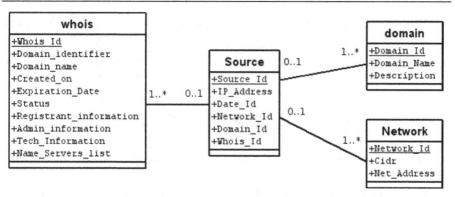

Figure 6. Network and Domain information

4.3.2 Examples

Some interesting statistics can be done on the domain names. We have developed some parsers to extract the different levels of the name. The top 5 most attacking domains are respectively the .net, .com, .jp, .fr and .de first name levels. Other statistics can be done quite easily by checking if the attacking machine belongs to a company network or is more likely to be a home computer. For instance, simple extractions of patterns like '%dsl%', '%cable%', '%dial%' are a good indicators of home computers. On the other hand, patterns like '%web%', '%mail%', '%serv%' in the machine name are likely to show up for machines belonging to some industrial professional environment. Several other analyses are possible and this is an ongoing task in our project.

5. META DATA

5.1 *Meta-Data* Definition

We have explained here above the existence of redundant information in our database for the sake of querying efficiency. In the following, we call "meta-data" the content of these redundant tables. Meta data information is information that is saved in specific tables but that could also be derived by means of queries against the other tables. *Meta-data* tables are built by means of automated scripts that are run whenever new data are entered into the database. We provide in the following a non-exhaustive list of *meta-data* information that can be found today in the database:

- The duration of the observation of a given *Source*

- The average inter arrival time of requests sent to a given *Source*. This might help differentiate hand-written attacks from automated tools.

- An indicator on who starts the attack session (to efficiently verify that none of our honeypots has ever been seen initiating a connection outside).

- A simple attribute that indicates how many virtual machines are targeted

- The number of observed complete TCP connections in a given Tiny Session

- Some precisions on the observation date: working days, working hours, etc.;

- The sequence of ports that have been targeted during the attack on a virtual machine

- A Boolean value indicating if a given Source has already been observed or not

- An attribute to mark *Tiny sessions* that are likely due to backscatter activities

- Another Boolean value to indicate if attacks on multiple virtual machines were performed in sequence or simultaneously.

- etc.

The main idea is that we do not want to compute this *meta-data* information whenever we need it. It is considered to be useful enough to be part of the database information. The attentive reader will notice that, actually, the core notions of *Source, Tiny_Session* and *Large_Session* are already *meta-data*. They are attack representations we observe from our platforms based on the raw packets initially stored.

In conclusion to this Section, there are a multitude of *meta-data* we have found interesting to represent and analyze. Others will definitely appear along with our experiments. We explain in the following how they can be easily integrated into the database architecture.

5.2   Flexible Database Interface

As explained in Section 5.1, the *meta-data* list we present in this document is far from being exhaustive. There is a very easy way to figure out where to integrate new *meta-data* into the current architecture. It boils down to answering the following question:

☑ *What characterizes this new piece of Information?*

- The Source only?

- The attack session between one Source and one Environment, i.e., a *Large_Session*?

- The attack session between one Source and one virtual machine, i.e.; a *Tiny_Session*?

The following steps are simple updates of the appropriate tables. Once tables are created or modified, updating the whole database to reflect these changes is a matter of minutes, thanks to a couple of scripts. It is important to note that the updates concern only the addition of new data, thanks to new data structures. It does not imply changing some existing values in certain tables. If that was the case, adding new meta data could lead to update anomaly problems.

The *meta-data* described in Section 5.1 have all been treated this way. The resulting tables are presented in Figure 7.

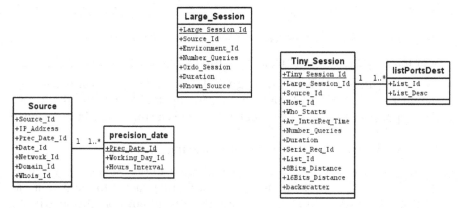

Figure 7. Meta Data Insertion

For the *Source* table, one major attribute has been added.

- The *Precision_Date* attribute gives more detailed information about the date of the observation of an attack. This information can be used to determine if the attack occurred during working days (Monday–Friday), or working hours (9h–17h). The *Working_Day_Id* is a Boolean value. The *Hours_Interval* attribute indicates the hour at which the Source has first been observed. This way, it is now quite easy to answer questions like: Are we less attacked during working days? Are attacks more virulent during night time? Some elements of responses are presented in Figure 8 for the VMWare platform which has been up and running for almost 2 years. All *Sources* that have been first observed between 00:00 and 01:00 are presented by the '0' bar. The 24 bars stem for the 24 hour intervals. This curve has a very nice shape, interesting to look at. We do not observe the same amount of attacks every hour. The curve clearly indicates that the attack time does not correspond to a random pattern. In addition, there is a weird peak of activities between 3pm. and 4pm.Thanks to the geographical location tables, we could identify if this shape is due to a particular country attacking at that specific time. We can also imagine many other possible investigations which lie beyond the scope of this paper.

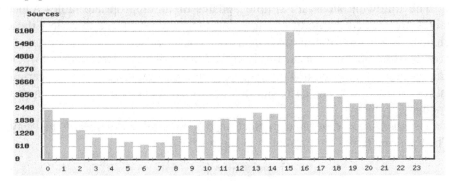

Figure 8. Attacks per Hour on our VMWare Platform

For the *Large_Session* table, a few attributes have also been added:

- *Number_Queries*: this attribute gives for each *Large_Session* the total number of packets that have been sent by the *Source* to the whole honeypot platform, i.e., *Environment*. There is a similar attribute assigned for the *Tiny_Session* table. It corresponds to the total number of packets sent by the same Source to one virtual machine, i.e., *Host*.

- *Duration*: This attribute corresponds in table *Large_Session* to the time period from the date the Source has sent its first packet to the date it has sent its last packet. In a similar way, there is a *Duration* attribute in the *Tiny_Session* table for packets sent to one *Host* only.

- *Ordo_Session*: This attribute indicates if *Hosts* have been attacked sequentially or in parallel. To get this information, it suffices to look at packet timestamps. If the first packet sent to the second virtual machine is posterior to the last one sent to the first virtual machine, they have been attacked sequentially. In other cases, they have been attacked in parallel.

- *Av_InterReq_Time*: This attribute provides the average time that occurs between two packets sent by the same *Source*. This attribute has been introduced with the goal of chasing traces due to non automated attacks. Our assumption is that attacks launched manually from a console by attackers will be characterized by a large inter arrival time of packets. This is true, for instance, when a user replies in an interactive way to an ftp server asking him his username and password. So far, we only have observed a very few number of attacks like this within the 2 year experiments.

For the *Tiny_Session* table, three main attributes have been added:

- *Who_Starts*: This attribute is an indicator to check who initiated the connection between the Source and the *Host*. By design, the *Host* should never initiate a connection to a *Source* unless if it has been compromised. We use this information as another method to verify that none of our hosts gets hacked.

- We make use of the definition *Ports Sequence* as an ordered list of ports targeted by an attack *Source* on a given Host. For instance, if source A sends requests on port 80 (HTTP), and then on ports 8080 (HTTP Alternate) and 1080 (SOCKS), the associated ports sequence will be {80;8080;1080}. The sequence of ports has been put in the *ListPortsDest* table. For all the *Tiny_Sessions* we have observed so far, the length of theses sequences of ports is usually very short. In this two-year experiment, we have observed only 9 scans on more than 500 ports. Thus, it seems more reasonable to store them once as strings and add in parallel a dedicated index in the *Tiny_Session* table.

- The *Backscatter* identification is quite straightforward. Indeed, backscatter packets are responses to connections requests issued by spoofed IP addresses, typically in the case of a Denial of Service attack against a third party. If our addresses are used (spoofed) in the course of this attack, we will see the responses of the victim sent to us without us having talked to him first. These attacks have been very well-analyzed by Moore et al. in [43], [44]. Figure 9 summarizes the various types of responses (column 'response from victim') that can be sent "against" our honeypots. These packets hit a large variety of ports that are traditionally unused, such as 27374 (TCP RST), 11224 (TCP SYN ACK), 9026 (RST ACK), etc.

Packet sent	Response from victim
TCP SYN (to open port)	TCP SYN/ACK
TCP SYN (to closed port)	TCP RST (ACK)
TCP ACK	TCP RST (ACK)
TCP DATA	TCP RST (ACK)
TCP RST	no response
TCP NULL	TCP RST (ACK)
ICMP ECHO Request	ICMP Echo Reply
ICMP TS Request	ICMP TS Reply
UDP pkt (to open port)	protocol dependent
UDP pkt (to closed port)	ICMP Port Unreach
...	...

Figure 9. Backscatter Packet Characteristics

5.3 Some Interesting Meta-Data Outputs

Insofar, the size of the database as described in the previous Sections is 27 Gbytes. Everyday, we insert around 13Mbytes of raw data. If we consider the global additional increase every day with all meta-data, this reaches 40 Mbytes per day. More specifically, the Source table is 36 Mbytes, the *Tiny_Session* is 97Mbytes, the *Large_Session* is 48 Mbytes, the *Source_To_Host_Traffic* table is 586 Mbytes, the *Host_To_Source_Traffic* table is 440 Mbytes, the *Geographical_Location* is 30 MBytes and finally the *Info_OS* table is 100 MBytes. These figures evolve every day but clearly indicate which tables are the largest.

Typically, it takes about 5 minutes to store the daily tcpdump file of one *Environment*. This means that we need less than two hours to store every day all data from all platforms. This is perfectly acceptable. To conclude, we can easily show the gain in terms of speed obtained thanks to the meta data. For this example, we do imagine that the meta data *listPortsDest* does not exist in the database and we want to know all ports sequences observed against all platforms. This comes down to running the following SQL query:

```
➤ SELECT group_concat(distinct(tcp_dport),distinct(udp_port))
  FROM Tiny_Session, Source_To_Host_Traffic, tcphdr, udphdr
  WHERE Tiny_Session.Tiny_Session_Id =
  Source_To_Host_Traffic.Tiny_Session_Id AND
  Source_To_Host_Traffic.Cid = tcphdr.cid AND
  Source_To_Host_Traffic.Cid = udphdr.cid GROUP BY
  Tiny_Session.Tiny_Session_Id
```

The answer is provided after 7 hours 48 minutes 21seconds during which almost 100 % of the CPU of the machine was devoted to this single request. The major reason of such an important delay is that the *tcphdr* table contains more than 17,700,000 entries. On the other hand, thanks to the integrated meta data, we can submit this Mysql query:

```
➤ SELECT list_desc FROM Tiny_Session, listPortsDest where
  Tiny_Session.List_Id=listPortsDest.list_id
```

Now, the time required to get an answer is reduced to 34seconds. This means that we gain almost two orders of magnitude in speed! In addition, the first SQL query does not give the exact sequence of ports with respect to the dates they were probed. It only gives the list of ports (TCP and UDP) that have been targeted. Asking for the *sequence* information would have made the request even more complex with an execution delay exceeding one day.

6. CONCLUSION

In this paper, we have presented in detail the design of the centralized database used in the context of the Leurré.com project. We have shown, step by step, the various tables that compose the databases, the reasoning beyond their creation as well as their usefulness to extract meaningful information easily from the database. We have explained why several tables have been created that do contain redundant information and we have motivated our choice for efficiency in the querying mechanism, at the cost of a greater storage need. Several examples have been given throughout the text to illustrate the various notions.

As shown in this paper, the richness of the database and the flexibility of its design are such that it enables a large diversity of analyses to be carried out on it. It is not the purpose of this paper to report on a specific analysis. Other publications have focused on some of these issues and some more work is ongoing. We have shown though by means of examples that this database helps in discovering trends in the attacks and in characterizing them. Being able to conduct such analysis in a systematic way is a prerequisite for establishing early warning information systems and, therefore, we believe our work constitutes a foundational element towards the creation of such centers.

It is our wish to share the data contained in this database with those interested in carrying some research on it. The authors can be reached by mail to get detailed information regarding how to join the project in order to gain access to the database.

7. REFERENCES

[1] WORM 2004, The 2nd Workshop on Rapid Malcode, held in Association with the 11th ACM Conference on Computer and Communication Security CCS, Oct. 2004, VA, USA, home page at: **http://www.acm.org/sigs/sigsac/ccs/CCS2004/worm.html**

[2] DIMVA 2004, The Detection of Intrusions and Malware & Vulnerability Assessment, July 2004, Dortmund, Germany, home page at: **http://www.dimva.org/dimva2005**

[3] SRUTI: Steps to Reducing Unwanted Traffic on the Internet, Usenix Workshop, July 2005, MA USA, home page at: **http://nms.lcs.mit.edu/~dina/SRUTI/**

[4] Staniford, S., V. Paxson, and N. Weaver, "How to Own the Internet in Your Spare Time." In the *Proceedings of the 11th USENIX Security Symposium*, pages 149–167, USENIX Association, 2002.

[5] Chen, Z., L. Gao, and K. Kwiat, "Modeling the Spread of Active Worms," in the *Proceedings of the IEEE INFOCOM 2003*, April 2003, CA, USA.

[6] Zou, C. C., W. Gong, and D. Towsley, "Worm Propagation Modeling and Analysis Under Dynamic Quarantine Defense," in *Proceedings of the 1st Workshop on Rapid Malcode (WORM'03)*, Oct. 2003, WA, USA.

[7] Spafford, E., "The Internet Worm Program: An Analysis," *Purdue Technical Report CSD-TR-823*, West Lafayette, IN 47907-2004, 1988.

[8] Moore, D., C. Shannon, G.M. Voelker, and S. Savage, "Code Red, a Case Study on the Spread and Victims of an Internet Worm," in *Proceedings of the ACM/USENIX Internet Measurement Workhop*, Nov. 2002.

[9] McAFEE Security Antivirus. "Virus Profile: W32/deloder worm." Available at: **http://us.mcafee.com/virusInfo/**

[10] F-Secure Corporation. "Deloder worm analysis." Available at: **http://www.f-secure.com**

[11] McHugh J., "Sets, Bags, and Rock and Roll Analyzing Large Data Sets of Network Data," in *Proceedings of the 9th European Symposium on Research in Computer Security USENIX'04*, Sept. 2004, Sophia-Antipolis, France.

[12] Honeyd Virtual Honeypot from N. Provos, home page: **http://www.honeyd.org**

[13] Dacier, M., F. Pouget, and H. Debar. "Honeypots, A Practical Mean to Validate Malicious Fault Assumptions," in *Proceedings of the 10th Pacific Ream Dependable Computing Conference (PRDC'04)*, Feb. 2004.

[14] Pouget, F. and M. Dacier. "Honeypot-based Forensics," in *Proceedings of the AusCERT Asia Pacific Information Technology Security Conference 2004 (AusCERT2004)*, May 2004, Australia.

[15] Pouget, F., M. Dacier, and V.H. Pham, "Understanding Threats: a Prerequisite to Enhance Survivability of Computing Systems," in *Proceedings of the International Infrastructure Survivability Workshop (IISW 2004)*, Dec. 2004, Portugal.

[16] Pouget, F., M. Dacier, and H. Debar, "Attack Processes found on the Internet," in *Proceedings of the NATO Symposium IST-041/RSY-013*, April 2004, France.

[17] VMWare Corporation. User's Manual version 4.1 available at: **http://www.vmware.com**

[18] TCPDUMP utility home page: **http://www.tcpdump.org**

[19] LEURRE.COM, the Eurecom Honeypot Project home page: **http://www.eurecom.fr/~pouget/leurrecom.html**

[20] Pouget, F., M. Dacier, and V.H. Pham, "On the Advantages of Deploying a Large Scale Distributed Honeypot Platform," to appear in the *Proceedings of the E-Crime and Computer Evidence Conference 2005*, Monaco, Feb. 2005.

[21] Garcia-Molina, H., J. D. Ullman, and J. D. Widom, "Database Systems: the Complete Book," 2002.

[22] Ullman, J. D., "A First Course in Database Systems," 2nd Edition, 1989.

[23] SNORT Intrusion Detection Sytem home page: http://www.snort.org

[24] MySQL Open Source Database home page: http://www.mysql.com

[25] "Blacklist Scanner" in Security Focus Home Tools:
http://www.securityfocu.com/tools/1962

[26] CAIDA Project. "Netgeo utility—the Internet geographical database," home page:
http://www.caida.org/tools/utilities/netgeo/

[27] Rosin, A., "Measuring Availability in Peer-to-Peer Networks," Sept. 2003, available at:
http://www.wiwi.hu-berlin.de/fis/p2pe/paper_A_Rosin.pdf

[28] Zeitoun, A., C. N. Chuah, S. Bhattacharyya, and C. Diot, "An AS-level study of Internet path delay characteristics," technical report, 2003, available at:
http://ipmon.sprint.com/pubs_trs/trs/RR03-ATL-051699-AS-delay.pdf

[29] Hook, S. H., H. Jeong, and A.L. Barabasi, "Modeling the Internet's large scale topology," in *PNAS –vol. 99*, Oct. 2002, available at:
http://www.nd.edu/networks/PDF/Modeling

[30] Eugene, T. S., Ng, and H. Zhang, "Predicting Internet Network Distance with Coordinates-based Approaches," in *Proceedings of INFOCOM 2002*, available at:
http://www-2.cs.cmu.edu/eugeneng/papers/INFOCOM02.pdf

[31] MaxMind GeoIP Country Database Commercial Product, home page:
http://www.maxmind.com/app/products

[32] IP2location products, home page: http://www.ip2location.com

[33] GeoBytes IP Address Locator Tool, home page:
http://www.geobytes.com/IPLocator.htm

[34] ISO 3166-1 alpha-2, Introduction to the 2-letter code for countries names, available at:
http://encyclopedia.thefreedictionary.com/ISO%203166-1

[35] Symantec Antivirus Corporation. Symantec Security Response w32.welchia.worm, 2004, available at
http://response.symantec.com/avcentr/venc/data/w32.welchia.b.worm.html

[36] "Internet Worm squirms into Linux Servers," CNET tech report available at:
http://news.com.com/2100-1001-251071.html?legacy=cnet

[37] "Ramen Linux Worm seen in Wild," InfoWorld News available at:
http://www.infoworld.com/articles/hn/xml/
01/01/25/010125hnramen.html?p=br&s=3

[38] Disco Passive Fingerprinting Tool home page: http://www.altmode.com/disco

[39] P0f Passive Fingerprinting Tool, version 2.0 home page:
http://lcamtuf.coredump.cx/p0f-beta.tgz

[40] Ettercap NG-0.7.1 Sourceforge Project available at: http://ettercap.sourceforge.net

[41] Comprehensive Perl Archive Network CPAN home page: http://www.cpan.org

[42] "Exchanging Routing Information Across Provider Boundaries in the CIDR Environment," IETF RFC 1520, available at: http://www.ietf.org/rfc/rfc1520.txt

[43] CAIDA Project: The UCSD Network Telescope,
http://www.caida.org/outreach/papers/2001/BackScatter/

[44] Moore, D., G. Voelker, and S. Savage, "Infering Internet Denial-of-Service activity," in *Proceedings of the 2001 USENIX Security Symposium*, Aug. 2001, CA, USA.

IRIS BIOMETRICS FOR SECURE REMOTE ACCESS

Andrzej Pacut, Adam Czajka, Przemek Strzelczyk
Warsaw University of Technology,
Institute of Control and Computation Engineering, Poland
Research and Academic Computer Network NASK,
Biometrics Laboratory, Poland

Abstract: We propose a new iris texture coding technique with optimal feature extraction, and design a secure remote (internet) access system using the proposed biometrics. The proposed iris coding method is based on Zak-Gabor coefficients sequence, and additionally uses an optimal selection of a subset of iris features. The secure access involves a communication scenario that employs a usual client-server network model, thus incorporating standard security mechanisms with biometric enhancements. The proposed access scenario enables to include the aliveness detection capability and the biometric replay attack prevention.

Keywords: Biometrics; iris; optimal features; remote access security

1. INTRODUCTION

The ideal biometrics may be envisioned as a physical or behavioral characterization of a person and a method of its symbolic description, fused in a system that is resistant to counterfeits, produces no authentication errors, is immune to aging and diseases, brings no social, religious, ethical, and other objections, and finally, is comfortable in use.

Biometrics research is still looking for this ideal. A wide variety of biometric modalities have been investigated and applied to various access control scenarios, including fingerprints, iris, face, voice recognition, hand geometry, handwritten signatures, etc. At present, fingerprint analysis is quite widely used, yet iris-based authentication is another important candidate for being a source of highly distinctive attributes characterizing identity with high reliability. It is fast, highly reliable and completely non-invasive, is stable throughout the human life and independent of genetic

---

259

J. S. Kowalik et al. (eds.), Cyberspace Security and Defense: Research Issues, 259–278.

features [A2], and raises little social objections. The iris-based authentication seems to be close to ideal and is likely to prevail over its competitors.

The iris texture complexity is very high and may need non-trivial feature extraction and coding algorithms and large computation times. The iris authentication methodology has been pioneered by John Daugman, and the commercial solutions are based on his algorithms. There still may be a need for new solutions, aiming into fast robust feature extracting.

In the paper we propose a new method of iris texture coding and feature extraction, and its application to internet security. We shortly introduce the iris coding method based on Zak-Gabor coefficients sequence, the routines for optimal iris features selection, and we show how these ideas may be implemented into a secure remote access system. A prototype of remote such authentication device was built and tested with the use of an iris database.

2. EYE IMAGING

2.1. Imaging Hardware

Before any type of processing, the iris images must first be captured. In this order, we use Iris Imaging Device which is a part of NASK Iris Recognition System prototype (Figure 1). The system consists of an eye imaging analogue camera with 570 TV lines resolution equipped with motorized lens, a framegrabber board for image acquisition, near-infrared illuminators placed on both sides of the lens, and a workstation controlling the hardware and processing acquired images. The imaging system interacts with a volunteer during the imaging process and helps him/her to position his/her head correctly behind the camera lens. Once the hardware encounters the eye existence in a proper distance and position, it starts to acquire a sequence of frames with varying focal length, thus compensating small depth-of-field that is common in imaging small targets as the human iris. The acquisition process takes approximately one second, and the whole iris image capturing including eye positioning approximates to 5 seconds. The iris images are compliant with the rectilinear iris image requirements as required by ISO/IEC 19794-6 Final Committee Draft [D3].

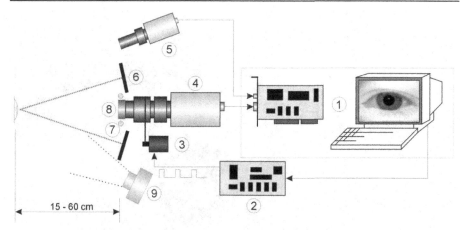

Figure 1. Iris image acquisition prototype as developed in NASK. The prototype consists of the workstation controlling the hardware and processing iris images (1), iris imaging camera (4), eye surroundings imaging camera (5), lens motor (2,3), positioning mirrors (6) and positioning LEDs (7), infrared filter (8), infrared illuminators (9).

The above hardware was used to create at NASK a multimodal biometric database BioBase, which at present contains images of iris, face, hand shape, and handwritten signatures, of couple of hundred volunteers. BioBase will be employed here to test the proposed approaches.

2.2 Iris Body and Occlusions Localization

Camera raw image contains the iris and its surroundings. Thus, the iris localization methods must be applied to extract the valuable iris texture information available within the image. Localization of both inner (i.e., between the pupil and the iris) and outer (i.e., between the iris and the sclera) iris boundaries makes use of local image gradient estimation. Consequently, we approximate the shape of inner and outer boundaries by two non-concentric circles. Figure 2 presents the camera raw image with iris both circular boundaries localized.

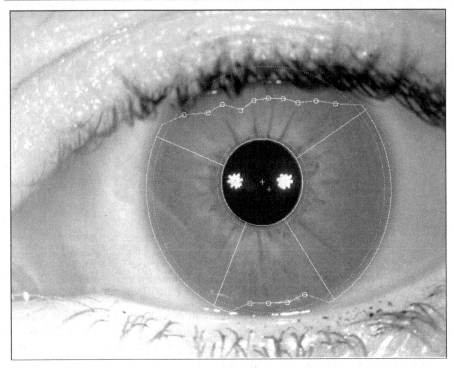

Figure 2. Pre-processing of the raw iris image: detection of occlusions (circled lines) and iris sectors free of occlusions (white lines).

The extracted iris body is almost always occluded by eyelids, or interfered with specular reflections as the effect of infrared illumination (cf. Figure 2). Thus, we apply the method of localizing the iris texture occlusions through detecting of inconsistent iris structure points. First, iris texture irregularity in radial direction is investigated at several angular positions. Afterward, estimating the maximal inconsistency for a particular iris image, we compare this result with inconsistency for radial directions determined for a number of angular sections. Consequently, we end up with a map of occlusion points for a number of angular sections.

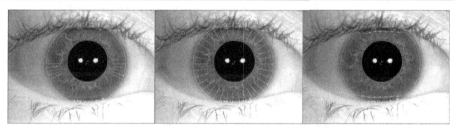

Figure 3. Image regularity determination in typically free of occlusions iris sections (left), irregularity check in all angular sections (middle), iris occlusions detected (right).

2.3 Iris Body Representation

Zak-Gabor algorithm makes use of a rectangular iris image representation. The inner and the outer iris boundaries are approximately circular, yet are not concentric. It is thus useful to transform the iris image to a rectangular representation by a resampling. Two iris sections free from eyelids and reflections, each of the angular width of 90°, are used in further image analysis, see Figure 4. Denote by P the iris sector angular width and by H its height.

The experiments (see also [A2]) revealed much higher correlation of the iris body in the radial direction as compared to the angular direction. Thus, instead of analyzing 2D images, we represent both iris sectors (in rectangular coordinates) as a collection of R iris stripes ($R/2$ stripes for each iris sector). Angular fluctuations of the iris structure are represented by the stripe variability, while radial fluctuations are averaged over a certain horizon.

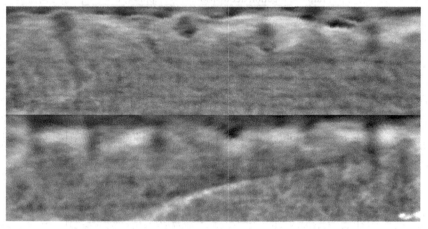

Figure 4. Left and right iris angular sectors in rectangular coordinates, as determined for iris image depicted in Figure 2.

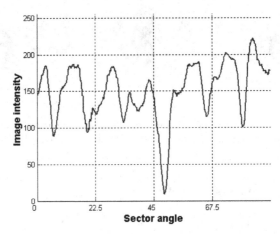

Figure 5. Intensity fluctuations in a single stripe,
as determined for angular sector shown in Figure 4.

Presented iris acquisition system is equipped with a coding method (see Section 3) to make it possible to observe and enhance the iris recognition process. Tables 1 and 2 present the average processing times in the current version of NASK Iris Recognition Device.

Table 1. Raw Iris Image Acquisition Times When Using NASK Iris Recognition Device

Task	Average processing time [s]
Skilled volunteer head and eye positioning	approx. 2.5
Frames collection acquisition	approx. 1.0
Best quality frame selection	approx. 1.5
Total	**approx. 5.0**

Table 2. Raw Iris Image Processing Times When Using NASK Iris Recognition Device

Task	Average processing time [s]
Iris boundaries localization and occlusions detection	2.819
Representation of iris image as a sequence of stripes	0.586
Zak-Gabor coefficients calculation and transformation into a features vector	0.06
Matching	< 0.01
Total	**3.47**

3. IRIS CODING

3.1. Gabor Expansion

It is often convenient to characterize a discrete-time signal in the frequency domain, or in a joint time-frequency domain, thus describing a stationary frequency distribution of energy. The common and well known mathematical tool for frequency analysis is the Fourier transform, typically in the form of Fast Fourier Transform. Sometimes, for non-stationary signals, it is fruitful to characterize the frequency locally, and find the distribution of signal energy in local—possibly overlapping—time segments. Typical examples of applications of this approach include sound analysis, like music applications, human voice recognition and biometric speaker verification. Pattern analysis is a second important application domain of time-frequency techniques, where the purpose of analysis is to differentiate (or recognize, segment, identify, etc.) local areas of incoming data by a use of local filters. In many cases it is fruitful to characterize these filters by position and scale instead of time and frequency.

Iris texture analysis may be qualified as a 2D pattern analysis task, yet it is often simplified to a set of 1-D tasks. The analysis aims at describing local features of iris, so that to construct a compact feature vector. Time-frequency or scale-frequency analysis seems to be a natural candidate to solve this problem. One of possible approaches is Gabor's signal expansion [C1], where a continuous-time signal is presented in a form of a set of properly shifted and modulated elementary (arbitrarily-shaped) signals. Typically, the elementary signals are Gaussian-shaped, since they result in best time-frequency resolution. In other words, Gaussian-shaped elementary signals (shifted and modulated) occupy the smallest possible area in the time-frequency domain. Gaussian-shaped elementary signals are yet not orthogonal, so Gabor's expansion coefficients cannot be determined in a simple way. Suggested algorithms include making the window function bi-orthonormal to the Gaussian-shaped elementary function [C3], the matrix-based algorithm [C6], and Zak transform [C3, C6]. Both matrix-based algorithm and the Zak-Gabor transform result in direct Gabor's coefficients calculation. Determination of Gabor's expansion coefficients through the Zak transform, developed by Martin J. Bastiaans [C3], is often called Zak-Gabor transform and is the fastest method for this purpose. We shortly describe this approach.

Denote by g a one-dimensional Gaussian function characterized by a scale parameter D, sampled at points $0 \ldots P-1$, namely

$$g[p] = 2^{\frac{1}{4}} e^{-\pi([p+\frac{1}{2}]/D)^2}, \quad p = 0 \ldots P - 1 \qquad (1)$$

We describe the Zak-Gabor transform for a single stripe and a chosen fixed scale parameter D. Let M be a number of translations of g, and K be the number of frequency shifts where we always take $M = P/K$. The Gabor elementary functions (GEF), are defined as shifted and modulated versions of g, namely

$$g_{mk}[p] = g[p - mK]e^{ikp2\pi/K}, \quad p = 0 \ldots P - 1 \tag{2}$$

where m and k denote position and frequency shifts, respectively ($m = 0$, 1, ..., M-1, $k = 0$, 1, ..., K-1), and g is wrapped around P point domain. Denote by f the intensity function defined on a stripe. The finite discrete Gabor transform of f is defined as a set of complex coefficients a_{mk} that satisfy the Gabor signal expansion relationship, namely

$$f[p] = \sum_{m=0}^{M-1} \sum_{k=0}^{K-1} a_{mk}g_{mk}[p], \quad p = 0 \ldots P - 1 \tag{3}$$

Following Bastiaans [C3], we set $K = D$ in further analysis so that the scale D parameter together with the stripe size P determine both M and K.

3.2. Zak Transform

The discrete finite Zak transform $Zf[\rho, \phi; K, M]$ of a signal f sampled equidistantly at P points is defined as the one-dimensional discrete Fourier transform of the sequence $f[\rho + nK]$, $n=0$, ..., M-1, namely [C3]

$$\mathcal{Z}f[\rho, \phi; K, M] = \sum_{n=0}^{M-1} f[\rho + nK]e^{-in\phi2\pi/M} \tag{4}$$

where $M = P/K$. The discrete Zak transform is periodic both in frequency ϕ (with the period $2\pi/M$) and in location ρ (with the period K), we choose the values of ρ and ϕ within the fundamental Zak interval, namely $\rho = 0$, 1, ..., K-1 and $\phi = 0$, 1, ..., M-1.

Similarly to the Fourier transformation, one may reconstruct the original function f from its Zak transform by way of the inverse discrete Zak transform, using the formula

$$f[\rho + nK] = \frac{1}{M} \sum_{n=0}^{M-1} \mathcal{Z}f[\rho, \phi; K, M]e^{in\phi2\pi/M} \tag{5}$$

simultaneously restricting the domain of the results to the fundamental Zak interval.

3.3. Application of Zak transform in Gabor transformation

Gabor's expansion coefficients can be recovered from the product form (8). In fact, application of the discrete Zak transform (5) to both sides of (3) yields

$$\mathcal{Z}f[\rho, \phi; K, M] = \sum_{n}^{M-1} \left[\sum_{m}^{M-1} \sum_{k}^{K-1} a_{mk} g[\rho + nK - mK] e^{ik\rho 2\pi/K} \right] e^{-in\phi 2\pi/M} \qquad (6)$$

Rearranging the factors in (6) to

$$\mathcal{Z}f[\rho, \phi; K, M] =$$

$$\sum_{n=0}^{M-1} \left[\sum_{m=0}^{M-1} \sum_{k=0}^{K-1} a_{mk} g[\rho + nK - mK] e^{ik\rho 2\pi/K} e^{-im\phi 2\pi/M} e^{im\phi 2\pi/M} \right] e^{-in\phi 2\pi/M} =$$

$$\sum_{m=0}^{M-1} \sum_{k=0}^{K-1} a_{mk} e^{-i2\pi(m\phi/M - k\rho/K)} \left[\sum_{n=0}^{M-1} g[\rho + (n-m)K] e^{-i2\pi(n-m)\phi/M} \right] \qquad (7)$$

results in

$$\mathcal{Z}f[\rho, \phi; K, M] = \mathcal{F}a[\rho, \phi; K, M] \, \mathcal{Z}g[\rho, \phi; K, M] \qquad (8)$$

where $Fa[\rho, \phi; K, M]$ denotes the discrete 2D Fourier transform of the signal a, and $Zg[\rho, \phi; K, M]$ is the discrete Zak transform of the Gaussian window used in the Gabor transformation. It shows that Gabor's expansion coefficients can be easily recovered from the product form (8). Once we choose K and M to be a power of 2 (hence the signal length P is a power of 2), calculation of both $Zf[\rho, \phi; K, M]$ and $Zg[\rho, \phi; K, M]$ and inverting 2D Fourier series rely on the Fast Fourier Transform, yielding computation times proportional to those in the FFT.

3.4. Determination of Iris Features Based on Zak-Gabor Coefficients

Gabor expansion coefficients (Sec. 3.1) were defined for a single scale parameter D and all strips $r = 0, \ldots, R\text{-}1$. To determine the iris features we determine Gabor expansion coefficients for chosen scales $D \in \boldsymbol{D}$, where $\boldsymbol{D}$ is the set of scales, ending up with a family of coefficients indexed by the quadruple: within-stripe position, frequency index, stripe index and scale (m, k, r, D). Identically as in Daugman's representation calculations, we define the features b_n as the signs of the real and imaginary parts of Zak-Gabor coefficients as features, namely

$$\text{sgn}(\Re(a_{mk;rD})), \quad \text{sgn}(\Im(a_{mk;rD})) \tag{9}$$

where $m = 0..., M\text{-}1$, $k=0...K\text{-}1$, $r=0,..., R\text{-}1$, $D \in \boldsymbol{D}$. The total possible number of Zak-Gabor coefficients PR #$\boldsymbol{D}$, where # denotes the number of elements in a set, thus leads to the *maximal feature vector b* of $N=2PR$ #$\boldsymbol{D}$ elements. We later select a subset of features to be included in an *optimal feature vector b**. We will keep the order of features identical for all images. Hence, the matching requires only XOR operation between two feature vectors, and the Hamming distance is used as the matching score between two irises.

3.5. Choice of Optimal Features

The number of features in the maximal feature vector, of order of hundreds of thousands, is too big to be useful in practice, due to such issues like data transmission through the net, data storage in databases, templates comparison made in smart card processors or biometric standalone devices, etc. To reduce the number of features, we will look for a feature vector that leads to minimum sample equal error rate determined on available iris images database.

3.5.1. Optimization of Features

To find features that carry most information, we will first analyze the sample variances of features. Since the set of all data can be divided into classes, each corresponding to a different eye, we can define average within-class sample variance $s_n^{(w)}$, and between-class sample variances by $s_n^{(b)}$, for each feature b_n given by (9). The features can now be selected in such a way that the between class separation is maximized and the within class separation is minimized, with the separations measured by the respective sample variances. Intuitively, a feature is useful if at least $s_{min}^{(b)} < s_n^{(y)} < s_n^{(w)}$ where $s_{min}^{(b)}$ is a between-class variance low threshold. Typically, the number of bits that meet this requirement is still too high. Moreover, the features are often highly correlated, thus carrying similar information. It is thus useful to introduce stronger selection mechanisms that select features b_n of low within-class sample variance and high between-class sample variance. This prioritizing my be done by sorting the features by a decreasing values of the variance quotient q_n, defined as

$$q_n = \frac{s_n^{(b)}}{s_n^{(w)}} \tag{10}$$

In order to minimize the sample correlation while sorting the features, we select only those consecutive elements for which the sample correlation coefficients with all the elements already selected does not exceed an assumed correlation threshold. We denote the selected bits by b_n^*, $n = 0, \ldots,$ N^*-1 where $N^* \leq N$. They are related to Zak-Gabor coefficients characterized by various quadruples (m,k,r,D), cf (9).

To study the relation between the number of features and the system quality, we may use one of standard measures that characterize the difference between two random variables. Assume that the scores c_b and c_w, related to comparisons between different and the identical eyes, are independent random variables. The *decidability* (or *detectability*) [A2] is defined as

$$d = \frac{|\bar{c}_b - \bar{c}_w|}{\sqrt{\frac{1}{2}(\bar{\bar{c}}_b + \bar{\bar{c}}_w)}} \qquad (12)$$

where $\bar{c}_b, \bar{c}_w$ denote the sample means and $\bar{\bar{c}}_b, \bar{\bar{c}}_w$ denote sample variances of c_b and c_w, respectively. The value of d estimates the degree by which the distributions of c_b and c_w overlap (the higher d is, the lower is the overlap). The decidability changes with the number of features included in the feature vector (Fig. 6). We estimated d using the iris data in BioBase, and found out that with the number of features (sorted as described above) growing to more that 100 000, the decidability first grows to reach a maximum for 324 features, and then decreases. At the maximum, there is no overlap of c_b and c_w distributions, i.e., there are no false matches and no false non-match examples. This 324-bit vector is an intermediate iris feature vector employed in the second selection stage.

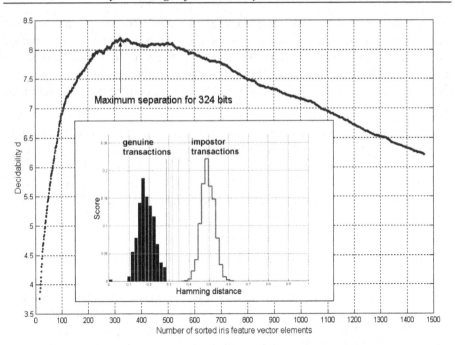

Figure 6. Decidability coefficient d vs. the number of sorted iris features.
Best d was obtained for 324 bits. The corresponding genuine and impostor
score distributions are presented in the inset.

3.5.2. Optimization of Feature Classes

The scales and frequencies of Zak-Gabor coefficients included into the code have a strong influence on the overall method's efficiency. Since D and k are dependent, they should be considered simultaneously. Their optimal selection is complicated, since we cannot a priori guess the most common frequencies that characterize all iris images, due to huge and unknown iris texture variability.

One may assume a uniform distribution of the information along the iris and aim into selecting "the best" frequency-scale pairs (k, D). This can be done by grouping in one class all coefficients of the same frequency-scale pair (k, D), and enlarging the feature vector by all features in a class. In other words, the problem is to find the best frequency-scale pairs.

Note that the number of features included in the feature vector b^* is not identical for all classes. The sorting rule for the classes of features mirrors the rule used for features: we sort the classes by the decreasing number of elements included into the feature vector. This enables to find the frequency-scale pairs for which the distributions of c_b and c_w are best separated. In other words, this procedure selects the features most sensitive to eye texture variability that characterize the individuals.

If there are no false matches and no false non-match errors for the tested database, we define the separation margin s as the difference between the worst (the lowest) between-class comparison score and the worst (the highest) within-class comparison score.

We calculated both d and s for various numbers of feature classes used in features calculations, and chose classes (scale-frequency pairs) characterized by the maximal d. This leads to the iris feature vector of 1152 bits (144 bytes) containing only four feature classes (Figure 7). Simultaneously, for those four selected feature classes we achieved the maximal non-zero separation s.

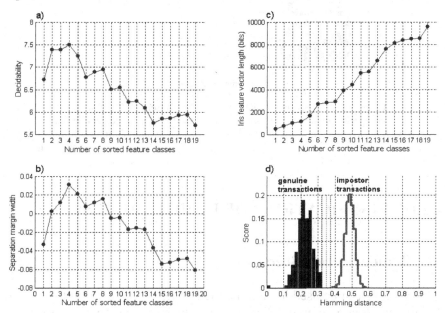

Figure 7. a) Decidability d vs. number of sorted frequency-scale pairs included in the feature vector, b) the separation margin s, c) the length of the iris feature vector, d) distribution of comparison scores for the same and different irises for the best final 144 byte iris feature vector.

We verified the above feature vector using the iris data for 180 individuals included in BioBase, with four images per volunteer available, three used for template creation and one employed in verification trials (Figure 8). We obtained zero false matches and zero false non-matches.

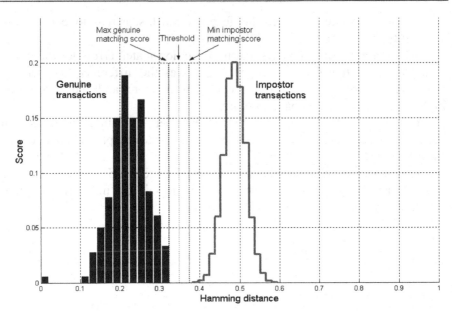

Figure 8. Comparison scores for iris data in NASK BioBase. 180 (N) genuine and 32220 (N(N-1)) comparisons impostor transactions were used. The average genuine transaction score 0.22, the average impostor transaction score 0.48, the minimal impostor transaction score 0.37, maximal genuine transaction score 0.32, Threshold = 0.35 results in no sample false match and no sample false non-match errors.

4. IRIS VERIFICATION FOR REMOTE ACCESS

4.1. Remote Access Scenario

Biometrics can be used in granting the remote access to the network. The scenario employs a common client-server network model, thus incorporating standard security mechanisms with biometric enhancements. The client terminal (see Figure 9) is a biometric-based host, equipped with the capturing device and the processing unit that measures the biometric trait and calculates the features vector (biometric template). The client capabilities may be understood in a wider sense, thus enabling the client to be equipped with sensors related to more than one biometric modality. The proposed access scenario enables to include the aliveness detection capability and the biometric replay attack prevention. To insert the necessary elements into the communication flow, capture-dependent parameters will be retrieved by the client terminal prior to the biometric trait measurement.

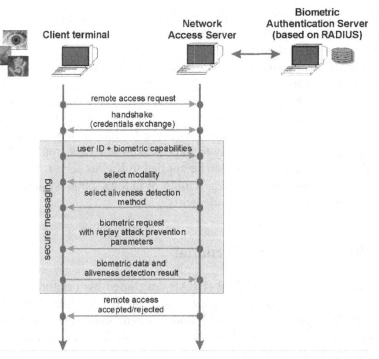

Figure 9. Biometric remote network access scenario. Single remote network access is depicted in a form of the EAP packets exchange between the biometric client and the biometric authentication server.

A flexible solution of biometric remote authentication can be based on biometric enhanced EAP protocol included in RADIUS server. RADIUS can incorporate a number of authentication protocols, e.g., PAP, SPAP, CHAP, MS-CHAP, EAP, depending on the distribution. The EAP protocol (*Extensible Authentication Protocol*)—among those available—can be extended for additional authentication methodology. Figure 9 presents the proposed EAP packets exchange in case of the biometric remote authentication, with aliveness detection and biometric replay attack prevention. Note that the client terminal may require some volunteer-dependent parameters prior to the capturing process (e.g., position and size of the iris sectors, left/right eye/hand/ear, the fingerprint index, the handwritten signature phrase, etc.). These additional parameters may be used for biometric replay attack prevention, since the server may require different parts of the biometric traits in each transaction. Additionally, the same mechanism of using additional parameters may be useful in dynamic biometrics implementations (e.g., phrase-dependent voice verification), when the challenge-response mechanism is necessary.

The above scenario is generic and may be applied to iris-based authentication. In particular, iris recognition with Zak-Gabor iris coding methodology can be applied here.

The client workstation can be established on Windows 2000 system and configured to enable for VPN connection to the remote network. Windows 2003 Server can be used as Network Access Server (NAS) for this purpose. The Radius biometric server can be installed on the same machine as NAS. The server may use MS SQL 2000 database for biometric templates storage. MS SQL database makes it easy to import biometric data from BioBase. MS SQL database interface must then be applied to Radius server. The enrolment station can be established on a remote Windows 2000 system. The next subsections depict the scenario elements.

4.2. Biometric Client Terminal

A biometric variant of EAP (BEAP developed by Telefonica I&D, may serve as an example) can be enhanced with the Iris Module. This enables to adapt Iris Recognition Device with Radius client and consequently to setup a remote access scenario based on iris pattern analysis. The Iris Module has the following proposed functionality:

- It controls Iris Imaging hardware and captures iris images with the desired quality and speed,
- It processes the acquired images, i.e., a) detects the inner and outer iris boundaries within the raw camera image, b) localizes the eyelids and specular reflections, c) extracts two iris sectors based on the localized occlusions, d) transforms the iris sectors to the collection of R stripes,
- It calculates the biometric template based on the representation of the iris image as the sequence of signs of the Zak-Gabor expansion coefficients.

The Iris Module consists of the device library used for high-level hardware management and image capture, and the algorithms library, which deals with image processing, quality measurement, iris and occlusions detection, and features extraction functions. Figure 10 depicts the entire Client Terminal structure.

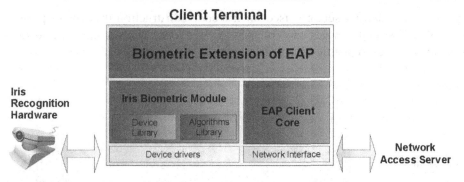

Figure 10. The Remote Client Terminal Architecture

4.3. Biometric Authentication Server

Radius server was configured to use MS-SQL BioBase server to store the templates. NASK BioBase Access Module add-on enables to make loading and storage of templates transparent to EAP Server Core. The server was also expanded by the iris matching algorithms, cf. Figure 11.

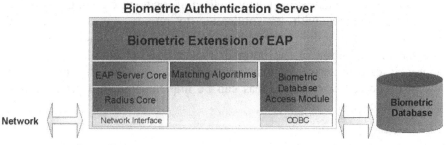

Figure 11. Biometric Authentication Server based on Radius servers,
with remote Biometric Database

4.4. Enrolment Terminal

The Enrolment Terminal (cf. Figure 12) uses the NASK Iris Module and BioBase Access Module. A separate application is developed that uses common elements of NASK biometrics modules, namely, the device library to control the hardware, and the algorithms library to process iris images and calculate iris features vectors.

The enrolment terminal captures a certain number of images of volunteer's eye. The raw image is processed to detect the inner and outer iris boundaries and eyelid occlusions. As an additional security mechanism, the occlusions may be used to determine volunteer-dependent free of occlusions

(FOC) angular iris sectors, used for iris code construction in place of pre-set angles. The FOC angles can enhance the iris code. The enrolment hardware helps the user to position his or head correctly behind the camera.

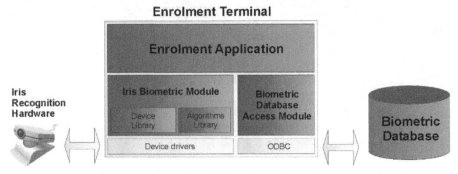

Figure 12. Iris biometrics enrolment terminal, developed at NASK for use with the remote access scenario

5. CONCLUSIONS

In the paper we described a new method of iris texture coding and feature extraction, together with its application to remote access security. We introduced the iris coding method based on Zak-Gabor coefficients sequence and the methodology of the optimal iris features selection. The proposed approach leads to zero false match and zero false non-match sample errors. We also showed how these ideas can be implemented in a secure remote access framework.

ACKNOWLEDGEMENTS

Most of the above results were obtained as a part of BioSec European integrated project IST-2002-001766.

REFERENCES

Iris recognition methods and devices

[A1]   Flom and Safir, "Iris recognition system," United States Patent 4.641.349, February 3, 1987

[A2]   Daugman, John, "Biometric identification system based on iris analysis," United States Patent 5.291.560, March 1, 1994

[A3]   Wildes, Richard P., et al., "Automated, non-invasive iris recognition system and method," United States Patent 5.572.596, November 5, 1996

[A4]   Kim, Daniel Daehoon, et al., "Iris identification system and method of identifying a person through iris recognition," United States Patent 6.247.813, June 19, 2001

[A5]   Zhu, Y., T. Tan, and Y. Wang, "Iris image acquisition system," Chinese Patent Application No. 99217063.X, 1999

[A6]   Zhu, Y., T. Tan, and Y. Wang, "Biometric Personal Identification System Based on Iris Pattern," Chinese Patent Application No. 9911025.6, 1999

[A7]   Matsushita, et al., "Iris identification system and iris identification method," United States Patent 5.901.238, May 4, 1999

[A8]   Doster, et al., "Iris recognition apparatus and method," United States Patent 5.956.122, September 21, 1999

[A9]   Mann, et al., "System and method for aircraft passenger check-in and boarding using iris recognition," United States Patent 6.119.096, September 12, 2000

[A10] McHugh, et al., "Handheld iris imaging apparatus and method," United States Patent 6.289.113, September 11, 2001

[A11] Musgrave, et al., "Iris imaging telephone security module and method," United States Patent 6.377.699, April 23, 2002

[A12] Boles, W. W. and B. Boashash, "A Human Identification Technique Using Images of te Iris and Wavelet Transform," IEEE Transactions on Signal Processing, Vol. 46, No. 4, April 1998

[A13] Tieniu, Tan, "Identity identifying method based on iris identification and its equipment," State Intellectual Property Office of the People's Republic of China, No. 1282048, applicant: Institute of Automation, Chinese Academy of Science, January 31, 2001

[A14] Wildes, Richard Patrick, Jane Circle Asmuth, Keith James Hanna, Stephen Charles Hsu, Raymond Joseph Kolczynski, James Regis Matey, and Sterling Eduard McBridge, "Automated, non-invasive iris recognition system and method," United States Patent US 5,572,596, assignee: David Sarnoff Research Center Inc., Princeton, N.J., USA, November 5, 1996

[A15] Czajka, Adam and Andrzej Pacut, "Zak's transform for automatic identity verification," *Proceedings of the 4th International Conference on Recent Advances in Soft Computing RASC2002*, 12-13 December 2002, Nottingham, United Kingdom, pp. 374-379, 2002

Eye structure and anatomy

[B1]   Adler, F. H., "Physiology of the Eye," St. Louis, MO: Mosby, 1965

[B2]   Davson, H., "The Physiology of the Eye," 2nd ed. Boston, MA: Little, Brown & Co., 1963

[B3]   Snell, R. S. and M. A. Lemp, "Clinical anatomy of the eye," 2nd Edition, Blackwell Science, 1998

[B4]   Ivins, James P. and John Porrill, "A deformable model of the human iris for measuring small three-dimensional eye movements," Machine Vision and Applications, vol. 11, str. 42-51, 1998

Time-frequency analysis

[C1]   Gabor, Denis, "Theory of communication," *Proc. Inst. Electr. Eng.*, Vol. 93 (III), pp. 429-457, 1946

[C2]   Chinen, Troy T. and Todd R. Reed, "A Performance Analysis of Fast Gabor Transform Methods," Graphical Models And Image Processing, Vol. 59, No. 3, pp. 117-127, May 1997

[C3]   Bastiaans, Martin J., "Gabor's Expansion and the Zak Transform for Continuous-Time and Discrete-Time Signals," w Josh Zeevi and Ronald Coifman (ed.), Signal and Image Representation in Combined Spaces, pp. 1–43, Academic Press, Inc., 1995

[C4]   Fisher, B., S. Perkins, A. Walker, and E.Wolfart, Hypermedia Image Processing Reference, available online: **http://www.cee.hw.ac.uk/hipr/html/hipr_top.html**

[C5]   Mallat, S. G., "Zero-crossing of wavelet transform," IEEE Transactions Information Theory, vol. 37, no. 14, pp. 1019-1033, 1991

[C6]   Chinen, Troy T., "A Performance Analysis of Fast Gabor Transform Methods," Graphical Models and Image Processing, Vol. 59, No. 3, pp. 117-127, 1997

Performance evaluation, standards

[D1]   Mansfield, A. J. and J.L. Wayman, "Best Practises in Testing and Reporting Performance of Biometric Devices," NPL Report CMSC 14/02, August 2002

[D2]   Common Criteria Biometric Evaluation Methodology Working Group, "Common Methodology for Information Technology Security Evaluation. Biometric Evaluation Methodology Supplement," August 2002

[D3]   Cambier, Jim, "Biometric Data Interchange Formats—Part 6: Iris image data," ISO/IEC 19794 Final Committee Draft

NEW DIRECTIONS IN ACCESS CONTROL

Sabrina De Capitani di Vimercati, Pierangela Samarati
Dipartimento di Tecnologie dell'Informazione Universit`
a di Milano 26013 Crema -Italy
{decapita,samarati}@dti.unimi.it

Abstract: Access control is the process of mediating every request to resources and data maintained by a system and determining whether the request should be granted or denied. Traditionally, the access control process is based on a simple paradigm with basic functionalities (e.g., simple authorization tuples), the access control rules are under the control of a single party, and relying on user's authentication. The emerging open-based scenarios make inapplicable traditional assumptions. In this paper we illustrate recent proposals and ongoing work addressing access control in emerging applications and new scenarios.

Keywords: Access control policies and languages; attribute and certificate-based authorizations; security policy composition; semantic-based access control

1. INTRODUCTION

Access control is the process of controlling every request to a system and determine, based on specified rules, whether the request should be granted or denied [20]. Traditionally, an access control system is based on a simple paradigm where access restrictions are represented by simple authorization tuples stating that a subject s can perform an action a on an object o. These access control rules are usually under the control of a single party and relying on user's authentication. However, the emerging open-based scenarios make inapplicable these traditional assumptions. Also, it is widely recognized that a well-understood model and a highly expressive language for access control are of paramount importance in today's global network environment. Many solutions have been proposed to increase expressiveness and flexibility of authorization languages [11, 14, 15, 17, 23]. However, even these rich approaches result limiting. First, current approaches to enforcing access

J. S. Kowalik et al. (eds.), Cyberspace Security and Defense: Research Issues, 279–293.
© 2005 *Springer. Printed in the Netherlands.*

control are all based on monolithic and complete authorization specifications. This is a limitation in many situations where the restrictions to be enforced come from different input requirements, possibly under the control of different authorities, and where the specifics of some requirements may not even been known a priori. This situation calls for a policy composition framework by which different component policies can be integrated while retaining their independence. Second, traditional assumptions for establishing and enforcing access control regulations do not hold anymore, since the traditional separation between authentication and access control does not apply, and alternative access control solutions should be devised. Writing access control policies where both requesters and resources to be protected are pointed at via data identifiers and access conditions evaluated against their generic *properties/attribute* seems to be a solution that can be used in open environments.

The remainder of this paper is organized as follows. Section 2 addresses the problem of combining authorization specifications that may be independently stated. We describe the characteristics that a policy composition framework should have and illustrate some current approaches and open issues. Section 3 addresses the problem of defining an access control system in open environments such as the Internet. We present the main requirements that an access control system should satisfy and describe current approaches and open issues. Finally, Section 4 concludes the paper.

2.   Policy Composition

Traditionally, authorization policies are expressed and managed in a centralized manner: one party administers and enforces the access control requirements. In many cases however, policy control has to be decentralized. For instance, in distributed environments, there may be multiple, independent and geographically distributed *entities* (i.e., individuals, organizations, institutes, and so on) with authority to control access to their local resources. Each of these parties is responsible for defining access control rules to protect resources and each brings its own set of constraints. To address these issues, a *policy composition framework* by which different component policies can be integrated while retaining their independence should be designed. The framework should be flexible to support different kinds of composition, yet remain simple so to keep control over complex compound policies. It should be based on a solid formal framework and a clear semantics to avoid ambiguities and enable correctness proofs.

In the following, we first describe the different requirements that must be addressed for a successful development and use of a policy composition framework. We then illustrate the main characteristics of some proposals and present some open issues.

2.1. Requirements of a Policy Composition Framework

A first step in the definition of a framework for composing policy is the identification of the characteristics that it should have. In particular, we have identified the following [6]:

- *Heterogeneous policy support.* The composition framework should be able to combine policies expressed in arbitrary languages and possibly enforced by different mechanisms. For instance, a datawarehouse may collect data from different data sources where the security restrictions autonomously stated by the sources and associated with the data are stated with different specification languages, or refer to different paradigms (e.g., open vs. closed policy).

- *Support of unknown policies.* It should be possible to account for policies which may be not completely known or even be specified and enforced in external systems. These policies are like "blackboxes" for which no (complete) specification is provided, but that can be queried at access control time. Think, for instance, of a situation where given accesses are subject, in addition to other policies, to a policy P enforcing "central administration approval". Neither the description of P, nor the specific accesses that it allows might be available; whereas P can respond yes or no to each specific request. Run-time evaluation is therefore the only possible option for P. In the context of a more complex and complete policy including P as a component, the specification could be partially compiled, leaving only P (and its possible consequences) to be evaluated at run time.

- *Controlled interference.* Policies cannot always be combined by simply merging their specifications (even if they are formulated in the same language), as this could have undesired side effects. The accesses granted/denied might not correctly reflect the specifications anymore. As a simple example, consider the combination of two systems P_{closed}, which applies a closed policy, based on rules of the form "grant access if $(s, o, +a)$", and P_{open} which applies an open policy, based on rules of the form "grant access if $(s, o, -a)$". Merging the two specifications would cause the latter decision rule to derive all authorizations not blocked by P_{open}, regardless of the contents of P_{closed}. Similar problems may arise from uncontrolled interaction of the derivation rules of the two specifications. Besides, if the adopted language is a logic language with negation, the merged program might not be stratified (which may lead to ambiguous or undefined semantics).

- *Expressiveness*. The language should be able to conveniently express a wide range of combinations (spanning from minimum privileges to maximum privileges, encompassing priority levels, overriding, confinement, refinement etc.) in a uniform language. The different kinds of combinations must be expressed without changing the input specifications (as it would be necessary even in most recent and flexible approaches) and without ad-hoc extensions to authorizations (like those introduced to support priorities). For instance, consider a policy P_1 regulating access to given documents and the central administration policy P_2. Assume that access to administrative documents can be granted only if authorized by both P_1 and P_2. This requisite can be expressed in existing approaches only by explicitly extending all the rules possibly referred to administrative documents to include the additional conditions specified by P_2. Among the drawbacks of this approach is the rule explosion that it would cause and the complex structure and loss of controls of two specifications; which, in particular, cannot be maintained and managed autonomously anymore.

- *Support of different abstraction levels*. The composition language should highlight the different components and their interplay at different levels of abstraction. This is important to: *i)* facilitate specification analysis and design; *ii)* facilitate cooperative administration and agreement on global policies; *iii)* support incremental specification by refinement.

- *Support for dynamic expressions and controlled modifications*. Mobile policies that follow (*stick with*) the data and can be enriched, subject to constraints, as the data move.

- *Formal semantics*. The composition language should be declarative, implementation independent, and based on a solid formal framework. The need of an underlying formal framework is widely recognized and in particular it is important to *i)* ensure non-ambiguous behavior, and *ii)* reason about and prove specifications properties and correctness [16]. In our framework this is particular important in the presence of *incomplete* specifications.

2.2. Summary of Current Policy Composition Frameworks

Various models have been proposed to reason about security policies [1, 11, 13, 18]. In [1, 13] the authors focused on the secure behavior of program modules. McLean [18] proposed a formal approach including combination operators: he introduced an algebra of security which enables to reason about the problem of policy conflict that can arise when different policies are combined. However, even though this approach permits to detect conflicts between policies, it did not propose a method to resolve the conflicts and to construct a security policy from inconsistent sub-policies. Hosmer [11] introduced the notion of meta-policies (i.e., policies about policies), an informal framework for combining security policies. Subsequently, Bell [2] formalized the combination of two policies with a function, called *policy combiner*, and introduced the notion of *policy attenuation* to allow the composition of conflicting security policies. Other approaches are targeted to the development of a uniform framework to express possibly heterogeneous policies [3, 14, 15, 17, 23]. Recently, Bonatti et al. [6] proposed an algebra for combining security policies together with its formal semantics. Following Bonatti et al.'s work, Jajodia et al. [22] presented a propositional algebra for policies with a syntax consisting of abstract symbols for atomic policy expressions and composition operators. The basic idea of these two proposals is to define a set of policy operators used for combining different policies. In particular, in [6] a policy is defined as a set of triples of the form (s, o, a), where s is a constant in (or a variable over) the set of subjects S, o is a constant in (or a variable over) the set of objects O, and a is a constant in (or a variable over) the set of actions A. Here, complex policies can then be obtained by combining policy identifiers, denoted P_i, through the following *algebra operators*.

- *Addition* (+) merges two policies by returning their set union. For instance, in an organization composed of different divisions, access to the main gate can be authorized by any of the administrator of the divisions (each of them knows users who needs the access to get to their division). The totality of the accesses through the main gate to be authorized would then be the union of the statements of each single division. Intuitively, additions can be applied in any situation where accesses can be authorized if allowed by any of the component (operand) policies.

- *Conjunction* (&) merges two policies by returning their intersection. For instance, consider an organization in which divisions share certain documents (e.g., clinical folders of patients). Access to the documents is to be allowed only if all the authorities that have a say on the document agree on it. Intuitively, while addition enforces maximum privilege, conjunction enforces minimum privilege.

- *Subtraction* (-) restricts a policy by eliminating all the accesses in the second policy. Intuitively, subtraction specifies exceptions to statements made by a policy and it encompasses the functionality of negative authorizations in existing approaches, while probably providing a clearer view of the combination of positive and negative statements. The advantages of subtraction over explicit denials include a simplification of the conflict resolution policies and a clearer semantics. In particular, the scoping of a difference operation allows to clearly and unambiguously express the two different uses of negative authorizations, namely *exceptions to positive statements* and *explicit prohibitions*, which are often confused in the models or requires explicit ad-hoc extension to the authorization form [19]. The use of subtraction provides extensible as the policy can be enriched to include different overriding/conflict resolution criteria as needed in each specific context, without affecting the form of the authorizations.

- *Closure* (∗) closes a policy under a set of inference (derivation) rules.

  Intuitively, derivation rules can be thought of as logic rules whose head is the authorization to be derived and whose body is the condition under which the authorization can be derived. Example of derivation rules can be found in essentially all logic based authorization languages proposed in the literature, where derivation rules are used, for example, to enforce propagation of authorizations along hierarchies in the data system, or to enforce more general forms of implication, related to the presence or absence of other authorizations, or depending on properties of the authorizations [14].

- *Scoping restriction* (^) restricts the application of a policy to a given set of subjects, objects, and actions. Scoping is particularly useful to "limit" the statements that can be established by a policy and, in some way, enforcing authority confinement. Intuitively, all authorizations in the policy which do not satisfy the scoping restriction are ignored, and therefore ineffective. For instance, the global policy of an organization can identify several component policies which need to be merged together; each component policy may be restricted in terms of properties of the subjects, objects and actions occurring in its authorizations.[1]

- *Overriding* (o) replaces part of a policy with a corresponding fragment of the second policy. The portion to be replaced is specified by means of a third policy. For instance, consider the case where users of a library who have passed the due date for returning a book cannot borrow the same

---

[1] A simple example of scoping constraint is the limitation of authorizations that can be stated by a policy to a specific portion of the data system hierarchy [15].

book anymore *unless* the responsible librarian vouchers for (authorizes) the loan. While the accesses otherwise granted by the library are stated as a policy P_{lib}, blacklist of accesses, meaning triples (user, book, loan) are stated as a policy P_{block}. In the absence of the *unless* portion of the policy, the accesses to be allowed would simply be $P_{lib} - P_{block}$. By allowing the librarian discretion for "overriding" the black list, calling P_{vouch} the triples authorized by the librarians, we can express the overall policy as $o\ (P_{lib}, P_{vouch}, P_{block})$.

- *Template* (τ) defines a partially specified policy that can be completed by supplying the parameters. Templates are useful for representing partially specified policies, where some component X is to be specified at a later stage. For instance, X might be the result of further policy refinement, or it might be specified by a different authority.

To fix ideas and make concrete examples, consider a drug-effects warehouse that might draw information from many hospitals. We assume that the warehouse receives information from three hospitals, denoted h_1, h_2, and h_3, respectively. These hospitals are responsible for granting access to information under their (possibly overlapping) authority domains, where domains are specified by a scoping function. The statements made by the hospitals are then unioned meaning that an access is authorized if any of the hospital policy states so. In term of the algebra, the warehouse policy can be represented as an expression of the form $P_1\hat{}[o \leq O_{h_1}] + P_2\hat{}[o \leq O_{h_2}] + P_3\hat{}[o \leq O_{h_3}]$, where P_i denotes the policy defined by hospital h_i, and the scope restriction $\hat{}[o \leq O_{h_i}]$ selects the authorizations referred to objects released by hospital h_i.[2] Each policy P_i can then be further refined. For instance, consider policy P1. Suppose that hospital h1 defines a policy P_{drug} regulating the access to drug-effects information. Assume also that the drug-effects information can be released only if the hospital's researchers obtain a patient's consent; $P_{consents}$ reports accesses to drug-effects information that the patients agree to release. We can then express P_1 as $P_{drug}\ \&\ P_{consents}$.

---

[2] We assume that the information collected from the hospitals can be organized in abstractions defining groups of objects that can be collectively referred to with a given name. Objects and groups thereof define a partial order that naturally introduces a hierarchy, where O_{h_i} contains objects obtained from hospital h_i.

2.3. Open Issues

We briefly describe some open issues that need to be taken into consideration in the future development of a policy composition framework.

- Investigate different *algebra operators and formal languages* for enforcing the algebra and proving properties. The proposed policy composition frameworks can be enriched by adding new operators. For instance, an *application operator* could be added that allows to take into consideration a policy only if the associated conditions evaluate to true. Also, the influence of different rule languages on the expressiveness of the algebra has not been yet investigated in the proposed approaches.

- *Administrative policies and language* with support for multiple authorities. The proposed approaches could be enriched by adding administrative policies that define who can specify authorizations/rules (i.e., who can define a component policy) governing access control.

- *Policy enforcement.* The resolution of the algebraic expression defining a policy P determines a set of ground authorization terms, that define exactly the accesses to be granted according to P. Different strategies can be used to evaluate the algebraic expression for enforcing access control: materialization, run-time evaluation, and partial evaluation. The first one allows a one-time compilation of the policy against which all accesses can be efficiently evaluated and which will then need to be updated only if the policy changes. The second strategy consists in enforcing a run-time evaluation of each request (access triple) against the policy expression to determine whether the access should be allowed. Between these two extremes, possibly combining the advantages of them, there are partial evaluation approaches, which can enforce different degrees of computation/materialization.

- Incremental approaches to enforce *changes to component policies*. When a materialization approach is used to evaluate the algebraic expression for enforcing access control, incremental approaches [21] can be applied to minimize the recomputation of the policy.

- *Mobile policies.* Intuitively, a *mobile policy* is the policy associated with an object and that follows the object when it is passed to another site. Because different and possibly independent authorities can define different parts of the mobile policy in different time instants, the policy can be expressed as a policy expression. In such a context, there is the problem on how ensure the obedience of policies when the associated objects move around.

3. ACCESS CONTROL IN OPEN SYSTEMS

In open environments such as the Internet resource/service requesters are not identified by unique names but depend upon their *attributes* (usually substantiated by certificates) to gain accesses to resources. Basing authorization on attributes of the resource/service requester provides flexibility and scalability that is essential in the context of large distributed open systems, where subjects are identified by their characteristics. Attribute-based access control differs from the traditional discretionary access control model by replacing both the *subject* by a set of attributes and *objects* by descriptions in terms of available properties associated with them. The meaning of a stated attribute may be a granted capability for a service, an identity or a non-identifying characteristic of a user (e.g., a skill). Here, the basic idea is that not all access control decisions are identity-based. For instance, information about a user's current role (e.g., physician) or a client's ability to pay for a resource access may be more important than the client's identity.

As before, we first describe the different requirements that must be addressed by an attribute-based access control system. We then illustrate the main characteristics of some proposals and present some open issues.

3.1. Requirements of an Attributed-Based Access Control System

Figure 1 depicts the basic scenario we consider. We are given different parties that interact with each other to offer services. A party can act both as a server and a client and each party has *i)* a set of services it provides and *ii)* a *portfolio* of properties (attributes) that the party enjoys. Access restrictions to the services are expressed by policies that specified the properties that a requester should enjoy to gain access to the services. The services are meant to offer certain functionalities that depend on the input parameters supplied by its users. Often input parameters must fulfill certain conditions to assure correct behavior of a

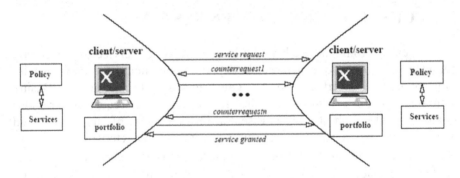

Figure 1. Client/Server Interaction

service. We identified the following requirements for specifying attribute-based access control for services.

- *Attribute interchange.* A server should be able to communicate to the client the requirements it need to satisfy to get access. Also, a client should be able to prove its eligibility for a service. This communication interchange could be performed in different ways (e.g., the involved parties can apply different strategies with respect to which properties are submitted).

- *Support for fine-grained reference to attributes within a credential.* The system should allow the selective disclosure of credentials which is a requirement that is not usually supported because users attributes are defined according to functional needs, making it easier to collect all credentials in a row instead of iteratively asking for the ones strictly necessary for a given service only.

- *Support for hierarchical relationships and abstractions on services and portfolio.* Attribute-based access control policies should be able to specify accesses to collection of services based upon collection of attributes processed by the requester.

- *Expressiveness and flexibility.* The system must support the specification of complex access control requirements. For instance, consider a service that offers telephone contracts and requires that the customer is at least 18 years of age. The telephone selling service has two input parameters, namely homeAddress and noticePeriod. The homeAddress must be a valid address in Italy and noticePeriod must be either one or three months. Further, the service's access control policy requires that contracts with one month notice period and home address outside a particular geographical region are closed only with users who can prove their AAA membership. Hence, we see that the access control requirements of a service may require more than one interaction between a client and a server.

- *Support for meta-policies.* The system should provide meta-policies for protecting the policy when communication requisites. This happens when a list of alternatives (policies) that must be fulfilled to gain the access to the data/service is returned to the counterpart. For instance, suppose that the policy returned by the system is "citizenship=EU". The party can decide to return to the client either the policy as it is or a modified policy simply requesting the user to prove its nationality (then protecting the information that access is restricted to EU citizens).

3.2. Summary of Current Attribute-Based Proposals

To address the problems described in the previous section, some proposals have been developed that use *digital certificates*. Traditionally, the widely adopted digital certificate has been the identity certificate. An *identity certificate* is an electronic document used to recognize an individual, a server, or some other entity, and to connect that identity with a public key [4, 5, 8]. Identity certificates are certified by given entities (e.g., certification authorities). The certificate authority generally uses published verification procedures to ensure that an entity requesting a certificate is who it claims to be. When a certificate authority issues an identity certificate, it binds a particular public key to the name of the entity identified in the certificate (such as the name of a doctor). In addition to a public key, a certificate always includes additional information such as the name of the entity it identifies, an expiration date, the name of the certificate authority that issued the certificate, the digital signature of the issuing certificate authority, and so on.

More recent research and development efforts have resulted in a second kind of digital certificate, the *attribute certificate* [10] that can be used for supporting attribute-based access control systems. An attribute certificate has a structure similar to an identity certificate but contains attributes that specify access control information associated with the certificate holder (e.g., group membership, role, security clearance). Note that in principle these attributes can be placed in the extension fields of identity certificates [12]. However, this is not a viable solution for two main reasons. First, the certificate authorities who issue the identity certificates are not usually responsible for this kind of authorization information. As a result, certificate authorities must take additional steps to obtain access control information from the source. Second, the lifetime associated with attribute-based information is different from the lifetime associated with identity-based certificates. In an attribute certificate, attributes need to be protected in a similar way to an identity certificate: they are therefore digitally signed sets of attributes created by *attribute authorities*. Attribute authorities are responsible for their certificates during their whole lifetime, as well as issuing them.

A first attempt to provide a uniform framework for attribute-based access control specification and enforcement was presented by Bonatti and Samarati in [7]. They propose a uniform framework for regulating service access and information disclosure in an open, distributed network system like the Web. Like in previous proposals, access regulations are specified as logical rules, where some predicates are explicitly identified. Attribute certificates are modeled as *credential expressions* of the form a ground value or a variable. Besides credentials, the proposal also allows to reason about declarations (i.e., unsigned statements) and user-profiles that the server can maintain and exploit for taking the access decision. Communication of requisites to be satisfied by the requester is based on a filtering and renaming process applied on the server's policy, which exploits partial evaluation techniques in logic programs. Yu et al. [24, 25, 26] developed a service negotiation framework for requesters and providers to gradually expose their attributes.

3.3. Open Issues

Although current approaches supporting attribute-based access control are technically mature enough to be used in practical scenarios, there are still some issues that need to be investigated in more detail to enable more complex applications. We summarize these issues as follows [7].

- *Ontologies.* Due to the openness of the scenario and the richness and variety of security requirements and attributes that may need to be considered, it is important to provide parties with a means to understand each other with respect to the properties they enjoy (or request the counterpart to enjoy). Therefore, common languages, dictionaries, and ontologies must be developed.

- *Access control evaluation and outcome.* Users may be occasional and they may not know under what conditions a service can be accessed. Therefore, to make a service "usable", access control mechanisms cannot simply return "yes" or "no" answers. It may be necessary to explain why authorizations are denied—or better how—to obtain the desired permissions. Therefore, the system can return an undefined response meaning that current information is insufficient to determine whether the request can be granted or denied. For instance, suppose that a user can access a service if she is at least eighteen and can provide a credit card number. Two cases can occur: *i)* the system knows that the user is not yet eighteen and therefore returns a negative response; *ii)* the user has proved that she is eighteen and the system returns an undefined response together with the request to provide the number of a credit card.

- *Filtering and renaming of policies.* As discussed above, since access control does not return only a "yes" or "no" access decision, but it returns the information about which conditions need to be satisfied for the access to be granted ("undefined" decision), the problem of communicating such conditions to the counterpart arises. To fix the ideas, let us see the problem from the point of view of the server (the client's point of view is symmetrical). The naive way to formulate a credential request, that is, giving the client a list with all the possible sets of credentials that would enable the service, is not feasible, due to the large number of possible alternatives. Also, the communication process should not disclose "too much" of the underlying security policy, which might also be regarded as sensitive information.

- *Negotiation strategy.* Credentials grant parties different choices with respect to what release (or ask) the counterpart and when to do it, thus allowing for multiple trust negotiation strategies [25]. For instance, an *eager* strategy, requires parties to turn over all their credentials if the release policy for them is satisfied, without waiting for the credentials to be requested. By contrast, a *parsimonious* strategy requires that parties only release credentials upon explicit request by the server (avoiding unnecessary releases).

- *Composite services.* In case of a composite service (i.e., a service that is decomposable into other services called component services) there must be some semi-automatic mechanisms to calculate the access control policy of a composite service from the access control policies of its component services.

- *Semantics-aware rules.* Although attribute-based access control systems allow the specifications of access control rules with reference to generic attributes or properties of the requestor and the resources, they do not fully exploit the semantic power and reasoning capabilities of emerging web applications. It is therefore important to be able to specify access control rules about subjects accessing the information and about resources to be accessed in terms of rich ontology-based metadata (e.g., Semantic Web-style ones) increasingly available in advanced e-services applications [9].

4. CONCLUSIONS

Traditional access control models and languages result limiting for emerging Web applications. The open and dynamic nature of such scenario requires the development of new ways of enforcing access control. In this paper, we investigated recent proposals and ongoing work addressing access control in emerging applications and new scenarios.

5. ACKNOWLEDGMENTS

This work was supported in part by the European Union within the PRIME Project in the FP6/IST Programme under contract IST-2002-507591 and by the Italian MIUR within the KIWI and MAPS projects.

REFERENCES

[1] Abadi, M., and L. Lamport, Composing specifications, *ACM Transactions on Programming Languages*, 14(4):1–60, October 1992.

[2] Bell, D. E., Modeling the multipolicy machine, in *Proc. of the New Security Paradigm Workshop*, August 1994.

[3] Bertino, E., S. Jajodia, and P. Samarati, A flexible authorization mechanism for relational data management systems, *ACM Transactions on Information Systems*, 17(2):101–140, April 1999.

[4] Blaze, M., J. Feigenbaum, J. Ioannidis, and A.D. Keromytis, The role of trust management in distributed systems security, *Secure Internet Programming: Issues in Distributed and Mobile Object Systems*, Springer Verlag LNCS State-ofthe-Art series, 1998.

[5] Blaze, M., J. Feigenbaum, and J. Lacy, Decentralized trust management, in *Proc. of the 1996 IEEE Symposiumon Security and Privacy*, Oakland, CA, USA, May 1996.

[6] Bonatti, P., S. De Capitani di Vimercati, and P. Samarati, An algebra for composing access control policies, *ACM Transactions on Information and System Security*, 5(1):1–35, February 2002.

[7] Bonatti, P. and P. Samarati, A unified framework for regulating access and information release on the web, *Journal of Computer Security*, 10(3):241–272, 2002.

[8] Chu, Y-H., J. Feigenbaum, B. LaMacchia, P. Resnick, and M. Strauss, Referee: trust management forweb applications, *WorldWide Web Journal*, 2(3):706–734, 1997.

[9] Damiani, E., S. De Capitani di Vimercati, C. Fugazza, and P. Samarati, Extending policy languages to the semantic web, in *Proc. of the International Conference on Web Engineering*, Munich, Germany, July 2004.

[10] Farrell, S. and R. Housley, An internet attribute certificate profile for authorization. RFC 3281, April 2002.

[11] Hosmer, H., Metapolicies ii, in *Proc. of the 15th National Computer Security Conference*, 1992.

[12] Information technology—open systems interconnection—the directory: Authentication framework, 2000. Recommendation X.509 (03/00).

[13] Jaeger, T., Access control in configurable systems, *Lecture Notes in Computer Science*, 1603:289–316, 2001.

[14] Jajodia, S., P. Samarati, M.L. Sapino, and V.S. Subrahmanian, Flexible support for multiple access control policies, *ACM Transactions on Database Systems*, 26(2):214–260, June 2001.

[15] Jajodia, S., P. Samarati, V.S. Subrahmanian, and E. Bertino, A unified framework for enforcing multiple access control policies, in *Proc. of the 1997 ACM International SIGMOD Conference on Management of Data*, Tucson, AZ, May 1997.

[16] Landwehr, C., Formal models for computer security, *Computing Surveys*, 13(3):247–278, September 1981.

[17] Li, N., J. Feigenbaum, and B. Grosof, A logic-based knowledge representation for authorization with delegation, in *Proc. of the 12th IEEE Computer Security Foundations Workshop*, pages 162–174, July 1999.

[18] McLean, J., The algebra of security, in *Proc. of the 1988 IEEE Computer Society Symposium on Security and Privacy*, Oakland, CA, USA, April 1988.

[19] Rabitti, F., E. Bertino, W. Kim, and D. Woelk, A model of authorization for next-generation database systems, *ACM TODS*, 16(1):89–131, March 1991.

[20] Samarati, P. and S. De Capitani di Vimercati, Access control: Policies, models, and mechanisms, in R. Focardi and R. Gorrieri, editors, *Foundations of Security Analysis and Design*, LNCS 2171. Springer-Verlag, 2001.

[21] Subrahmanian, V. S., S. Adali, A. Brink, J.J. Lu, A. Rajput, T.J. Rogers, R. Ross, and C. Ward, Hermes: Heterogeneous reasoning and mediator system. **http://www.cs.umd.edu/projects/hermes**

[22] Wijesekera, D. and S. Jajodia, A propositional policy algebra for access control, *ACM Transactions on Information and System Security*, 6(2):286–325, May 2003.

[23] Woo, T.Y.C. and S.S. Lam, Authorizations in distributed systems: A new approach, *Journal of Computer Security*, 2(2,3):107–136, 1993.

[24] Yu, T., M. Winslett, and K.E. Seamons, Prunes: An efficient and complete strategy for automated trust negotiation over the internet, in *Proc. of the 7th ACM Conference on Computer and Communications Security*, Athens, Greece, November 2000.

[25] Yu, T., M. Winslett, and K.E. Seamons, Interoperable strategies in automated trust negotiation, in *Proc. of the 8th ACM Conference on Computer and Communications Security*, Philadelphia, PA, USA, November 2001.

[26] Yu, T., M. Winslett, and K.E. Seamons, Supporting structured credentials and sensistive policies trough interoperable strategies for automated trust, *ACM Transactions on Information and System Security (TISSEC)*, 6(1):1–42, 2003.

PART 5

CRYPTOGRAPHY

IMPROVED BLOCK CIPHER COUNTER MODE OF OPERATION SCHEMES

IVAN GORBENKO
Kharkov National University of Radioelectronics, Ukraine

SERGIY GOLOVASHYCH
Kharkov National University of Radioelectronics, Ukraine
serg_golov@mail.ru

Abstract: The main goals of presented research were the analysis of the base block cipher protectability from cryptanalytic attacks in standard modes of operation and the ways to increase the stream modes of operation security. We also paid special attention to the problem of the gamma overlapping. Therefore, we selected the counter mode as a basis for the new perspective modes, and investigated its property for the case of multiple encryption restarts with the same key. As result of our research, we are proposing two new schemes of modes of operation. They have advanced security.

Keywords: Cryptography; block ciphers; modes of operation; Counter mode (CTR); known plaintext attacks; gamma period; gamma overlapping

INTRODUCTION

Modern computer systems are often used for processing, storing and transferring restricted information. These information systems have certain safety requirements and should maintain confidentiality. The easiest way of solving this problem in open systems is using cryptography.

One of the essential components of the modern cryptographic security systems is the symmetric ciphers. They are divided into two classes: stream ciphers and block ciphers.

The block ciphers are more widespread in open computer systems, but the classical stream ciphers usually are hardware implementation oriented, secret and used in special-purpose communication systems.

J. S. Kowalik et al. (eds.), Cyberspace Security and Defense: Research Issues, 297–314.
© 2005 *Springer. Printed in the Netherlands.*

The block cipher can be considered as key-dependent permutation on a set of binary vectors corresponding to separate blocks. For the purpose of weakness elimination of permutation ciphers, for block ciphers several modes of operation were designed. They are intended for processing a large amount of information. These modes actually define the schemes of stream ciphering on basis of a block cipher.

The most effective classes of cryptanalytical attacks on block ciphers are "known plaintext" and "chosen plaintext" attacks. They assume that cryptanalyst knows the plaintext that corresponds to the intercepted cryptogram or can control the data input of the cipher respectively. As a result of this the security of block cipher-based stream cipher depends on both the block cipher security and the properties of the mode of operation scheme.

The main goals of our research were the analysis of the base block cipher protectability from cryptanalytic attacks in standard modes of operation and the ways to increase the stream modes of operation security. We also paid special attention to the problem of the gamma overlapping; therefore, we selected the counter mode as a basis for the new perspective modes. The counter mode is a unique mode of operation, which has the "fixed period" and the "random access" properties. We investigated its property for the case of multiple encryption restarts with the same key. As result of our research, we are proposing two new schemes of modes of operation. They have advanced security.

NOTATION

In the article we used following notation:

E – block cipher encryption: $O_i = E_K (I_i)$;

D – block cipher decryption: $I_i = D_K (O_i)$;

G – generator of "synchronization sequences";

K – secret key for block cipher;

I_i – input block to base block cipher;

O_i – output block from base block cipher;

Γ_i – one block of encryption gamma;

M_i – one block of plaintext (message);

C_i – one block of cryptogram;

IV – initialization vector;

S_i – internal state of stream cipher;

n – bit-size of base cipher block;

m – bit-size of gamma-output block;

r – bit-size of feedback.

According to the NIST Sp. Pub. №800-38A [1], it is specified 5 modes of operation (and see also [2,3,4,5]). The first of them (ECB) is a pure block cipher; all other modes define stream ciphers. Let's consider each of them and analyze the possibility to extract the base cipher input and output values from the known plaintext and cipher text. If this is possible for some mode then the class of known plaintext attacks is applicable to this mode.

1. THE OUTPUT FEEDBACK MODE

On all following layouts of modes of operation the encryption transformation is presented at the left and the decryption is at the right. The Output Feedback (OFB) mode defines synchronous stream cipher (Figure 1).

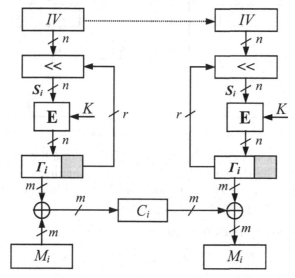

Figure 1. The Output Feedback Mode

The next block of gamma is determined by one or a few of the preceding blocks of gamma. As we can see from the expressions the output of base cipher can be obtained as XOR of cryptogram and known plaintext blocks, but input of base cipher at current step equal to its previous output.

Known plaintext attack ($m = r = n$):

$$I_i = O_{i-1}, \quad O_i = C_i \oplus M_i, \quad I_0 = IV$$

Therefore, the OFB mode doesn't protect the base cipher from known plaintext attacks.

2. THE CIPHER FEEDBACK MODE

The Cipher Feedback (CFB) mode defines self-synchronized stream cipher (Figure 2).

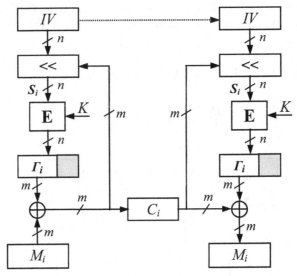

Figure 2. The Cipher Feedback Mode

The next block of gamma is determined by one or a few preceding blocks of cryptogram. The output of the base cipher, as before, can be obtained as XOR of cryptogram and known plaintext blocks, and input of the base cipher at current step is the previous cryptogram block.

Known plaintext attack (m = n):

$$I_i = C_{i-1}, \quad O_i = C_i \oplus M_i, \quad I_0 = IV$$

Therefore, the CFB mode doesn't protect base cipher from the known plaintext attacks too.

3. THE CIPHER BLOCK CHAINING MODE

The Cipher Block Chaining (CBC) mode (Figure 3) utilizes the scheme that is the inverse to CFB mode therefore it has similar property. The input of the base cipher can be obtained as XOR of the previous cryptogram block and the current plaintext block, but the output of the base cipher corresponds to the cryptogram block. So the CBC mode also doesn't protect base cipher from the known plaintext attacks.

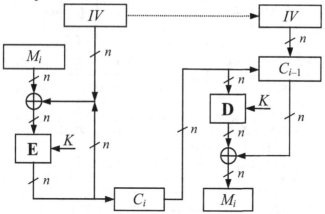

Figure 3. The Cipher Block Chaining Mode

Known plaintext attack:

$$I_i = C_{i-1} \oplus M_i, \quad O_i = C_i$$

4. THE COUNTER MODE

The last standard mode is the Counter (CTR) mode. The layout that is shown on the Figure 4 describes the CTR mode with the secret synchronization sequence. The same scheme is utilized at the 2nd mode of GOST 28147 89. The blocks of gamma are produced by means of the base block encryption of corresponding blocks of the synchronization sequence. The synchronization sequence (S) is produced from the encrypted initial vector (IV) using some recurrent generator (G). In the easiest case the generator G can be defined as the simple n-bit-length summary counter with fixed increment value (W). We shall call this value *the one-step "weight" value*. The module of such generator is equal to the n-th power of two.

In the same way as the OFB mode, the base cipher output can be obtained as XOR of cryptogram and known plaintext. Its input values can't be obtained, but the differences between them are known and potentially it can be used for mounting some differential attack. Therefore, the Counter mode also doesn't protect base cipher from the known plaintext attacks.

Known plaintext attack (m = n):

$$I_i = ?, \quad \forall i : \Delta I_{i,i+1} = W, \quad O_i = C_i \oplus M_i$$

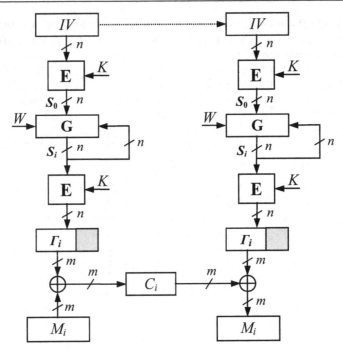

Figure 4. The Counter Mode

5. "FIXED STEP COUNTERS"

Let's consider internal structure of the generator G. As it was mentioned above, in the simplest case it can be simple summary counter with fixed increment value (W). It is quite enough to produce suitable synchronization sequence, because the single requirement for that sequence is to have no repetition on a given length. Such generator can be described by the next recurrent expression:

$$S_i = (S_{i-1} + W) \bmod 2^n,$$

where S_i –   internal state at step i;

W –   one step "weight" value.

We call such generator the "*Fixed Step Counter,*" because its parameter W is fixed within the bounds of one sequence.

As we can see from the following expression:

$$S_i = (S_0 + W \times i) \bmod 2^n,$$

the difference between any pair of the elements is fixed and can be expressed from the parameter W. Potentially this property can be used for the differential cryptoanalysis, especially when the W is known.

We can divide Fixed Step Counters on two classes by usage period of step "weight" value (W):

1. *Constant public parameter* W (in this case, the parameter W is a part of the mode).

2. *Variable (session) secret parameter* W (it changes together with IV at each session).

Let's consider the periodic properties of each of them.

5.1. Period of Fixed Step Counters

Let's consider the rules of step "weight" value selecting. Let's assume that message length is always limited by L_{max} blocks, and make use of following notations: the required quantity of binary digits for representing value L_{max} denoted by small letter l, the period of generator denoted by capital letter T. Moreover, the value of l must be at the least four times less than block-bit-length n.

$$T = 2^n /(W, 2^n), \qquad l = \lceil \log_2 (L_{max} + 1) \rceil, \quad l \le n/4$$

5.1.1. Constant Public "Weight"

If the used value of parameter W is odd, then the period of binary counter is maximum and equal to the transformation module. For the first case the step "weight" value is constant and public, therefore parameter W may be any odd number with a respective width. In that case, an assaulter knows parameter W and can calculate the difference between any pair of counter states S_i.

$$W = 2 \times x + 1 \quad \Rightarrow \quad (W, 2^n) = 1 \quad \Rightarrow \quad T = 2^n$$

The difference is calculated at the ring of natural numbers by the module n-th power of two.

Assaulter knowledge: $\qquad \Delta S_{i,j} = W \times (j - i) \bmod 2^n$.

5.1.2. Variable (Session) Secret "Weight"

In the second case, the parameter W is secret; therefore, it must be generated randomly. It must also satisfy to some requirements in order to provide a period that is larger than L_{max}.

The period of the counter is inversely proportional to the greatest common divisor of the module and increment value W. We propose next very simple procedure to form parameter W:

1.   Generate a random n-bit-length number.

$$R \leftarrow RANDOM$$

2.   If the $n-l$ least significant bits are zero, then set the least significant bit to one.

$$R = x \times 2^{n-l} + y$$

$$W \leftarrow \begin{cases} R, & y > 0 \\ R \vee 1, & y = 0 \end{cases} \Rightarrow \quad T > L_{\text{max}}$$

The number is produced by this way can be used as secret parameter W.

In the second case, the assaulter knows only that the differences between generator states S_i located at on the same distance are equal. This considerably decreases the assaulter known information in comparison to the first case.

Assaulter knowledge: $\forall i, j, t: \Delta S_{i,\,i+t} = \Delta S_{j,\,j+t}$.

5.2.   Gamma Overlapping

Let's consider the problem of gamma overlapping.

*The **gamma overlapping** term we shall use for designation of the event that consists of a block repetition within one of the sequences of encryption gamma or at least two blocks repetition in any pair of different sequences, produced by the same key.*

For the task simplification, consider the counter mode construction where the encryption-gamma utilizes the full output block of base cipher. In this case, taking into consideration that the block encryption is bijective mapping we may replace the gamma overlapping problem by the synchronization sequence overlapping problem and may consider only generator G accordingly.

As stated above blocks repetition within of one sequence can be prevented by appropriate selection of W parameter.

Now let's consider the overlapping event of two synchronization sequences for both case of counter mode building.

5.2.1. Gamma Overlapping Event for Constant Step "Weight"

For the first case when the step "weight" value is constant, we have following situation (Figure 5). If two different synchronization sequences i and j have at least one (not last) common element than all elements following to them coincide in pairs. In that way *the overlapping event depend from the sequences start points only.*

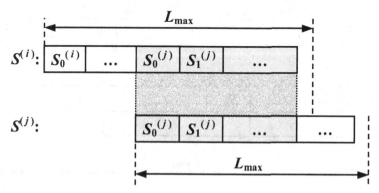

Figure 5. Gamma Overlapping Event for Constant Step "Weight"

Gamma overlapping condition:

$$\left| S_0^{(i)} - S_0^{(j)} \right| \leq W \times (L_{max} - 2)$$

Overlapping probability for one pair of sequences:

$$P_{1\,max} = \frac{2 \times L_{max} - 3}{2^n} \cong 2^{-(n-l-1)}$$

Overlapping probability for multitude sequences:

$$P_{max} = P_{1\,max} \times (N^2 - N)/2$$

From the overlapping probability expressions, we derive expressions for Allowable number of cipher restarts without key change:

$$N_A \approx \sqrt{2 \times P_A / P_{1\,max}} = \sqrt{2^{n-l} \times P_A}$$

where P_A – allowable overlapping probability.

5.2.2. Gamma Overlapping Event for Variable Step "Weight"

For the second case when the step "weight" value is variable, we have another situation (Figure 6). The one pair coincidence of not last elements isn't enough for the overlapping event occurs. Distances to the elements of next coincident pair depend from the correlation between step "weight" values used for the sequences producing. In order to overlapping event is possible the distances between elements of the nearest coincident pairs must be less than L_{max}. In that way *the overlapping event depends from both the sequences start points and the correlation between step "weight" values.*

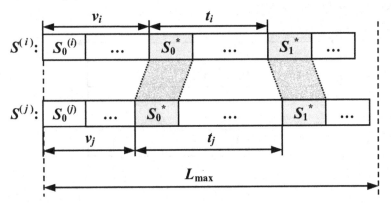

Figure 6. Gamma Overlapping Event for Variable Step "Weight"

Gamma overlapping condition:

$$\begin{cases} S^{(i)}_{v_i} = S^{(j)}_{v_j} = S^*_0 \\ S^{(i)}_{v_i+t_i} = S^{(j)}_{v_j+t_j} = S^*_1 \\ (v_i+t_i) \le L_{max} \\ (v_j+t_j) \le L_{max} \\ t_i \ne 0, \quad t_j \ne 0 \\ S^*_0 = S^*_1 \end{cases} \Rightarrow \begin{cases} t_j \times W_j - t_i \times W_i \equiv 0 \,(\mathrm{mod}\,2^n) \\ v_j \times W_j - v_i \times W_i \equiv \Delta S^{(i,j)}_0 \,(\mathrm{mod}\,2^n) \\ (v_i+t_i) \le L_{max}, \quad (v_j+t_j) \le L_{max} \\ t_i \ne 0, \quad t_j \ne 0 \end{cases}$$

where t_i – minimum number of steps between repeated states;
   v_i – minimum number of steps to first repeated state;

$\Delta S^{(i,j)}_0$ – initial states difference:

$$\Delta S^{(i,j)}_0 = \left(S^{(i)}_0 - S^{(j)}_0\right) \mathrm{mod}\,2^n$$

Gamma overlapping condition **1**:

$$\begin{cases} t_j \times W_j - t_i \times W_i \equiv 0 \pmod{2^n} \\ 0 < t_i \le L_{\max}, \quad 0 < t_j \le L_{\max} \end{cases}$$

1st condition fulfillment probability:

$$P'_{1\max} = L_{\max}^2 / 2^n$$

Gamma overlapping condition **2**:

$$\begin{cases} v_j \times W_j - v_i \times W_i \equiv \Delta S_{i,j}^{(0)} \pmod{2^n} \\ 0 \le v_i < L_{\max}, \quad 0 \le v_j < L_{\max} \end{cases}$$

2nd condition fulfillment probability:

$$P''_{1\max} = (L_{\max} + 1)^2 / 2^n$$

Overlapping probability for one pair of sequences:

$$P_{1\max} \cong \frac{1}{2} \times \left(\frac{3}{4} \times \frac{L_{\max}^2}{2^n} \right)^2 \cong \frac{1}{4} \times \frac{L_{\max}^4}{2^{2n}} \cong 2^{-(2n-4l+2)}$$

Overlapping probability for multitude sequences:

$$P_{\max} = P_{1\max} \times (N^2 - N)/2$$

From the overlapping probability expressions, we derive expressions for Allowable number of cipher restarts without key change:

$$N_A \approx \sqrt{2 \times P_A / P_{1\max}} = 2^{n-2l+1} \times \sqrt{2 \times P_A} \,,$$

where P_A – allowable overlapping probability.

In the Table 1, the estimated values of upper bounds of the gamma overlapping probability for one pair of sequences ($P_{1\max}$) and the allowable number of cipher restarts with same key (N_A) are presented. Taking into account the limitation on the value l, which must be at most a quarter of the value n we can see that the overlapping probability of one pair of sequences for the case of variable W is significantly smaller than for the case of constant W.

Table 1. Upper Bounds of the Gamma Overlapping Properties

Counter type	P_{1max}	N_A
Constant step "weight"	$2^{-(n-l-1)}$	$\sqrt{2^{n-l} \times P_A}$
Variable step "weight"	$2^{-(2n-4l+2)}$	$2^{n-2l+1} \times \sqrt{2 \times P_A}$

5.2.3. Gamma Overlapping for IP-Traffic Encryption by Counter Mode

To illustrate considerable difference of overlapping probability between these two variants of counter mode, consider the example of the gamma overlapping properties calculation for the case of IP-traffic encryption.

Block length n = 128 bit   **1 day = 216,4 sec.**

Min. packet size = 28 byte,   **Max. packet size = 216 byte**

L_{max} = (216 × 8) / 128 = 212 blocks $\Rightarrow$ l = 12

We assumed the each packet is a separate message with individual session parameters. It is used following notation: subscript *CSW* means the *Constant Step "Weight"* and subscript *VSW* means the *Variable Step "Weight"*.

We performed calculation of overlapping probability for two most widespread cases of transfer rate: 100 Mbps and 1 Gbps. For shown results we assumed that all packets have maximal size, but P_{CSW}-values can be slightly less if we accept model with minimal packet size. As you can see the absolute value of binary logarithm of overlapping probability for the Variable step "weight" in two and half times more then for the Constant step "weight".

The upper bounds of the gamma overlapping probability:

$$P_{CSW} \approx 2^{-115} \times N^2 : \qquad 100\,\text{Mbps}: \quad P_{CSW} \approx 2^{-67} \times D^2$$
$$1\,\text{Gbps}: \qquad P_{CSW} \approx 2^{-60} \times D^2$$
$$P_{VSW} \approx 2^{-210} \times N^2 : \qquad 100\,\text{Mbps}: \quad P_{VSW} \approx 2^{-162} \times D^2$$
$$1\,\text{Gbps}: \qquad P_{VSW} \approx 2^{-155} \times D^2$$

where D – days number in one key usage period.

The allowable number of cipher restarts:

$$N_{A,CSW} \approx 2^{58} \times \sqrt{P_A}$$

$$N_{A,VSW} \approx 2^{105,5} \times \sqrt{P_A}$$

So the Variable "weight" counter has two advantages under the Constant "weight" counter:

1. the step "weight" value is unknown for assaulter;
2. the gamma overlapping probability for the case of multi-session key usage is incomparably smaller.

The main drawback of the Variable step "weight" counter is the two times increasing of the session initialization vector.

6. CONSTRUCTION PRINCIPLES OF SECURE STREAM CIPHERING MODES

Now consider the ways of security improving of stream modes of operation. As was shown above the all standard modes of operation allow application of the known plaintext attack to their base block cipher. And also synchronous OFB mode doesn't guarantee the some lower bound of gamma's period.

On purpose to eliminate the mentioned defects of the standard modes of operation, we have defined three design principles of construction stream modes with advanced security:

- Gamma's period must always satisfy some lower bound (T_{min}) independently from used key and initialization vector.
- The state change function (same as the gamma output function) must be non-linear and key dependent.
- The cipher must hide self internal state, i.e. the states' space must exceed the gamma-output block space.

Common structure of "secure" stream cipher, which satisfies mentioned principles, is presented on Figure 7.

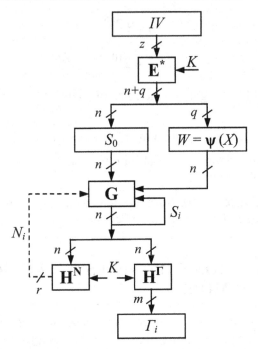

Figure 7. Common Structure of "Secure" Stream Cipher

At Figure 7 are used following additional symbols:

N_i – number of steps to the next state $i+1$;

Γ_i – gamma-output block;

ψ – "weight"-selection function;

E^* – init encryption function;

$\mathbf{H^N}$ – keyed feedback function;

$\mathbf{H^G}$ – keyed gamma-output function.

7. "DYNAMIC STEP COUNTER"

In concordance with these principles we propose the new construction of stream modes. We called it the "Dynamic Step Counter". It has following analytical description:

$$S_{i+1} = (S_i + W \times N_i) \bmod 2^n$$

$$N_i = f_K(S_i), \quad 0 < N_i < 2^r, \quad r + m \leq n$$

$$W = 2^{n/2} + 2^{n/4+1} + 1 \quad (for \ r = n/2)$$

$$(W, 2^n) = 1 \quad \Rightarrow \quad \mathbf{2^{n-r} < T \leq 2^n}$$

where S_i − internal state at step i;

               W − one step "weight" value;

               N_i − number of elementary W-increments on the step i;

               f_K − a non-linear key-depended feedback function.

This construction based on the simple Counter with constant step "weight" but the number of elementary incrementations by W-value is different on each step and depends from the previous state. In other words we can say that the incrementation value changes dynamically on each step proportionally to W-value. This incrementation value is secret and mustn't leak out from the cipher.

The zero output value for f_K function is forbidden. This function may utilize a part of the base cipher output. The W-value must be coprime to counter module, in that case, the period of internal states is variable, but it is always bounded by the presented range.

The most optimal length of feedback function is half of the base cipher block length ($r = n / 2$), because it is directly proportional to the assaulter vagueness and inversely proportional to the lower bound of period.

Assaulter Vagueness: $N_i = ?$

For simplification of this mode implementation we propose to use the rare W-value with only three unit bits. In such case the multiplication can be replaced by a few additions.

The synchronization sequence generator built according to such scheme has guaranteed lower bound of period and hides the differential property of base cipher input sequence.

Now let's consider the modes' schemes constructed on the basis of the "Dynamic step counter."

7.1. Strengthened Stream Ciphering Mode

The scheme of strengthened stream ciphering mode is presented on the Figure 8. It is constructed according to the given above design principles. It scheme define synchronous stream cipher with half block output. The base cipher output block is divided on two non-overlapped parts of equal length. One half of it is used as gamma-output and another—as the feedback (or N_i– vector).

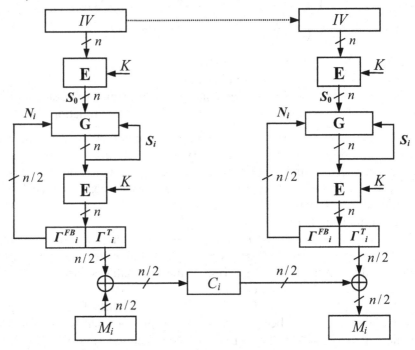

Figure 8. Strengthened Stream Ciphering Mode

We can view this mode as combination of the Counter mode and the Output Feedback mode (CTR+OFB).

The initial internal state is hided by initial encryption of initialization vector (*IV*). Further states' hiding is provided by the "Dynamic step counter" utilization. This scheme has guaranteed lower bound of the internal states' period.

7.2. Strengthened Stream Ciphering and Authentication Mode

The last scheme (Figure 8) can be modified for ciphering and authentication tasks performing simultaneously (Figure 9).

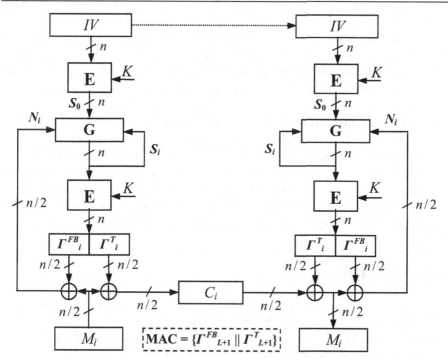

Figure 9. Strengthened Stream Ciphering and Authentication Mode

Shown scheme defines strengthened stream ciphering and authentication mode. This mode is similar to previous mode but has one distinction—the feedback value N_i depends on the message block too. As a result the current internal state depends on all processed plaintext blocks.

We can view this mode as combination of the Counter mode and the Cipher Feedback mode (CTR+CFB). After processing all message blocks the cipher internal state (S_i) depends linearly on the last block and non-linearly on all other message blocks (M_i), encryption key (K) and initialization vector (IV). In order to get Message Authentication Code (MAC) it is necessary to perform yet one blank encryption. The obtained base cipher output block or its part can be used as MAC.

CONCLUSION

Now let's summarize the all presented results.

1. In standard modes of operation (excluding CTR) the base block cipher is vulnerable to known plaintext attacks.
2. In the Counter mode the synchronization sequence has fixed known differential property and therefore the base block cipher is potentially vulnerable to differential cryptanalysis attack.

3. In the OFB mode the minimal gamma period depends on the base block cipher properties and therefore it doesn't guarantee any lower bound.

4. The Counter mode with session step "weight" value has increased security and can be recommended for encryption of information with the random access requirement and strict limitation to gamma overlapping in the case of multi-session key usage. Both proposed schemes of improved "counter mode" utilize "dynamic step" principle and protect base block cipher from known plaintexts and differential attacks. Their performance is practically equivalent to the performance of standard Counter mode with half block size output. The implementation of "Dynamic Step Counter" for 128-bit block-size requires about 10 non-paralleled micro operations on the 32-bit Intel Architecture (for comparison—the standard Counter mode requires 4 non-paralleled micro operations).

REFERENCES

1. Morris Dworkin. Recommendation for Block Cipher Modes of Operation. Methods and Techniques. NIST Special Publication 800-38A, 2001.

2. FIPS 81, "DES Modes of Operation," Federal Information Processing Standards Publication 81, U.S. Department of Commerce / National Bureau of Standards, National Technical Information Service, Springfield, Virginia, 1980.

3. ANSI X3.106, "American National Standard for Information Systems—Data Encryption Algorithm—Modes of Operation," American National Standards Institute, 1983.

4. ISO 8732, "Banking—Key Management (wholesale)," International Organization for Standardization, Geneva, Switzerland, 1988 (first edition).

5. ISO/IEC 10116, "Information Processing—Modes of Operation for an n–bit Block Cipher Algorithm," International Organization for Standardization, Geneva, Switzerland, 1991 (first edition).

ELECTRONIC SIGNATURE IN REAL WORLD

Vlasta Joškova
ICZ a.s., Czech Republic
vlasta.joskova@i.cz

Abstract: This paper looks for an answer to the question of why electronically signed documents are used less than expected. Obstacles to using electronic signature are described and a solution of how to address some of them is suggested.

Key words: Electronic signature; Public Key Infrastructure

1. INTRODUCTION

Six years ago, Public Key Infrastructure (PKI)—as any popular buzzword—seemed to be a remedy for (almost) every security problem and the electronic signature was supposed to be used by (almost) everyone very soon. Today, we are not much closer to the paperless world. Based on experience coming from a number of PKI projects, the author of this paper points out some obstacles preventing people from using the electronic signature and looks for solutions.

2. DEFINITIONS

Since the terms *digital signature* and *electronic signature* are often used confusingly we would like to clarify their meaning for this article.

A *digital signature* is a technical concept, a technical means of protecting data and providing proof of its authenticity and integrity. Digital signature technology is used both for authenticating data and authenticating entities in a digital dialog, e.g. in on-line communication protocols.

An *electronic signature* is a legal concept that was defined in [DIR] as data in electronic form that is attached to, or logically associated with, other electronic data, and which serve as a method of authentication. That definition has a very wide sense to be open to various technologies, both current ones and those that may come in future. An electronic signature refers to data authentication, not to the authentication of entities.

315

J. S. Kowalik et al. (eds.), Cyberspace Security and Defense: Research Issues, 315–321.
© 2005 *Springer. Printed in the Netherlands.*

An *advanced electronic signature* is defined in [DIR] as an electronic signature that is

- uniquely linked to the signatory;
- capable of identifying the signatory;
- created using means that the signatory can maintain under his sole control; and
- linked to the data to which it relates in such a manner that any subsequent change of the data is detectable.

That notion is also quite broad, and not associated with specific technology. In practice, it is implemented using digital signature technology, based on digital certificates and PKI (see [ETSI]). The electronic signature, based on PKI, having similar functions in the electronic world as a signature in real world, is a subject of this paper. Whenever the term electronic signature is further used, it means an electronic signature based on PKI, having similar functions in electronic world as a signature in real world.

3. OBSTACLES FOR COMMON USERS

Let us consider common users first; people who are not worried about the strengths of cryptographic algorithms or the quality of the implementation, but who are interested in value for money, and want value for effort and ease of use.

3.1 PKI Itself is Difficult to Use

PKI, as the underlying technology for digital signatures, is the first obstacle of wider acceptance of the electronic signature. PKI is difficult for common users to understand and use. Several non-trivial steps must be completed before a person can start using digital certificates. A key pair must be generated and an electronic request for certificate created. After a certificate is issued, it must be installed into software, together with certificates of trusted certification authorities. When using other people certificates, fresh information about certificate revocation must be available. Only experienced users, or users with substantial support of trusted personnel, can do those steps properly and with all security precautions.

The complexity of PKI can be partly avoided by simplifying some processes connected with issuing certificates and by automating others. If users are provided with smart cards, where a key pair with all relevant certificates is installed, it reminds the user of procedures they are already used to: procedures for issuing credit cards. If software accesses certificate revocation information automatically, based on CRL distribution point certificate extension or by OCSP protocol, life is easier for users. On the other hand, using smart cards means installing smart card readers and appropriate device drives, which again may not be straightforward for some users.

Trusted and experienced support personnel are therefore vital for successful PKI implementation and usage. Support people have to set up and maintain all the PKI components to make PKI as seamless as possible and reasonable and help users with tasks done exceptionally. Proper support is usually available in closed communities, enterprises and organizations, but not for people outside closed communities, like citizens who want to use PKI in communication with government.

Using PKI is often painful and so there must be a "reward" for doing that. If users have attractive applications that help them in saving their time and/or money, they are willing to invest their effort into them. Unfortunately, the lack of an attractive application is another obstacle of using electronic signatures. This issue will be dealt with in 3.3.

3.2 Cost of Establishing and Running PKI

A trusted certification authority is the cornerstone of the Public Key Infrastructure. The complexity of the solution is derived from what the certificates are used for, and even in the simplest electronic signature implementation, in a closed community, the certification authority is a trusted institution that must be built and operated with adequate care. The technological part of the certification authority is usually the easiest part to set up. It is not the cost of technology, but mainly the cost of non-technological components of PKI, which makes building certification authority a complicated and expensive process. There is always a significant portion of non-technical activities associated with establishing a certification authority: creating certificate policy, certification practice statement, security policy and all the necessary regulations and guidelines, training the certification authority personnel, etc. And after all that is created, it must be maintained and audited continuously.

All the costs are multiplied many times for public certification authorities selling their services to general public, which are subject to various legal regulations.

For closed communities, outsourcing of certification services can be a way to save costs. The external services provider covers costs for establishing and running the certification authority; on the other hand, the certificates will be paid for and must be renewed regularly. Even if using certificates issued by an external institution, there are always some in-house activities that cannot be delegated to the external organization. Therefore, a cost model must be worked out before deciding whether internal or external certification services are better in the specific case.

If an internal certification authority is built, certification procedures should be as close as possible to existing administrative processes to avoid additional personnel costs.

3.3   Lack of Attractive Applications

The lack of attractive and useful application is probably the most important obstacle for common users. What are the applications available?

E-mail is probably the most widespread ready-made application where electronic signature can be used and is used. Work flow and document management applications are other examples of information systems where an electronic signature is needed. Those applications are mainly dedicated to closed communities of users and documents with a limited validity period. The "paperless office" is the type of application that may be most promising for coming years.

E-banking is often presented as a field where electronic signature is used most. E-banking applications use many means of authenticating transactions. Electronic signature based on PKI is just one of them, and probably not the most convenient and user friendly one.

E-government is another area with a big potential to growth. On the contrary to pictures of every citizen using electronic signature to communicate with government, the area of growth will lay in communication among governmental institutions and between commercial and governmental institutions.

Only a deep analysis of users' needs leads to applications attractive enough and a wider usage of electronic signatures. We should not expect a "killer application" to appear soon.

3.4   Lifetime of the Electronically Signed Documents

Another obvious reason why people hesitate to use electronically signed documents is a lack of assurance about how long the signed electronic documents can be stored and validated.

Hardware is changing rapidly and many computer users can remember media they used to use and that are hardly readable today, like 8-inch floppy discs. The same is true for software. Formats of electronic documents are changing and the backward compatibility may not be assured for a longer period.

The issue is even more complicated for electronically signed documents. What is the lifetime of electronic signatures created today? For creating and validating signatures, keys of certain "secure" lengths and algorithms considered unbreakable today are used. But what about the progress in cryptography and brute-force attacks? Certificates and other evidence used for validating electronic signature have therefore limited validity.

All questions above can be answered and the problems can be handled reasonably, but not at a level of a common user and by simple means. Special institutions, trusted archives of electronically signed documents must be established. Since these must be trusted institutions, some rules and regulations for them must be worked out, like for certification authorities and time stamp authorities.

Widely adopted technical standards for this area are also still missing. A format for Archival Electronic Signature (ES-A) has been defined in [ETSI]. An IETF working group is working in this field (see [DOS] and [WAL]), but most documents are at the level of Internet Drafts and they are works in progress.

4. OBSTACLES FOR EXPERIENCED USERS

Experienced users with certain level of knowledge in IT and cryptography can hesitate even more.

A personal computer with a piece of software is usually used for creating electronic signatures. Unless it is maintained, updated and protected properly, it can hardly be considered being a "means that the signatory can maintain under his sole control," as [DIR] requests for Advanced Electronic Signatures. There are so many "intangible" and "invisible" components between a signatory and an electronically signed document that the risk may be unbearable for some users. Properly maintained and protected computers are found in closed communities where a strict security policy is announced and implemented.

Another question is associated with the security of the device used for creating and validating the signature and presentation of the document. How can a user be sure that he signs what he sees at the screen? And the other way round: an electronic signature of a document was validated. How can a user be sure that the document presented on the screen is the document that was validated?

Cryptographic algorithms can be unbreakable in theory, but they must be implemented in practice. The implementation may not be flaws free, and the private key of a signatory can be compromised. Cryptographic tokens, where keys are stored and cryptographic operations are performed, may improve the security and trustworthiness of a solution.

[DIR] addresses those issues by defining a secure signature-creation device, which should reasonably protect the signatory's private key, do not alter the data being signed and present them correctly. Sometimes, smart cards or other cryptographic tokens are considered to be secure signature-creation devices, which is not true, since the presentation of the document to be signed is done by a piece of software outside the token. In fact, such a device must consist of more than a cryptographic token and should go through a security assessment, which makes the device expensive and prevents its wider usage.

5. CONCLUSION

Unless qualified help is available to individual users (natural persons) the usage of PKI and electronic signatures based on it will be limited to closed communities with trusted IT personnel. Furthermore, PKI as it is today may not be a good underlying technology for electronic signatures. The gap between the complexity of PKI-based electronic signatures and the simplicity of signatures in the real world may be too wide to be overcome in a wider scope.

Electronic signatures will be used for electronic documents with a limited validity until a good system of trusted electronic archives is built.

The signature in the real world is an institution rooted deeply in human culture. Therefore, multidisciplinary research is needed to achieve wider acceptance of electronic signatures.

REFERENCES AND FURTHER READING

[DIR]   Directive 1999/93/EC of the European Parliament and of the Council of 13 December 1999 on a Community framework for electronic signatures, **http://europa.eu.int/ eur-lex/pri/en/oj/dat/2000/l_013/l_01320000119en00120020.pdf**

[DOS]   DOSTALEK, L., VOHNOUTOVA, M., "Long-term Archive Architecture," Internet Draft, November 2003, **http://ltans.edelweb.fr/draft-ietf-ltans-arch-00.pdf**

[DUM]   DUMORTIER, J., "E-Government and Digital Preservation," E-Government: Legal, Technical and Pedagogical Aspects, Publicaciones del Seminario de Informatica y Derecho, Universidad de Zaragoza, 2003, p. 93–104, ISBN 84-95480-96-4

[ETSI] ETSI TS 101 733 V1.5.1 (2003-12) Electronic Signatures and Infrastructures (ESI); Electronic Signature Formats, **http://www.ictsb.org/EESSI_home.htm**

[LEG] "The legal and market aspects of electronic signatures," Study for the European Commission—DG Information Society, September 2003, **http://europa.eu.int/ information_society/eeurope/2005/all_about/security/electronic_sig_report.pdf**

[WAL] WALLACE, C., PORDESCH, U., BRANDNER, R., "Long term archive service requirements," Internet Draft, October 2004, **http://www.ietf.org/internet-drafts/draft-ietf-ltans-reqs-03.txt**

A NOTE ON TWO SIGNIFICANT DEVELOPMENTS IN CYBERSPACE SECURITY AND DEFENSE

Janusz Kowalik
j.kowalik@comcast.net
Seattle, Washington, U.S.A.

Abstract: Among recent scientific and technological developments two of them stand out and have significant potential for contributing to cyberspace security and defense. These two developments are: theory of large scale-free networks developed in the last decade and quantum cryptography which is rapidly maturing and soon may be ready for implementation. The paper explains why these two developments deserve special attention and further study.

Keywords: Scale-free networks; Internet structure; quantum key distribution; cryptography

1. INTRODUCTION

Internet offers great advantages for scientists, businesses and average citizens of the world community .But at the same time it opens new opportunities for abuse and crime. To limit or eliminate these negative consequences of the global networking we have to understand how large networks behave, and how computer users can be protected against these abuses and criminal activities.

The list of possible criminal acts is long and includes: computer viruses, worms, denial of service, illegal spying and retrieving unauthorized information.

One of the pioneers of the network security and reliability who investigated large communication networks in 1960s was Paul Baran from the RAND Corporation [1].Another pioneer was Leonard Kleinrock. At about the same time the famous mathematical genius Paul Erdos and his collaborator Alfred Renyi investigated random networks.

A major breakthrough in the theory of large randomly evolving networks took place in the last decade of the 20th century when Albert-Laszlo

J. S. Kowalik et al. (eds.), Cyberspace Security and Defense: Research Issues, 323–330.

Barabasi and his collaborators [2]–[3] researched and established foundations for the real large random networks called scale-free.

One of the key discoveries was the realization that very many real networks in nature, technology (e.g., the Internet and WWW) and human relations have similar structure and growth patterns, and can be described by the same mathematical formulas. All of them share similar properties and behavior. This discovery and the new theory have created an unprecedented opportunity for investigating resilience and vulnerabilities of the Internet and the WWW. For this reason we consider the scale-free network theory and related empirical results as being a significant development in the Cyberspace Security and Defense.

Unlike the new theory of scale-free networks the beginnings of cryptography can be found in antiquity. Basic ideas of secret communication are old but only recently two major innovations were created; the public key systems (PKS) [4] and quantum key distribution (QKD) [5]. PKS is based on the current inability of solving efficiently certain computationally intractable problems. Quantum key distribution is using immutable laws of physics and if successfully implemented QKD will become a practical secure technique for supporting cryptographic message exchange. Hence we have included QKD as the second significant development contributing to Cyberspace Security and Defense.

2. SCALE-FREE NETWORKS

The classic graph theory deals with static and usually human designed graphs. In contrast to the graph theory the new network theories are dealing with evolving in time large random networks whose structure and properties are determined by the rules of growth [6].

First random networks research was conducted around 1959 and 1960 by famous Erdos and his collaborator Renyi. Investigating random networks they made two key assumptions:

1. The number of network nodes was fixed

2. Nodes were connected by random edges without any preference

In the resulting network most of the nodes had approximately equal number of attached edges. They are so to speak "democratic."

One of the simple but important stochastic characterizations of random networks is the node degree distribution function $P(k)$ which is the probability of a node having k nearest neighbors.

The family of classic random networks considered by Erdos and Renyi is characterized by the Poisson (bell-shaped) distribution function

$$P(k) = \frac{e^{-\bar{k}}\bar{k}^k}{k!}$$

where "$k\ bar$" is the average node degree.

This function is reached asymptotically when the number of nodes approaches infinity and if the mean node degree is fixed.

Random networks were a significant contribution to the future theory of large real networks but the most dramatic and useful development took place about forty years later when A-L Barabasi and his collaborators made empirical mapping of the Internet and using different growth principles created the theory of nets called *scale-free networks*.

The scale-free networks investigated by A-L Barabasi and his collaborators follow a different growth rule than the rules for creating random networks. All scale-free networks are characterized by distribution functions $P(k)$ which are powers of k.

$$P(k) \propto k^{-\gamma}$$

where the typical range of the power is

$$2 \leq \gamma \leq 3$$

The pattern of growth for scale-free networks follows the rule of *preferential attachment* [7]. According to this rule a new node prefers attaching itself to the highly connected nodes. For example a simple linear version of this rule can be expressed formally as

$$\prod(k_i) = k_i / \sum_j k_j$$

where the left hand side is the probability of attaching a new node to the node i with k_i nearest neighbors. The summation on the right side applies to the entire existing network or some neighborhood of the node i.

The most dramatic result of the preferential attachment growth rule is the appearance of highly connected nodes called *hubs*. The scale-free networks do not have typical nodes with average number of edges. The concept of average connectivity does not have meaning for these nets.

Scale-free networks have few very highly connected hubs and most of the nodes have only few edges. This difference in the structure between the classic random networks and the scale-free networks results in very different behaviors of the two networks.

Scale free networks are common in nature, human relations, economy and technology. The Internet and WWW are important examples of scale-free networks. A possible reason for popularity of scale-free nets in nature may be their robustness in the presence of random node failures. Computer experiments have shown that Internet would not fall apart even if 80% of all routers fail [7].

This structural robustness could be attributed to the existence of hubs in scale-free networks. Similar experiments indicate that by removing a few hubs the Internet would disintegrate into disjoint components.

A coordinated simultaneous attack on Internet hubs could be devastating. Hubs are the key to the random failure robustness as well as to the Internet vulnerability to targeted assault. Defending hubs against malicious or hostile damage is a must. They also need to be protected against viral infections. Being linked to many computers Internet hubs can transmit massively infections to the neighbors. This would suggest targeting hubs for virus immunization [8].

3. QUANTUM KEY DISTRIBUTION

In conventional cryptography there is only one key used for encryption and decryption. The entire process for sending secret messages has two major components:

1. the key distribution to recipients, and

2. encrypting a plain message, transmitting cryptotext and decrypting it at the destination

Figure 1 illustrates the process. Secure key distribution is hard for conventional encryption. It requires a secure transmission which is not available in the world of conventional cryptography.

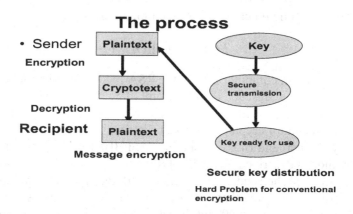

Figure 1. Process for Sending Secret Messages

Once the key has been safely delivered to the recipient and the plaintext has been encrypted any brute force attack on the cryptotext must deal with a huge number of possible keys. For example if the key has 128 binary digits the number of all possible keys is approximately 10^{38}.

The key distribution problem can be avoided by the Public Key System (PKS) which was invented in the 1970s.The idea is based on each secret communication participant having two keys. One public key for encryption and the second private key for decryption. If Alice wants to send a confidential message to Bob she encryptsher plain message using Bob's public key. Bob decrypts the cryptotext using his private key which is complementary to his public key.

The most popular version of PKS is the system called RSA which is implemented in banking, many businesses and industrial companies .To break the system requires computing factors of a product of two large primes. The most efficient known algorithm for computing prime factors is so inefficient that RSA is regarded safe as long as a better method is not invented.

The current best algorithm computes prime factors in time that is an exponential function of their product *n*.

$$T(n) = \exp[c(\ln n)^{1/3}(\ln\ln n)^{2/3}]$$

For large primes (over 100 digits long) the computing time *T(n)* is astronomical even if we would do computation on parallel supercomputers. This very long computing time becomes reasonably short if we use a different model of computation.

Peter Shor from The AT&T Bell Laboratories showed in 1994 that in principle a quantum computer could factor products of prime numbers in practical times.

The solution time function of his quantum algorithm is:

$$T(n) = O[(\ln n)^3]$$

Once a quantum computer is built the RSA method would not be safe.

Fortunately the rescue comes from the same direction, quantum mechanics.

The first quantum cryptographic key distribution protocol was published in 1984 by Bennett and Brassard and is called BB84. An informal description of this method is described below [9]–[10].

In this method the sender Alice sends randomly polarized photons to the receiver Bob. We assume that each of them has two polarizers. One aligned with the rectilinear basis 0/90 and the second aligned with the diagonal basis 45/135.

Alice and Bob communicate via a quantum channel such as an optical fiber wire.

Alice sends photons randomly polarized in one of the four orientations: 0, 90, 45, 135. Bob measures each photon with his polarizers chosen at random.

Bob's choice of polarizers may or may not match polarizers used by Alice. If his choice is correct Bob's measurement will agree with the polarization used by Alice. If not the result of his measurement will be random.

After sending and measuring a stream of photons Alice and Bob discuss the transmission using an open channel. Bob tells Alice which polarizers he used and Alice tells him if they match polarizers used by her. In the next step they discard all data for which there was no match. The remaining data can be converted to a bit string of 0s and 1s and this string represents the transmitted encryption key.

There is a potential important third player in this process. She is Eve the eavesdropper. Eve interferes with the transmission process by measuring and resending photons sent by Alice. Eve is also using randomly selected polarizers and may or may not match polarizers used by Alice. If she chooses the correct polarizer she will send to Bob a photon matching Alice's original photon polarization and she will be undetected. But if Eve chooses a wrong polarizer her interference could be detected. If the number if suspected interferences is high enough Alice and Bob can discard the entire stream and repeat transmission from scratch.

4. CONCLUSIONS

Both developments, scale-free network theory and quantum key distribution offer new opportunities for Cyberspace Security and Defense. In both areas several practical issues are still open and require further work. For example, can scale-free networks theory help us to understand and prevent cascading collapses of power grids? Can Internet collapse as power grids do?

Another issue is related to spreading viruses in the Internet. It is not entirely clear that in practice the spread of viruses is intensified by hubs. Viruses target individual computer systems or companies not hubs. Interesting network issues have been mentioned by Peter Denning [11]. He points out that network theories can help us to understand how innovations spread and how modern network-centric military and industrial organizations function.

In the area of quantum key distribution the most important difficulties are in practical implementations, for example, implementing QKD over long distances. A significant progress in QKD has been made by the National Institute of Standards and Technology [12]. The NIST system uses an infrared laser to generate the photons and telescopes with 8-inch mirrors to send and receive photons over the air.

The NIST system transmitted a stream of individual photons to create an encryption key (used to encrypt messages) at the rate of 1Million bits per second. A very impressive speed but this transmission was between two NIST buildings that are 730 meters apart. One of the issues is how to built repeaters which can allow long quantum channels. A 67 kilometers quantum transmission achieved in 2001 at the University of Geneva may be the longest possible distance with current technology.

One of the investigated alternatives is using satellites. Richard Hughes from the Los Alamos National Laboratories is investigating methods for sending photons through the open air. One of the obstacles is bad weather in some parts of the world, e.g., the Northwest of the United States. Initial research results in this area are not encouraging [13].

Sending photons via open air requires identifying QKD photons from others such as coming from the sun. In the NIST system QKD photons are time stamped and looked for only when they are expected to arrive.

For additional information on the NIST system, see [14]. Two commercial companies sell optical-fiber based systems that send quantum cryptographic keys over the distances of tens of kilometers. One of them is MagiQ Technologies in New York City. The other is a Swiss company id Quantique in Geneva, Switzerland [15].

5. REFERENCES

1. Baran, Paul, "Introduction to Distributed Communication Networks," RM-1420, PR, 1964.

2.   A-L Barabasi and Albert Reka, "Emergence of Scaling in Random Networks," Science 286 (1999): P509–512.

3.   Barabasi, A.-L., Albert Reka, and Jeong Hawoong, Mean-Field Theory for Scale-Free Random Networks, Physics A, 272, (1999): 173–187.

4.   Stallings, W., "Cryptography and Network Security Principles and Practice," Prentice-Hall, 1998.

5.   Nielsen, M. A. and Isaac L. Chuang, "Quantum Computation and Quantum Information, Cambridge University Press, 2000.

6.   Dorogovtse, S. N. and J. F. F. Mendes, "Evolution of Networks," From Biological to the Internet and WWW, Oxford University Press, 2003.

7.   Barabasi, A-L., Linked, The new Science of Networks, Perseus Publishing, 2002.

8.   Dezso, Zoltan and A-L. Barabasi, "Halting viruses in scale- free networks," Phys Rev. E, 65, 055103(R)

9.   Vittorio, Salvatore, "Quantum Cryptography: Privacy Through Uncertainty," released October 2002, **http://www.cs.csa.com/hottopics/crypt/oview/**

10. Quantum Cryptography Tutorial, **http://www.cs.dartmouth.edu/~jford/crypto.html**

11. Denning, Peter, *Communications of the ACM*, November 2004, Vol.47, Number 11, pp15–20.

12. NIST Quantum Keys System Sets Speed Record for Encryption, HPCwire, May 6th 2004.

13. McNeely, Bill, The Boeing Company, private communication.

14. **http://www.nist.gov/public_affairs/releases/quantumkeys_background.htm**

15. Stix, G., "Best Kept Secrets," *Scientific American*, Vol.292, No. 1, pages 79–83, January 2005.

A CRYPTOGRAPHIC MOBILE AGENT IMPLEMENTING SECURE PERSONAL CONTENT DELIVERY PROTOCOL

Bartłomiej Ziółkowski and Janusz Stokłosa
Pozna University of Technology
Division of Information System Security
Pozna , Poland
ziolkowski@sk-kari.put.poznan.pl
stoklosa@sk-kari.put.poznan.pl

Abstract: This paper describes a proposal of a protocol for secure personal content delivery based on a cryptographic mobile agent. The proposed protocol allows a controlled and secured delivery of personal content (e.g., photo, text message, etc.) to the target device. Furthermore, the protocol is enhanced with time-based constraints in order to impose control over point in time when the content becomes available. The preliminary analysis of the protocol is presented and also some practical applications are discussed. The idea of cryptographic mobile agents is briefly explained to give the reader an understanding of the properties of such agents. The research is based upon leading agent standard, the Foundation for Intelligent Physical Agents, and the protocol is specified using Agent Unified Modeling Language. The paper also describes a prototype of mobile agent implementing the proposed protocol.

Keywords: cryptography; mobile agents; personal content; FIPA; AUML; DRM; JADE; JADE-S; security

1. INTRODUCTION

The proliferation of the feature-rich mobile devices, for example mobile phones or network-enabled Personal Digital Assistants (PDA), provides means for creation of distributed mobile agents platforms. Unique properties of mobile agents, like ability to migrate data together with agent's code from host to host, or ability to make decisions on behalf of the owner, open a new

J. S. Kowalik et al. (eds.), Cyberspace Security and Defense: Research Issues, 331–345.

area of their applications. The increased interest in the commercial applications of mobile agent systems requires greater attention to security issues. Therefore the agent-based protocols must be designed on the solid cryptographic basis to assure satisfying level of security.

Through combination of agent decisive capabilities and security mechanisms it is possible to create an agent that acts as an intelligent guard to carried data. Only when certain, operational conditions are true agent 'makes a decision' to decrypt the carried data and present it to the target user—another agent or a real person. However, after agent arrives to a host its code and data can be thoroughly analyzed and conditions can be forged by an attacker. Hence, there is a need to make the agent resistant to analysis.

The secure personal content delivery protocol proposed by authors in this paper allows creating agents that act as a guard to carried content. This is a new approach in the area of personal content management and enhancing it further could lead to creation of agent-based Digital Rights Management solution.

2. CLUELESS AGENTS

In the traditional cryptographic systems two parties willing to exchange information in a secure manner need to share the same secret key for encryption and decryption. Such a key has to be exchanged prior to communication and must not be revealed to third parties. The key is static by nature, i.e., it does not depend on temporal or operational conditions. In a distributed multi-agent system such conditions play very important role as mobile agents function and move through a wide variety of environments. Security properties of these environments are very different. That creates an additional challenge when the mobile agent needs to carry sensitive or private data. If on its way agent has to pass through insecure network or stop on non-trusted agent host it may be captured and analyzed so that any information carried by the agent becomes available to the attacker.

Clueless agent is a mobile agent that carries encrypted data, for example a text message, and does not carry any information that allows decryption of the data, such as an encryption key.

The greatest advantage of such an approach is that attacker is not able to decrypt the data even after bit-by-bit analysis of the agent code. The clueless agent, however, needs a method of constructing the decryption key. One of the methods is environmental key generation [1].

After arrival to a certain location, the agent searches the environment. When the proper information is located, the decryption key is generated and ciphertext is decrypted. Without the environmentally supplied input, the agent is not able to decrypt carried data and act upon them, i.e., it is clueless.

In case the attacker has access to agent's code and data as well as to all environmental information the agent is able to gather, the attacker may try to analyze what the agent searches for and forge this information. One of the methods to prevent such analysis is the use of hash functions [2] in a way that the agent does not reveal the required environmental information, i.e., searched information is not embedded in agent's code or carried data.

Let *ob* be an integer corresponding to an environmental observation, *h* a hash function, *m* the hash value *h(ob)* of the observation *ob* needed for activation, and *k* a key. The value *m* is carried by the agent. Then, for example, we can use the following construction [1]: if *h(ob)* = *m* then let *k := ob*.

3. TOOLS AND STANDARDS

3.1 FIPA

The Foundation for Intelligent Physical Agents (FIPA) is a non-profit organization aimed at producing standards for interoperation of heterogeneous software agents [3]. It specifies communication, interoperability, and external behavior of the agents. To date FIPA specifications have formed the leading standard.

3.2 JADE, JADE-LEAP and JADE-S

JADE (Java Agent Development Framework) is a software framework implemented in Java language [4]. It aids the implementation of multi-agent systems through a middle-ware that claims to comply with the FIPA specifications, and through a set of tools that support the debugging and deployment phase. The agent platform is operating system-independent and can be distributed across different machines and the configuration can be controlled via a remote Graphical User Interface. The configuration can even be changed at run-time by moving agents from one machine to another, as and when required. The distributed multi-agent system created in JADE is modeled through two different components:

- Containers—the local runtime environment where agents are executed, the platform consists of a number of containers.

- Agents—autonomous components interacting with theirs hosting containers and communicating with theirs local or remote peers.

One of the drawbacks of JADE framework is that it does not support full mobility of agents. By default, JADE agents communicate with each other using Java Remote Method Invocation (RMI, [5]) or Common Object Request Broker Architecture (CORBA, [6]). However, a mobile agent can be created and it can travel between hosts within the same agent platform but not between different platforms. Currently, there is a research work on going to enhance JADE to support mobility between different agent platforms.

The JADE LEAP (Lightweight Extensible Agent Platform) [7] is a JADE enhancement that allows obtaining a FIPA-complaint agent platform with reduced footprint and compatibility with mobile Java environments. The platform can be run on mobile terminals supporting mobile Java (e.g., mobile phones, PDAs, etc.). Possibility of having agents on mobile terminals opens a new area for their application. Currently, JADE LEAP does not support agent mobility.

The JADE-S (i.e., Secure-JADE) add-on to JADE is a third party enhancement to the framework that implements numbers of security services, including user/agent authentication, authorization and secure intra-platform communication. It makes the platform a multi-user environment where all components (i.e., agents and containers) are owned by users who are responsible for their actions. Additionally, a security policy can be enforced in order to allow or deny actions only on chosen subset of agents or users.

3.3 AUML

The Agent Unified Modeling Language (AUML) is a set of UML idioms and extensions tailored for agent-based software development [8]. The AUML represents agent interaction protocols using a three-layer approach: (1) templates and packages to represent the protocol as a whole; (2) sequence and collaboration diagrams to capture inter-agents dynamics; and (3) activity diagrams and state charts to capture both intra-agent and inter-agent dynamics. The AUML is widely used to represent agent protocols for FIPA standards. It is also used to represent the secure personal content delivery protocol proposed in this paper.

4. PERSONAL CONTENT

All the person's distinct intellectual or artistic creation stored in digital form is understood here as a personal content. The assumption is that person creates the content using its mobile device or some other external tool and uploads it to the device. Examples of personal content include a photo, a text message, a music fragment, or a drawing.

The person who created or owns the content is called a rights holder, and the person who is a user of the content is called an end consumer. Right holder defines restrictions and limitations of the distributed content that end consumer should comply with.

Additionally, all the content to which ownership has been transferred to a person, for example by purchase, also becomes personal content. For example, a digital certificate issued by a Certification Authority, and purchased by the person, becomes personal content as it contains a public key that is bound to the person's private key.

A purchased piece of music (e.g., a ring tone) or a picture (e.g., desktop background) does not become a personal content, as a person who purchased it did not create it and usually does not have full rights over it. In the traditional Digital Rights Management solutions a forward lock mechanism [9] might be implemented that prevents such content from leaving the device.

In many situations it is very important for the original creator to know what happened with his creation or whether license agreement is fulfilled. If there are no mechanisms in place, usually, the creator loses control over his creation as soon as it leaves his terminal (i.e., computer, mobile phone, PDA, etc.).

In the world, where convergence between IT and telecommunication is a fact, it is equally easy to create content and to distribute it. Hence, there is a need to provide simple mechanisms that allows the creator imposing control over his creation.

The protocol proposed in this paper does not allow a creation of fully functional Digital Rights Management system for all kinds of content but rather provides a mobile agent-based solution for secure delivery of the personal content.

5. A USE CASE

Let us imagine that Bob took a photo with his mobile phone. He would like to send the photo to his friend Alice but he wouldn't like Eve, who might be eavesdropping the channel, to capture the photo during transfer. Additionally, Bob would like to control what Alice can do with the photo he sends. He would like the photo to be shown only on Alice's own terminal. Moreover, she should not be able to forward this photo to anyone else and claim it to be her own creation.

In order to achieve it Bob creates a mobile agent, gives the photo as a load to carry, sets the policy, and provides Alice's number as destination. Mobile agent queries Alice's session key from a trusted third party, encrypts the load, and travels to the destination. Upon arrival it searches for the decryption key and if the key is found the photo is decrypted and presented on Alice's terminal.

If Alice wants to perform any operations on this photo (e.g., copying, forwarding, modifying, etc.), the agent will first check the policy and will allow only the operations permitted by the policy.

Moreover, Bob might demand that photo is removed from Alice's terminal after certain period of time. In such a case the agent will repeatedly query a timeserver and remove the photo when time set in the policy is up.

If Eve captures the agent she is not able to decrypt the carried content (i.e., the photo) if she has no access to Alice's decryption key. She is also not able to forward this photo to anybody else than Alice, as the recipients also do not have access to Alice's decryption key. The only thing Eve can do is to prevent the delivery of photo to Alice's terminal. However, Bob might request delivery receipt and react if receipt is not received.

By using a mobile agent, Bob is able to control his personal content and to deliver his content in a secure manner.

6. REQUIREMENTS

In order to enable a service that implements a scenario described in the previous paragraph, there are a number of mandatory and optional requirements that should be fulfilled.

First, on all of the mobile terminals an agent server should be running. The server is registered within the agent platform and accepts incoming agents. Such an agent server is called an agent container further on.

All containers share a common secret key k_{ID}, with the Platform Manager that is used for secure communication between a container and the Platform Manager. For each container there is a different secret key generated. Platform Manager is an agent that manages other agents running within a distributed agent platform and acts as a trusted third party. An initial shared secret key k_{INIT}, is generated by Platform Manager and delivered to the end user manually upon service purchase from network operator. When container is started for the first time, initial key k_{INIT}, is used for secure exchange of shared secret key k_{ID}. Afterwards, the initial key is deleted from the container. The shared secret key is renewed either according to defined platform's security policy or on demand.

All containers are registered with a unique ID within the platform, which is kept by Platform Manager and is associated with shared secret key k_{ID}. The ID could be randomly generated or constructed based on, for example, the combination of device serial number and owner's identification number.

Shared secret key k_{ID}, stored on the terminal is not revealed to mobile agents executed within the container. There is a service available which allows an agent to request the decryption of some data with container's secret key. The agent requests the container either to encrypt or to decrypt a set of data. For that purpose there could be also another agent implemented that serves the encryption/decryption requests from other agents and, additionally, manages the secret key of the container. Such an agent, however, should implement some mechanisms preventing a known plaintext attack or denial-of-service attacks.

There are two additional requirements, which are not mandatory for the proposed protocol. The first is availability of the secure timeserver [1] to implement time-based enhancements to the protocol. That allows the right holder restricting when the content is presented, for example, only before 8 p.m. or only after 8 p.m. That feature enables presenting the content to all end consumers at the same time or enables expiration of content if not delivered on time.

The second one requires an agent container to be a trusted agent platform. That means that code running the container must be signed and only containers with valid code signature are able to register within the platform. Additionally, agents arriving to such container need some means to verify if container is not compromised. Fulfilling of this requirement enables implementation of security policy for agents [10].

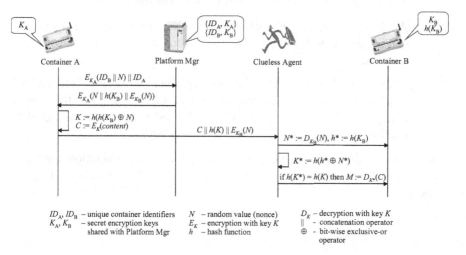

Figure 1. Secure Content Delivery Protocol

7. PROTOCOL PROPOSAL

The original method for clueless agents as proposed in [1] requires that agent knows the way of constructing the decryption key from environment after arrival to the destination. This secret key could be created based on some observation of, for example, traffic incoming on the network interface or the value of some system variable. The requirement precondition is that the sender knows something about the target environment. However, there is a risk this information is also known by someone else. In order to design the secure personal content delivery protocol it is assumed that the method of constructing the key in target environment is bound with some information that is only known by the owner of that environment, like, for example, the container's secret key. To assure that the sender is always able to get required information about the target environment, a trusted third party is introduced. Here, it is the Platform Manager.

The secure content delivery protocol is depicted in Figure 1. Let's assume that, PM denotes the Platform Manager. All other symbols are explained in the picture. There are following steps of the protocol:

I.   A → PM: $E_{Ka}(ID_B \| N) \| ID_A$—application running in container A sends a request to the Platform Manager that it wants to send an agent to container B, request is encrypted with shared key K_A.

II.   PM → A: $E_{Ka}(N \| h(K_B) \| E_{Kb}(N))$—PM responds with hash of K_B, the secret key of container B, and random value N.

III. Application computes the session encryption key $K := h(h(K_B) \oplus N)$, and encrypts the content with it, $C := E_K(content)$.

IV.   A → B: $C \| h(K) \| E_{Kb}(N)$—application creates a mobile agent that carries encrypted content and this agent travels to the destination container.

V.   After arrival agent requests the container to decrypt the carried random value with container's secret key $N^* := D_{Kb}(N)$, then agent computes $K^* := h(h(K_B) \oplus N^*)$, if hashed result $h(K^*)$ is equal to carried $h(K)$ agent uses this as decryption key.

Finally, the decrypted content is presented on the destination terminal. The receiver is able to see the content and perform operations allowed by the policy, if set.

8. PROTOCOL PROPERTIES

The proposed secure personal content delivery protocol allows a controlled delivery of personal content to a target environment.

Carried content is protected during transport, i.e.,all the data sent over the network is encrypted. And after arrival content is only decrypted when the correct information is found.

Encryption key used for the carried content is always different as random value is used for its computation.

There is only one secret key needed per mobile terminal (or per container) that is distributed manually upon service purchase. This secret key is stored in the container and is shared with the Platform Manager. It is used for secure and authenticated communication between the container and the Platform Manager.

This solution simplifies the key management and reduces number of keys needed. For n mobile containers that communicate with each other in pairs we need $n*(n-1)/2$ keys. Here we only need n keys for n agent containers.

Communication between an agent container and the Platform Manager is authenticated due to the fact that only the owner of the container, whose identity was verified and who received the shared key upon service purchase, can create encrypted request to Platform Manager. And Platform Manager looks up the shared key in its data storage where the key is associated to container's unique identifier

9. TIME-BASED CONSTRUCTIONS

The proposed secure personal content delivery protocol can be enhanced in such a way that time is used to control when the content should be presented on the end customer's terminal.

For that purpose a secure timeserver is introduced. In this role an agent running within the platform is acting. The time agent supports two modes of operation as described in [1]: forward-time hash function and backward-time hash function. The forward-time constructions permit key generation only after a given time. And the backward-time constructions permit key generation only before it.

The former construction is used to create mobile agents that present the carried content simultaneously on many devices after certain point in time. That feature depends, however, on availability of the time agent—if there is latency in the network the content might be presented on some devices a bit later than on the others.

The latter construction is used to create mobile agents with expiration date. That means if the agent content was not presented by the given point in time it is considered as expired.

If s denotes the secret belonging to the time agent and h denotes a hash function, the forward-time hash function construction has the following steps [1]:

- The agent sends the target time t^*, and a random value v, to the time agent.
- The time agent sets t to the current time and returns to the agent t and $h(h(s,t^*), h(v,t))$.
- The agent assigns $p := h(v,t)$ and $k := h(h(s,t^*), h(v,t))$ and uses k to encrypt the carried content, the value p is also carried by the agent.
- The agent continuously queries the time agent for the current time's secret, the time agent returns $s_i := h(s,t_i)$.
- The agent tries to use $k := h(s_i,p)$ to decrypt carried content, it will only succeed when $s_i = h(s,t^*)$, which is when $t_i = t^*$.

The use of current time t in the construction of p prevents an attacker from using the time agent to mount a dictionary attack. Additionally, the use of random value v complicates the forward time dictionary attack.

The backward-time hash function construction has the following steps (symbols as in the previous example) [1]:

- The agent sends the target time t^* and a random value v to the time agent.
- The agent returns $h(s,v,t^*)$ if and only if t^* is in the future.
- The agent assigns $k := h(s,v,t^*)$ and used it to encrypt the carried content, the values v and t^* are also carried by the agent.
- At time t, the agent sends the target time t^* and a random value v to the time agent, it will receive the valid key k in return, if and only if t^* is not later than t.

10. FORWARD TIME-ENHANCED PROTOCOL

The proposed secure personal content delivery protocol does not use time construction by default. There are additional steps required in the protocol. Let TA denotes the Time Agent and s denotes the secret belonging to the Time Agent. In order to use forward-time hash function constructions the protocol has the following steps:

- A → PM: $E_{Ka}(ID_B \| N) \| ID_A$—application running in container A sends a request to the Platform Manager that it wants to send an agent to container B, request is encrypted with shared key K_A.

- PM → A: $E_{Ka}(N \| h(K_B) \| E_{Kb}(N))$—PM responds with hash of K_B, the secret key of container B, and random value N.

- A → TA: t^*, N – the application sends the target time t^* and the random value N to the Time Agent.

- TA → A: $K_T := h(h(s,t^*), h(N,t))$—the Time Agent sets t to the current time and returns current time t together with hashed value of its secret s combined with time and random value.

- Application computes the session encryption key $K := h(h(K_B) \oplus N \oplus K_T)$, and encrypts the content with it, $C := E_K(content)$.

- A → B: $C \| h(K) \| E_{Kb}(N) \| h(N,t)$—application creates a mobile agent that carries encrypted content and this agent travels to the destination container.

- After arrival the agent requests the container to decrypt the carried random value with container's secret key $N^* := D_{Kb}(N)$.

- Then the agent queries the Time Agent for the current time's secret, the Time Agent returns $s_i := h(s,t_i)$.

- Finally the agent computes $K^* := h(h(K_B) \oplus N^* \oplus h(s_i, h(N,t)))$, if the hashed result $h(K^*)$ is equal to carried $h(K)$ then agent uses this as decryption key.

The computed secret key $h(K^*)$ is equal to the carried key $h(K)$ if and only if:

- The random value N^* decrypted with target container's secret key K_B equals initial random value N.

- The hash value of target container's secret key $h(K_B)$ equals the hash value returned by the Platform Manager.

- The current time's secret $h(s,t_i)$ returned by the Time Agent equals $h(s,t^*)$ used by the agent for secret key K construction.

11. BACKWARD TIME-ENHANCED PROTOCOL

Similarly, in order to use backward-time hash function construction there are additional steps required in the protocol. However, this time application first queries the Time Agent for the target time's secret and only then queries the Platform Manager for target container's secret. In the backward-time hash function construction, as described in the previous paragraph, the target time t^* is carried by the mobile agent in plain text form. If agent gets captured, the attacker is able to extract the expiration date/time t^* of the agent and prevent the agent to reach its destination container till it expires.

Let us use the same symbols as in the previous protocol. Now, the protocol has the following steps:

- A → TA: t^*, *N*—the application sends the target time t^* and the random value N to the Time Agent.

- TA → A: $K_T := h(s,N,t^*)$—the Time Agent returns the hash value of own secret *s*, random value *N*, and target time t^*, if and only if t^* is in the future.

- A → PM: $E_{Ka}(ID_B \,\|\, N \,\|\, t^*) \,\|\, ID_A$—application running in container A sends a request to the Platform Manager that it wants to send an agent to container B, request is encrypted with shared key K_A.

- PM → A: $EK_a(N \,\|\, h(K_B) \,\|\, EK_b(N) \,\|\, EK_b(t^*))$—PM responds with hash of K_B, the secret key of container B, and random value *N*.

- Application computes the session encryption key $K := h(h(K_B) \oplus N \oplus K_T)$, and encrypts the content with it, $C := EK(content)$.

- A → B: $C \,\|\, h(K) \,\|\, EK_b(N) \,\|\, EK_b(t^*)$—application creates a mobile agent that carries encrypted content and this agent travels to the destination container.

- After arrival the agent requests the container to decrypt the carried random value with container's secret key $N^* := DK_b(N)$.

- Afterwards the agent request the container to decrypt the carried target time with container's secret key $t^{**} := DK_b(t^*)$.

- At the time *t*, the agent sends the decrypted target time t^{**}, and the decrypted random value N^*, to the Time Agent.

- The Time Agent in return sends $K_T := h(s,N^*,t^{**})$, if and only if t^{**} is not later than the current time *t*.

- Finally the agent computes $K^* := h(h(K_B) \oplus N^* \oplus K_T)$, if hashed result $h(K^*)$ is equal to carried $h(K)$ agent uses this as the decryption key.

The carried content is decrypted if and only if values decrypted with container's secret key are equal to the values used for creation of the session encryption key, and if the current time is not later than the expiration date (i.e., target time).

In both, a forward- and backward-time hash function protocol enhancement, the communication between the applications running in the container and the Time Agent is not secured. Assuming that the Time Agent is a mandatory part of the agent platform it could be running together with the Platform Manager in the same main container and have the access to the shared key storage. Then the application could use the shared key to encrypt requests to the Time Agent, the corresponding steps of the protocol would look like the following:

- A → TA: $EK_a(t^*,N) \parallel ID_A$—the application sends the target time t^* and the random value N to the Time Agent, encrypted with the shared key of container A.

- TA → A: $EK_a(K_T := h(s,N,t^*))$—the Time Agent returns hash of own secret s, random value N, and target time t^*, if and only if t^* is in the future.

This method prevents the attacker from sniffing the communication between mobile agents and the Time Agent and the attacker is not able to find out the expiration date of an agent.

12. VIATOR—PROTOCOL IMPLEMENATION

Viator (*Latin*: messenger, traveler) is a cryptographic mobile agent that implements secure personal content delivery, proposed in this paper. It has been implemented in JADE framework and is a proof-of-concept for the protocol. Currently, JADE-LEAP version of JADE does not support agent mobility on mobile terminals. Hence, Viator was implemented on the Linux platform. It will be ported to mobile device version as soon as support for mobility is available. There were a number of agents implemented:

- Platform Manager is an agent that serves all the incoming requests required for protocol functioning. There is one instance of the Platform Manager running in the distributed agent platform.

- Viator is a mobile agent that implements the secure personal content delivery protocol. Viator implements plain version of the proposed protocol as well as time-enhanced version of the protocol.

- Container Manager is an agent that manages the container's secret key (i.e., performs initial key exchange and renews the key) and serves agents requesting encryption or decryption of data with container's secret key. One instance of the Container Manager is running per container.

- Time Agent is an agent that implements forward- and backward-time hash function constructions. There is a one instance of the Time Agent running in the agent platform.

All the implemented agents exchanged messages between each other using Agent Communication Language as specified by FIPA [3]. The key search mechanism on the target platform is implemented as agent's behavior.

Secret encryption keys are stored in the file system. The containers IDs are random numbers combined with container's name that make them unique within the platform.

The Viator mobile agent presents a GUI to the user. The user chooses the file containing the personal content, the variant of the secure personal content delivery protocol, plain or time-enhanced, and destination container. Then the agent reads the file containing the content to carry, e.g., a photo. Next it sends the request to Platform Manager agent to get a hash value of other's container key. If time-enhanced protocol is chosen, the agent queries the Time Agent to get the time construct. Then the session key is computed and the content is encrypted. Viator travels to the destination container, searches for the decryption key, and when it is found the content is decrypted and presented. If requested, the Viator contacts the Time Agent prior to decrypting the content.

13. FINAL REMARKS

In the world of convergence between IT and telecommunications the paradigm of mobile agents opens up a new area for their applications. It is fairly easy to create personal content and distribute it due to high availability of rich-featured interconnected mobile devices. Hence, there is a need to provide some mechanisms that prevents misusing of someone's property.

The existing Digital Right Management architectures [11] require complicated infrastructure and are designed for commercial content with strictly defined copyrights. There is a number of different DRM solutions on the market that do not interoperate with each other.

In the recent years the mobile devices gained more processing power and allow running custom made Java-based applications. That makes possible installation and execution of different agent platforms. The notion of mobile agent taking role of always-available personal assistant is becoming real.

The idea of clueless agents helps creating the agents resistant to attacker's analysis and able to create decryption key based on temporal or operational conditions.

The secure personal content delivery protocol allows controlled and secure delivery of personal content to the target environment. It protects personal content during transport and decrypts carried content only after the correct information is found.

The forward- and backward time hash functions allows the creation of mobile agents that are able to display the content simultaneously on many target devices after certain point in time or the agents carrying the content with expiration date set.

There are software tools available on the market, which allow creation of standardized mobile agents and help running them on computers as well as on mobile terminals of all kinds (e.g., mobile phones, PDAs, etc.). One of those is the open-source JADE framework that aids implementation of mobile agents complying with the FIPA specifications.

Viator is a mobile agent implemented in Java using JADE framework that is a proof-of-concept for secure personal content delivery protocol. The implementation of Viator will be enhanced in order to create an agent-based Digital Rights Management solution.

14. REFERENCES

1. Riordan J. and B. Schneier, "Environmental Key Generation Towards Clueless Agents," in Vigna G. (ed.), Mobile Agents and Security, LNCS 1419, Springer, Berlin 1998, 15–24

2. Menezes A.J., van Oorschot, S. A. Vanstone, "Handbook of Applied Cryptography," CRC Press, Boca Raton, FL, 1997

3. The Foundation for Intelligent Physical Agents, web page **http://www.fipa.org**

4. The Java Agent Development Framework, web page **http://jade.cselt.it**

5. The Java Remote Method Invocation, web page **http://java.sun.com/products/jdk/rmi**

6. The CORBA Standard, web page **http://www.omg.org/gettingstarted**

7. The Lightweight Extensible Agent Platform, web page **http://leap.crm-paris.com**

8. Odell J., H. Van Dyke Parunak, and B. Bauer, "Representing Agent Interaction Protocols in UML," in Ciancarini P., Wooldrige M. (eds.), Agent-Oriented Software Engineering, Springer, Berlin 2001, 121–140

9. Ianella, R., "Mobile Digital Rights Management," whitepaper, IPR Systems, 2003, available at **http://www.iprsystems.com/whitepapers/Mobile-DRM-WP.pdf**

10. Jansen W.A., "Determining Privileges of Mobile Agents," National Institute of Standards and Technology, in *Proceedings of the Computer Security Applications Conference*, December 2001

11. Ianella R., "Digital Rights Management (DRM) Architectures," in D-Lib Magazine, vol. 7, nr 6, June 2001, available at **http://www.dlib.org/dlib/june01/ianella/06ianella.html**

PART 6

INTRUSION DETECTION

AN INFRASTRUCTURE FOR DISTRIBUTED EVENT ACQUISITION

Hervé Debar (*herve.debar@francetelecom.com*),
Benjamin Morin (*benjamin.morin@francetelecom.com*),
Vincent Boissée (*vincent.boissee@francetelecom.com*), and
Didier Guérin (*didier.guerin@francetelecom.com*)
France Télécom R&D, 42 Rue des Coutures, F–14000 Caen, France

Abstract: This paper describes a distributed application for acquiring events from different equipment in a lightweight fashion. The architecture of the application is fully distributed, and takes advantage of standard tools such as web servers and relational databases. Several prototypes of the application have been deployed in our corporate network to monitor multiple environments. This paper defines the architecture of the distributed application around four axes, ac cording to the interaction they have with the data repository and the outside world. It also defines the kind of information that is stored in the database according to three categories.

Keywords: intrusion detection; alert management; operational security; security information management

1. INTRODUCTION

The background of this work comes from the need expressed by the security group of our corporation to have a visibility of the security state of the information system. Our information system is extremely large and diverse, and the volume of logs collected is enormous. As such, analyzing the logs requires time, and we have been looking at automating this task. This has led to three kinds of actions, deploying additional sensors with better logging capability, concentrating and consolidating existing log files, and developing a visualization and correlation platform.

In this paper, we present a distributed application for acquiring events. The application is fully distributed and has the ability to concentrate information from multiple heterogeneous formats into a single database for event correlation and visualization. An *event* in the context of this paper

J. S. Kowalik et al. (eds.), Cyberspace Security and Defense: Research Issues, 349–365.

represents a generic piece of information that is generated by a *sensor* or *probe*. An event carries a *message* or *signature*, qualifying the event, and a *timestamp*. Sensor, signature and timestamp must be present for an event to be inserted in the database. In addition, we provide space for storing host information (the host on which the event occurs for host-based event sources, or source and destination addresses for network-based event sources) and user information. Finally, we use an IDMEF-like *additionaldata* structure (Curry et al., 2004) to store sensor-specific information.

Most of our events represent some sort of security information, or activity happening on the information system that is relevant from a security point of view. In particular, events all have a priority attribute, measuring how security-critical the event is. We measure this severity on a scale of 1 to 4, with 5 reserved for unqualified events (usually internal error messages from sensor or from the application). Operators have to deal with events of priority 1, the others being kept for trending and forensics. Given the volume of events handled by the system (on the order of 4 million events over a period of four months in a small deployment), we have designed and developed an application for correlating and presenting the information to system operators.

2. RELATED WORK

Similar approaches have been followed in the Tivoli Risk Manager (TRM) product (Debar and Wespi, 2001) and in the Prelude open-source project (Vandorselaere and Oudot, 2003), for example. Tivoli is a universal system management environment and as such is clearly overkill for our needs. This as also been understood by the TRM developers, which have moved away from the Tivoli framework. Prelude also requires cryptographic capabilities on the host and is quite cumbersome for handling large numbers of sensors. While we do not exclude the possibility of moving to one of these frameworks in the future, we believe that there is room for a lighter and simpler design.

There are many commercial tools available that allow this kind of information collection. They can roughly be divided in two families, log consolidation tools and security management consoles. Log consolidation tools (e.g., Netsecure log) are capable of collecting extremely high volumes of events into a central database. Security Management Consoles (e.g., NetForensics, NetIQ) cannot handle as much volume, but process the information to ensure consistency and support correlation. We are interested in this second family.

Unfortunately, most of these tools are extremely expensive, and are fairly complex to deploy, requiring a database backend for alert storage. Surprisingly, they also have limited correlation capabilities, only providing a dozen or so rules as example for the development of environment-specific correlation rules. They should be viewed as a development framework for writing correlation rules. Since our correlation needs are very diverse, we could not find a platform that would allow us to run multiple correlation processes in parallel, from dynamic statistical analysis to vulnerability assessment. Also, manipulation of contextual data with interfaces to the inventory and configuration databases of the companies, was a strong requirement that no commercial tool satisfied at the time we launched the project.

3. OBJECTIVES AND ARCHITECTURE

The main goal of the application is to provide system operators with a view of the security status of the information system. As such, it collects events generated by multiple components of the information system and normalizes them into a generic format. Events are then homogenized to facilitate the display in a generic web application. The architecture of the application is presented in Figure 1.

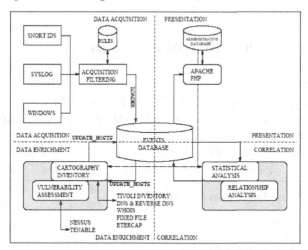

Figure 1. Architecture of the Distributed Application

This architecture is segmented in four functions, data acquisition, data enrichment, correlation and user interface. All these functions interact with a relational database, which serves as a reliable and persistent data bus for all components. All information is therefore easily accessed through standard interfaces; the main issue being database performance.

The application is naturally distributed, in the sense that each of the components in each quarter can reside on a different host, communications being handled by remote database connections over ssh tunnels.

The apache web server can also interact with multiple databases: events are generated throughout all the company, and this requires the ability to remotely interact with data sources. Also, we want the overhead of transporting data to be small, which implies that a central web server will interact with multiple event data bases. In addition, we need to support different groups located in multiple places that need access to the console. Event gathering can store events in multiple databases. In addition to event databases, each installation uses an administrative database for storing the properties of the web site, users, roles and processes. All background processes connect to the administrative database to obtain information about the event databases they need to process (enrichment, correlation, etc.).

However, events are not currently consolidated over multiple databases. We are planning to add this functionality at a hierarchical level for the alert presentation modules, so that a central database can rely on other event databases to provide a consolidated view of alert information. We are also interested in associating multiple databases as input of a correlation component, so that aggregated information improves correlation results.

3.1. Analysis of the Different Functions

The different functions are separated because they have different requirements for accessing the database, for interacting with the external world, for performance and for localization. These requirements are summarized in Table 1.

Table 1. Summary of the Characteristics of the Different Functions.

Function	Privileges	Performance	Localization	Interactions
Acquisition	Partial write access	High	Mostly remote	External to database
Enrichment	Read + update on events, Insert + update on context	Low	Possibly remote	Database + external to database
Correlation	Insert, update, read on all database tables	High	Usually local	Database to database

Function	Privileges	Performance	Localization	Interactions
Presentation	Read, update depending on user needs	Varying	Local	From database

Data acquisition needs privileges for inserting data into the database, but not for modifying it. It must be distributed and concurrent. It needs high performance remote access, because it is extremely likely that it will not reside in the same server as the database. It must have a high priority to ensure that event storms are properly handled.

Data enrichment needs access to external information sources that are not necessarily accessible from the system hosting the database or the web server. It needs update privileges on tables that are outside the core event tables. As such, it may need to be distributed, but not necessarily concurrent. In fact, our implementation locks data enrichment processes at the database level, to ensure that two installations of the application will not attempt the same enrichment procedure. Regarding performance, data enrichment can be delayed by data acquisition.

Correlation is usually co-located on the database server, because it also needs rapid access to all the tables in the database, and does not need to interact with the outside world. Performance is an issue because events need to be properly cleaned before they are presented to the operators. As such, correlation comes second after data acquisition for performance needs. It also needs read, write and update privileges on almost all areas of the database.

Finally, presentation is also usually co-located on the database server, hosting also the web server. Access privileges vary according to the tables that need to be accessed by the users. Some users have only read privileges to access event data, while others will be able to modify event information manually. The performance requirements of the presentation function vary; they need to be consistent with user needs, and thus directly depend on the capabilities of the hosting platform.

3.2. Data Acquisition

Data acquisition is presented in the upper left corner of Figure 1. The information is read from multiple heterogeneous sources and transformed in our standard format. The acquisition mechanism understands the IDMEF format, our private database format, and several dedicated log sources such as firewall logs (Cisco, Netscreen, Checkpoint, IPtables), access control mechanisms (TCP-wrappers, login), VPN concentrators, IDS sensors and routers.

The **loader** translates the application-specific format into our own, and decides whether the event needs to be inserted in the database. For this purpose, the **loader** uses a Snort-like ruleset (Roesch, 1999) that check the type of event and its content to decide if it should be logged or not. The advantage of using the Snort rule format is that this formalism is already used in the Snort sensors configuration and in many other commercial sensors or anti-viruses; the operators need to understand a single syntax for configuring the entire system. This simple technique not only filters the incoming event stream, but also adds contextual information through message, references, classification and priority. This is particularly useful in the context of firewall or VPN logs, which contain very short and cryptic messages.

Our data acquisition process is designed to be extremely lightweight to install and operate, as it is the most distributed part of the application. The **loader** is written in Perl and inserts events in a relational database directly. We do not have transport-layer security, as multiple VPN mechanisms (IPSec, stunnel, etc.) can be used for this, are reliable and provide solid management features. Nevertheless, the default installation procedure proposes the creation of SSH tunnels and SSH port replication to create a simple VPN, as SSH is available on all devices that we need to access. When SSH is not available on the target platform or it is impossible to install additional software (e.g. in routers), we deploy a syslog server that collect the logs. While we understand that syslog is insecure and could loose log entries, we have not found an environment that would actually suffer from this in a noticeable fashion. Moreover, syslog is ubiquitous and is already used in operations for centralizing logs, hence the capability to capitalize on a distributed and already deployed event acquisition framework.

3.3. Data Enrichment

Data enrichment is presented at the lower left corner of Figure 1. Data enrichment occurs when heterogeneous contextual information is entered in the event database. The same object can be represented by heterogeneous information depending on the data source. For example, the Windows NT event log can give us a host name, the network intrusion detection system a host IP address, and the wireless access point a MAC address, this for the same machine. The data enrichment functions attempt to complete and reconcile heterogeneous information entered in the database.

The **update_hosts** process is currently based on DNS and reverse DNS queries, Whois queries and inventory queries. Inventory is maintained by system administrators to track the evolution of the information system, and this detailed information source allows us to precisely locate machines within a subsidiary or a building. It also inserts vulnerability assessment information into the database to enable event severity assessment in the correlation processes. Data enrichment may be fairly costly. As such, it monitors the activity of the event database and runs with lower priority when event storms occur.

Data enrichment currently only deals with host information and vulnerability assessment information, although additional sources are under investigation, such as the Cisco Threat Response (CTR) technology[1] that provides on-the-spot scan ability for IDS alert assessment. Both functions are presented in greater detail in Section 5.

3.4. Correlation

Correlation is presented at the lower right corner of Figure 1. The difference between data enrichment and correlation is that correlation does not interact with the outside world, but processes only information available within the database. Also, correlation manipulates event information and can insert or change events in broad ways, whereas enrichment does not modify event information.

The main role of the correlation processes is to reduce the volume of information presented to the operator. This is done in two ways, by modifying existing events and by linking existing raw events with synthetic events. Modification of raw events occurs when the severity of an event is modified or when the context needs to be simplified (when two machines are identified to be the same, for example). Linkage occurs when multiple events can be linked together and represented by a single one, either an original event or one inserted by the correlation process.

As such, all these processes create hierarchies of events, with only the top-level events being presented to the operator. This greatly simplifies the linear visualization of events. It also has the effect of masking a high-priority event by lower-priority one if the original event is later found to be innocuous. Note that the correlation processes are generally cumulative, i.e., two correlation processes can associate raw events with two different top-level ones. If one of the correlation processes is later found to be erroneous, the other relationship remains and continues to mask the raw event.

We believe that it is extremely important to separate enrichment from correlation, to ensure the stability of multiple parallel correlation processes.

---

[1] **http://www.cisco.com/en/US/products/sw/secursw/ps5054/**

3.5. Presentation

Presentation is presented at the upper right corner of Figure 1. Presentation is the provider of information from our application to the outside world. Events are accessed by the operators through a web application. This web application supports both synthetic visualization for on-the-spot event handling and in-depth digging for forensics and trending purposes.

Installation of the presentation application is considered an installation of the application server. It installs and configures an apache web server and creates an administrative database. The administrative database holds the configuration of the web site (users, roles, graphics, languages, events databases) and the configuration of the enrichment and correlation processes with respect to each event database known to the web site. An event database does not need to reside on the presentation server, but is specified using a connection string. An event database can be accessed from multiple presentation sites.

Also, our application deals with security data, but does not have the ability to act on the monitored information system. For this purpose, we send messages to the general management console, where operators can take the appropriate actions. We use syslog messaging for this purpose, as all management applications that we need to interface to are capable of receiving syslog messages.

4. DATA REPRESENTATION

To support these functions, we have organized our data model as a set of concentric circles. Our data model is inspired from the Snort relational database schema, the IDMEF message format (Curry et al., 2004), and the M2D2 model (Morin et al., 2002). We participated in deploying these tools and developing these models, so they naturally were used as a starting point for our development. However, we believe that event and contextual information are not equivalent and this is not obvious in the three models cited before. Hence, we choose to provide a different representation shown in Figure 2.

4.1. Event Information

The inner circle represents core event information, sensor, signature and timestamp. Note that the two first bits (sensor and signature) are in fact quite complex, comprising several tables and attributes in our database schema. These more complex bits are stored in the second circle, and each event links to the second circle for sensor and signature reference. This mechanism naturally takes into account differences in volume, as there are only a few hundred different sensors and a few thousand signatures for several million events. It also naturally renders the fact that sensor and signature information evolves on a much longer timeframe than event information.

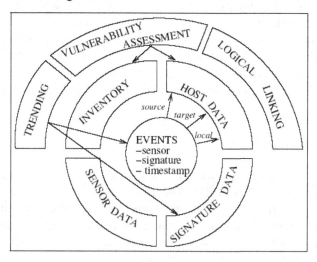

Figure 2. Circular Representation of the Data Model

4.2. Contextual Information

The second circle represents contextual information. This core event information links to host and user information in the second circle. Signature information links to sensor configuration, to indicate whether a sensor is able to detect an attack or not, and under which condition. Contextual information is mostly generated by the data enrichment processes (see 3.3) and by statically entered configuration information. While this contextual information evolves slowly over time, there is a need to track changes, as they have an impact on the signification of the events. Signatures are tracked using revision numbers that reflect improvements in their design. As such, events attached to the same signature message but with a higher revision number are considered more reliable than earlier events. The same process is used to track the evolution of sensor properties, each property change being tagged with the appropriate timestamp.

4.3. Transient Information

The third circle represents transient information that is generated by correlation processes (see 3.4). For example, statistical processes need to store numerical values associated with the statistical model; we use this area for the EWMA control values that monitor signature activity (Viinikka and Debar, 2004). This circle also links to the first two.

For example, the signature trending tool associates signature information in the second circle and event flows stored in the first circle.

The arrows of Figure 2 represent examples of links between contextual information and event information. A network event links to host information with source and destination of the network connection. A system event links to local host information indicating on which host the event occurred.

4.4. Implementation

Each circle is implemented by a set of tables in a relational database model (Date, 2003). Referential integrity constraints are used within each circle and between circles to ensure consistency of the event information. Triggers and constraints are used within each circle to facilitate data insertion and removal. There are no cross-circle constraints and triggers due to the unequal relationship between these two circles.

Referential integrity unfortunately introduces a heavy insertion performance penalty. Checking constraints between sensors, signatures and events works correctly because of the small size of the key, but is terribly expensive when checking the correspondence between events and hosts, because of the size of the host key (64 bits integer) and because of the number of hosts. It slows down bulk insertion by two to three orders of magnitude. When manipulating high volume databases, we recommend that referential integrity between hosts and events is dropped. Since there is no cascading upon delete of events, this behaviour is considered acceptable.

5. TOPOLOGICAL INFORMATION

Topological information is quite important to the application, as successful event handling requires the capability to identify the impact of the observed events on the host, and to physically locate it for intervention. As event collection is distributed and heterogeneous, we need to address the different representations of a host that are found in logs.

5.1. Structure of Host Representation

Logs represent host by three different keys, a host *name*, a host *IP address*, and a host *MAC address*. The name is either fully qualified or a simple machine name, depending on the information source. This type of information is often provided by host-based information sources, or by devices configured to do on-the-fly reverse DNS mapping. An IP address is often provided by network-based IDS sensors and other network equipments. Finally, MAC addresses are provided by low-level networking devices such as wireless access points and switches, when specific network or wireless attacks are detected. All three keys are frequently found in event logs.

Different information sources will describe the host using different keys. To ensure that the same device is recognized by different sources, these three keys are associated in the same structure. Each key is associated with a Boolean value indicating whether this key was used by an information source or was derived from a data enrichment process. Upon insertion of an event, the process will first retrieve the appropriate host key with the Boolean set to *TRUE*, checking whether the same device has already been accessed. It will then re-query the same host key with the Boolean set to *FALSE*, checking whether enrichment of the host has taken place for an already existing host. If this is the case, it means that the host was previously inserted using another key coming from another source. For example, an IP address could be used for the first insertion, then a reverse DNS resolution could provide the host name that could then be encountered in host events. If such a host entry is found, the Boolean associated with the key will be set to *TRUE* to facilitate future insertions, and the host entry found will be used to insert the event. If both searches fail, it will create a new host entry.

The enrichment process (update_hosts) attempt among other things to complete the key information associated with a host in the database. If a host is identified by an IP address, then a reverse DNS lookup is attempted to obtain the host name. If a host is identified by a host name, a DNS lookup is also attempted. Both operations are costly and would result in undue delays upon insertion of a new host, hence the choice of off-loading the loader and pushing such task to a background process.

5.2. Issues with Network Host Information

While defining the keys vas fairly straightforward, it happens that there are a number of issues with the keys that we have designed.

5.2.1. Host Information Collection Point

The first remark is that we collect host information in a different location that event information. Most if not all of our sensors are passive devices, to limit the risk of attack against them. Therefore, they do not have the capability of adding host information to events. As a result, the gathered host information is from the vantage point of the application server and not the sensor. The advantage is that all events are tagged from the same viewpoint, thus normalizing the events. The disadvantage is that the application server needs to be able to access all host information, and that static local information (e.g., host names stored in /etc/hosts) will not be accessible. Even though one could fear that the visibility from the application server and from the sensor is different, we have not observed wrong host information as a result of this process.

5.2.2. Network Address Translation

Network address translation (Egevang and Francis, 1994) is frequently used by private companies and internet service providers to mask the internal structure of their environment and to lessen address space requirements. As such, different machines may be seen as a single one by our application. When NAT is in place, the name resolved through DNS is the name of the NAT device and does not reflect the exact name of the target or source of the event. As a result, our application in this configuration identifies a domain but not the exact target or source.

This problem rarely occurs for hosts under our control. This means that we usually can still precisely identify hosts that are within our realm.

5.2.3. Dynamic Host configuration

The dynamic host configuration protocol (DHCP (Droms, 1997)) allows the same machine to have multiple IP addresses over time. Moreover, host name information is sometimes generic as well, reusing for example the two last bytes of the IP address. When this is the case, our application is not able to uniquely identify a machine.

DHCP is a frequent occurrence in the environments monitored by our application. Our update_hosts tool attempts to determine whether the host is within a DHCP environment. When this is recognized, the host is identified by its host name, which is stored in our DNS servers during DHCP handshake and is uniquely generated in the corporation. When such a host is identified by an IP address, the update_hosts reconfigures the event-host associations a posteriori, using DNS queries. This is a domain-specific solution and may not be applicable to other environments. In particular, ISPs tend to use generic names, as mentioned earlier. Another solution would be to use the MAC address, but this key is very rarely available.

5.2.4. Mobility

Mobility is a frequent occurrence in our corporate environment. Laptops and the use of DHCP facilitate remote connections, as well as the generalization of VPN connectivity. However, this poses a problem when such a host is the subject of a security problem, particularly a viral or worm infection. We need to distinguish the case of laptops connected internally into a site that is not their home site, and laptops using VPN connections to access the information system.

In the case of locally-connected laptops, it is often the case that the resolution between host name and host IP address is wrong. Let's take the case of a virus infection. This virus infection is logged into the NT Event Log of the laptop, which in turns connects to a central server to deliver the infection alert. This infection alert is based on the host name, which is a unique key in our corporate network. As such, the event will be correctly assigned to the host. Unfortunately, geographic information is based on the IP address. If an IP address already exists for the host name, this information is not systematically refreshed as this is a costly process. Therefore, getting the current geographic coordinates of the infected laptop requires an additional DNS lookup to retrieve the current IP address and its associated geographical location. This process is quite time consuming and correct information may not be immediately available; if this process takes too much time the connection is terminated.

In the case of VPN-connected laptops (which is also used for wireless connections), the IP address of the laptop resolves to the IP address of the VPN concentrator. Therefore, it is impossible to retrieve the physical location of the infected machine and the connection is terminated.

5.2.5. Traceroute

A generic solution that has been proposed for these issues is to systematically trace the route between a known point inside our network and the victim/source host. We could then retrieve the location of the last router or switch, than is fixed and known in the inventory, and thus strongly reduce the physical search space for the machine.

We have not implemented this solution, as traceroute is filtered on most internal routers. If the reference point is external, then it may be an interesting alternative solution for identifying machines that are not within our realm. We believe that this solution would provide an interesting solution for tracing intruders at least to the peering point where they enter our networks, thus allowing us to push back countermeasures as far away from our systems as possible.

Unless the Host Identity Protocol[2] provides a solution to these issues, we anticipate that they will remain and that event correlation will suffer from the fuzziness of host identification.

5.3. Issues with Vulnerability Assessment Information

We also need to precisely assess the relevance of the collected events to the information systems. If these events are IDS alerts indicating an attack, we need to infer whether there is a risk that this attack may succeed and damage the information system.

This information is collected by the vulnerability assessment process. A vulnerability report is generated by a vulnerability assessment tool (for example Nessus[3]) as an XML file. Information in this file is imported in the events database as contextual information associated with hosts. Since vulnerability reports are associated with security references (bugtraq, CVE, etc.) and IDS signatures are also associated with the same information, it is fairly straightforward to infer the events that create a serious risk for the information system. If an event has as target the host associated with vulnerability X, and as signature one also associated with vulnerability X, then the risk is serious. This is a standard process that is in use in most intrusion-detection products.

5.3.1. Temporal Validity of Audit Information

The timestamp of the report does not provide information about the temporal validity of audit information. It is likely that the vulnerability did exist before the audit time. As a conservative measure, we consider that vulnerability exists before the current audit report and up to the time of the previous report if it exists, forever otherwise. When a new report becomes available, events generated after the time of the previous report are re-evaluated in the light of the current report. They remain as is they were

---

[2] http://www.ietf.org/html.charters/hip-charter.html
[3] http://www.nessus.org/

already involved in a correlation and they are upgraded if new vulnerabilities have been discovered (i.e., we consider that vulnerabilities that existed in the previous report have not been closed until the current one).

This simple algorithm could be improved by tracking patch management over time. Patches carry information about the vulnerability they close, often also as a bugtraq or CVE reference. Obtaining patch event information with timestamp and reference would allow us to precisely define the window of vulnerability for each IDS signature. We do not have this feature in our application yet.

5.3.2. Absence of Audit Information

Another annoying "feature" of most audit assessment tools is that they provide information about the vulnerabilities found, and not the ones that do not exist in the information system. It is therefore difficult to practice "anti-correlation" and degrade the severity of events that are not security risks for the information system. To obtain this effect, we currently manually maintain a set of simple rules indicating which vulnerability sets cannot be found in our corporate network. For example, we exclude all IIS vulnerabilities from events coming from hosting zones, as we do not offer this platform in our services. Note that we do not consider here the case where the vulnerability assessment tool fails to discover the vulnerability. Audit information is considered trusted.

We hope to improve this situation by using active port information and assessment configuration information coming from the vulnerability assessment tools. Most of these tools provide a global configuration section that lists all the tests that will be run. These tests are associated with a port number, and each tested host is associated with a list of open ports. For the ports of each open host, we can infer the list of tests that have been run against the host, and deduce that all these not included in the vulnerability report have had a negative outcome.

6. CONCLUSION

In this paper, we have described the design and implementation of a distributed event gathering application. The application relies on standard software tools such as databases and web servers for ensuring identification and authentication of users and storing data in a secure and reliable fashion. It also uses well-known transport layer security tools, such as SSH or virtual private networks, for ensuring identification, authentication and confidentiality at the transport layer.

The contribution of this paper is the definition of four different kinds of components for distributed event collection, according to the way they interact with the database and with the outside world. It also generically defines three types of information that are handled by the application. This structure is very important in terms of security, because it allows a strong separation of privileges at the table and column level (for databases that support it), between insertions, modifications, access and deletion. We are also able to effectively leverage the consistency mechanisms of SQL (foreign keys and references) to ensure that event information remains consistent over time.

This application has been successfully deployed in several corporate environments, monitoring IDS sensors on internal networks and hosting zones, monitoring VPN accesses, and monitoring core routers. In all cases, it has proven efficient in collecting detailed event information and displaying it to the operators. In particular, event storms characteristic of worm propagation are handled correctly. The correlation processes quickly identify the infected machines, and the enrichment process precisely locates them. As such, the cleanup phase of worm infections has been significantly improved.

A number of issues remain related to the reliability of host information. We are currently investigating the possible use of traceroute to more precisely locate hosts within a geographic area. We are also looking into the capture of DHCP messages or logs, which would provide a temporal view of the evolution of IP addresses.

Going forward, we plan to improve the presentation of information with geographical and organizational data, to ensure that complete contextual information on any given object (host, sensor, user, signature) is available to the operators. We are also moving to a change-detection visualization mode, where operators will see the evolution of the information contained in the database, and will rely on dynamic changes for decision making, in addition to static displays.

REFERENCES

Curry, D., H. Debar, and B. Feinstein, 'The Intrusion Detection Message Exchange Format,' Internet Draft, work in progress, expires July 8th, 2004.

Date, C., *An Introduction to Database Systems*, Eighth Edition. Pearson Addison Wesley, ISBN 0321197844, 2003.

Debar, H. and A. Wespi, 'Aggregation and Correlation of Intrusion-Detection Alerts,' In: W. Lee, L. Mé, and A. Wespi (eds.): *Proceedings of the 4th International Symposium on*

Recent Advances in Intrusion Detection (RAID 2001), Davis, CA, USA, pp. 85–103, Springer, 2001.

Droms, R., 'Dynamic Host Configuration Protocol,' RFC 2131, 1997.

Egevang, K. and P. Francis, 'The IP Network Address Translator (NAT),' RFC 1631, 1994.

Morin, B., L. Mé, H. Debar, and M. Ducassé, 'M2D2 : A Formal Data Model for IDS Alert Correlation,' in: *Proceedings of the Fifth International Symposium on Recent Advances in Intrusion Detection (RAID)*, 2002.

Roesch, M., 'Snort—Lightweight Intrusion Detection for Networks,' in: *Proceedings of LISA'99*, Seattle, Washington, USA, 1999.

Vandorselaere, Y. and L. Oudot, 'Intrusion Detection System -Hybrid, Distributed and Open-source,' in: *FOSDEM 2003*. Bruxelles, Belgium, 2003, **http://www.prelude-ids.org/**

Viinikka, J. and H. Debar, 'Monitoring IDS Background Noise Using EWMA Control Charts and Alert Information,' in: *Proceedings of the 7th International Symposium on Recent Advances in Intrusion Detection (RAID 2004)*, Springer-Verlag, 2004.

SOME ASPECTS OF NEURAL NETWORK APPROACH FOR INTRUSION DETECTION

Vladimir Golovko, Pavel Kochurko
Brest State Technical University,
Moskovskaja str. 267, 224017 Brest, Belarus,
gva@bstu.by

Abstract: Intrusion detection techniques are of great importance for computer network protecting because of increasing the number of remote attack using TCP/IP protocols. There exist a number of intrusion detection systems, which are based on different approaches for anomalous behavior detection. This paper focuses on applying neural networks for intrusion detection and recognition. It is based on nonlinear PCA network and multilayer perceptron. The 1999 KDD Cup data set is used for training and testing neural networks. The results of experiments are discussed in the paper.

Keywords: neural networks; intrusion detection systems; PCA; network attacks; attack recognition and identification

1. INTRODUCTION

The rapid and extensive growth of Internet technology increases the importance of protecting computer networks from attacks. In the last years the number of network attacks has been raised very promptly that has led to significant problems in different companies. For instance some companies like Yahoo were attacked by DoS (denial of service), costing them millions of dollars.

Intrusion detection systems (IDS) are used as a computer network security tool and permit to alert an administrator in case of attack. The main goal of IDS is to detect and recognize network attacks in real time. Nowadays there exist different approaches for intrusion detection. It is signature analysis, rule-based method, embedded sensors, neural networks, artificial immune systems [1]–[6] and so on. The most of these IDS can detect the known attacks and have poor ability to detect new attacks.

J. S. Kowalik et al. (eds.), Cyberspace Security and Defense: Research Issues, 367–382.
© 2005 *Springer. Printed in the Netherlands.*

In last years a neural network techniques have been applied and investigated for intrusion detection [7]–[10]. Such approaches are based on different strategies. So, one of them for anomaly detection use analysis of the audit records, produced by the operating system [8]. The other one is based on network protocol analysis [9].

Among the most wide-spread neural networks are feedforward networks, namely multilayer perceptron (MLP). This network type has been proven to be universal function approximators [11]. Another important feature of MLP is the ability to generalization. Therefore MLP can be powerful tool for design of intrusion detection systems.

This paper presents applying of neural networks for intrusion detection through an examination of network traffic data. It has been shown that denial of service and other network-based attacks are presented in the network traffic data. Therefore using neural networks permits to extract nonlinear relationships between variables from network traffic and to design real-time intrusion detection systems.

We describe the intrusion detection system, which consists of two different neural networks. The first neural network is nonlinear PCA (principal component analysis) network, which permits to identify normal or anomalous system behavior. The second one is multilayer perceptron (MLP), which can recognize type of attack.

The rest of the paper is organized as follows. The Section 2 describes attack classification and training data set. In the Section 3 the intrusion detection system is described, based on neural network approach. Section 4 presents the nonlinear PCA neural network and multilayer perceptron for identification and classification of computer network attack. In Section 5 the results of experiments are presented. Conclusion is given in Section 6.

2. ATTACK CLASSIFICATION AND KDD DATA SET

An event is a minimal unit with which modern protection tools operate. As soon as event breaks a policy of security, it at once is considered as a part of attack. Action or sequence of the connected actions of the intruder resulting in realization of threat by use of vulnerabilities is called attack to information system.

There are various types of classification of attacks. For example, division into passive and active, external and internal attacks, deliberate and unintentional. It should be mentioned that many models of attacks are currently well known: "one-to-one" or "one-to-many," i.e., attack proceeds from one point; "many-to-one" and "many-to-many," i.e., distributed or coordinated attacks; hybrid attacks also named the blended threat [12].

In the 1998 DARPA intrusion detection evaluation program, an environment was set up to acquire raw TCP/IP dump data for a network by simulating a typical U.S. Air Force LAN. The LAN was operated like a true environment, but being blasted with multiple attacks [13]. In 1999 sample data set of network traffic was presented at KDD'99 conference [14].

Attacks can be classified on the purposes of intrusion. Some of these categories were used in KDD data set [12, 14]:

- Remote penetration, R2L—attacks which allow to realize the remote control of a computer through a network: unauthorized access from a remote machine.

- Local penetration, U2R—the attack resulting in assigning of non-authorized access to the site on which it is started, unauthorized access to local su-peruser (root) privileges.

- Remote denial of service, DoS—attack which allows to break functioning of system or to overload a computer through Internet.

- Local denial of service, DoS—the attack, allowing to break functioning system or to overload a computer on which it is realized. An example of such attack is the hostile applet which loads the central processor an infinite cycle that results in impossibility of transaction processing of other applications.

- Scanners, probing—analysis of the topology of a network, services accessible to attack, carrying out search of vulnerabilities on network hosts.

- Sniffers—programs which "listen" to the network traffic. Using these programs it is possible to search automatically for identifiers and passwords of users, the information on credit cards, etc.

Table 1 describes main attack types used in KDD data set.

Table 1. Attack Descriptions [13]

Attack Type	Attack Class	Description
back	DOS	Denial of service attack against apache webserver where a client requests a URL containing many backslashes.
ftp-write	R2L	Remote FTP user creates .rhost file in world writable anonymous FTP directory and obtains local login.
guess_passwd	R2L	Try to guess password via telnet for guest account.
imap	R2L	Remote buffer overflow using imap port leads to root shell
ipsweep	probing	Surveillance sweep performing either a port sweep or ping on multiple host addresses.
land	DOS	Denial of service where a remote host is sent a UDP packet with the same source and destination.
loadmodule	U2R	Non-stealthy loadmodule attack which resets IFS for a normal

Attack Type	Attack Class	Description
		user and creates a root shell
multihop	R2L	Multi-day scenario in which a user first breaks into one machine
neptune	DOS	Syn flood denial of service on one or more ports.
Attack Type	**Attack Class**	**Description**
nmap	probing	Network mapping using the nmap tool. Mode of exploring network will vary– options include SYN
perl	U2R	Perl attack which sets the user id to root in a perl script and creates a root shell
phf	R2L	Exploitable CGI script which allows a client to execute arbitrary commands on a machine with a misconfigured web server.
pod	DOS	Denial of service ping of death
portsweep	probing	Surveillance sweep through many ports to determine which services are supported on a single host
rootkit	U2R	Multi-day scenario where a user installs one or more components of a rootkit
satan	probing	Network probing tool which looks for well-known weaknesses. Operates at three different levels. Level 0 is light.
smurf	DOS	Denial of service icmp echo reply flood.
spy	R2L	Multi-day scenario in which a user breaks into a machine with the purpose of finding important information where the user tries to avoid detection. Uses several different exploit methods to gain access.
teardrop	DOS	Denial of service where mis-fragmented UDP packetscause some systems to reboot.
warezclient	R2L	Users downloading illegal software which was previously posted via anonymous FTP by the warezmaster.
warezmaster	R2L	Anonymous FTP upload of Warez (usually illegal copies of copywrited software) onto FTP server.

KDD database consists of 4940210 records where every record describes one TCP/IP connection. Only 20% of records represent normal connections. A connection is by a sequence of TCP packets during a duration whose starting time and ending time are both well defined, and data flow during this duration from a source IP address to a target IP address under some well defined protocol. Each connection is labeled as either normal or attack. In the latter case, the connection should be with exactly one specific attack type.

For each TCP/IP connection, 41 various quantitative and qualitative features were extracted. Table 2 shows the list of 41 features of the data [14]. This features can be divided into three categories: intrinsic features, i.e., general information related to the connection; traffic features, i.e., statistics related to past connections similar to the current one e.g., number of connections with the same destination host or connections related to the same service in a given time window or within a predefined number of past connections; content features, i. e., features containing information about the data content of packets that could be relevant to discover an intrusion [15]. Each connection record consists of approximately 100 bytes.

Table 2. List of Features (type C is continuous, while D is discrete.)

#	Feature name	Description	Type
1	duration	Length (# of seconds) of the connection	C
2	protocol type	Type of the protocol, e.g. tcp, udp, etc.	D
3	service	Network service on the destination, e.g., http, telnet, etc.	D
4	flag	Normal or error status of the connection	D
5	src bytes	# of data bytes from source to destination	C
6	dst bytes	# of data bytes from destination to source	C
7	land	1 if connection is from/to the same host/port; 0 otherwise	D
8	wrong fragment	# of "wrong" fragments	C
9	urgent	# of urgent packets	C
10	hot	# of "hot" indicators	C
11	num failed logins	# of failed login attempts	C
12	logged in	1 if successfully logged in; 0 otherwise	D
13	num compromised	# of compromised conditions	C
14	root shell	1 if root shell is obtained; 0 otherwise	D
15	su attempted	1 if "su root" command attempted; 0 otherwise	D
16	num root	# of "root" accesses	C
17	num file creations	# of file creation operations	C
18	num shells	# of shell prompts	C
19	num access files	# of operations on access control files	C
20	num outbound cmds	# of outbound commands in an ftp session	C
21	is host login	1 if the login belongs to the "hot" list; 0 otherwise	D
22	is guest login	1 if the login is a "guest' login; 0 otherwise	D
23	count	# connections to the same host as the current one during past two seconds	C
24	srv count	# of connections to the same service as the current connection in the past two seconds	C
25	serror rate	% of connections that have "SYN" errors	C
26	srv serror rate	% of connections that have "SYN" errors	C
27	rerror rate	% of connections that have "REJ" errors	C
28	srv rerror rate	% of connections that have "REJ" errors	C
29	same srv rate	% of connections to the same service	C
30	diff srv rate	% of connections to different services	C
31	srv diff host rate	% of connections to different hosts	C
32	dst host count		C
33	dst host srv count		C
34	dst host same srv rate		C
35	dst host diff srv rate		C
36	dst host same src port rate		C
37	dst host srv diff host rate		C
38	dst host serror rate		C

#	Feature name	Description	Type
39	dst host srv serror rate		C
40	dst host rerror rate		C
41	dst host srv rerror rate		C

3. SYSTEM DESCRIPTION

Two approaches to intrusion detection are currently used. The first one, called misuse detection is based on the knowledge of attacker behavior. Intrusion detection system compares current network activity with the known patterns of behaviors of attackers attempting to penetrate the system. The second one, called anomaly detection involves identifying activities that vary from established behavior of users, or groups of users. Anomaly detection though is often highly difficult, as it must be tailored system to system, and sometimes even user to user, as behavior patterns and system usage can vary widely [12], [9], [16].

Let's examine the block-diagram of the intrusion detection system (Figure 1). It consists of several stages. At the beginning the system reads traffic data and sends it to the preprocessing module. The task of preprocessing module is to collect necessary data for neural networks from network traffic.

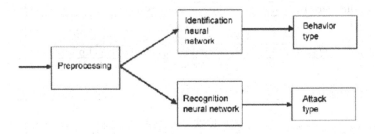

Figure 1. Block Diagram of the Network Traffic Processing

Our intrusion detection system uses its own sniffer based on WinPCap driver to collect raw traffic data [17]. WinPCap is Windows port of UNIX pcap and used for sniffing of network devices. It provides gathering data from IP, TCP, UDP, ICMP protocols. Every packet we receive from WinPCap has its header and body. The system analyzes the header data and calculates the parameters of TCP-connections. Every incoming and outgoing packet is analyzed and its parameters are added to the connection parameters. The following set of parameters of TCP-connections (Table 3) are selected by preprocessing module for training and testing of neural networks, like it is shown in Tables 5–9.

Table 3: Selected Network Traffic Elements

Feature Name	Description	Type
duration	length (number of seconds) of the connection	continuous
protocol_type	type of the protocol, e.g. tcp, udp, etc.	discrete
service	network service on the destination, e.g., http, telnet, etc.	discrete
src_bytes	number of data bytes from source to destination	continuous
dst_bytes	number of data bytes from destination to source	continuous
logged_in	1 if successfully logged in; 0 otherwise	discrete
flags	TCP/IP network flags	discrete

The neural network for identification is nonlinear PCA (NPCA) network [18]. As input data in this case, four features: service, duration, src_bytes, and dst_bytes are used. The neural network for recognition is multilayer perceptron. In this case, all of the listed features above (Table 3) are used as input data. Such a system permits to identify and recognize the network attacks.

4. NEURAL NETWORK STRUCTURE

As it is mentioned before, the goal of nonlinear PCA network (NPCA) is to identify an attack. The NPCA architecture consists of five fully connected layers with 3 input nodes and 3 output units. The number of nodes in the hidden layers is shown in Figure 2.

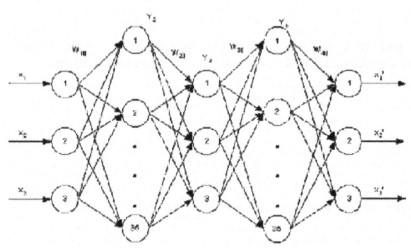

Figure 2. NPCA Network Structure

The output of unit j in the hidden layer k is computed as:

$$Y_{kj} = F(S_{kj}),$$

(1)

$$S_{kj} = \sum_i \omega_{kij} Y_{(k-1)i}.$$

(2)

The j-th output unit is given by

$$X'_j = F(S_j),$$

(3)

$$S_j = \sum_i \omega_{4ij} Y_{4j},$$

(4)

where F is the activation function, Sj is weighted sum, ω_{kij} is the weight from the i-th unit to the j-th unit of layer k.

The purpose of NPCA is to reconstruct the original data set at the output layer. The level by level method is used for training of NPCA network [19]. It consists of several separate phases of the training. At the first phase the definition of the weight matrix of last layer W_4 and desired output units of 4th layer Y_4 is performed. The purpose of the training is to minimize the mean squared error (MSE):

$$Es = \frac{1}{2} \sum_{p=1}^{L} \sum_j (\overline{X}_j^p - X_j^p)^2,$$

(5)

where L is the number of test training patterns. The gradient method is used for minimization of the equation (5). In accordance with them

$$\omega_{4ij}(t+1) = \omega_{4ij}(t) - \alpha \frac{\partial E}{\partial \omega_{4ij}},$$

(6)

$$Y_{4i}(t+1) = Y_{4i}(t) - \alpha \frac{\partial E}{\partial Y_{4i}}.$$

(7)

The cost function for one sample is defined by:

$$E = \frac{1}{2} \sum_j (\overline{X}_j - X_j)^2.$$

(8)

Differentiating (8) with respect to ω_{4ij} and Y_4 we can get the following equations:

$$w_{4ij}(t+1) = w_{4ij}(t) - \alpha F'(S_j)(\overline{X}_j - X_j)Y_{4i},$$
(9)

$$Y_{4i}(t+1) = Y_{4i}(t) - \alpha \sum_j F'(S_j)(\overline{X}_j - X_j)w_{4ij}.$$
(10)

At the second stage the weight matrix of the next layer W_3 and target output units Y_3 are determined. As the desired outputs of this layer the vector Y_4 is used, which has been obtained previously. Then the aim of the training at the second stage is to minimize the following expression:

$$E_S = \frac{1}{2} \sum_{p=1}^{L} \sum_j (Y_{4j} - \overline{Y}_{4j})^2.$$
(11)

The weights and outputs of this layer are updated iteratively in accordance with the following rule:

$$w_{3ij}(t+1) = w_{3ij}(t) - \alpha F'(S_{4j})(Y_{4j} - \overline{Y}_{4j})Y_{3i},$$
(12)

$$Y_{3i}(t+1) = Y_{3i}(t) - \alpha \sum_j F'(S_{4j})(Y_{4j} - \overline{Y}_{4j})w_{3ij}.$$
(13)

The same approach is applied for the other layer of neural network. As a result we can train the NPCA to reproduce original data set.

It should be noted that the first layer of NPCA (Figure 1) performs the processing of the input data by the following way:

$$X_i = \frac{1}{1 + e^{-\log X_i}}.$$
(14)

After training of NPCA we can define reconstruction error for every input pattern:

$$E(k) = \frac{1}{L} \sum_j (\overline{X}_j^k - X_j^k)^2.$$
(15)

Let $E'(k)$ be the measure of outlyingness. Then we can detect network attack by comparison of reconstruction error with measure of outlyingness. If $E(k) > E'(k)$ then it is network attack. In other case there are normal behavior.

Let's consider the neural network for recognition of attack. This network is multilayer perceptron with 6 input units, 40 hidden units and 23 output units, where the number of the unit with maximal value shows the type of recognized attack. The backpropagation algorithm is used for training MLP. It should be noted that one MLP for each services has been used.

The results of experiments are discussed in the next section.

5. EXPERIMENTAL RESULTS

To assess the effectiveness of the proposed intrusion detection approach, the experiments were conducted on the KDD Cup network intrusion detection data set [14]. We have used training data sets for anomaly detection made up of 400–700 randomly selected normal samples for each service. Training data sets for identification of attack made up of normal samples and attacks (Table 4) for each service.

Table 4.

Attack Type	# of normal samples	Total samples
auth	220	328
bgp	0	106
domain	3	116
eco_i	109	207
finger	468	670
ftp	190	407
ftp data	350	457
http	219	442
pop_3	79	202
private	180	458
smtp	79	99
telnet	219	513

Tables 5–6 show experimental results of trained NPCA networks for some services-based attacks. The measure of outlyingness was chosen to maximize ration of number of true attack alarms to false attack alarms.

Table 5. NPCA Results for Some Services

Measure	True attack alarms, %	False attack alarms, %	Service
0,001	99,96 (2406)	9,94 (6151)	
0,0011	99,96 (2406)	9,63 (5961)	
0,0012	99,79 (2402)	9,53 (5898)	HTTP
0,0013– optimal	99,50 (2395)	9,50 (5580)	
0,0014	98,46 (2370)	9,49 (5872)	
0,0015	10,14 (244)	9,47 (5861)	
0,001	99,76 (424)	2,68 (10)	FTP
0,003	99,29 (422)	1,34 (5)	
0,005	97,65 (415)	1,07 (4)	
0,006 – optimal	97,41 (414)	0,8 (3)	

Measure	True attack alarms, %	False attack alarms, %	Service
0,007	97,18 (413)	0,8 (3)	
0,01	96 (408)	0,8 (3)	
0,0005	36,84 (340)	14,09 (535)	
0,001	36,84 (340)	9,35 (355)	
0,002	36,84 (340)	8,14 (309)	
0,004	36,84 (340)	3,74 (142)	
0,005	35,97 (332)	3,19 (121)	
0,007	35,97 (332)	2,61 (99)	FTP DATA
0,010	35,97 (332)	1,76 (67)	
0,011	35,97 (332)	1,11 (42)	
0,012	35,97 (332)	0,95 (36)	
0,013 – optimal	35,97 (332)	0,90 (34)	
0,027	35,97 (332)	0,90 (34)	
0,028	16,79 (155)	0,84 (32)	
0,001	99,2 (124)	77,75 (7462)	SMTP
0,002	99,2 (124)	70,57 (6773)	
0,005	99,2 (124)	59,63 (5723)	
0,01	99,2 (124)	53,76 (5160)	
0,02	99,2 (124)	0,68 (65)	
0,03 – optimal	99,2 (124)	0,30 (29)	
0,05	98,4 (123)	0,30 (29)	

Table 6: Optimal Results for Main Services

Service	Measure	True attack alarms, %	False attack alarms, %
HTTP	0,0013	99,50 (2395)	9,50 (5580)
FTP	0,006	97,41 (414)	0,8 (3)
FTP_DATA	0,013	35,97 (332)	0,90 (34)
SMTP	0,03	99,2 (124)	0,30 (29)

As can be seen PCA network can detect 99,81% attack from KDD data set and only 0,41% of normal traffic raise false attack alarms.

Let's examine the recognition of attack types (Table 7). Table 8 show the statistic of recognition and detection of attacks depending on attack type. Table 9 shows the common results concerning attack recognition and detection for four categories. As can be seen MLP network can recognize 94,49% attack.

Table 7: Identification and Recognition Statistics Depending on Service

Service	# of records	# of attacks	True attack alarms	False attack alarms	Recognized correctly
1 auth	328	108	108 (100%)	0	108 (100%)
2 bgp	106	106	106	0	0 (0%)

Service	# of records	# of attacks	True attack alarms	False attack alarms	Recognized correctly
			(100%)		
3 courier	108	108	*108 (100%)*	0	*88 (81,48%)*
4 csnet_ns	126	126	*126 (100%)*	0	*100 (79,37%)*
5 ctf	97	97	*97 (100%)*	0	78 (80,41%)
6 daytime	103	103	*103 (100%)*	0	*102 (99,03%)*
7 discard	116	116	*116 (100%)*	0	89 (76,72%)
7 domain	116	113	113 (100%)	0	112 (99,12%)
8 domain_u	5863	1	0 (0%)	0	0 (0%)
9 echo	112	112	*112 (100%)*	0	89 (79,46%)
10 eco_i	1642	1253	1253 (100%)	0	1149 (91,7%)
11 ecr_i	281400	281055	281049 (99,99%)	0	280790 (99,90%)
12 efs	103	103	*103 (100%)*	0	79 (76,7%)
13 exec	99	99	*99 (100%)*	0	*99 (100%)*
14 finger	670	202	200 (99,01%)	3 (0,64%)	180 (90%)
15 ftp	798	425	414 (97,41%)	3 (0,8%)	409 (98,79%)
16 ftp_data	4721	923	317 (34,34%)	5 (0,13%)	308 (97,16%)
17 gopher	117	117	*117 (100%)*	0	96 (82,05%)
18 host-names	104	104	*104 (100%)*	0	86 (82,69%)
19 http	64293	2407	2364 (98,21%)	220 (0,36%)	2362 (99,92%)
20 http_443	99	99	*99 (100%)*	0	81 (81,82%)
21 imap4	117	117	*116 (99,15%)*	0	82 (70,69%)
22 IRC	43	1	1 (100%)	31 (73,81%)	1 (100%)
23 iso_tsap	115	115	*115 (100%)*	0	96 (83,48%)
24 klogin	106	106	*106 (100%)*	0	82 (77,36%)
25 kshell	98	98	*98 (100%)*	0	82 (83,67%)

Service	# of records	# of attacks	True attack alarms	False attack alarms	Recognized correctly
26 ldap	101	101	*101 (100%)*	0	*0 (0%)*
27 link	102	102	*102 (100%)*	0	*80 (78,43%)*
28 login	104	104	*102 (98,08%)*	0	*102 (100%)*
29 mtp	107	·107	*107 (100%)*	0	*83 (77,57%)*
30 name	98	98	*98 (100%)*	0	*78 (79,59%)*
31 net-bios_dgm	99	99	*99 (100%)*	0	*0 (0%)*
32 net-bios_ns	102	102	*102 (100%)*	0	*82 (80,39%)*
33 net-bios_ssn	107	107	*107 (100%)*	0	*0 (0%)*
34 netstat	95	95	*95 (100%)*	0	*1 (1,05%)*
35 nnsp	105	105	*105 (100%)*	0	*86 (81,9%)*
36 nntp	108	108	*108 (100%)*	0	*106 (98,15%)*
37 ntp_u	380	0	0	0	0
38 other	7237	1605	*1602 (99,81%)*	93 (1,65%)	*1228 (76,65%)*
39 pm_dump	1	1	*0 (0%)*	0	*0 (0%)*
40 pop_2	101	101	*101 (100%)*	0	*82 (81,19%)*
41 pop_3	202	123	122 (99,19%)	0	119 (97,54%)
42 printer	109	109	*109 (100%)*	0	*107 (98,17%)*
43 private	110894	103527	103500 (99,97%)	2 (0,03%)	83900 (81,01%)
44 red_i	1	0	·0	0	0
45 remote_job	120	120	*120 (100%)*	0	*101 (84,17%)*
46 rje	111	111	*111 (100%)*	0	*83 (74,77%)*
47 shell	112	111	111 (100%)	0	111 (100%)
48 smtp	9723	125	122 (97,6%)	28 (0,29%)	120 (98,36%)
49 sql_net	110	110	*110 (100%)*	0	*0 (0%)*
50 ssh	105	104	104 (100%)	0	102 (98,08%)
51 sunrpc	107	107	*107*	0	*86 (80,37%)*

Service	# of records	# of attacks	True attack alarms	False attack alarms	Recognized correctly
			(100%)		
52 supdup	105	105	*105 (100%)*	0	*77 (73,33%)*
53 systat	115	115	*115 (100%)*	0	*92 (80%)*
54 telnet	513	294	250 (85,03%)	3 (1,37%)	246 (98,4%)
55 tftp_u	1	0	0	1 (100%)	0
56 tim_i	7	5	*0 (0%)*	0	*0 (0%)*
57 time	157	105	103 (100%)	2 (3,85%)	103 (100%)
58 urh_i	14	0	0	0	0
59 urp_i	538	1	0 (0%)	0	0 (0%)
60 uucp	106	106	*106 (100%)*	0	*80 (75,47%)*
61 uucp_path	106	106	*106 (100%)*	0	*87 (82,08%)*
62 vmnet	106	106	*106 (100%)*	0	*1 (0,94%)*
63 whois	110	110	*110 (100%)*	0	*90 (81,82%)*
64X11	11	2	*2 (100%)*	8 (88,89%)	2 (100%)
65 Z39_50	92	92	*92 (%)*	0	*0 (0%)*

Table 8. Identification and Recognition Statistics Depending on Attack Type

Attack	Category	Count	Detected	Recognized
1 back	dos	2203	2192 (99,5%)	2192 (100%)
2 buffer overflow	u2r	30	0 (0%)	0 (0%)
3 ftp_write	r2l	8	2 (25%)	2 (100%)
4 guess passwd	r2l	53	49 (92,45%)	49 (100%)
5 imap	r2l	12	11 (91,67%)	1 (9,09%)
6 ipsweep	probe	1247	1236 (99,12%)	1161 (93,93%)
7 land	dos	21	21 (100%)	0 (0%)
8 loadmodule	u2r	9	0 (0%)	0 (0%)
9 multihop	r2l	7	1 (14,29%)	0 (0%)
10 neptune	dos	107201	107177 (99,98%)	86445 (80,6%)
11 nmap	probe	231	205 (88,74%)	99 (48,29%)
12 perl	u2r	3	0 (0%)	0 (0%)
13 phf	r2l	4	2 (50%)	2 (100%)
14 pod	dos	264	259 (98,11%)	0 (0%)
15 portsweep	probe	1040	1038 (99,81%)	498 (47,98%)
16 rootkit	u2r	10	2 (20%)	2 (100%)
17 satan	probe	1589	1578 (99,31%)	1522 (96,45%)
18 smurf	dos	280790	280790 (100%)	280790 (100%)
19 spy	R2l	2	0 (0%)	0 (0%)
20 teardrop	dos	979	977 (99,8%)	977 (100%)
21 warezclient	R2l	1020	427 (41,86%)	427 (100%)

Attack	Category	Count	Detected	Recognized
22 warezmaster	R2l	20	17 (85%)	16 (94,12%)

Table 9: Identification and Recognition Statistics Depending on Attack Category

Category	Count	Detected	Recognized
1 dos	391458	391416 (99,98%)	370404 (94,62%)
2 u2r	52	2 (3,84%)	0 (0%)
3 r2l	1126	509 (45,2%)	497 (97,64%)
4 probe	4107	4057 (98,78%)	3280 (79,86%)

In this paper some aspects of neural networks applying for intrusion detection have been addressed. By using two different neural networks namely NPCA and MLP, we can identify and recognize the computer network attacks. In comparison with other approaches the neural networks permit to design the intrusion detection systems, which have ability to training and working in real time. The experiments have shown the efficiency of neural networks techniques.

7. ACKNOWLEDGMENT

This research is supported by the Grant of Belarus National Academy of sciences.

REFERENCE

[1] Bishop, M., S. Cheung, C. Wee, J. Frank, J. Hoagland, and S. Samorodin, The treat from the Net, *IEEE Spectrum*, 34(8), pp. 56–53, 1993.

[2] Anderson, D., T. Frivold, and A. Valdes, Next-generation Intrusion Detection Expert Systems (NIDES): A Summary, SRI International Technical Report SRI-CSL-95-07, 1995.

[3] Spafford, E. and D. Zamboni, Data collection mechanisms for intrusion detection systems, CERIAS Technical Report 2000-08, CERIAS, Purdue University, 1315 Recitation Building, West Lafayette, IN, 2000.

[4] Debar, H., M. Becke, and D.Simboni, A Neural Network Component for an Intrusion Detection System, in *Proceedings of the IEEE Computer Society Symposium on Research in Security and Privacy*, 1992.

[5] Jirapummin, C., and N. Wattanapongsakorn, Visual Intrusion Detection using Self-Organizing Maps, *Proc. of Electrical and Electronic Conference (EECON-24)*, Thailand, Vol. 2, pp. 1343–1349, 2001.

[6] Lee, S. C., and D.V. Heinbuch, Training a Neural Network Based Intrusion Detector to Recognize Novel Attacks, *Information Assistance and Security*, pp. 40–46, 2000.

[7]   Lee, S. C., D. V. Heinbuch, Training a Neural-Network Based Intrusion Detector to Recognize Novel Attacks, *IEEE Trans. on Systems, Man, and Cybernetics, Part A*, 31, 2001, pp. 294–299.

[8]   Ghosh, A. K., and A. Schwartzbard, A Study in Using Neural Networks for Anomaly and Misuse Detection, *Proc. of the USENIX Security Symposium*, August 23–26, 1999, Washington, USA.

[9]   Cannady, J., An adaptive neural network approach to intrusion detection and response, Ph.D. Thesis, School of Comp. and Inf. Sci., Nova Southeastern University,

[10] Bonifacio, J. M., et al., Neural Networks applied in intrusion detection systems, *Proc. of the IEEE World congress on Comp. Intell. WCCI'98*, 1998.

[11] Hornik, K., M. Stinchcombe, H. White, Multy-layer feedforward networks are universal approximators, *Neural Networks*, 2 pp. 359–366, 1989.

[12] Lukatsky, A., Intrusion detection. Saint-Petersburg: BHV-Peterburg, 2003.

[13] MIT Lincoln Laboratory—DARPA Intrusion Detection Evaluation Web Page Template. Training Data Attack Descriptions **http://www.ll.mit.edu/IST/ideval/docs/ 1998/attacks.html**

[14] 1999 KDD Cup Competition. **http://kdd.ics.uci.edu/databases/kddcup99/kddcup99.html**

[15] Lee, W. and S. J. Stolfo, A framework for constructing features and models for intrusion detection systems, *ACM Trans. on Inform. and System Security*, 3(4), 200, 227–261.

[16] Cannady, J., Applying Neural Networks to Misuse Detection, in *Proceedings of the 21ˢᵗ National Information Systems Security Conference.*

[17] WinPcap: the Free Packet Capture Architecture for Windows, NetGroup, Politecnico di Torino, Italy, **http://winpcap.polito.it, 1999–2004**

[18] Hawkins, S., H. He, G. Williams, and R. Baxter, Outlier Detection Using Replicator Neural Networks, *Proceedings of the 4th International Conference on Data Warehousing and Knowledge Discovery (DaWaK02)*, lecture notes in computer Science, Vol. 2454, Springer, Pages 170–180, ISBN 3-540-44123-9, 2002

[19] Golovko, V., O. Ignatiuk, Yu. Savitsky, T. Laopoulos, A. Sachenko, and L. Grandinetti, Unsupervised learning for dimensionality reduction, *Proc. of Second Int. ICSC Symposium on Engineering of Intelligent Systems EIS'2000*, University of Paisley, Scotland, June 2000, Canada/Switzerland: ICSS Academic Press, pp. 140–144, 2000.